# DAVE ELLIS

# Becoming a Master Student

## CONCISE

### FOURTEENTH EDITION

**Doug Toft**
*Contributing Editor*

inquisitive

CARING

RESPONSIBLE

CREATIVE

Willing to change

Spontaneous

willing to work

WILLING TO TAKE RISKS

SELF-directed

CENGAGE
Learning®

Australia • Brazil • Japan • Korea • Mexico • Singapore • Spain • United Kingdom • United States

CENGAGE
Learning®

**Becoming a Master Student Concise, Fourteenth Edition**
Ellis

Product Director: Annie Todd

Senior Product Manager: Shani Fisher

Senior Content Developer: Marita Sermolins

Content Coordinator: Erin Nixon

Product Assistant: Kayla Gagne

Media Developer: Amy Gibbons

Marketing Manager: Lydia LeStar

Content Project Manager: Jill Quinn

Senior Art Director: Pam Galbreath

Manufacturing Planner: Sandee Milewski

Rights Acquisition Specialist: Shalice Shah-Caldwell

Production Service: MPS Limited

Cover Image: Oliver Cleve/Photographer's Choice/Getty Images

Compositor: MPS Limited

For product information and technology assistance, contact us at
**Cengage Learning Customer & Sales Support, 1-800-354-9706**

For permission to use material from this text or product,
submit all requests online at **www.cengage.com/permissions**.
Further permissions questions can be emailed to
**permissionrequest@cengage.com.**

Library of Congress Control Number: 2013949368

Student Edition:

ISBN-13: 978-1-133-31158-4

ISBN-10: 1-133-31158-X

Annotated Instructor's Edition:

ISBN-13: 978-1-285-43863-4

ISBN-10: 1-285-43863-9

**Cengage Learning**
200 First Stamford Place, 4th Floor
Stamford, CT 06902
USA

Cengage Learning is a leading provider of customized learning solutions with office locations around the globe, including Singapore, the United Kingdom, Australia, Mexico, Brazil and Japan. Locate your local office at **international.cengage.com/region**.

Cengage Learning products are represented in Canada by Nelson Education, Ltd.

For your course and learning solutions, visit **www.cengage.com**.

Purchase any of our products at your local college store or at our preferred online store **www.cengagebrain.com**.

**Instructors:** Please visit **login.cengage.com** and log in to access instructor-specific resources.

Printed in the United States of America
1 2 3 4 5 6 7 17 16 15 14 13

# Brief Contents

Images: Oliver Cleve/Getty Images

# Contents

Oliver Cleve/Getty Images

what if ⟵┄┄┄┄ ┄┄┄⟶ why

how ⟵┄┄┄ ┄┄┄⟶ what

# CHAPTER 2 Time and Money **51**

iStockphoto.com/parema

# CHAPTER 3 Memory 79

# CHAPTER 4 Reading 97

©Istockphoto.com/Tatiana Popova

© Chris Pancewicz/Alamy

# CHAPTER 5 Notes **117**

iStockphoto.com/Chad McDermott

# CHAPTER 6 Tests **137**

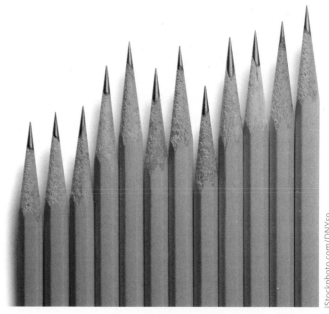

iStockphoto.com/DNY59

# CHAPTER 7 Thinking **157**

Steve Cole/Getty Images

# CHAPTER 8 Communicating **177**

# CHAPTER 9 Health **197**

# CHAPTER 10 What's Next? 215

iStockphoto.com/esolla

# ACKNOWLEDGMENTS

## ADVISORY BOARD

**Faculty Advisor:** Dean Mancina, Golden West College

Annette McCreedy, Nashville State Community College

Paula Wimbish, Hinds Community College

Leigh Smith, Lamar Institute of Technology

Charlene Aldrich, Trident Technical College

Krista Clay-Lieffring, Neosho County Community College

## FACULTY REVIEWERS

Johanna Bacik, Cuyahoga Community College

Colleen Baker, Lassen Community College

Frank Baker, Golden West College

Marla Barbee, South Plains College

Victoria Basnett, St. Johns River State College

Laura Bazan, Central Piedmont Community College

Donald Becker, Delaware State University

Mark Binkley, South Dakota State University

Barbara Braid, Bakersfield College

Paula Calahan, Middle Tennessee State University

Carole Comarcho, Broward College

Dennis Congos, University of Central Florida

Tim Cook, Clark College

Dana Dildine, Eastern New Mexico University, Ruidoso Branch

Marnice Emerson, Sierra College

Shirley Flor, San Diego Mesa College

Joseph Fly, South Plains College, Reese Campus

Beth Giroir, Arkansas Tech University

Brent Green, Salt Lake Community College

Dale S. Haralson, Hinds Community College

Sellestine Hunt, Angelina College

Judith Isonhood, Hinds Community College

Jon Jones, Shasta Community College

Mary LeVan, Brown Mackie Community College—Atlanta

Leila A. Llewelyn Rowe, Delaware State University

Rajone Lyman, Houston Community College, NE

Judy Lynch, Kansas State University

Angel Moore, Mesa Community College

Maria Parnell, Brevard Community College

Karey Pharris, Pikes Peak Community College

Berta Parrish, Cuesta College

Terry Lee Rafter Carles, Valencia Community College

Anthony Reuss, San Diego Mesa College

Star Rivera, San Diego Mesa College

Margaret Seymour, South Plains College

Dawn Shaffer, Central Piedmont Community College

Patricia Sheriff-Taylor, Jackson State University

Londell Smith, James A. Rhodes State College

Jane Speer, Alpena Community College

Karen Tunistra, Colorado Mesa University

Deborah Warfield, Seminole State College of Florida

Brandy Whitlock, Anne Arundel Community College

## STUDENT REVIEWERS

NyKailia Bailey, Hinds Community College, Rankin Campus

Jonathan M. Brown, Hinds Community College, Rankin Campus

Scott Bruning, Alpena Community College

Alissa Bullock, Hinds Community College, Rankin Campus

Morgan Callahan, Hinds Community College, Rankin Campus

Bennie Carey, Hinds Community College

Brianna Creson, Nashville State Community College

Jack Daniel Stewart, Hinds Community College, Rankin Campus

Carson Drennan, South Plains College

Micah Elliott, Nashville State Community College

Shelby Ellis, Hinds Community College

Kendale Enoch, Hinds Community College, Rankin Campus

Adrian Flores, South Plains College

Katie Garrett, Hinds Community College

Taylor Gehrer, Neosho County Community College

Lorri Haddix Fetty, Alpena Community College

Randall Hicks, South Plains College

Asisah Johnson, Hinds Community College

Esmi Lee, South Plains College

Alex Logan, Hinds Community College

Kelly Martin Lalair, Nashville State Community College

Jacob McCord, Nashville State Community College

Amanda Mink, Alpena Community College

Tracey Mitchell, Hinds Community College, Rankin Campus

Jean M. Mixon, Hinds Community College

Walter Moore, Hinds Community College

Sanyonette Myles, Hinds Community College

Eric Newman, Hinds Community College, Rankin Campus

Kim Nguyen, Golden West College

Percy Nichols, Hinds Community College, Rankin Campus

Lauren Plagens, South Plains College

Deidra Powell, Hinds Community College

Christina Rodgers, Hinds Community College, Rankin Campus

Akeem Ruhman Hall, Nashville State Community College

Joseph Schlink, Hinds Community College

Shelby Self, Hinds Community College, Rankin Campus

Jonathan Steinke, Mesa Community College

Kamesha Stokes, Hinds Community College

Betty Vittitoe, Hinds Community College, Rankin Campus

Emily Watkins, Hinds Community College

# The Master Student

Use this **Master Student Map** to ask yourself,

**WHY** THE INTRODUCTION MATTERS . . .
- You can ease your transition to higher education and set up a lifelong pattern of success by starting with some key strategies.

**WHAT** IS INCLUDED . . .

**HOW** CAN I USE THIS INTRODUCTION . . .
- Connect with the natural learner within you.
- Discover a way to interact with books that multiplies their value.
- Use a journal to translate personal discoveries into powerful new behaviors.

**WHAT** IF . . .
- I could use the ideas in this book to more consistently get what I want in my life?

## ✔ EXERCISE 1

### Textbook reconnaissance

Start becoming a master student this moment by doing a 15-minute "textbook reconnaissance." First, read this book's Table of Contents. Do it in 3 minutes or less. Next, look at every page in the book. Move quickly. Scan headlines. Look at pictures. Notice forms, charts, and diagrams.

Look especially for ideas you can use. When you find one, write the page number and a short description of the idea here. You also can use sticky notes to flag pages that look useful. (If you're reading *Becoming a Master Student* as an ebook, you can flag pages electronically.)

_____
_____
_____
_____
_____
_____
_____
_____
_____
_____
_____

© Ruslan Ivantsov/Shutterstock.com

# POWER process

# Discover what you want

Imagine a person who walks up to a counter at the airport to buy a plane ticket for his next vacation. "Just give me a ticket," he says to the reservation agent. "Anywhere will do."

The agent stares back at him in disbelief. "I'm sorry, sir," she replies. "I'll need some more details. Just minor things—such as the name of your destination city and your arrival and departure dates."

"Oh, I'm not fussy," says the would-be vacationer. "I just want to get away. You choose for me."

Compare this person to another traveler who walks up to the counter and says, "I'd like a ticket to Ixtapa, Mexico, departing on Saturday, March 23, and returning Sunday, April 7. Please give me a window seat, first class, with vegetarian meals."

Now, ask yourself which traveler is more likely to end up with a vacation that he'll enjoy.

The same principle applies in any area of life. Knowing where we want to go increases the probability that we will arrive at our destination. Discovering what we want makes it more likely that we'll attain it.

Okay, so the example about the traveler with no destination is far-fetched. Before you dismiss it, though, do an informal experiment: Ask three other students what they want to get out of their education. Be prepared for hemming and hawing, vague generalities, and maybe even a helping of pie in the sky à la mode.

This is amazing, considering the stakes involved. Students routinely invest years of their lives and thousands of dollars, with only a hazy idea of their destination in life.

Now suppose that you asked someone what she wanted from her education and you got this answer: "I plan to get a degree in journalism, with double minors in earth science and Portuguese, so that I can work as a reporter covering the environment in Brazil." The details of a person's vision offer clues to his or her skills and sense of purpose.

Another clue is the presence of "stretch goals"—those that are big *and* achievable. A 40-year-old might spend years talking about his desire to be a professional athlete some day. Chances are, that's no longer achievable. However, setting a goal to lose 10 pounds by playing basketball at the gym 3 days a week is another matter. That's a stretch—a challenge. It's also doable.

Discovering what you want helps you succeed in higher education. Many students quit school simply because they are unsure about what they want from it. With well-defined goals in mind, you can look for connections between what you want and what you study. The more connections, the more likely you'll stay in school—and get what you want in every area of life.[1]

**You're One Click Away...**
*from accessing Power Process media online and finding out more about "Discovering what you want."*

# Master student *qualities*

## This book is about something that cannot be taught. It's about becoming a master student.

Mastery means attaining a level of skill that goes beyond technique. For a master, work is effortless; struggle evaporates. The master carpenter is so familiar with her tools that they are part of her. To a master chef, utensils are old friends. Because these masters don't have to think about the details of the process, they bring more of themselves to their work.

Mastery can lead to flashy results: an incredible painting, for example, or a gem of a short story. In basketball, mastery might result in an unbelievable shot at the buzzer. For a musician, it might be the performance of a lifetime, the moment when everything comes together. You could describe the experience as "flow" or being "in the zone."

Often, the result of mastery is a sense of profound satisfaction, well-being, and timelessness. Distractions fade. Time stops. Work becomes play. After hours of patient practice, after setting clear goals and getting precise feedback, the master has learned to be fully in control.

At the same time, he lets go of control. Results happen without effort, struggle, or worry. Work seems self-propelled. The master is in control by being out of control. He lets go and allows the creative process to take over. That's why after a spectacular performance by an athlete or performer, observers often say, "He played full out—and made it look like he wasn't even trying."

Likewise, the master student is one who makes learning look easy. She works hard without seeming to make any effort. She's relaxed *and* alert, disciplined *and* spontaneous, focused *and* fun-loving.

You might say that those statements don't make sense. Actually, mastery does *not* make sense. It cannot be captured with words. It defies analysis. Mastery cannot be taught. It can only be learned and experienced.

By design, you are a learning machine. As an infant, you learned to walk. As a toddler, you learned to talk. By the time you reached age 5, you'd mastered many skills needed to thrive in the world. And you learned all these things without formal instruction, without lectures, without books, without conscious effort, and without fear.

Shortly after we start school, however, something happens to us. Somehow we start forgetting about the master student inside us. Even under the best teachers, we experience the discomfort that sometimes accompanies learning. We start avoiding situations that might lead to embarrassment. We turn away from experiences that could lead to mistakes. We accumulate a growing list of ideas to defend, a catalog of familiar experiences that discourages us from learning anything new. Slowly, we restrict our possibilities and potentials.

However, the story doesn't end there. You can open a new chapter in your life, starting today. You can rediscover the natural learner within you. Each chapter of this book is about a step you can take on this path.

Master students share certain qualities. These are attitudes and core values. Though they imply various strategies for learning,

inquisitive
CARING
RESPONSIBLE
CREATIVE
Willing to change
Spontaneous
willing to work
WILLING TO TAKE RISKS
SELF-directed

Oliver Cleve/Getty Images

they ultimately go beyond what you do. Master student qualities are ways of *being* exceptional.

Following is a list of master student qualities. Remember that the list is not complete. It merely points in a direction.

As you read the following list, look to yourself. Put a check mark next to each quality that you've already demonstrated. Put another mark, say an exclamation point, next to each quality you want to actively work on possessing. This is not a test. It is simply a chance to celebrate what you've accomplished so far—and start thinking about what's possible for your future.

☐ **Inquisitive.** The master student is curious about everything. By posing questions, she can generate interest in the most mundane, humdrum situations. When she is bored during a biology lecture, she thinks to herself, "I always get bored when I listen to this instructor. Why is that? Maybe it's because he reminds me of my boring Uncle Ralph, who always tells those endless fishing stories. He even looks like Uncle Ralph. Amazing! Boredom is certainly interesting." Then she asks herself, "What can I do to get value out of this lecture, even though it seems boring?" And she finds an answer.

☐ **Able to focus attention.** Watch a 2-year-old at play. Pay attention to his eyes. The wide-eyed look reveals an energy and a capacity for amazement that keep his attention absolutely focused in the here and now. The master student's focused attention has a childlike quality. The world, to a child, is always new. Because the master student can focus attention, to him the world is always new too.

☐ **Willing to change.** The unknown does not frighten the master student. In fact, she welcomes it—even the unknown in herself. We all have pictures of who we think we are, and these pictures can be useful. But they also can prevent learning and growth. The master student is open to changes in her environment and in herself.

☐ **Able to organize and sort.** The master student can take a large body of information and sift through it to discover relationships. He can play with information, organizing data by size, color, function, timeliness, and hundreds of other categories. He has the guts to set big goals—and the precision to plan carefully so that those goals can be achieved.

☐ **Competent.** Mastery of skills is important to the master student. When she learns mathematical formulas, she studies them until they become second nature. She practices until she knows them cold, then puts in a few extra minutes. She also is able to apply what she learns to new and different situations.

☐ **Joyful.** More often than not, the master student is seen with a smile on his face—sometimes a smile at nothing in particular other than amazement at the world and his experience of it.

> For example, if a master student takes a required class that most students consider boring, she chooses to take responsibility for her interest level. She looks for ways to link the class to one of her goals. She sees the class as an opportunity to experiment with new study techniques that will enhance her performance in any course.

☐ **Able to suspend judgment.** The master student has opinions and positions, and she is able to let go of them when appropriate. She realizes she is more than her thoughts. She can quiet her internal dialogue and listen to an opposing viewpoint. She doesn't let judgment get in the way of learning. Rather than approaching discussions with a "Prove it to me, and then I'll believe it" attitude, she asks herself, "What if this is true?" and explores possibilities.

☐ **Energetic.** Notice the student with a spring in his step, the one who is enthusiastic and involved in class. When he reads, he often sits on the very edge of his chair, and he plays with the same intensity. He is determined and persistent. He is a master student.

☐ **Well.** Health is important to the master student, though not necessarily in the sense of being free of illness. Rather, she values her body and treats it with respect. She tends to her emotional and spiritual health as well as her physical health.

☐ **Self-aware.** The master student is willing to evaluate himself and his behavior. He regularly tells the truth about his strengths and those aspects that could be improved.

☐ **Responsible.** There is a difference between responsibility and blame, and the master student knows it well. She is willing to take responsibility for everything in her life—even for events that most people would blame on others. For example, if a master student takes a required class that most students consider boring, she chooses to take responsibility for her interest level. She looks for ways to link the class to one of her goals. She sees the class as an opportunity to experiment with new study techniques that will enhance her performance in any course. She remembers that by choosing her thoughts and behaviors, she can create interesting classes, enjoyable relationships, fulfilling work experiences, or just about anything else she wants.

☐ **Willing to take risks.** The master student often takes on projects with no guarantee of success. He participates in class dialogues at the risk of looking foolish. He tackles difficult subjects in term papers. He welcomes the risk of a challenging course.

☐ **Willing to participate.** Don't look for the master student on the sidelines. She's in the game. She is a team player who can be counted on. She is engaged at school, at work, and with friends and family. She is willing to make a commitment and to follow through on it.

☐ **A generalist.** The master student is interested in everything around him. In the classroom, he is fully present. Outside the classroom, he actively seeks out ways to deepen his learning—through study groups, campus events, student organizations, and team-based projects. Through such experiences, he develops a broad base of knowledge in many fields that can apply to his specialties.

☐ **Willing to accept paradox.** The word *paradox* comes from two Greek words, *para* ("beyond") and *doxen* ("opinion"). A paradox is something that is beyond opinion or, more accurately, something that might seem contradictory or absurd yet might actually have meaning. For example, the master student can be committed to managing money and reaching her financial goals. At the same time, she can be totally detached from money, knowing that her real worth is independent of how much money she has. The master student recognizes the limitations of the mind and is at home with paradox. She can accept that ambiguity.

☐ **Courageous.** The master student admits his fear and fully experiences it. For example, he will approach a tough exam as an opportunity to explore feelings of anxiety and tension related to the pressure to perform. He does not deny fear; he embraces it. If he doesn't understand something or if he makes a mistake, he admits it. When he faces a challenge and bumps into his limits, he asks for help. And he's just as willing to give help as to receive it.

☐ **Self-directed.** Rewards or punishments provided by others do not motivate the master student. Her desire to learn comes from within, and her goals come from herself. She competes like a star athlete—not to defeat other people, but to push herself to the next level of excellence.

☐ **Spontaneous.** The master student is truly in the here and now. He is able to respond to the moment in fresh, surprising, and unplanned ways.

☐ **Relaxed about grades.** Grades make the master student neither depressed nor euphoric. She recognizes that sometimes grades are important. At the same time, grades are not the only reason she studies. She does not measure her worth as a human being by the grades she receives.

☐ **"Tech" savvy.** A master student defines "technology" as any tool that's used to achieve a human purpose. From this point of view, computers become tools for deeper learning, higher productivity, and greater success in the workplace. When faced with a task to accomplish, the master student chooses effectively from the latest options in hardware and software. He searches for information efficiently, thinks critically about data, and uses technology to create online communities. If he isn't familiar with a type of technology, he doesn't get overwhelmed. Instead, he embraces learning about the new technology and finding ways to use the technology to help him succeed at the given task. He also knows when to go "offline" and fully engage with his personal community of friends, family members, classmates, instructors, and coworkers.

☐ **Intuitive.** The master student has an inner sense that cannot be explained by logic alone. She trusts her "gut instincts" as well as her mind.

☐ **Creative.** Where others see dull details and trivia, the master student sees opportunities to create. He can gather pieces of knowledge from a wide range of subjects and put them together in new ways. The master student is creative in every aspect of his life.

☐ **Willing to be uncomfortable.** The master student does not place comfort first. When discomfort is necessary to reach a goal, she is willing to experience it. She can endure personal hardships and can look at unpleasant things with detachment.

☐ **Optimistic.** The master student sees setbacks as temporary and isolated, knowing that he can choose his response to any circumstance.

☐ **Willing to laugh.** The master student might laugh at any moment, and her sense of humor includes the ability to laugh at herself. Although going to school is a big investment, with high stakes, you don't have to enroll in the deferred-fun program. A master student celebrates learning, and one of the best ways of doing that is to laugh now and then.

**Hungry.** Human beings begin life with a natural appetite for knowledge. In some people, it soon gets dulled. The master student has tapped that hunger, and it gives him a desire to learn for the sake of learning.

**Willing to work.** Once inspired, the master student is willing to follow through with sweat. She knows that genius and creativity are the result of persistence and work. When in high gear, the master student works with the intensity of a child at play.

**Caring.** A master student cares about knowledge and has a passion for ideas. He also cares about people and appreciates learning from others. He collaborates on projects and thrives on teams. He flourishes in a community that values win-win outcomes, cooperation, and love. ■

# ✔️ EXERCISE 2

## The master student in you

The purpose of this exercise is to demonstrate to yourself that you truly are a master student. Start by remembering a time in your life when you learned something well or demonstrated mastery. This experience does not have to relate to school. It might be a time when you aced a test, played a flawless soccer game, created a work of art that won recognition, or burst forth with a blazing guitar solo. It might be a time when you spoke from your heart in a way that moved someone else. Or it might be a time when you listened deeply to another person who was in pain, comforted him, and connected with him at a level beyond words.

Describe the details of such an experience in your life. Include the place, time, and people involved. Describe what happened and how you felt about it.

_____

_____

_____

_____

_____

_____

_____

Now, review the article "Master student qualities" and take a look at the master student qualities that you checked off. These are the qualities that apply to you.

Give a brief example of how you demonstrated at least one of those qualities.

_____

_____

_____

_____

_____

_____

_____

_____

_____

_____

Now think of other qualities of a master student—characteristics that were not mentioned in the article. List those qualities here, along with a one-sentence description of each.

_____

_____

_____

_____

_____

_____

_____

_____

_____

_____

# This book is worthless— *if you just read it*

The first edition of this book began with the sentence *This book is worthless.* Many students thought that this was a trick to get their attention. It wasn't. Others thought it was reverse psychology. It wasn't that either. Still others thought it meant that the book was worthless if they didn't read it. It meant more than that.

This book is worthless *even if you read it*—if reading it is all you do. What was true of that first edition is true of this one as well. Until you take action and use the ideas in it, *Becoming a Master Student* really is worthless.

So, get something for your money by committing to becoming a master student. Here's what's in it for you.

**Pitch #1: You can save money now and make more money later.** As a master student, you control the value you get out of your education, and that value can be considerable. The joy of learning aside, higher levels of education relate to higher lifetime income and more consistent employment.[2] It pays to be a master student.

**Pitch #2: You can rediscover the natural learner in you.** Joy is important too. As you become a master student, you will learn to gain knowledge in the most effective way possible—by discovering the joyful, natural learner within you.

**Pitch #3: You can choose from hundreds of techniques.** *Becoming a Master Student* is packed with practical, nuts-and-bolts techniques. And you can begin using them immediately.

**Pitch #4: You get the best suggestions from thousands of students.** The concepts and techniques in this book are here not just because learning theorists, educators, and psychologists say they work. Tens of thousands of students from all kinds of backgrounds have tried them and agree that they work.

**Pitch #5: You can use a proven product.** The strategies that successful students use are well-known. You have hundreds of them at your fingertips right now, in this book. Use them. Modify them. Invent new ones. You're the authority on what works for you.

What makes any technique work is commitment—and action. Without them, the pages of *Becoming a Master Student Concise* are just 2.1 pounds of expensive mulch. Add your participation to the mulch, and these pages become priceless. ∎

## ✓ EXERCISE 3

## Commitment

This book is worthless unless you actively participate in its activities and exercises. One powerful way to begin taking action is to make a commitment. Conversely, if you don't make a commitment, then sustained action is unlikely. The result is a worthless book. Therefore, in the interest of saving your valuable time and energy, this exercise gives you a chance to declare your level of involvement upfront. From the options below, choose the sentence that best reflects your commitment to using this book.

1. "Well, I'm reading this book right now, aren't I?"
2. "I will skim the book and read the interesting parts."
3. "I will read the book, think about it, and do the exercises that look interesting."
4. "I will read the book, do some exercises, and complete some of the Journal Entries."
5. "I will read the book, do some exercises and Journal Entries, and use some of the techniques."
6. "I will read the book, do most of the exercises and Journal Entries, and use some of the techniques."
7. "I will study this book, do most of the exercises and Journal Entries, and use some of the techniques."
8. "I will study this book, do most of the exercises and Journal Entries, and experiment with many of the techniques in order to discover what works best for me."
9. "I promise myself that I will create value from this course by studying this book, doing all the exercises and Journal Entries, and experimenting with most of the techniques."
10. "I will use this book as if the quality of my education depended on it—doing all the exercises and Journal Entries, experimenting with most of the techniques, inventing techniques of my own, and planning to reread this book in the future."

Write the sentence number that best describes your commitment level and today's date here:

Commitment level _____ Date _____

If you selected commitment level 1 or 2, you probably won't create a lot of value in this class, and you might consider passing this book on to a friend. If your commitment level is 9 or 10, you are on your way to terrific success in school. If your level is somewhere in between, experiment with the techniques and learning strategies in this book. If you find that they work, consider returning to this exercise and raising your level of commitment.

# Get the most out of this book

**Get used to a new look and tone.** This book looks different from traditional textbooks. *Becoming a Master Student* presents major ideas in magazine-style articles. There are lots of lists, blurbs, one-liners, pictures, charts, graphs, illustrations, and even a joke or two.

**Rip 'em out.** The pages of *Becoming a Master Student* are perforated because some of the information here is too important to leave in the book. You can rip out pages, then reinsert them later by sticking them into the spine of the book. A piece of tape will hold them in place.

**Skip around.** Feel free to use this book in several different ways. Read it straight through. Or pick it up, turn to any page, and find an idea you can use right now.

You might find that this book presents similar ideas in several places. This repetition is intentional. Repetition reinforces key points. A technique that works in one area of your life might work in others as well.

**If it works, use it. If it doesn't, lose it.** If there are sections of this book that don't apply to you at all, skip them—unless, of course, they are assigned. In that case, see whether you can gain value from those sections anyway. When you commit to get value from this book, even an idea that seems irrelevant or ineffective at first can turn out to be a powerful tool in the future.

**Listen to your peers.** Throughout this book, you will find features titled Master Students in Action. These are short quotations from students who used this text. As you dig into the following chapters, think about what you would say if you could add your voice to theirs.

**Own this book.** Determine what you want to get out of school, and create a record of how you intend to get it by completing the Journal Entries throughout this book. Every time your pen touches a page, you move closer to mastery.

## Master Students IN ACTION

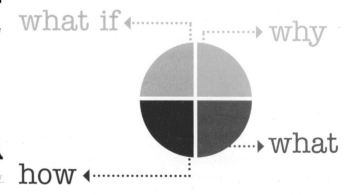

" *When studying for a test, the first thing I usually do is to read over my notes. Sometimes I reread the chapter just to make sure I comprehend what the chapter is saying. I find it very helpful to go online to the publisher's Web site and do the practice exams. By doing the practice exams, I get a better perspective of what the critical points are in the chapters. I like to go through the chapter outline because sometimes the answers are in the outlines.* "

—Lea Dean, Central Michigan University

**Do the exercises.** Action makes this book work. To get the most out of this book, do most of the exercises. (It's never too late to go back and do the ones you skipped.) Exercises invite you to write, touch, feel, move, see, search, ponder, speak, listen, recall, choose, commit, and create. You might even sing and dance. Learning often works best when it involves action.

**Practice critical thinking.** Practicing Critical Thinking activities appear throughout this book. Other elements of this text, including Chapter 7: Thinking, the exercises, and Journal Entries, also promote critical thinking.

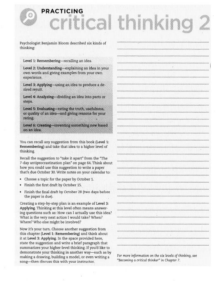

**Learn about learning styles.** Check out the Learning Styles Inventory and related articles in Chapter 1. This material can help you discover your preferred learning styles and allow you to explore new styles. Then, throughout the rest of this book, you'll find suggestions for applying your knowledge of learning styles. The modes of learning can be accessed by asking four basic questions: *Why? What? How?* and *What if?*

what if ⟵ ⟶ why

how ⟵ ⟶ what

**Navigate through learning experiences with the Master Student Map.** You can orient yourself for maximum learning every time you open this book by asking those same four questions: *Why? What? How?* and *What if?* That's the idea behind the Master Student Map included on the first page of each chapter, which includes sample answers to those questions. Remember that you can use the four-part structure of this map to effectively learn anything.

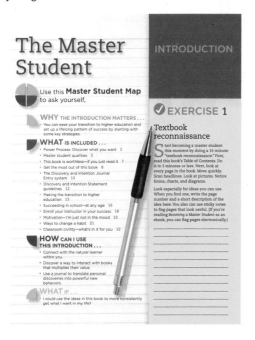

**Experience the power of the Power Processes.** A Power Process is a suggestion to shift your perspective or try on a new behavior. Look for this feature on the second page of each chapter. Users of *Becoming a Master Student* often refer to these articles as their favorite part of the book. Approach them with a sense of play and possibility. Start with an open mind, experiment with the ideas, and see what works.

**Link to the Web.** Throughout this book, you'll notice reminders to visit the College Success Coursemate for *Becoming a Master Student*. There you'll discover ways to take your involvement with this book to a deeper level. For example, access the Web site to do an online version of the Discovery Wheel exercise. Also look for videos, additional exercises, articles, practice tests, and forms. Scan this code with your smartphone to go directly to CengageBrain.com and login to CourseMate.

You're One Click Away...

IN

To get access, visit CengageBrain.com

**Read the sidebars.** Look for sidebars—short bursts of words placed between longer articles—throughout this book. These short pieces might offer insights that transform your experience of higher education. ■

### Have some FUN!

Contrary to popular belief, finals week does not have to be a drag. In fact, if you have used techniques in this chapter, exam week can be fun. You will have done most of your studying long before finals arrive.

When you are well prepared for tests, you can even use fun as a technique to enhance your performance. The day before a final, go for a run or play a game of basketball. Take in a movie or a concert. A relaxed brain is a more effective brain. If you have studied for a test, your mind will continue to prepare itself even while you're at the movies. Get plenty of rest too. There's no need to cram until 3:00 A.M. when you have reviewed material throughout the term.

# This book is worth $1,000

Cengage Learning is proud to present three students each year with a $1,000 scholarship for tuition reimbursement. Any post-secondary school in the United States and Canada can nominate one student for the scholarship. To be considered, write an essay that answers the question, "How do you define success?"

 You're One Click Away...
*from finding more details online at the College Success CourseMate for* Becoming a Master Student.

# The **Discovery** and *Intention Journal* Entry system

One way to become a better student is to grit your teeth and try harder. There is a better way: The Discovery and Intention Journal Entry system. This system can increase your effectiveness by showing you how to focus your energy.

GOAL

AIRPORT

Using the Discovery and Intention Journal Entry system is a little like flying a plane. Airplanes are seldom exactly on course. Human and automatic pilots are always checking an airplane's positions and making corrections. The resulting flight path looks like a zigzag. The plane is almost always flying in the wrong direction, but because of constant observation and course correction, it arrives at the right destination.

As a student, you can use a similar approach. Journal Entries throughout this book are labeled as Discovery Statements, Intention Statements, or Discovery/Intention Statements. Each Journal Entry contains a short set of suggestions that involve writing.

Through Discovery Statements, you gain **awareness** of "where you are." These statements are a record of what you are learning about yourself as a student—both your strengths and your weaknesses. **Discovery Statements can also be declarations of your goals, descriptions of your attitudes, statements of your feelings, transcripts of your thoughts, and chronicles of your behavior.**

Sometimes Discovery Statements chronicle an "aha!" moment—a flash of insight that results when you connect a new idea with your prior experiences, preferred styles of learning, or both. Perhaps a solution to a long-standing problem suddenly occurs to you. Or a life-changing insight wells up from the deepest recesses of your mind. Don't let such moments disappear. Capture them in Discovery Statements.

**Intention Statements can be used to alter your course.** These statements are about your **commitment** to take action based on increased awareness. An intention arises out of your choice to direct your energy toward a specific task and to aim at a particular goal. The processes of discovery and intention reinforce each other.

Even simple changes in behavior can produce results. If you feel like procrastinating, then tackle just one small, specific task related to your intention. Find something you can complete in 5 minutes or less, and do it *now*. For example, access just one Web site related to the topic of your next assigned paper. Spend just 3 minutes previewing a reading assignment. Taking "baby steps" like these can move you into action with grace and ease.

*Hello Author*
*I Agree* :)

. . . . . . . . . . . . . . . . . . . . . . . . . . . . . . . . . . . . . .

# That's the system in a nutshell. Discovery leads to awareness. Intention leads to commitment, which naturally leads to focused action.

. . . . . . . . . . . . . . . . . . . . . . . . . . . . . . . . . . . . . .

The purpose of this system is not to get you pumped up and excited to go out there and try harder. In fact, Discovery and Intention Statements are intended to help you work smarter rather than harder.

The process of discovery, intention, and action creates a dynamic and efficient cycle. First, you write Discovery Statements about where you are now. Next, you write Intention Statements about where you want to be and the specific steps you will take to get there. Finally, you follow up with action—the sooner, the better.

Then you start the cycle again. Write Discovery Statements about whether or how you act on your Intention Statements—and what you learn in the process. Follow up with more Intention Statements about what you will do differently in the future. Then move into action and describe what happens next.

This process never ends. Each time you repeat the cycle, you get new results. It's all about getting what you want and becoming more effective in everything you do. This is the path of mastery—a path that you can travel for the rest of your life.

Sometimes a Discovery or Intention Statement will be long and detailed. Usually, it will be short—maybe just a line or two. With practice, the cycle will become automatic.

Don't panic when you fail to complete an intended task. Straying off course is normal. Simply make the necessary corrections. Consider the first word in the title of this book—*becoming*. This word implies that mastery is not an end state or final goal. Rather, mastery is a process that never ends.

Miraculous progress might not come immediately. Do not be concerned. Stay with the cycle. Give it time. Use Discovery Statements to get a clear view of your world. Then use Intention Statements to direct your actions. Whenever you notice progress, record it.

The following statement might strike you as improbable, but it is true: It can take the same amount of energy to get what you *don't* want in school as it takes to get what you do want. Sometimes getting what you don't want takes even more effort. An airplane burns the same amount of fuel flying away from its destination as it does flying toward it. It pays to stay on course.

You can use the Discovery and Intention Journal Entry system to stay on your own course and get what you want out of school. Start with the Journal Entries included in the text. Then go beyond them. Write Discovery and Intention Statements of your own at any time, for any purpose. Create new strategies whenever you need them, based on your current situation.

Once you get the hang of it, you might discover you can fly. ▪

# Discovery and Intention Statement Guidelines

**W**riting Journal Entries helps you to develop self-awareness, self-direction, and other master student qualities. Use the following guidelines as a checklist. Consider removing this page from the book and posting it in a prominent place where you'll typically be writing your responses to the Journal Entries.

## DISCOVERY STATEMENTS

☐ **Record the specifics about your thoughts, feelings, and behavior.** Notice your thoughts, observe your actions, and record them accurately. Get the facts. If you spent 90 minutes chatting online with a favorite cousin instead of reading your anatomy text, write about it. Include details.

☐ **Use discomfort as a signal.** When you approach a daunting task, such as a difficult math problem, notice your physical sensations. Feeling uncomfortable, bored, or tired might be a signal that you're about to do valuable work. Stick with it. Write about it. Tell yourself you can handle the discomfort just a little bit longer. You will be rewarded with a new insight.

☐ **Suspend judgment.** When you are discovering yourself, be gentle. Suspend self-judgment. If you continually judge your behaviors as "bad" or "stupid," your mind will quit making discoveries. For your own benefit, be kind to yourself.

☐ **Tell the truth.** Suspending judgment helps you tell the truth about yourself. "The truth will set you free" is a saying that endures for a reason. The closer you get to the truth, the more powerful your Discovery Statements. If you notice that you are avoiding the truth, don't blame yourself. Just tell the truth about it.

## INTENTION STATEMENTS

☐ **Make intentions positive.** The purpose of writing Intention Statements is to focus on what you want rather than what you don't want. Instead of writing "I will not fall asleep while studying chemistry," write, "I intend to stay awake when studying chemistry." Also avoid the word *try*. Trying is not doing. When we hedge our bets with *try,* we can always tell ourselves, "Well, I *tried* to stay awake."

☐ **Make intentions observable.** Rather than writing "I intend to work harder on my history assignments," write, "I intend to review my class notes, and I intend to make summary sheets of my reading."

☐ **Make intentions small and achievable.** Break large goals into small, specific tasks that can be accomplished quickly. Small and simple changes in behavior—when practiced consistently over time—can have large and lasting effects.

When setting your goals, anticipate self-sabotage. Be aware of what you might do, consciously or unconsciously, to undermine your best intentions. Also, be careful with intentions that depend on other people. If you intend for your study group to complete an assignment by Monday, then your success depends on the students in the group. Likewise, you can support your group's success by following through on your stated intentions.

☐ **Set time lines.** For example, if you are assigned a paper to write, break the assignment into small tasks and set a precise due date for each one: "I intend to select a topic for my paper by 9:00 A.M. Wednesday."

☐ **Move from intention to action.** Intention Statements are of little use until you act on them. If you want new results in your life, then take action. Life responds to what you *do*. ∎

---

## JOURNAL ENTRY 1
### *Discovery Statement*

# Declare what you want

**R**eview the Power Process: "Discover what you want" on page 2. Then, writing on separate paper, brainstorm possible ways to complete the following sentence. When you're done, choose the ending that feels best to you and write it below.

I discovered that what I want most from my education is . . .

_____

_____

_____

_____

_____

_____

_____

# MAKING THE TRANSITION TO higher education

You share one thing in common with other students at your vocational school, college, or university: Entering higher education represents a major change in your life. You've joined a new culture with its own set of rules, both spoken and unspoken.

**W**hether you've just graduated from high school or have been out of the classroom for decades, you'll discover many differences between secondary and post-secondary education. The sooner you understand such differences, the sooner you can deal with them. Some examples of what you might face include the following:

- **New academic standards.** Once you enter higher education, you'll probably find yourself working harder in school than ever before. Instructors will often present more material at a faster pace. There probably will be fewer tests in higher education than in high school, and the grading might be tougher. Compared to high school, you'll have more to read, more to write, more problems to solve, and more to remember.

- **A new level of independence.** College instructors typically give less guidance about how or when to study. You may not get reminders about when assignments are due or when quizzes and tests will take place. You probably won't get study sheets before a test. And anything that's said in class or included in assigned readings might appear on an exam. Overall, you might receive less consistent feedback about how well you are doing in each of your courses. Don't let this tempt you into putting off work until the last minute. You will still be held accountable for all course work. And anything that's said in class or included in assigned readings might appear on an exam.

- **Differences in teaching styles.** Instructors at colleges, universities, and vocational schools are often steeped in their subject matter. Many did not take courses on how to teach and might not be as interesting as some of your high school teachers. And some professors might seem more focused on research than on teaching.

- **A larger playing field.** The institution you've just joined might seem immense, impersonal, and even frightening. The sheer size of the campus, the variety of courses offered, the large number of departments—all of these opportunities can add up to a confusing array of options.

- **More students and more diversity.** The school you're attending right now might enroll hundreds or thousands more students than your high school. And the range of diversity among these students might surprise you.

In summary, you are now responsible for structuring your time and creating new relationships. Perhaps more

iStockphoto.com/Mahazabin Gori

than ever before, you'll find that your life is your own creation. You are free to set different goals, explore alternative ways of thinking, change habits, and expand your circle of friends. All this can add up to a new identity—a new way of being in the world.

At first, this world of choices might seem overwhelming or even frightening. You might feel that you're just going through the motions of being a student or playing a role that you've never rehearsed.

That feeling is understandable. Use it to your advantage. Consider that you *are* assuming a new role in life—that of being a student in higher education. And just as actors enter the minds of the characters that they portray, you can take on the character of a master student.

When you're willing to take responsibility for the quality of your education, you can create the future of your dreams. Keep the following strategies in mind.

**Decrease the unknowns.** To reduce surprise, anticipate changes. Before classes begin, get a map of the school property and walk through your first day's schedule, perhaps with a class-mate or friend. Visit your instructors in their offices and introduce yourself. Anything you can do to get familiar with the new routine will help. In addition, consider buying your textbooks before class begins. Scan them to get a preview of your courses.

**Admit your feelings—whatever they are.** School can be an in-timidating experience for new students. People of diverse cultures, adult learners, commuters, and people with disabilities may feel excluded. Anyone can feel anxious, isolated, homesick, or worried.

Those emotions are common among new students, and there's nothing wrong with them. Simply admitting the truth about how you feel—to yourself and to someone else—can help you cope. And you can almost always do something constructive in the present moment, no matter how you feel.

If your feelings about this transition make it hard for you to carry out the activities of daily life—going to class, working, study-ing, and relating to people—then get professional help. Start with a counselor at the student health service on your campus. The mere act of seeking help can make a difference.

**Allow time for transition.** You don't have to master the transi-tion to higher education right away. Give it some time. Also, plan your academic schedule with your needs for transition in mind. Balance time-intensive courses with others that don't make as many demands.

**Find resources.** A supercharger increases the air supply to an in-ternal combustion engine. The resulting difference in power can be dramatic. You can make just as powerful a difference in your educa-tion if you supercharge it by using all of the resources available to students. In this case, your "air supply" includes people, campus clubs and organizations, and school and community services.

Of all resources, people are the most important. You can isolate yourself, study hard, and get a good education. However, doing this is not the most powerful use of your tuition money. When you es-tablish relationships with teachers, staff members, fellow students,

and employers, you can get a *great* education. Build a network of people who will personally support your success in school.

Accessing resources is especially important if you are the first person in your family to enter higher education. As a first-generation student, you are having experiences that people in your family may not understand. Talk to your relatives about your activities at school. If they ask how they can help you, give specific answers. Also, ask your instructors about programs for first-generation students on your campus.

**Make peace with new technology.** Turn back the clock to 2001. Google was just a few years old. There was no Facebook, no Twitter, no iPad, and no iPhone. Compare that to today's world, when these services and products are used by millions of people.

If you don't feel comfortable with the latest technology, welcome to the club. Students in higher education are asked to engage with technology at a level that has no precedent in our history.

To make the transition to this world, remember that it's okay to admit the truth whenever you're outside of your comfort zone. It's also okay to get help.

Go to your academic advisor and ask about "help desks," technology workshops, classes, and other campus resources for getting up to speed with technology. Find out how to access your school's computer network, wireless network, Web site, email system, and public computers and printers.

One way to overcome fear of change is to get hands-on experi-ence with digital tools as soon as possible.

# Master Students
# IN ACTION

*Photo courtesy of Timothy Alley/American River College*

"*Use all of the resources on campus. Get to know your instructors and professors, attend every class, accept all new challenges, get a support group, have outside hobbies and passions, believe in yourself.*"

—Timothy Allen, American River College

**You're One Click Away...**
*from a video about Master Students in Action.*

**Meet with your academic advisor.** One person in particular—your academic advisor—can help you access resources and make the transition to higher education. Meet with this person regularly. Advisors generally know about course requirements, options for declaring majors, and the resources available at your school. Peer advisors might also be available.

When you work with an advisor, remember that you're a paying customer and have a right to be satisfied with the service you get. Don't be afraid to change advisors when that seems appropriate.

**Learn the language of higher education.** Terms such as *grade point average (GPA), prerequisite, accreditation, matriculation, tenure,* and *syllabus* might be new to you. Ease your transition to higher education by checking your school catalog or school Web site for definitions of these words and others that you don't understand. Also ask your academic advisor for clarification.

**Show up for class.** In higher education, teachers generally don't take attendance. Yet you'll find that attending class is essential to your success. The amount that you pay in tuition and fees makes a powerful argument for going to classes regularly and getting your money's worth. In large part, the material that you're tested on comes from events that take place in class.

Showing up for class occurs on two levels. The most visible level is being physically present in the classroom. Even more important, though, is showing up mentally. This kind of attendance includes taking detailed notes, asking questions, and contributing to class discussions.

Research on college freshmen indicates a link between regular class attendance and academic success.[3] Succeeding in school can help you get almost anything you want, including the career, income, and relationships you desire. Attending class is an investment in yourself.

**Manage out-of-class time.** For students in higher education, time management takes on a new meaning. What you do *outside* class matters as much as—or even more than—what you do in class. Instructors give you the raw materials for understanding a subject while a class meets. You then take those materials, combine them, and *teach yourself* outside of class.

To allow for this process, schedule 2 hours of study time for each hour that you spend in class. Also, get a calendar that covers the entire academic year. With the syllabus for each of your courses in hand, note key events for the entire term—dates for tests, papers, and other projects. Getting a big picture of your course load makes it easier to get assignments done on time and prevent all-night study sessions.

**Experiment with new ways to study.** You can cope with increased workloads and higher academic expectations by putting all of your study habits on the table and evaluating them. Don't assume that the learning strategies you used in the past—in high school or the workplace—will automatically transfer to your new role in higher education. Keep the habits that serve you, drop those that hold you back, and adopt new ones to promote your success. On every page of this book, you'll find helpful suggestions.

# Rewrite IN
## this book

Some books should be preserved in pristine condition. This book isn't one of them.

Something happens when you interact with your book by writing in it. *Becoming a Master Student* is about learning, and learning results when you are active. When you make notes in the margin, you can hear yourself talking with the author. When you doodle and underline, you see the author's ideas taking shape. You can even argue with the author and come up with your own theories and explanations. In all of these ways, you can become a coauthor of this book. Rewrite it to make it yours.

While you're at it, you can create symbols or codes that will help you when reviewing the text later on. You might insert a "Q" where you have questions or put exclamation points or stars next to important ideas. You could also circle words to look up in a dictionary.

Remember, if any idea in this book doesn't work for you, you can rewrite it. Change the exercises to fit your needs. Create a new technique by combining several others. Create a technique out of thin air!

Find something you agree or disagree with on this page, and write a short note in the margin about it. Or draw a diagram. Better yet, do both. Let creativity be your guide. Have fun.

Begin rewriting now.

**Take the initiative in meeting new people.** Introduce yourself to classmates and instructors. Just before or after class is a good time. Realize that most of the people in this new world of higher education are waiting to be welcomed. You can help them and help yourself at the same time.

Perhaps you imagined that higher education would be a hotbed of social activity—and now find yourself feeling lonely and disconnected. Your feelings are common. Remember that plugging into the social networks at any school takes time. And it's worth the effort. Connecting to school socially as well as academically promotes your success and your enjoyment. ■

# Succeeding in school—
## at any age

David Buffington/Getty Images

David Buffington/Blend Images/Getty Images

B eing an adult learner puts you on a strong footing. With a rich store of life experiences, you can ask meaningful questions and make connections between course work and daily life. Any abilities that you've developed to work on teams, manage projects, meet deadlines, and solve problems are assets. Many instructors will especially enjoy working with you.

Following are some suggestions for adult learners who want to ease their transition to higher education. If you're a younger student, commuting student, or community college student, look for useful ideas here as well.

**Acknowledge your concerns.** Adult learners might express any of the following fears:

- *I'll be the oldest person in all my classes.*
- *I've been out of the classroom too long.*
- *I'm concerned about my math, reading, and writing skills.*

- *I'm worried about making tuition payments.*
- *How will I ever make the time to study, on top of everything else I'm doing?*
- *I won't be able to keep up with all the new technology.*

Those concerns are understandable. Now consider some facts:

- College classrooms are more diverse than ever before. According to the U.S. Census Bureau, 37 percent of students in the nation's colleges are age 25 and older. The majority of these older students attend school part-time.[4]
- Adult learners can take advantage of evening classes, weekend classes, summer classes, distance learning, and online courses. Also look for classes in off-campus locations, closer to where you work or live.
- Colleges offer financial aid for students of all ages, including scholarships, grants, and low-interest loans.

- You can meet other students and make new friends by taking part in orientation programs. Look for programs that are targeted to adult learners.

- You are now enrolled in a course that can help boost your skills at math, reading, writing, note taking, time management, and other key skills.

**Ease into it.** If you're new to higher education, consider easing into it. You can choose to attend school part-time before making a full-time commitment. If you've taken college-level classes in the past, find out if any of those credits will transfer into your current program.

**Plan ahead.** By planning a week or month at a time, you get a bigger picture of your multiple roles as a student, an employee, and a family member. With that awareness, you can make conscious adjustments in the number of hours you devote to each domain of activity in your life. For example:

- If your responsibilities at work or home will be heavy in the near future, then register for fewer classes next term.

- Choose recreational activities carefully, focusing on those that relax you and recharge you the most.

- Don't load your schedule with classes that require unusually heavy amounts of reading or writing.

For related suggestions, see Chapter 2: Time and Money.

**Delegate tasks.** If you have children, delegate some of the household chores to them. Or start a meal co-op in your neighborhood. Cook dinner for yourself and someone else one night each week. In return, ask that person to furnish you with a meal on another night. A similar strategy can apply to child care and other household tasks.

**Get to know other returning students.** Introduce yourself to other adult learners. Being in the same classroom gives you an immediate bond. You can exchange work, home, or cell phone numbers and build a network of mutual support. Some students adopt a buddy system, pairing up with another student in each class to complete assignments and prepare for tests.

In addition, learn about student services and organizations. Many schools have a learning assistance center with workshops geared to adult learners. Sign up and attend. Meet people on campus. Personal connections are key to your success.

**Find common ground with traditional students.** Traditional and nontraditional students have many things in common. They seek to gain knowledge and skills for their chosen careers. They desire financial stability and personal fulfillment. And, like their older peers, many younger students are concerned about whether they have the skills to succeed in higher education.

Consider pooling resources with younger students. Share notes, edit one another's papers, and form study groups. Look for ways to build on one another's strengths. If you want help with using a computer for assignments, you might ask a younger student for help. In group projects and case studies, you can expand the discussion by sharing insights from your experiences.

**Enlist your employer's support.** Let your employer in on your educational plans. Point out how the skills you gain in the classroom will help you meet work objectives. Offer informal seminars at work to share what you're learning in school. You might find that your company reimburses its employees for some tuition costs or even grants time off to attend classes.

**Get extra mileage out of your current tasks.** Look for ways to relate your schoolwork to your job. For example, when you're assigned a research paper, choose a topic that relates to your current job tasks. Some schools even offer academic credit for work and life experience.

**Review your subjects before you start classes.** Say that you've registered for trigonometry and you haven't taken a math class since high school. Consider brushing up on the subject before classes begin. Also, talk with future instructors about ways to prepare for their classes.

**"Publish" your schedule.** After you plan your study and class sessions for the week, write up your schedule and post it in a place where others who live with you will see it. If you use an online calendar, print out copies to put in your school binder or on your refrigerator door, bathroom mirror, or kitchen cupboard.

**Enroll family and friends in your success.** School can cut into your social life. Prepare friends and family members by discussing this issue ahead of time. See Chapter 8: Communicating for ways to prevent and resolve conflict.

You can also involve your spouse, partner, children, or close friends in your schooling. Offer to give them a tour of the campus, introduce them to your instructors and classmates, and encourage them to attend social events at school with you. Share ideas from this book, and from your other courses.

Take this process a step further, and ask the key people in your life for help. Share your reason for getting a degree, and talk about what your whole family has to gain from this change in your life. Ask them to think of ways that they can support your success in school and to commit to those actions. Make your own education a joint mission that benefits everyone. ■

**You're One Click Away...**
*from finding more strategies for adult learners online.*

# Enroll your instructor in your SUCCESS

Thinkstock/Getty

Faced with an instructor you don't like, you have two basic choices. One is to label the instructor a "dud" and let it go at that. When you make this choice, you get to endure class and complain to other students.

There is another option. Don't give away your power. Instead, take responsibility for your education. Enlist instructors as partners in getting what you want from higher education.

**Research the instructor.** When deciding what classes to take, look for formal and informal sources of information about instructors. One source is the school catalog. Alumni magazines or newsletters or the school newspaper might run articles on teachers. At some schools, students post informal evaluations of instructors on Web sites. Also talk to students who have taken courses from the instructor you're researching.

**Show interest in class.** Students give teachers moment-by-moment feedback in class. That feedback comes through posture, eye contact, responses to questions, and participation in class discussions. If you find a class boring, recreate the instructor through a massive display of interest. Ask lots of questions. Sit up straight, make eye contact, and take detailed notes. Your enthusiasm might enliven your instructor. If not, you are still creating a more enjoyable class for yourself.

**Release judgments.** Maybe your instructor reminds you of someone you don't like—your annoying Aunt Edna, a rude store clerk, or the fifth-grade teacher who kept you after school. Your attitudes are in your own head and beyond the instructor's control. Likewise, an instructor's beliefs about politics, religion, or feminism are not related to teaching ability. Being aware of such things can help you let go of negative judgments.

**Get to know the instructor.** Meet with your instructor during office hours. Teachers who seem boring in class can be fascinating in person.

Come to the meeting prepared with a list of questions and any materials you'll need. During the meeting, relax. This activity is not graded. However, avoid questions that might offend your instructor, such as: "I missed class on Monday. Did we do anything important?"

**Open up to diversity.** A Hispanic person can teach English literature. A white teacher can have something valid to say about African music. A teacher in a wheelchair can command the attention of a hundred people in a lecture hall. Don't let assumptions about race, gender, and disability hinder your learning.

**Separate liking from learning.** Remember that you don't have to like an instructor in order to learn from her.

**Form your own opinion about each instructor.** You might hear conflicting reports about teachers from other students. The same instructor could be described by two different students as a riveting speaker and as completely lacking in charisma. Decide for yourself.

**Seek alternatives.** You might feel more comfortable with another teacher's style or method of organizing course materials. Consider changing teachers, asking another teacher for help outside class, or attending an additional section taught by a different instructor.

**Avoid excuses.** Instructors know them all. Most teachers can see a snow job coming before the first flake hits the ground.

**Submit professional work.** Prepare papers and projects as if you were submitting them to an employer.

**Accept criticism.** Learn from your teachers' comments about your work. It is a teacher's job to give feedback. Don't take it personally.

**Use course evaluations.** In many classes, you'll have an opportunity to evaluate the instructor. Write about the aspects of the class that did not work well for you. Offer specific ideas for improvement. Also note what *did* work well.

**Communicate effectively by phone and email.** Find out how your instructors prefer to be contacted outside of class. Most have specific preferences about what they want you to include in a voice mail or email.

**Take further steps, if appropriate.** Sometimes severe conflict develops between students and instructors. In such cases, you might decide to file a complaint or ask for help from an administrator. Be prepared to document your case in writing. Describe specific actions that created problems. Stick to the facts—events that other class members can verify. Your school has grievance procedures that apply in these cases. Use them. You are a consumer of education and have a right to fair treatment. ■

**You're One Click Away...**
*from discovering more ways to create positive relationships with instructors online.*

# MOTIVATION—
## *I'm just not in the mood*

In large part, this chapter is about your motivation to succeed in school. There are at least two ways to think about motivation. One is that the terms *self-discipline, willpower,* and *motivation* describe something missing in ourselves. We use these words to explain another person's success—or our own shortcomings: "If I were more motivated, I'd be more successful in school."

A second approach to thinking about motivation is to stop assuming that motivation is mysterious, determined at birth, or hard to come by. Motivation could be something that you *already* possess—the ability to do a task even when you don't feel like it. This is a habit that you can develop with practice.

**Promise it.** Motivation can come simply from being clear about your goals and acting on them. Say that you want to start a study group. You can commit yourself to inviting people and setting a time and place to meet. Promise your classmates that you'll do this, and ask them to hold you accountable. Self-discipline, willpower, motivation—none of these mysterious characteristics has to get in your way. Just make a promise and keep your word.

**Befriend your discomfort.** Once you're aware of your discomfort, stay with it a few minutes longer. Don't judge it as good or bad. Accepting discomfort robs it of power. It might still be there, but in time it can stop being a barrier for you. Discomfort can be a gift—an opportunity to do valuable work on yourself. On the other side of discomfort lies mastery.

**Change your mind—and your body.** You can also get past discomfort by planting new thoughts in your mind or changing your physical stance. For example, instead of slumping in a chair, sit up straight or stand up. Get physically active by taking a short walk. Notice what happens to your discomfort.

Work with your thoughts as well. Replace "I can't stand this" with "I'll feel great when this is done" or "Doing this will help me get something I want."

**Sweeten the task.** Sometimes it's just one aspect of a task that holds you back. You can stop procrastinating merely by changing that aspect. If distaste for your physical environment keeps you from studying, for example, then change that environment. Reading about social psychology might seem like a yawner when you're alone in a dark corner of the house. Moving to a cheery, well-lit library can sweeten the task.

**Turn up the pressure.** Sometimes motivation is a luxury. Pretend that the due date for your project has been moved up 1 month, 1 week, or 1 day. Raising the stress level slightly can spur you into action. Then the issue of motivation seems beside the point, and meeting the due date moves to the forefront.

**Turn down the pressure.** The mere thought of starting a huge task can induce anxiety. To get past this feeling, turn down the pressure by taking "baby steps." Divide a large project into small tasks. In 30 minutes or less, you could preview a book, create a rough outline for a paper, or solve two or three math problems. Careful planning can help you discover many such steps to make a big job doable.

**Ask for support.** Other people can become your allies in overcoming procrastination. For example, form a support group and declare what you intend to accomplish before each meeting. Then ask members to hold you accountable. If you want to begin exercising regularly, ask another person to walk with you three times weekly. People in support groups ranging from Alcoholics Anonymous to Weight Watchers know the power of this strategy.

**Compare the payoffs to the costs.** Skipping a reading assignment can give you time to go to the movies. However, you might be unprepared for class and have twice as much to read the following week. Maybe there is another way to get the payoff (going to the movies) without paying the cost (skipping the

Galina Barskaya/Shutterstock.com

reading assignment). With some thoughtful weekly planning, you might choose to give up a few hours of television and end up with enough time to read the assignment *and* go to the movies.

**Heed the message.** Sometimes lack of motivation carries a message that's worth heeding. An example is the student who majors in accounting but seizes every chance to be with children. His chronic reluctance to read accounting textbooks might not be a problem. Instead, it might reveal his desire to major in elementary education. His original career choice might have come from the belief that "real men don't teach kindergarten." In such cases, an apparent lack of motivation signals a deeper wisdom trying to get through. ■

# ATTITUDES, AFFIRMATIONS, ## AND VISUALIZATIONS

Visible measures of success—such as top grades and résumés filled with accomplishments—start with invisible assets called attitudes. Some attitudes will help you benefit from all the money and time you invest in higher education. Consider these examples: "Every course is worthwhile." "I learn something from any instructor." "The most important factors in the quality of my education are my own choices."

Other attitudes will render your investment worthless: "This required class is a total waste of time." "You can't learn anything from some instructors." "Success depends on luck more than anything else." "I've never been good at school."

You can change your attitudes through regular practice with affirmations and visualizations.

**Affirm it.** An affirmation is a statement describing what you want. The most effective affirmations are personal, positive, and written in the present tense.

To use affirmations, first determine what you want, then describe yourself as if you already have it. To get what you want from your education, you could write, "I, Malika Jones, am a master student. I take full responsibility for my education. I learn with joy, and I use my experiences in each course to create the life that I want."

If you decide that you want a wonderful job, you might write, "I, Peter Webster, have a wonderful job.

I respect and love my colleagues, and they feel the same way about me. I look forward to going to work each day."

Effective affirmations include detail. Use brand names, people's names, and your own name. Involve all of your senses—sight, sound, smell, taste, touch. Take a positive approach. Instead of saying, "I am not fat," say, "I am slender."

Once you have written an affirmation, repeat it. Practice saying it out loud several times a day.

**Visualize it.** Here's one way to begin. Choose what you want to improve. Then describe in writing what it would look like, sound like, and feel like to have that improvement in your life. If you are learning to play the piano, write down briefly what you would see, hear, and feel if you were playing skillfully. If you want to improve your relationships with your children, write down what you would see, hear, and feel if you were communicating with them successfully.

Once you have a sketch of what it would be like to be successful, practice seeing it in your mind's eye. Whenever you toss the basketball, it swishes through the net. Every time you invite someone out on a date, the person says "yes." Each test the teacher hands back to you is graded an A. Practice at least once a day. Then wait for the results to unfold in your life.

Be clear about what you want, and then practice it.

# Ways to
# *change a habit*

One way of thinking about success or failure is to focus on habits. Behaviors such as ignoring reading assignments or skipping class might be habits leading to outcomes that "could not" be avoided—including dropping out of school. In the same way, behaviors such as completing assignments and attending class might lead to the outcome of getting an A.

When you confront a behavior that undermines your goals or creates a circumstance that you don't want, consider a new attitude: That behavior is just a habit. And it can be changed.

Thinking about ourselves as creatures of habit actually gives us power. Then we are not faced with the monumental task of changing our very nature. Rather, we can take on the doable job of changing our habits. One consistent change in behavior that seems insignificant at first can have effects that ripple throughout your life. Following are ways to test this idea for yourself.

## TELL THE TRUTH

Telling the truth about any habit—from chewing our fingernails to cheating on tests—frees us. Without taking this step, our efforts to change can be as ineffective as rearranging the deck chairs on the *Titanic*. Telling the truth allows us to see what's actually sinking the ship.

## CHOOSE AND COMMIT TO A NEW BEHAVIOR

Richard Malott, a psychologist who specializes in helping people overcome procrastination, lists three key steps in committing to a new behavior.[5] First, *specify* your goal in numerical terms whenever possible. For example, commit to reading 30 pages per day, Monday through Friday. Second, *observe* your behavior and record the results—in this case, the number of pages that you actually read every day. Finally, set up a small *consequence* for failing to keep your commitment. For instance, pay a friend one quarter for each day that you read less than 30 pages.

## START WITH A SMALL CHANGE

You can sometimes rearrange a whole pattern of behaviors by changing one small habit. If you have a habit of always being late for classes, then be on time for one class. As soon as you change the old pattern by getting ready and going on time to one class, you might find yourself arriving at all of your classes on time. You might even start arriving everywhere else on time, too.

## GET FEEDBACK AND SUPPORT

Getting feedback and support is a crucial step in adopting a new behavior. It is also a point at which many plans for change break down. It's easy to practice your new behavior with great enthusiasm for a few days. After the initial rush of excitement, though, things can get a little tougher.

One way to get feedback is to bring other people into the picture. Ask others to remind you that you are changing your habit if they see you backsliding. Support from others can be as simple as a quick phone call: "Hi. Have you started that outline for your research paper yet?" Or it can be as formal as a support group that meets once a week to review everyone's goals and action plans.

One effective source of feedback is yourself. Create your own charts to track your behavior, or write about your progress in your journal. Figure out a way to monitor your progress.

## PRACTICE, PRACTICE, PRACTICE— WITHOUT SELF-JUDGMENT

Psychologists such as B. F. Skinner define learning as a stable change in behavior that comes as a result of practice.[6] This widely accepted idea is key to changing habits. Act on your intention over and over again. If you fail or forget, let go of any self-judgment. Just keep practicing the new habit. Allow whatever time it takes to make a change.

Accept the feelings of discomfort that might come with a new habit. Keep practicing the new behavior, even if it feels unnatural. Trust the process. Grow into the new behavior. However, if this new habit doesn't work, simply note what happened (without guilt or blame), select a new behavior, and begin this cycle of steps over again.

Making mistakes as you practice doesn't mean that you've failed. Even when you don't get the results you want from a new behavior, you learn something valuable in the process. Once you understand ways to change one habit, you understand ways to change almost any habit. ■

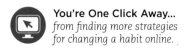

**You're One Click Away...**
*from finding more strategies for changing a habit online.*

# CLASSROOM CIVILITY—
# what's in it for you

**This topic might seem like common sense, yet some students forget that simple behaviors create a sense of safety, mutual respect, and community.**

Consider an example: A student arrives 15 minutes late to a lecture and lets the door slam behind her. She pulls a fast-food burger out of a crackling paper bag. Then her cell phone rings at full volume—and she answers it. Behaviors like these send a message to everyone in the room: "I'm ignoring you."

**Without civility, you lose.** Even a small problem with classroom civility can create a barrier for everyone. Learning gets interrupted. Trust breaks down. Your tuition dollars go down the drain. You deserve to enter classrooms that are free of discipline problems and bullies. Many schools have formal policies about classroom civility. Find out what policies apply to you. The consequences for violating them can be serious and may include dismissal or legal action.

**With civility, you win.** When you treat instructors with respect, you're more likely to be treated that way in return. A respectful relationship with an instructor could turn into a favorable reference letter, a mentorship, a job referral, or a friendship that lasts for years after you graduate. Politeness pays.

Classroom civility does not mean that you have to be passive or insincere. You can present your opinions with passion and even disagree with an instructor in a way that leaves everyone enriched rather than threatened.

Lack of civility boils down to a group of habits. Like any other habits, these can be changed. The following suggestions reflect common sense, and they make an uncommon difference.

**Attend classes regularly and on time.** If you know that you're going to miss a class or be late, let your instructor know. Take the initiative to ask your instructor or another student about what you missed.

If you arrive late, do not disrupt class. Close the door quietly and take a seat. When you know that you will have to leave class early, tell your instructor before class begins, and sit near an exit. If you leave class to use the restroom or handle an emergency, do so quietly.

**During class, participate fully.** Take notes and join in discussions. Turn off your cell phone or any other electronic device that you don't need for class. Remember that sleeping, texting, or doing work for another class is a waste of your time and money. Instructors notice distracting activities and take them as a sign of your lack of interest and commitment. So do employers.

Before packing up your notebooks and other materials, wait until class has been dismissed. Instructors often give assignments or make a key point at the end of a class period. Be there when it happens.

**Communicate respect.** When you speak in class, begin by addressing your instructor as *Ms., Mrs., Mr., Dr., Professor,* or whatever the teacher prefers.

Discussions gain value when everyone gets a chance to speak. Show respect for others by not monopolizing class discussions. Refrain from side conversations and profanity. When presenting viewpoints that conflict with those of classmates or your instructor, combine the passion for your opinion with respect for the opinions of others. Similarly, if you disagree with a class requirement or grade you received, then talk to your instructor about it after class in a respectful way. In a private setting, your ideas will get more attention.

Respect gets communicated in small details. Don't make distracting noises. Cover your mouth if you yawn or cough. Avoid wearing inappropriate clothing. And even if you meet your future spouse in class, refrain from public displays of affection.

**Embrace diversity.** Master students—and teachers—come in endless variety. They are old and young, male and female. They come from every culture, race, and ethnic group. Part of civility is staying open to the value that other people have to offer.

**See civility as a contribution.** Every class you enter has the potential to become a community of people who talk openly, listen fully, share laughter, and arrive at life-changing insights. These are master student qualities. Every time you demonstrate them, you make a contribution to your community. ◼

# First Steps

Use this **Master Student Map** to ask yourself,

## WHY THIS CHAPTER MATTERS . . .

- Success starts with telling the truth about what *is* working—and what *isn't*—in our lives right now.

## WHAT IS INCLUDED . . .

## HOW CAN I USE THIS CHAPTER . . .

- Experience the power of telling the truth about your current skills.
- Discover your preferred learning styles.
- Choose learning strategies that promote your success.

## WHAT IF . . .

- I could start to create new outcomes in my life by accepting the way I am right now?

---

**JOURNAL ENTRY 2**
*Intention Statement*

## Create value from this chapter

Skim this chapter for three techniques that you'd like to use in school or in your personal life during the upcoming week. List each technique and a related page number here.

I intend to use . . .

_____

_____

_____

_____

_____

_____

_____

_____

_____

_____

_____

_____

_____

_____

_____

_____

_____

_____

_____

© Ruslan Vantsov/Shutterstock.com

# POWER process

# Ideas are tools

There are many ideas in this book. When you first encounter them, don't believe any of them. Instead, think of the ideas as tools.

For example, you use a hammer for a purpose—to drive a nail. You don't try to figure out whether the hammer is "right." You just use it. If it works, you use it again. If it doesn't work, you get a different hammer.

People have plenty of room in their lives for different kinds of hammers, but they tend to limit their openness to different kinds of ideas. A new idea, at some level, is a threat to their very being—unlike a new hammer, which is simply a new hammer.

Most of us have a built-in desire to be right. Our ideas, we often think, represent ourselves.

Some ideas are worth dying for. But please note: This book does not contain any of those ideas. The ideas on these pages are strictly "hammers."

Imagine someone defending a hammer. Picture this person holding up a hammer and declaring, "I hold this hammer to be self-evident. Give me this hammer or give me death. Those other hammers are flawed. There are only two kinds of people in this world: people who believe in this hammer and people who don't."

That ridiculous picture makes a point. This book is not a manifesto. It's a toolbox, and tools are meant to be used.

If you read about a tool in this book that doesn't sound "right" or one that sounds a little goofy, remember that the ideas here are for using, not necessarily for believing. Suspend your judgment. Test the idea for yourself. If it works, use it. If it doesn't, don't use it.

Any tool—whether it's a hammer, a computer program, or a study technique based on your knowledge of learning styles—is designed to do a specific job. A master mechanic carries a variety of tools, because no single tool works for all jobs. If you throw a tool away because it doesn't work in one situation, you won't be able to pull it out later when it's just what you need. So if an idea doesn't work for you and you are satisfied that you gave it a fair chance, don't throw it away. File it away instead. The idea might come in handy soon.

And remember, this book is not about figuring out the "right" way. Even the "ideas are tools" approach is not "right."

It's a hammer . . . (or maybe a saw).

 **You're One Click Away...**
*from accessing the Power Process Media online and finding out more about how "ideas are tools."*

akva/Shutterstock.com

# First Step: Truth is a
# key to mastery

The First Step technique is simple: Tell the truth about who you are and what you want.

End of discussion. Now, proceed to Chapter 2.

Well . . . it's not *quite* that simple.

The First Step is one of the most valuable tools in this book. It magnifies the power of all the other techniques. It is a key to becoming a master student.

To succeed in school, tell the truth about what kind of student you are and what kind of student you want to become. Success starts with telling the truth about what *is* working—and what is *not* working—in our lives right now. When we acknowledge our strengths, we gain an accurate picture of what we can accomplish. When we admit that we have a problem, we are free to find a solution. Ignoring the truth, on the other hand, can lead to problems that stick around for decades.

## FIRST STEPS ARE UNIVERSAL

An article about telling the truth might sound like pie-in-the-sky moralizing. However, there is nothing pie-in-the-sky or moralizing about a First Step. It is a practical, down-to-earth principle to use whenever we want to change our behavior.

When you see a doctor, the First Step is to tell the truth about your current symptoms. That way you can get an accurate diagnosis and effective treatment plan. This principle is universal. It works for just about any problem in any area of life.

First Steps are used by millions of people who want to turn their lives around. No technique in this book has been field-tested more often or more successfully—or under tougher circumstances.

For example, members of Alcoholics Anonymous start by telling the truth about their drinking. Their First Step is to admit that they are powerless over alcohol. That's when their lives start to change.

When people join Weight Watchers, their First Step is telling the truth about how much they currently weigh.

When people go for credit counseling, their First Step is telling the truth about how much money they earn, how much they spend, and how much they owe.

People dealing with a variety of other challenges—including troubled relationships with food, drugs, sex, and work—also start by telling the truth. They use First Steps to change their behavior, and they do it for a reason: First Steps work.

## FIRST STEPS ARE CHALLENGING— AND REWARDING

Let's be truthful: It's not easy to tell the truth about ourselves.

It's not fun to admit our weaknesses. Many of us approach a frank evaluation of ourselves about as enthusiastically as we'd greet a phone call from the bank about an overdrawn account. We might end up admitting that we're afraid of algebra, that we don't complete term papers on time, or that coming up with the money to pay for tuition is a constant challenge.

There is another way to think about self-evaluations. If we could see them as opportunities to solve problems and take charge of our lives, we might welcome them. Believe it or not, we can begin working with our list of weaknesses by celebrating them.

Consider the most accomplished, "together" people you know. If they were totally candid with you, they would talk about their mistakes and regrets as well as their rewards and recognition. The most successful people tend to be the most willing to look at their flaws.

It may seem natural to judge our own shortcomings and feel bad about them. Some people believe that such feelings are necessary to correct their errors. Others think that a healthy dose of shame can prevent the moral decay of our society.

Think again. In fact, consider the opposite idea: We can gain skill without feeling rotten about the past. We can change the way things *are* without having to criticize the way things *have been*. We can learn to see shame or blame as excess baggage and just set them aside.

If the whole idea of telling the truth about yourself puts a knot in your stomach, that's good. Notice the knot. It is your friend. It is a reminder that First Steps call for courage and compassion. These are qualities of a master student.

## FIRST STEPS FREE US TO CHANGE

Master students get the most value from a First Step by turning their perceived shortcomings into goals. "I don't exercise enough" turns into "I will walk briskly for 30 minutes at least three times per week."

"I don't take clear notes" turns into "I will review my notes within 24 hours after class and rewrite them for clarity."

"I am in conflict with my parents" turns into "When my parents call, I will take time to understand their point of view before disagreeing with them."

"I get so nervous during the night before a big test that I find it hard to sleep" turns into "I will find ways to reduce stress during the 24 hours before a test so that I sleep better."

Another quality of master students is that they refuse to let their First Steps turn into excuses. These students avoid using the phrase "I can't" and its endless variations.

The key is to state First Steps in a way that allows for new possibilities in the future. Use language in a way that reinforces your freedom to change.

For example, "I can't succeed in math" is better stated like this: "During math courses, I tend to get confused early in the term and find it hard to ask questions. I could be more assertive in asking for help right away."

"I can't say no to my underage friends who like to drink until they get drunk" is better stated as "I have friends who drink illegally and drink too much. I want to be alcohol-free and still be friends with them."

Telling the truth about what we don't want gives us more clarity about what we *do* want. By taking a First Step, we can free up all the energy that it takes to deny our problems and avoid change. We can redirect that energy and use it to take actions that align with our values.

## FIRST STEPS INCLUDE STRENGTHS

For some of us, it's even harder to recognize our strengths than to recognize our weaknesses. Maybe we don't want to brag. Maybe we're attached to a poor self-image.

The reasons don't matter. The point is that using the First Step technique in *Becoming a Master Student* means telling the truth about our positive qualities too.

Remember that weaknesses are often strengths taken to an extreme. The student who carefully revises her writing can make significant improvements in a term paper. If she revises too much and hands in the paper late, though, her grade might suffer. Any success strategy carried too far can backfire.

## FIRST STEPS ARE SPECIFIC

Whether written or verbal, the ways that we express our First Steps are more powerful when they are specific.

For example, if you want to improve your note-taking skills, you might write, "I am an awful note taker"; but it would be more effective to write, "I can't read 80 percent of the notes I took in Introduction to Psychology last week, and I have no idea what was important in that class."

Be just as specific about what you plan to achieve. You might declare, "I want to take legible notes that help me predict what questions will be on the final exam."

The exercises and Journal Entries in this chapter are all about getting specific. They can help you tap resources you never knew you had. For example, do the Discovery Wheel to get a big-picture view of your personal effectiveness. And use the Learning Styles Inventory, along with the articles about multiple intelligences and the VAK system, to tell the truth about how you perceive and process information.

As you use these elements of *Becoming a Master Student*, you might feel surprised at what you discover. You might even disagree with the results of an exercise. That's fine. Just tell the truth about it. Use your disagreement as a tool for further discussion and self-discovery.

This book is full of First Steps. It's just that simple. The truth has power. ■

# ✓EXERCISE 4

## Taking the First Step

The purpose of this exercise is to give you a chance to discover and acknowledge your own strengths, as well as areas for improvement. For many students, this exercise is the most difficult one in the book. To make the exercise worthwhile, do it with courage.

Some people suggest that looking at areas for improvement means focusing on personal weaknesses. They view it as a negative approach that runs counter to positive thinking. Well, perhaps. Positive thinking is a great technique. So is telling the truth, especially when we see the whole picture—the negative aspects as well as the positive ones.

If you admit that you can't add or subtract and that's the truth, then you have taken a strong, positive First Step toward learning basic math. On the other hand, if you say that you are a terrible math student and that's not the truth, then you are programming yourself to accept unnecessary failure.

The point is to tell the truth. This exercise is similar to the Discovery Statements that appear throughout the chapters. The difference is that, in this case, for reasons of confidentiality, you won't write down your discoveries in the book.

You are likely to disclose some things about yourself that you wouldn't want others to read. You might even write down some truths that could get you into trouble. Do this exercise on separate sheets of paper; then hide or destroy them. Protect your privacy. To make this exercise work, follow these suggestions.

**Be specific.** It is not effective to write, "I can improve my communication skills." Of course you can. Instead, write down precisely what you can *do* to improve your communication skills—for example, "I can spend more time really listening while the other person is talking, instead of thinking about what I'm going to say next."

**Be self-aware.** Look beyond the classroom. What goes on outside school often has the greatest impact on your ability to be an effective student. Consider your strengths and weaknesses that you may think have nothing to do with school.

**Be courageous.** This exercise calls for an important master student quality—courage. It is a waste of time

if this exercise is done half-heartedly. Be willing to take risks. You might open a door that reveals a part of yourself that you didn't want to admit was there. The power of this technique is that once you know what is there, you can do something about it.

### Part 1

Time yourself, and for 10 minutes write as fast as you can, completing each of the following sentences at least 10 times with anything that comes to mind. If you get stuck, don't stop. Just write something—even if it seems crazy.

> I never succeed when I . . .
>
> I'm not very good at . . .
>
> Something I'd like to change about myself is . . .

### Part 2

When you have completed the first part of the exercise, review what you have written, crossing off things that don't make any sense. The sentences that remain suggest possible goals for becoming a master student.

### Part 3

Here's the tough part. Time yourself, and for 10 minutes write as fast as you can, completing the following sentences with anything that comes to mind. As in Part 1, complete each sentence at least 10 times. Just keep writing, even if it sounds silly.

> I always succeed when I . . .
>
> I am very good at . . .
>
> Something I like about myself is . . .

### Part 4

Review what you have written, and circle the things that you can fully celebrate. This list is a good thing to keep for those times when you question your own value and worth.

**You're One Click Away...**
*from completing this exercise online under Exercises.*

# ✓ EXERCISE 5
# THE DISCOVERY WHEEL

The Discovery Wheel is another opportunity to tell the truth about the kind of student you are and the kind of student you want to become. Like many other students, you might find the Discovery Wheel to be the most valuable exercise in the book.

This is not a test. There are no trick questions, and the answers will have meaning only for you.

Here are two suggestions to make this exercise more effective. First, think of it as the beginning of an opportunity to change. There is another Discovery Wheel at the end of this book. You will have a chance to measure your progress there, so be honest about where you are now. Second, lighten up. A little laughter can make self-evaluations a lot more effective.

Here's how the Discovery Wheel works. By the end of this exercise, you will have filled in a circle similar to the one on this page. The Discovery Wheel circle is a picture of how you see yourself as a student. The closer the shading comes to the outer edge of the circle, the higher the evaluation of a specific skill. In the example given here, the student has rated her reading skills low and her note-taking skills high.

The terms *high* and *low* are not meant to reflect judgment. The Discovery Wheel is not a permanent picture of who you are. It is a picture of how you view your strengths and weaknesses as a student today. To begin this exercise, read the following statements and award yourself points for each one, using the point system described below. Then add up your point total for each section, and shade the Discovery Wheel on page 31 to the appropriate level.

**5 points:** This statement is always or almost always true of me.

**4 points:** This statement is often true of me.

**3 points:** This statement is true of me about half the time.

**2 points:** This statement is seldom true of me.

**1 point:** This statement is never or almost never true of me.

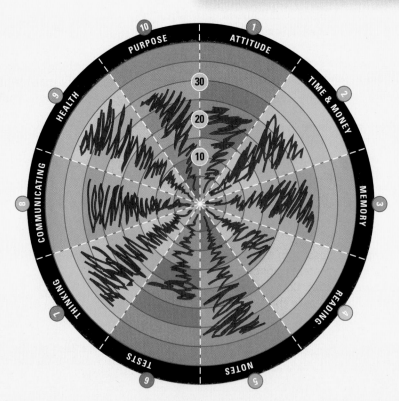

1. _____ I enjoy learning.

2. _____ I understand and apply the concept of multiple intelligences.

3. _____ I connect my courses to my purpose for being in school.

4. _____ I make a habit of assessing my personal strengths and areas for improvement.

5. _____ I am satisfied with how I am progressing toward achieving my goals.

6. _____ I use my knowledge of learning styles to support my success in school.

7. _____ I am willing to consider any idea that can help me succeed in school—even if I initially disagree with that idea.

8. _____ I regularly remind myself of the benefits I intend to get from my education.

_____ Total score (1) Attitude

1. _____ I set long-term goals and periodically review them.

2. _____ I set short-term goals to support my long-term goals.

3. _____ I write a plan for each day and each week.

4. _____ I assign priorities to what I choose to do each day.

5. _____ I am confident that I will have enough money to complete my education.

6. _____ I make regular deposits to a savings account.

7. _____ I pay off the balance on credit card accounts each month.

8. _____ I can have fun without spending money.

_____ Total score (2) Time and Money

1. _____ I am confident of my ability to remember.

2. _____ I can remember people's names.

3. _____ At the end of a lecture, I can summarize what was presented.

4. _____ I apply techniques that enhance my memory skills.

5. _____ I can recall information when I'm under pressure.

6. _____ I remember important information clearly and easily.

7. _____ I can jog my memory when I have difficulty recalling.

8. _____ I can relate new information to what I've already learned.

_____ Total score (3) Memory

1. _____ I preview and review reading assignments.

2. _____ When reading, I ask myself questions about the material.

3. _____ I underline or highlight important passages when reading.

4. _____ When I read textbooks, I am alert and awake.

5. _____ I relate what I read to my life.

6. _____ I select a reading strategy to fit the type of material I'm reading.

7. _____ I take effective notes when I read.

8. _____ When I don't understand what I'm reading, I note my questions and find answers.

_____ Total score (4) Reading

1. _____ When I am in class, I focus my attention.

2. _____ I take notes in class.

3. _____ I am aware of various methods for taking notes and choose those that work best for me.

4. _____ I distinguish important material and note key phrases in a lecture.

5. _____ I copy down material that the instructor writes on the board or overhead display.

6. _____ I can put important concepts into my own words.

7. _____ My notes are valuable for review.

8. _____ I review class notes within 24 hours.

_____ Total score (5) Notes

1. _____ I use techniques to manage stress related to exams.

2. _____ I manage my time during exams and am able to complete them.

3. _____ I am able to predict test questions.

4. _____ I adapt my test-taking strategy to the kind of test I'm taking.

5. _____ I understand what essay questions ask and can answer them completely and accurately.

6. _____ I start reviewing for tests at the beginning of the term.

7. _____ I continue reviewing for tests throughout the term.

8. _____ My sense of personal worth is independent of my test scores.

_____ Total score (6) Tests

1. _____ I have flashes of insight and think of solutions to problems at unusual times.

2. _____ I use brainstorming to generate solutions to a variety of problems.

3. _____ When I get stuck on a creative project, I use specific methods to get unstuck.

4. _____ I learn by thinking about ways to contribute to the lives of other people.

5. _____ I am willing to consider different points of view and alternative solutions.

6. _____ I can detect common errors in logic.

7. _____ I construct viewpoints by drawing on information and ideas from many sources.

8. _____ As I share my viewpoints with others, I am open to their feedback.

_____ **Total score (7) Thinking**

1. _____ I am honest with others about who I am, what I feel, and what I want.

2. _____ Other people tell me that I am a good listener.

3. _____ I can communicate my upset and anger without blaming others.

4. _____ I can make friends and create valuable relationships in a new setting.

5. _____ I am open to being with people I don't especially like in order to learn from them.

6. _____ I build rewarding relationships with people from diverse backgrounds.

7. _____ I can effectively plan and research a large writing assignment.

8. _____ I know ways to prepare and deliver effective speeches.

_____ **Total score (8) Communicating**

1. _____ I have enough energy to study and work—and still enjoy other areas of my life.

2. _____ If the situation calls for it, I have enough reserve energy to put in a long day.

3. _____ The way I eat supports my long-term health.

4. _____ The way I eat is independent of my feelings of self-worth.

5. _____ I exercise regularly to maintain a healthful weight.

6. _____ My emotional health supports my ability to learn.

7. _____ I notice changes in my physical condition and respond effectively.

8. _____ I am in control of any alcohol or other drugs I put into my body.

_____ **Total score (9) Health**

1. _____ I see learning as a lifelong process.

2. _____ I relate school to what I plan to do for the rest of my life.

3. _____ I see problems and tough choices as opportunities for learning and personal growth.

4. _____ I have a written career plan and update it regularly.

5. _____ I am gaining skills to support my success in the workplace.

6. _____ I take responsibility for the quality of my education—and my life.

7. _____ I live by a set of values that translates into daily actions.

8. _____ I am willing to accept challenges even when I'm not sure how to meet them.

_____ **Total score (10) Purpose**

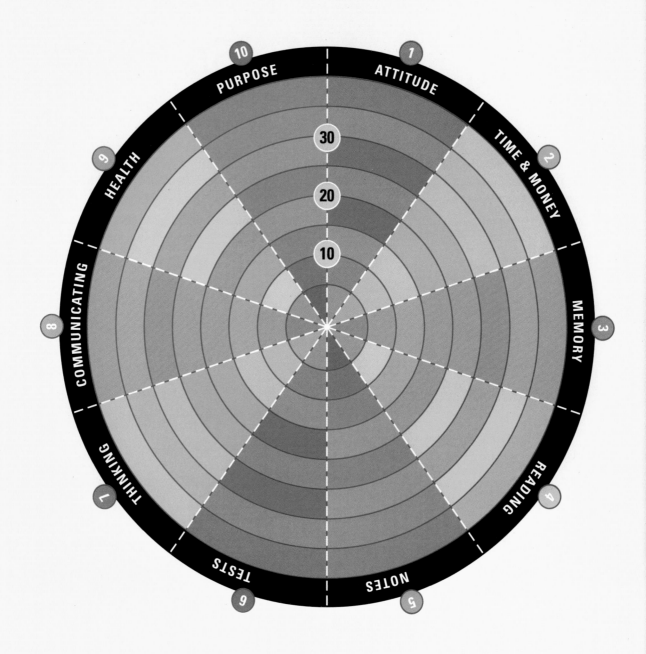

# FILLING IN YOUR DISCOVERY WHEEL

Using the total score from each category, shade in each section of the Discovery Wheel. Use different colors, if you want. For example, you could use green to denote areas you want to work on. When you have finished, complete the Skills Snapshot on the next page. ■

**You're One Click Away...**
*from having your Discovery Wheel scores calculated automatically for you online.*

# ⦿ SKILLS *Snapshot*

**N**ow that you have completed your Discovery Wheel, it's time to get a sense of its weight, shape, and balance. Can you imagine running your hands around it? If you could lift it, would it feel light or heavy? How would it sound if it rolled down a hill? Would it roll very far? Would it wobble? Make your observations without judging the wheel as good or bad. Simply be with the picture you have created.

After you have spent a few minutes studying your Discovery Wheel, complete the following sentences in the spaces below them. Don't worry about what to write. Just put down whatever comes to mind. Remember, this is not a test.

## OVERVIEW

This wheel is an accurate picture of my ability as a student because . . .


My self-evaluation surprises me because . . .


## STRENGTHS

One area where I show strong skills is . . .


Another area of strength is . . .


## GOALS

The area in which I most want to improve is . . .


It is also important for me to get better at . . .


I want to concentrate on improving these areas because . . .


To meet my goals for improvement, I intend to . . .


**Note:** You'll get an opportunity to reflect on your progress when you do the Discovery Wheel exercise again in Chapter 10.

# LEARNING STYLES
## Discovering how you learn

Right now, you are investing substantial amounts of time, money, and energy in your education. What you get in return for this investment depends on how well you understand the process of learning and use it to your advantage.

If you don't understand learning, you might feel bored or confused in class. After getting a low grade, you might have no idea how to respond. Over time, frustration can mount to the point where you question the value of being in school.

Some students answer that question by dropping out of school. These students lose a chance to create the life they want, and society loses the contributions of educated workers.

You can prevent that outcome. Gain strategies for going beyond boredom and confusion. Discover new options for achieving goals, solving problems, listening more fully, speaking more persuasively, and resolving conflicts between people. Start by understanding the different ways that people create meaning from their experience and change their behavior. In other words, learn about *how* we learn.

### WE LEARN BY PERCEIVING AND PROCESSING

When we learn well, says psychologist David Kolb, two things happen.[1] First, we *perceive*. That is, we notice events and "take in" new experiences.

Second, we *process*. We "deal with" experiences in a way that helps us make sense of them.

Some people especially prefer to perceive through *feeling* (also called *concrete experience*). They like to absorb information through their five senses. They learn by getting directly involved in new experiences. When solving problems, they rely on intuition as much as intellect. These people typically function well in unstructured classes that allow them to take initiative.

Some people prefer to process by *watching* (also called *reflective observation*). They prefer to stand back, watch what is going on, and think about it. They consider several points of view as they attempt to make sense of things and generate many ideas about how something happens. They value patience, good judgment, and a thorough approach to learning.

Other people like to perceive by *thinking* (also called *abstract conceptualization*). They take in information best when they can think about it as a subject separate from themselves. They analyze, intellectualize, and create theories. Often these people take a scientific approach to problem solving and excel in traditional classrooms.

Other people like to process by *doing* (also called *active experimentation*). They prefer to jump in and start doing things immediately. These people do not mind taking risks as they attempt to make sense of things; this helps them learn. They are results oriented and look for practical ways to apply what they have learned.

### PERCEIVING AND PROCESSING—AN EXAMPLE

Suppose that you get a new cell phone. It has more features than any phone you've used before. You have many options for learning how to use it. For example:

*   Just get your hands on the phone right away, press some buttons, and see whether you can dial a number or send a text message.
*   Recall experiences you've had with phones in the past and what you've learned by watching other people use their cell phones.
*   Read the instruction manual and view help screens on the phone before you try to make a call.
*   Ask a friend who owns the same type of phone to coach you as you experiment with making calls and sending messages.

These actions illustrate the different approaches to learning:

*   Getting your hands on the phone right away and seeing whether you can make it work is an example of learning through *feeling* (or *concrete experience*).
*   Recalling what you've experienced in the past is an example of learning through *watching* (or *reflective observation*).
*   Reading the manual and help screens before you use the phone is an example of learning through *thinking* (or *abstract conceptualization*).
*   Asking a friend to coach you through a "hands-on" activity with the phone is an example of learning through *doing* (or *active experimentation*).

In summary, your learning style is the unique way that you blend feeling, thinking, watching, and doing. You tend to use this approach in learning anything—from cell phones to English composition to calculus. Reading the next few pages and doing the recommended activities will help you explore your learning style in more detail. ■

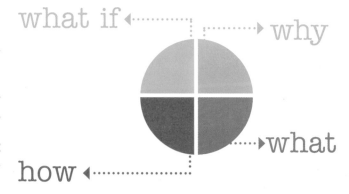

## JOURNAL ENTRY 3
*Discovery Statement*

# Prepare for the Learning Style Inventory (LSI)

As a "warm-up" for the Learning Style Inventory that follows, think about times when you felt successful at learning. Underline or highlight any of the following statements that describe those situations.

- I was in a structured setting, with a lot of directions about what to do.
- I was free to learn at my own pace and in my own way.
- I learned as part of a small group.
- I learned mainly by working alone in a quiet place.
- I learned in a place where there was a lot of activity going on.
- I formed pictures in my mind.
- I learned by *doing* something—moving around, touching something, or trying out a process for myself.
- I learned by talking to myself or explaining ideas to other people.
- I got the "big picture" before I tried to understand the details.
- I listened to a lecture and then thought about it after class.
- I read a book or article and then thought about it afterward.
- I used a variety of media—such as videos, films, audio recordings, or computers—to assist my learning.
- I was considering where to attend school and had to actually set foot on each campus before choosing.
- I was shopping for a car and paid more attention to how I felt about test-driving each one than to the sticker prices or mileage estimates.
- I was thinking about going to a movie and carefully read the reviews before choosing one.

Reviewing this list, do you see any patterns in the way you prefer to learn? If so, briefly describe them.

# Directions for completing the Learning Style Inventory

To help you become more aware of learning styles, a psychologist named David Kolb developed the Learning Style Inventory (LSI). This inventory is included on the next page. Responding to the items in the LSI can help you discover a lot about the ways you learn. Following the LSI are suggestions for using your results to promote your success.

**The LSI is not a test.** There are no right or wrong answers. Your goal is simply to develop a profile of your current learning style. So, take the LSI quickly. You might find it useful to recall a recent time when you learned something new at school, home, or work. However, do not agonize over your responses.

Note that the LSI consists of 12 sentences, each with four different endings. You will read each sentence, and then write a "4" next to the ending that best describes the way you currently learn. Then you will continue ranking the other endings with a "3," "2," or "1," representing the ending that least describes you. This is a forced-choice inventory, so you must rank each ending. Do not leave any endings blank. Use each number only once for each question.

Following are more specific directions:

1. Before you write on page LSI–1, remove the sheet of paper following page LSI–2.

2. Read the instructions at the top of page LSI–1. When you understand example A, you are ready to begin.

3. While writing on page LSI–1, *press firmly* so that your answers will show up on page LSI–3.

# Learning Style Inventory

**Complete items 1–12 below. Use the following example as a guide:**

**A. When I learn:** _2_ I am happy.   _3_ I am fast.   _4_ I am logical.   _1_ I am careful.

**Do not leave any endings blank. Use each number only once for each question. Before completing the items, remove the sheet of paper following this page. While writing, press firmly.**

| | | | | | | | |
|---|---|---|---|---|---|---|---|
| **1. When I learn:** | ____ | I like to deal with my feelings. | ____ | I like to think about ideas. | ____ | I like to be doing things. | ____ | I like to watch and listen. |
| **2. I learn best when:** | ____ | I listen and watch carefully. | ____ | I rely on logical thinking. | ____ | I trust my hunches and feelings. | ____ | I work hard to get things done. |
| **3. When I am learning:** | ____ | I tend to reason things out. | ____ | I am responsible about things. | ____ | I am quiet and reserved. | ____ | I have strong feelings and reactions. |
| **4. I learn by:** | ____ | feeling. | ____ | doing. | ____ | watching. | ____ | thinking. |
| **5. When I learn:** | ____ | I am open to new experiences. | ____ | I look at all sides of issues. | ____ | I like to analyze things, break them down into their parts. | ____ | I like to try things out. |
| **6. When I am learning:** | ____ | I am an observing person. | ____ | I am an active person. | ____ | I am an intuitive person. | ____ | I am a logical person. |
| **7. I learn best from:** | ____ | observation. | ____ | personal relationships. | ____ | rational theories. | ____ | a chance to try out and practice. |
| **8. When I learn:** | ____ | I like to see results from my work. | ____ | I like ideas and theories. | ____ | I take my time before acting. | ____ | I feel personally involved in things. |
| **9. I learn best when:** | ____ | I rely on my observations. | ____ | I rely on my feelings. | ____ | I can try things out for myself. | ____ | I rely on my ideas. |
| **10. When I am learning:** | ____ | I am a reserved person. | ____ | I am an accepting person. | ____ | I am a responsible person. | ____ | I am a rational person. |
| **11. When I learn:** | ____ | I get involved. | ____ | I like to observe. | ____ | I evaluate things. | ____ | I like to be active. |
| **12. I learn best when:** | ____ | I analyze ideas. | ____ | I am receptive and open-minded. | ____ | I am careful. | ____ | I am practical. |

# Taking the next steps

*Now that you've finished taking the Learning Style Inventory, you probably have some questions about what it means. You're about to discover some answers! In the following pages, you will find instructions for:*

- *Scoring your inventory (page LSI–3)*
- *Plotting your scores on to a Learning Style Graph that literally gives a "big picture" of your learning style (page LSI–5)*
- *Interpreting your Learning Style Graph by seeing how it relates to four distinct modes, or styles, of learning (page LSI–6)*
- *Developing all four modes of learning (page LSI–7)*
- *Balancing your learning preferences (page LSI–8)*

Take your time to absorb all this material. Be willing to read through it several times and ask questions.

Your efforts will be rewarded. In addition to discovering more details about *how* you learn, you'll gain a set of strategies for applying this knowledge to your courses. With these strategies, you can use your knowledge of learning styles to actively promote your success in school.

Above all, aim to recover your natural gift for learning—the defining quality of a master student. Rediscover a world where the boundaries between learning and fun, between work and play, all disappear. While immersing yourself in new experiences, blend the sophistication of an adult with the wonder of a child. This path is one that you can travel for the rest of your life.

# Remove this sheet before completing the Learning Style Inventory.

*This page is inserted to ensure that the other writing you do in this book doesn't show through on page LSI–3.*

# Remove this sheet before completing the Learning Style Inventory.

*This page is inserted to ensure that the other writing you do in this book doesn't show through on page LSI–3.*

# Scoring your Inventory

Now that you have taken the Learning Style Inventory, it's time to fill out the Learning Style Graph (page LSI–5) and interpret your results. To do this, follow these steps.

**STEP 1** First, add up all of the numbers you gave to the items marked with brown F letters. Then write down that total in the box to the right, next to **"Brown F."** Next, add up all of the numbers for **"Teal W,"**

"Purple T," and "Orange D," and also write down those totals in the box to the right.

**STEP 2** Add the four totals to arrive at a GRAND TOTAL, and write down that figure in the box to the right. (**Note:** The grand total should equal 120. If you have a different amount, go back and re-add the colored letters; it was probably just an addition error.) Now remove this page and continue with Step 3 on page LSI–5.

## SCORECARD

Brown **F** total \_\_\_\_\_

Teal **W** total \_\_\_\_\_

Purple **T** total \_\_\_\_\_

Orange **D** total \_\_\_\_\_

GRAND TOTAL \_\_\_\_\_

| | | | |
|---|---|---|---|
| F | T | D | W |
| W | T | F | D |
| T | D | W | F |
| F | D | W | T |
| F | W | T | D |
| W | D | F | T |
| W | F | T | D |
| D | T | W | F |
| W | F | D | T |
| W | F | D | T |
| F | W | T | D |
| T | F | W | D |

Remove this page after you have completed
Steps 1 and 2 on page LSI-3.
Then continue with Step 3 on page LSI-5.

# Learning Style Graph

**STEP 3** Remove the sheet of paper that follows this page. Then transfer your totals from Step 2 on page LSI–3 to the lines on the Learning Style Graph below. On the brown (F) line, find the number that corresponds to your "Brown F" total from page LSI–3. Then write an X on this number. Do the same for your "Teal W," "Purple T," and "Orange D" totals. The graph on this page is for you to keep. The graph on page LSI–7 is for you to turn in to your instructor if required to do so.

**STEP 4** Now, pressing firmly, draw four straight lines to connect the four X's, and shade in the area to form a "kite." This is your learning style profile. (For an example, see the illustration to the right.) Each X that you placed on these lines indicates your preference for a different aspect of learning:

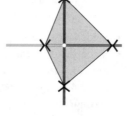

**F** **"Feeling" (Concrete Experience)** The number where you put your X on this line indicates your preference for learning things that have personal meaning. The higher your score on this line, the more you like to learn things that you feel are important and relevant to yourself.

**W** **"Watching" (Reflective Observation)** Your number on this line indicates how important it is for you to reflect on the things you are learning. If your score is high on this line, you probably find it important to watch others as they learn about an assignment and then report on it to the class. You probably like to plan things out and take the time to make sure that you fully understand a topic.

**T** **"Thinking" (Abstract Conceptualization)** Your number on this line indicates your preference for learning ideas, facts, and figures. If your score is high on this line, you probably like to absorb many concepts and gather lots of information on a new topic.

**D** **"Doing" (Active Experimentation)** Your number on this line indicates your preference for applying ideas, using trial and error, and practicing what you learn. If your score is high on this line, you probably enjoy hands-on activities that allow you to test out ideas to see what works.

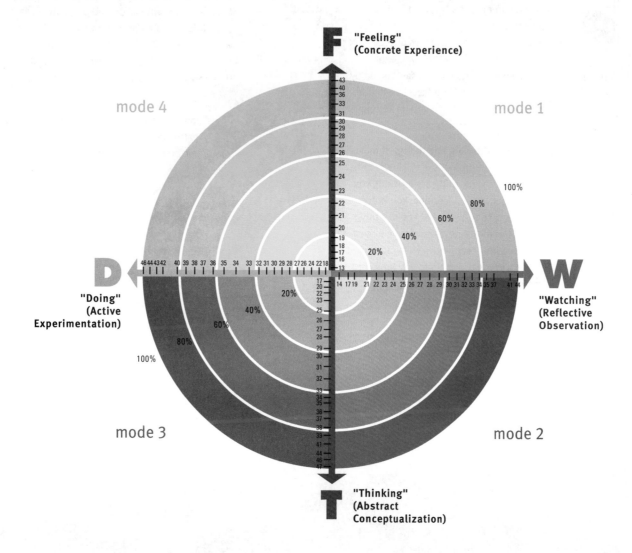

# Interpreting your Learning Style Graph

When you examine your completed Learning Style Graph on page LSI–5, you will notice that your learning style profile (the "kite" that you drew) might be located primarily in one part of the graph. This will give you an idea of your preferred **mode** of learning—the kind of behaviors that feel most comfortable and familiar to you when you are learning something.

Using the descriptions below and the sample graphs, identify your preferred learning mode.

 **Mode 1 blends feeling and watching.** If the majority of your learning style profile is in the upper right-hand corner of the Learning Style Graph, you probably prefer Mode 1 learning. You seek a purpose for new information and a personal connection with the content. You want to know why a course matters and how it challenges or fits in with what you already know. You embrace new ideas that relate directly to their current interests and goals.

 **Mode 2 blends watching and thinking.** If your learning style profile is mostly in the lower right-hand corner of the Learning Style Graph, you probably prefer Mode 2 learning. You are interested in knowing what ideas or techniques are important. You seek a theory to explain events and are interested in what experts have to say. You enjoy learning lots of facts and then arranging these facts in a logical and concise manner. You break a subject down into its key elements or steps and master each one in a systematic way.

 **Mode 3 blends thinking and doing.** If most of your learning style profile is in the lower left-hand corner of the Learning Style Graph, you probably prefer Mode 3 learning. You hunger for an opportunity to try out what you're studying. You get involved with new knowledge by testing it out. You investigate how ideas and techniques work, and you put into practice what you learn. You thrive when you have well-defined tasks, guided practice, and frequent feedback.

 **Mode 4 blends doing and feeling.** If most of your learning style profile is in the upper left-hand corner of the Learning Style Graph, you probably prefer Mode 4 learning. You get excited about going beyond classroom assignments. You like to take what you have practiced and find other uses for it. You seek ways to apply this newly gained skill or information at your workplace or in your personal relationships.

It might be easier for you to remember the modes if you summarize each one as a single question:

- Mode 1 means asking, *Why* learn this?
- Mode 2 means asking, *What* is this about?
- Mode 3 means asking, *How* does this work?
- Mode 4 means asking, *What if* I tried this in a different setting?

 **Combinations.** Some learning style profiles combine all four modes. The profile to the left reflects a learner who is focused primarily on gathering information—*lots* of information! People with this profile tend to ask for additional facts from an instructor, or they want to know where they can go to discover more about a subject.

 The profile to the left applies to learners who focus more on understanding what they learn and less on gathering lots of information. People with this profile prefer smaller chunks of data with plenty of time to process it. Long lectures can be difficult for these learners.

 The profile to the left indicates a learner whose preferences are fairly well balanced. People with this profile can be highly adaptable and tend to excel no matter what the instructor does in the classroom. ■

# Remove this sheet before completing the Learning Style Graph.

*This page is inserted to ensure that the other writing you do in this book does not show through on page LSI–7.*

# Remove this sheet before completing the Learning Style Graph.

*This page is inserted to ensure that the other writing you do in this book does not show through on page LSI–7.*

# Developing all four modes of learning

Each mode of learning represents a unique blend of feeling, watching, thinking, and doing. No matter which of these you've tended to prefer, you can develop the ability to use all four modes:

- **To develop Mode 1,** ask questions that help you understand *why* it is important for you to learn about a specific topic. You might also want to form a study group.
- **To develop Mode 2,** ask questions that help you understand *what* the main points and key facts are. Also, learn a new subject in stages. For example, divide a large reading assignment into sections and then read each section carefully before moving on to the next one.
- **To develop Mode 3,** ask questions about *how* a theory relates to daily life. Also allow time to practice what you learn. You can do experiments, conduct interviews, create presentations, find a relevant work or internship experience, or even write a song that summarizes key concepts. Learn through hands-on practice.
- **To develop Mode 4,** ask *what-if* questions about ways to use what you have just learned in several different situations. Also,

seek opportunities to demonstrate your understanding. You could coach a classmate about what you have learned, present findings from your research, explain how your project works, or perform your song.

Developing all four modes offers many potential benefits. For example, you can excel in many types of courses and find more opportunities to learn outside the classroom. You can expand your options for declaring a major and choosing a career. You can also work more effectively with people who learn differently from you.

In addition, you'll be able to learn from instructors no matter how they teach. Let go of statements such as "My teachers don't get me" and "The instructor doesn't teach to my learning style." Replace those excuses with attitudes such as "I am responsible for what I learn" and "I will master this subject by using several modes of learning."

*The graph on this page is here for you to turn in to your instructor if required to do so.*

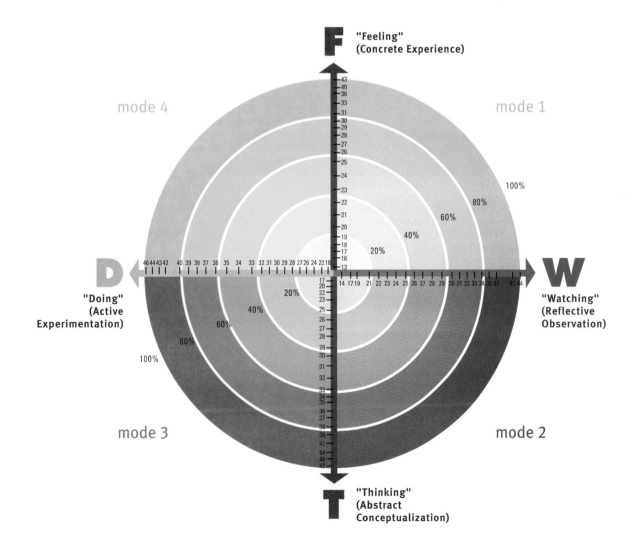

# Balancing your preferences

The chart below identifies some of the natural talents people have, as well as challenges for people who have a strong preference for any one mode of learning. For example, if most of your "kite" is in Mode 2 of the Learning Style Graph, then look at the lower right-hand corner of the following chart to see whether it gives an accurate description of you.

After reviewing the description of your preferred learning mode, read all of the sections that start with the words "People with other preferred modes." These sections explain what actions you can take to become a more balanced learner.

**Feeling**

**mode 4**

**Strengths:**
• Getting things done
• Leadership
• Risk taking

**Too much of this mode can lead to:**
• Trivial improvements
• Meaningless activity

**Too little of this mode can lead to:**
• Work not completed on time
• Impractical plans
• Lack of motivation to achieve goals

**People with other preferred modes can develop Mode 4 by:**
• Making a commitment to objectives
• Seeking new opportunities
• Influencing and leading others
• Being personally involved
• Dealing with people

**mode 1**

**Strengths:**
• Imaginative ability
• Understanding people
• Recognizing problems
• Brainstorming

**Too much of this mode can lead to:**
• Feeling paralyzed by alternatives
• Inability to make decisions

**Too little of this mode can lead to:**
• Lack of ideas
• Not recognizing problems and opportunities

**People with other preferred modes can develop Mode 1 by:**
• Being aware of other people's feelings
• Being sensitive to values
• Listening with an open mind
• Gathering information
• Imagining the implications of ambiguous situations

**Doing** ← → **Watching**

**mode 3**

**Strengths:**
• Problem solving
• Decision making
• Deductive reasoning
• Defining problems

**Too much of this mode can lead to:**
• Solving the wrong problem
• Hasty decision making

**Too little of this mode can lead to:**
• Lack of focus
• Reluctance to consider alternatives
• Scattered thoughts

**People with other preferred modes can develop Mode 3 by:**
• Creating new ways of thinking and doing
• Experimenting with fresh ideas
• Choosing the best solution
• Setting goals
• Making decisions

**mode 2**

**Strengths:**
• Planning
• Creating models
• Defining problems
• Developing theories

**Too much of this mode can lead to:**
• Vague ideals ("castles in the air")
• Lack of practical application

**Too little of this mode can lead to:**
• Inability to learn from mistakes
• No sound basis for work
• No systematic approach

**People with other preferred modes can develop Mode 2 by:**
• Organizing information
• Building conceptual models
• Testing theories and ideas
• Designing experiments
• Analyzing quantitative data

**Thinking**

# Using your
# LEARNING STYLE PROFILE
## to succeed

## DEVELOP ALL FOUR MODES OF LEARNING

Each mode of learning highlighted in the Learning Styles Inventory represents a unique blend of concrete experience, reflective observation, abstract conceptualization, and active experimentation. You can explore new learning styles simply by adopting new habits related to each of these activities. Consider the following suggestions as places to start.

**To gain concrete experiences:**

- See a live demonstration or performance related to your course content.
- Engage your emotions by reading a novel or seeing a video related to your course.
- Interview an expert in the subject you're learning or a master practitioner of a skill you want to gain.
- Conduct role-plays, exercises, or games based on your courses.
- Conduct an informational interview with someone in your chosen career or "shadow" that person for a day on the job.
- Look for a part-time job, internship, or volunteer experience that complements what you do in class.
- Deepen your understanding of another culture and extend your foreign language skills by studying abroad.

**To become more reflective:**

- Keep a personal journal, and write about connections among your courses.
- Form a study group to discuss and debate topics related to your courses.

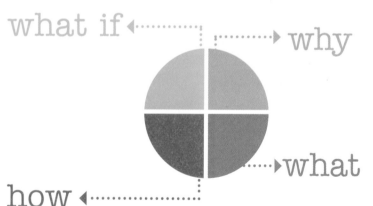

- Set up a Web site, blog, e-mail listserv, or online chat room related to your major.
- Create analogies to make sense of concepts; for instance, see if you can find similarities between career planning and putting together a puzzle.
- Visit your course instructor during office hours to ask questions.
- During social events with friends and relatives, briefly explain what your courses are about.

**To develop abstract thinking:**

- Take notes on your reading in outline form; consider using word-processing software with an outlining feature.
- Supplement assigned texts with other books, magazine and newspaper articles, and related Web sites.
- Attend lectures given by your current instructors and others who teach the same subjects.
- Take ideas presented in text or lectures and translate them into visual form—tables, charts, diagrams, and maps (see Chapter 5: Notes).
- Create visuals and use computer software to recreate them with more complex graphics and animation.

**To become more active:**

- Conduct laboratory experiments or field observations.
- Go to settings where theories are being applied or tested.
- Make predictions based on theories you learn, and then see if events in your daily life confirm your predictions.
- Try out a new behavior described in a lecture or reading, and observe its consequences in your life.

## USE THE MODES WHILE CHOOSING COURSES

Remember your learning style profile when you're thinking about which classes to take and how to study for each class. Look for a fit between your preferred mode of learning and your course work.

If you prefer Mode 1, for example, then look for courses that sound interesting and seem worthwhile to you. If you prefer Mode 2, then consider classes that center on lectures, reading, and discussion. If you prefer Mode 3, then choose courses that include demonstrations, lab sessions, role-playing, and others ways to take action. And if you enjoy Mode 4, then look for courses that could apply to many situations in your life—at work, at home, and in your relationships.

You won't always be able to match your courses to your learning styles. View those situations as opportunities to practice becoming a flexible learner. By developing your skills in all four modes, you can excel in many types of courses.

## USE THE MODES OF LEARNING TO EXPLORE YOUR CAREER

Knowing about learning styles becomes especially useful when planning your career.

People who excel at Mode 1 are often skilled at tuning in to the feelings of clients and coworkers. These people can listen with an open mind, tolerate confusion, be sensitive to people's feelings, open up to problems that are difficult to define, and brainstorm a variety of solutions. If you like Mode 1, you may be drawn to a career in counseling, social services, the ministry, or another field that centers on human relationships. You might also enjoy a career in the performing arts.

People who prefer Mode 2 like to do research and work with ideas. They are skilled at gathering data, interpreting information, and summarizing—arriving at the big picture. They may excel at careers that center on science, math, technical communications, or planning. Mode 2 learners may also work as college teachers, lawyers, technical writers, or journalists.

People who like Mode 3 are drawn to solving problems, making decisions, and checking on progress toward goals. Careers in medicine, engineering, information technology, or another applied science are often ideal for them.

People who enjoy Mode 4 like to influence and lead others. These people are often described as "doers" and "risk takers." They like to take action and complete projects. Mode 4 learners often excel at managing, negotiating, selling, training, and teaching. They might also work for a government agency.

Keep in mind that there is no strict match between certain learning styles and certain careers. Learning is essential to success in all careers. Also, any career can attract people with a variety of learning styles. For instance, the health care field is large enough to include people who prefer Mode 3 and become family physicians—*and* people who prefer Mode 2 and become medical researchers.

## EXPECT TO ENCOUNTER DIFFERENT STYLES

As higher education and the workplace become more diverse and technology creates a global marketplace, you'll meet people who differ from you in profound ways. Your fellow students and coworkers will behave in ways that express a variety of preferences for perceiving information, processing ideas, and acting on what they learn. Consider these examples:

- A roommate who's continually moving while studying—reciting facts out loud, pacing, and gesturing—probably prefers concrete experience and learning by taking action.

- A coworker who talks continually on the phone about a project may prefer to learn by listening, talking, and forging key relationships.

- A supervisor who excels at abstract conceptualization may want to see detailed project plans and budgets submitted in writing well before a project swings into high gear.

- A study group member who always takes the initiative, manages the discussion, delegates any work involved, and follows up with everyone probably prefers active experimentation.

Differences in learning style can be a stumbling block—or an opportunity. When differences intersect, there is the potential for conflict as well as for creativity. Succeeding with peers often means seeing the classroom and workplace as a laboratory for learning from experience. Resolving conflict and learning from mistakes are all part of the learning cycle.

## ACCEPT CHANGE—AND OCCASIONAL DISCOMFORT

Seek out chances to develop new modes of learning. If your instructor asks you to form a group to complete an assignment, avoid joining a group where everyone shares your learning style. Work on project teams with people who learn differently than you. Get together with people who both complement and challenge you.

Also look for situations where you can safely practice new skills. If you enjoy reading, for example, look for ways to express what you learn by speaking, such as leading a study group on a textbook chapter.

Discomfort is a natural part of the learning process. Allow yourself to notice any struggle with a task or lack of interest in completing it. Remember that such feelings are temporary and that you are balancing your learning preferences. By choosing to move through discomfort, you consciously expand your ability to learn in new ways. ■

> You won't always be able to match your courses to your learning styles. View those situations as opportunities to practice becoming a flexible learner.

# Claim your multiple INTELLIGENCES

**1**

People often think that being smart means the same thing as having a high IQ, and that having a high IQ automatically leads to success. However, psychologists are finding that IQ scores do not always foretell which students will do well in academic settings—or after they graduate.[2]

Howard Gardner of Harvard University believes that no single measure of intelligence can tell us how smart we are. Instead, Gardner defines intelligence in a flexible way as "the ability to solve problems, or to create products, that are valued within one or more cultural settings." He also identifies several types of intelligence, as described here.[3]

People using **verbal/linguistic intelligence** are adept at language skills and learn best by speaking, writing, reading, and listening. They are likely to enjoy activities such as telling stories and doing crossword puzzles.

People who use **mathematical/logical intelligence** are good with numbers, logic, problem solving, patterns, relationships, and categories. They are generally precise and methodical, and are likely to enjoy science.

When people learn visually and by organizing things spatially, they display **visual/spatial intelligence**. They think in images and pictures, and understand best by seeing the subject. They enjoy charts, graphs, maps, mazes, tables, illustrations, art, models, puzzles, and costumes.

People using **bodily/kinesthetic intelligence** prefer physical activity. They enjoy activities such as building things, woodworking, dancing, skiing, sewing, and crafts. They generally are coordinated and athletic, and they would rather participate in games than just watch.

Individuals using **musical/rhythmic intelligence** enjoy musical expression through songs, rhythms, and musical instruments. They are responsive to various kinds of sounds; remember melodies easily; and might enjoy drumming, humming, and whistling.

People using **intrapersonal intelligence** are exceptionally aware of their own feelings and values. They are generally reserved, self-motivated, and intuitive.

Outgoing people show evidence of **interpersonal intelligence.** They do well with cooperative learning and are sensitive to the feelings, intentions, and motivations of others. They often make good leaders.

People using **naturalist intelligence** love the outdoors and recognize details in plants, animals, rocks, clouds, and other natural formations. These people excel in observing fine distinctions among similar items.

Each of us has all of these intelligences to some degree. And each of us can learn to enhance them. Experiment with learning in ways that draw on a variety of intelligences—including those that might be less familiar. When we acknowledge all of our intelligences, we can constantly explore new ways of being smart. ■

# ✓ EXERCISE 6

## Develop your multiple intelligences

Gardner's theory of multiple intelligences complements the discussion of different learning styles in this chapter. The main point is that there are many ways to gain knowledge and acquire new behaviors. You can use Gardner's concepts to explore a range of options for achieving success in school, work, and relationships.

The chart on the next page summarizes the content of "Claim your multiple intelligences" and suggests ways to apply the main ideas. Instead of merely glancing through this chart, get active. Place a check mark next to any of the "Possible characteristics" that describe you. Also check off the "Possible learning strategies" that you intend to use. Finally, underline or highlight any of the "Possible careers" that spark your interest.

Remember that the chart is *not* an exhaustive list or a formal inventory. Take what you find merely as points of departure. You can invent strategies of your own to cultivate different intelligences.

| Type of intelligence | Possible characteristics | Possible learning strategies | Possible careers |
|---|---|---|---|
| Verbal/linguistic | ❑ You enjoy writing letters, stories, and papers.<br>❑ You prefer to write directions rather than draw maps.<br>❑ You take excellent notes from textbooks and lectures.<br>❑ You enjoy reading, telling stories, and listening to them. | ❑ Highlight, underline, and write notes in your textbooks.<br>❑ Recite new ideas in your own words.<br>❑ Rewrite and edit your class notes.<br>❑ Talk to other people often about what you're studying. | Librarian, lawyer, editor, journalist, English teacher, radio or television announcer |
| Mathematical/logical | ❑ You enjoy solving puzzles.<br>❑ You prefer math or science class to English class.<br>❑ You want to know how and why things work.<br>❑ You make careful, step-by-step plans. | ❑ Analyze tasks so you can order them in a sequence of steps.<br>❑ Group concepts into categories, and look for underlying patterns.<br>❑ Convert text into tables, charts, and graphs.<br>❑ Look for ways to quantify ideas—to express them in numerical terms. | Accountant, auditor, tax preparer, mathematician, computer programmer, actuary, economist, math or science teacher |
| Visual/spatial | ❑ You draw pictures to give an example or clarify an explanation.<br>❑ You understand maps and illustrations more readily than text.<br>❑ You assemble things from illustrated instructions.<br>❑ You especially enjoy books that have a lot of illustrations. | ❑ When taking notes, create concept maps, mind maps, and other visuals (see Chapter 5: Notes).<br>❑ Code your notes by using different colors to highlight main topics, major points, and key details.<br>❑ When your attention wanders, focus it by sketching or drawing.<br>❑ Before you try a new task, visualize yourself doing it well. | Architect, commercial artist, fine artist, graphic designer, photographer, interior decorator, engineer, cartographer |
| Bodily/kinesthetic | ❑ You enjoy physical exercise.<br>❑ You tend not to sit still for long periods of time.<br>❑ You enjoy working with your hands.<br>❑ You use a lot of gestures when talking. | ❑ Be active in ways that support concentration; for example, pace as you recite, read while standing up, and create flash cards.<br>❑ Carry materials with you, and practice studying in several different locations.<br>❑ Create hands-on activities related to key concepts; for example, create a game based on course content.<br>❑ Notice the sensations involved with learning something well. | Physical education teacher, athlete, athletic coach, physical therapist, chiropractor, massage therapist, yoga teacher, dancer, choreographer, actor |

| Type of intelligence | Possible characteristics | Possible learning strategies | Possible careers |
|---|---|---|---|
| Musical/rhythmic | ❑ You often sing in the car or shower.<br>❑ You easily tap your foot to the beat of a song.<br>❑ You play a musical instrument.<br>❑ You feel most engaged and productive when music is playing. | ❑ During a study break, play music or dance to restore energy.<br>❑ Put on background music that enhances your concentration while studying.<br>❑ Relate key concepts to songs you know.<br>❑ Write your own songs based on course content. | Professional musician, music teacher, music therapist, choral director, musical instrument sales representative, musical instrument maker, piano tuner |
| Intrapersonal | ❑ You enjoy writing in a journal and being alone with your thoughts.<br>❑ You think a lot about what you want in the future.<br>❑ You prefer to work on individual projects over group projects.<br>❑ You take time to think things through before talking or taking action. | ❑ Connect course content to your personal values and goals.<br>❑ Study a topic alone before attending a study group.<br>❑ Connect readings and lectures to a strong feeling or significant past experience.<br>❑ Keep a journal that relates your course work to events in your daily life. | Minister, priest, rabbi, professor of philosophy or religion, counseling psychologist, creator of a home-based or small business |
| Interpersonal | ❑ You enjoy group work over working alone.<br>❑ You have plenty of friends and regularly spend time with them.<br>❑ You prefer talking and listening over reading or writing.<br>❑ You thrive in positions of leadership. | ❑ Form and conduct study groups early in the term.<br>❑ Create flash cards, and use them to quiz study partners.<br>❑ Volunteer to give a speech or lead group presentations on course topics.<br>❑ Teach the topic you're studying to someone else. | Manager, school administrator, salesperson, teacher, counseling psychologist, arbitrator, police officer, nurse, travel agent, public relations specialist, creator of a midsize to large business |
| Naturalist | ❑ As a child, you enjoyed collecting insects, leaves, or other natural objects.<br>❑ You enjoy being outdoors.<br>❑ You find that important insights occur during times you spend in nature.<br>❑ You read books and magazines on nature-related topics. | ❑ During study breaks, take walks outside.<br>❑ Post pictures of outdoor scenes where you study, and play recordings of outdoor sounds while you read.<br>❑ Invite classmates to discuss course work while taking a hike or going on a camping trip.<br>❑ Focus on careers that hold the potential for working outdoors. | Environmental activist, park ranger, recreation supervisor, historian, museum curator, biologist, criminologist, mechanic, woodworker, construction worker, construction contractor or estimator |

1

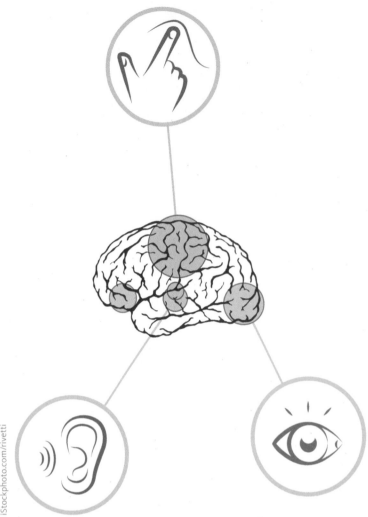

iStockphoto.com/rivetti

# LEARNING BY SEEING, HEARING, AND MOVING: the VAK system

Alternatively, you can approach the topic of learning styles with a simple and powerful system—one that focuses on just three ways of perceiving through your senses:

- Seeing, or visual learning
- Hearing, or auditory learning
- Movement, or kinesthetic learning

To recall this system, remember the letters **VAK**, which stand for **visual, auditory,** and **kinesthetic.** The theory is that each of us prefers to learn through one of these senses. And we can enrich our learning with activities that draw on the other channels.

To reflect on your VAK preferences, answer the following questions. Each question has three possible answers. Circle the answer that best describes how you would respond in the stated situation. This is not a formal inventory—just a way to prompt some self-discovery.

**When you have problems spelling a word, you prefer to:**

1. Look it up in the dictionary.

2. Say the word out loud several times before you write it down.

3. Write out the word with several different spellings and then choose one.

**You enjoy courses the most when you get to:**

1. View slides, overhead displays, videos, and readings with plenty of charts, tables, and illustrations.

2. Ask questions, engage in small-group discussions, and listen to guest speakers.

3. Take field trips, participate in lab sessions, or apply the course content while working as a volunteer or intern.

**When giving someone directions on how to drive to a destination, you prefer to:**

1. Pull out a piece of paper and sketch a map.

2. Give verbal instructions.

3. Say, "I'm driving to a place near there, so just follow me."

**When planning an extended vacation to a new destination, you prefer to:**

1. Read colorful, illustrated brochures or articles about that place.

2. Talk directly to someone who's been there.

3. Spend a day or two at that destination on a work-related trip before taking a vacation there.

**You've made a commitment to learn to play the guitar. The first thing you do is:**

1. Go to a library or music store and find an instruction book with plenty of diagrams and chord charts.

2. Pull out your favorite CDs, listen closely to the guitar solos, and see whether you can play along with them.

3. Buy or borrow a guitar, pluck the strings, and ask someone to show you how to play a few chords.

**You've saved up enough money to lease a car. When choosing from among several new models, the most important factor in your decision is:**

1. Reading information about the car from sources like *Consumer Reports*.

2. The information you get by talking to people who own the cars you're considering.

3. The overall impression you get by taking each car on a test drive.

**You've just bought a new computer system. When setting up the system, the first thing you do is:**

1. Skim through the printed instructions that come with the equipment.

2. Call someone with a similar system and ask her for directions.

3. Assemble the components as best as you can, see whether everything works, and consult the instructions only as a last resort.

**You get a scholarship to study abroad next semester, which starts in just three months. You will travel to a country where French is the most widely spoken language. To learn as much French as you can before you depart, you:**

1. Buy a video-based language course that's recorded on a DVD.

2. Set up tutoring sessions with a friend who's fluent in French.

3. Sign up for a short immersion course in an environment in which you speak only French, starting with the first class.

Now take a few minutes to reflect on the meaning of your responses. All of the answers numbered "1" are examples of visual learning. The "2's" refer to auditory learning, and the "3's" illustrate kinesthetic learning. Finding a consistent pattern in your answers indicates that you prefer learning through one sense channel more than the others. Or you might find that your preferences are fairly balanced.

Listed here are suggestions for learning through each sense channel. Experiment with these examples, and create more techniques of your own. Use the suggestions to build on your current preferences and develop new options for learning.

## TO ENHANCE VISUAL LEARNING:

- Preview reading assignments by looking for elements that are highlighted visually—bold headlines, charts, graphs, illustrations, and photographs.

- When taking notes in class, leave plenty of room to add your own charts, diagrams, tables, and other visuals later.

- Whenever an instructor writes information on a blackboard or overhead display, copy it exactly in your notes.

- Transfer your handwritten notes to your computer. Use word-processing software that allows you to format your notes in lists, add headings in different fonts, and create visuals in color.

- Before you begin an exam, quickly sketch a diagram on scratch paper. Use this diagram to summarize the key formulas or facts you want to remember.

- During tests, see whether you can visualize pages from your handwritten notes or images from your computer-based notes.

## TO ENHANCE AUDITORY LEARNING:

- Reinforce memory of your notes and readings by talking about them. When studying, stop often to recite key points and examples in your own words.

- After reciting several summaries of key points and examples, record your favorite version or write it out.
- Read difficult passages in your textbooks slowly and out loud.
- Join study groups, and create short presentations about course topics.
- Visit your instructors during office hours to ask questions.

## TO ENHANCE KINESTHETIC LEARNING:

- Look for ways to translate course content into three-dimensional models that you can build. While studying biology, for example, create a model of a human cell using different colors of clay.

- Supplement lectures with trips to museums, field observations, lab sessions, tutorials, and other hands-on activities.
- Recite key concepts from your courses while you walk or exercise.
- Intentionally set up situations in which you can learn by trial and error.
- Create a practice test, and write out the answers in the room where you will actually take the exam.

One variation of the VAK system has been called VARK.[4] The *R* describes a preference for learning by reading and writing. People with this preference might benefit from translating charts and diagrams into statements, taking notes in lists, and converting those lists into possible items on a multiple-choice test. ■

# Master Students
# IN ACTION

**You're One Click Away...**
*from a video about Master Students in Action.*

" *At the beginning of the term, I would have said that I learned best by doing (hands-on). But now that I have grown and expanded the boundaries of my mind's learning capabilities, I learn best with a mixture of all three (watching, listening, and doing). This is because I have come to realize that all three types of learning are connected through a balance; leading one to discover the "perfect" method of learning.* "

—Deondré Lucas, Valencia
Community College

# Choosing your purpose

Success is a choice—your choice. To *get* what you want, it helps to *know* what you want. That is the purpose of this two-part Journal Entry. You can begin choosing success by completing this Journal Entry right now. If you choose to do it later, then plan a date, time, and place and then block out the time on your calendar.

Date: _____ Time: _____ Place: _____

**1**

## Part 1

Select a time and place when you know you will not be disturbed for at least 20 minutes. (The library is a good place to do this exercise.) Relax for two or three minutes, clearing your mind. Next, complete the following sentences—and then keep writing. When you run out of things to write, stick with it just a bit longer. Be willing to experience a little discomfort. Keep writing. What you discover might be well worth the extra effort.

What I want from my education is . . . _____

_____

When I complete my education, I want to be able to . . . _____

_____

I also want . . . _____

_____

_____

_____

## Part 2

After completing Part 1, take a short break. Reward yourself by doing something that you enjoy. Then come back to this Journal Entry.

Now, review the list you just created of things that you want from your education. See whether you can summarize them in one sentence. Start this sentence with "My purpose for being in school is. . . ." Allow yourself to write many drafts of this mission statement, and review it periodically as you continue your education. With each draft, see whether you can capture the essence of what you want from higher education and from your life. State it in a vivid way—in a short sentence that you can easily memorize, one that sparks your enthusiasm and makes you want to get up in the morning.

You might find it difficult to express your purpose statement in one sentence. If so, write a paragraph or more. Then look for the sentence that seems most charged with energy for you. Following are some sample purpose statements:

- My purpose for being in school is to gain skills that I can use to contribute to others.

- My purpose for being in school is to live an abundant life that is filled with happiness, health, love, and wealth.

- My purpose for being in school is to enjoy myself by making lasting friendships and following the lead of my interests.

Write at least one draft of your purpose statement here:

_____

_____

_____

# EXTRACURRICULAR ACTIVITIES
## reap the benefits

As you enter higher education, you may find that you are busier than you've ever been before. Often that's due to the variety of extracurricular activities available to you: athletics, fraternities, sororities, student newspapers, debate teams, study groups, service learning projects, internships, student government, and political action groups, to name just a few. Your school might also offer conferences, films, concerts, museums, art galleries, and speakers—all for free or reduced prices. Student organizations help to make these activities possible, and you can join any of them.

People who participate in extracurricular activities gain many benefits. They bridge the worlds inside and outside the classroom. They expand their learning styles by testing theories in action and gaining concrete experiences. Through student organizations, they explore possible careers, make contacts for jobs, and build a lifelong habit of giving back to their communities. They make new friends among both students and faculty and work on teams with people from other cultures.

Getting involved in such organizations also comes with some risks. When students don't balance extracurricular activities with class work, their success in school can suffer. They can also compromise their health by losing sleep, neglecting exercise, skipping meals, or relying on fast food. These costs are easier to avoid if you keep a few suggestions in mind:

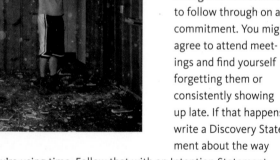

- **Make conscious choices** about how to divide your time between schoolwork and extracurricular activities. Decide up front how many hours each week or month you can devote to a student organization. Leave room in your schedule for relaxing and for unplanned events. For more ideas, see Chapter 2: Time and Money.

- **Look to the future** when making commitments. Write down three or four of the most important goals you'd like to achieve in your lifetime. Then choose extracurricular activities that directly support those goals.

- **Create a career plan** that includes a list of skills needed for your next job. Then choose extracurricular activities to develop those skills. If you're unsure of your career choice, then get involved in campus organizations to explore your options.

- **Whenever possible, develop leadership experience** by holding an office in an organization. If that's too much of a commitment, then volunteer to lead a committee or plan a special event.

- **Get involved** in a variety of extracurricular activities. Varying your activities demonstrates to future employers that you can work with a variety of people in a range of settings.

- **Recognize reluctance** to follow through on a commitment. You might agree to attend meetings and find yourself forgetting them or consistently showing up late. If that happens, write a Discovery Statement about the way you're using time. Follow that with an Intention Statement about ways to keep your agreements—or consider renegotiating those agreements.

- **Say no** to activities that fail to create value for you. Avoid joining groups only because you feel guilty or obligated to do so.

- **Check out the rules** before joining any student organization. Ask about dues and attendance requirements. ■

# SERVICE-LEARNING:
## The art of learning by contributing

As part of a service-learning project for a sociology course, students volunteer at a community center for older adults. For another service-learning project, history students interview people in veterans' hospitals about their war experiences. These students plan to share their interview results with a psychiatrist on the hospital staff.

Meanwhile, business students provide free tax-preparation help at a center for low-income people. Students in graphic arts classes create free promotional materials for charities. Other students staff a food cooperative and a community credit union.

These examples of actual projects from the National Service-Learning Clearinghouse demonstrate the working premise of service-learning: Volunteer work and other forms of contributing can become a vehicle for higher education.

### FILL YOURSELF UP AND GIVE IT BACK

In the spirit of the Power Process included earlier in this chapter, think of service-learning as a way to find new tools in new ideas. In fact, see service-learning as a tool based on one of the core values behind this book—making a positive contribution to the lives of other people.

Much of *Becoming a Master Student* is about filling yourself up, taking care of yourself, being selfish, and meeting your needs. The techniques and suggestions in these pages focus on ways to get what you want out of school, work, and the rest of your life.

One of the results of all this successful selfishness is the capacity to contribute. This means giving back to your community in ways that enhance the lives of other people.

### FIND SERVICE-LEARNING COURSES

Many schools offer service-learning programs. Look in the index of your school catalog under "service-learning," and search your school's Web site using those key words. There might be a service-learning office on your campus.

Also turn to national organizations that keep track of service-learning opportunities. One is the Corporation for National and Community Service, a federal government agency (**www.nationalservice.gov**, 202-606-5000). You can also contact the National Service-Learning Clearinghouse (**www.servicelearning.org**, 866-245-7378). These resources can lead you to others, including service-learning programs in your state.

### GETTING THE MOST FROM SERVICE-LEARNING

When you design a service-learning project, consider the following suggestions.

**Follow your interests.** Think of the persistent problems in the world—illiteracy, hunger, obesity, addictions, unemployment, poverty, and more. Which of them generate the strongest feelings in you? Which of them link to your possible career plans and choice of major? The place where passion intersects with planning often creates a useful opportunity for service-learning.

**Choose partners carefully.** Work with a community organization that has experience with students. Make sure that the organization has liability insurance to cover volunteers.

**Learn about the organization.** Once you connect with community organization, learn everything you can about it. Find its mission statement and explore its history. Find out what makes this organization unique. If the organization partners with others in the community, learn about those other organizations as well.

**Handle logistics.** Integrating service-learning into your schedule can call for detailed planning. If your volunteer work takes place off campus, arrange for transportation and allow for travel time.

**Build long-term impact into your project.** One potential pitfall of service-learning is that the programs are often short-lived. After students pack up and return to campus, programs can die. To avoid this outcome, make sure that other students or community members are willing to step in and take over for you when the semester ends.

**Connect service-learning to critical thinking.** To think critically and creatively about your service-learning project, ask questions such as these:

- What service did you perform?
- What roles did your service project include, and who filled those roles?
- What knowledge and skills did you bring to this project?
- After being involved in this project, what new knowledge and skills do you want to gain?
- What did you learn from this experience that can make another service-learning project more successful?
- Will this service-learning project affect your choice of a major? If so, how?
- Will this service-learning project affect your career plans? If so, how?

Service-learning provides an opportunity to combine theory and practice, reflection and action, "book learning" and "real-world" experience. Education takes place as we reflect on our experiences and turn them into new insights and intentions. Use service-learning as a way to take your thinking skills to a whole new level. ■

**You're One Click Away...**
*from finding more strategies online for effective service-learning.*

# MAKE THE CAREER
## *connection*

Starting now, read this book with a mental filter in place. Ask yourself, "How can I use this idea to meet my career goals? How can I apply this technique to my current job or the next job I see for myself?" The answers can help you thrive in any job, whether you work full time or part time.

Many articles in this book have workplace applications. Following are just a few examples. As you read, look for more.

The techniques presented in *Setting and achieving goals* (page 59) can help you plan and complete projects on time. Supplement these ideas with suggestions from *The ABC daily to-do list* (page 60) and *Stop procrastination now* (page 64).

*Get the most out of now* (page 65) is packed with ideas you can transfer to the workplace. For example, tackle difficult tasks first thing in the day, or at any other time when your energy peaks.

*Memory techniques* (page 84) will come in handy as you learn the policies and procedures for a new job. Those techniques can also help you remember names as you meet people during your job search, and as meet new coworkers.

Use the Muscle Reading method presented in Chapter 4 to keep up with journals and books in your career field.

Adapt the ideas mentioned in *Cooperative learning: Studying in groups* (page 144) in order to cooperate more effectively with members of a project team.

*Let go of test anxiety* (page 150) is full of strategies that can help you manage stress at work.

Thinking skills can help you create new products and services and sell them. See *Ways to create ideas* (page 164), *Becoming a critical thinker* (page 160), and *Four ways to solve problems* (page 169) for strategies.

Your own career path may require you to produce e-mails, reports, memos, articles, abstracts, proposals, job descriptions, and other business documents. *Strategies for effective writing* (page 189) offers a core process for completing all these assignments. You can also enhance your career with public speaking skills. Take the next step in developing these skills with *Strategies for public speaking* (page 191).

The suggestions in *Communicating across cultures* (page 186) can assist you in adapting to the culture of a new workplace.

Return to *Create your career now* (page 221) at any time in the future when you're redefining the kind of work that you want to do. Then hone your job-hunting skills with *Use résumés and interviews to "hire" an employer* (page 226).

*Now that you're done—begin* (page 233) opens up pathways to lifelong learning. Use these suggestions to continually update your job skills and explore new areas for personal development. ■

iStockphoto.com/Lise Gagne

# YOU DON'T *NEED* THIS COURSE
## —but you might *want* it

Some students don't believe they need a student success course. They might be right. These students may tell you that many schools don't even offer such a class. That's true.

### Consider the benefits of taking this course anyway.

Start with a single question: What's one new thing that you could do on a regular basis to make a significant, positive difference in your life? This question might be the most important thing you ask yourself this term. The answer does not have to involve a huge behavior change. Over weeks and months, even a small shift in the way you take notes, read a textbook, or interact with instructors can make a major difference in how well you do in school. A student success course gives you dozens of strategies for creating the life of your dreams.

Students who open up to this idea experience benefits. These comments from a recent student success course evaluation are typical:

*I didn't expect to get anything out of this course except an easy A. Boy, was I ever wrong. This course has changed my life.*

*I entered college with no confidence. Now that I have taken this class, I feel like I can succeed in any class.*

*This course has truly showed that I have the power to change any situation for the better.*

*I am now ready for the rest of my college years.*

It's possible that you might arrive at such results on your own, given enough time. Why wait, however? Approach this book and your course as if the quality of your education depended on them. Then watch the benefits start to unfold.

# PRACTICING
# critical thinking 1

Psychologist Benjamin Bloom described six kinds of thinking:

**Level 1: Remembering**—recalling an idea.

**Level 2: Understanding**—explaining an idea in your own words and giving examples from your own experience.

**Level 3: Applying**—using an idea to produce a desired result.

**Level 4: Analyzing**—dividing an idea into parts or steps.

**Level 5: Evaluating**—rating the truth, usefulness, or quality of an idea—and giving reasons for your rating.

**Level 6: Creating**—inventing something new based on an idea.

You can recall any suggestion from this book (**Level 1: Remembering**) and take that idea to a higher level of thinking. For example, the article "Extracurricular activities—reap the benefits," on page 44, includes this suggestion: "Get involved in a variety of extracurricular activities." You could take this suggestion to **Level 2: Understanding** by adding personal examples:

> *Extracurricular activities are worthwhile things to do while I'm in school. These activities go beyond the assignments in my classes and help me develop skills that I can use in my career after I graduate. At my school, for example, I could do volunteer fund raising for the campus radio station. I could also join an intramural volleyball team or run for student senate.*

Now it's your turn. Choose another suggestion from this chapter (**Level 1: Remembering**) and think about it at **Level 2: Understanding**. In the space below, state the suggestion and write a brief paragraph that summarizes your higher-level thinking.

_____

_____

_____

_____

_____

**Note:** If you'd like to demonstrate your thinking in another way—such as by making a drawing, building a model, or even writing a song—then discuss this with your instructor.

*For more information on the six levels of thinking, see "Becoming a critical thinker" in Chapter 7.*

# MASTER STUDENT
# profiles

In each chapter of this text, there is an example of a person who embodies one or more of the master student qualities mentioned in the Introduction to this book. As you read about these people and others like them, ask yourself: "How can I apply this?" Look for the timeless qualities in the people you read about. Many of the strategies used by master students from another time or place are tools that you can use today.

The master students in this book demonstrated unusual and effective ways to learn. Remember that these are just 10 examples of master students (one for each chapter). You can read more about them in the Master Student Hall of Fame on the Web site.

As you read the Master Student Profiles, ask questions based on each mode of learning: Why is this person considered a master student? What attitudes or behaviors helped to create her mastery? How can I develop those qualities? What if I could use his example to create positive new results in my own life?

Also reflect on other master students you've read about or know personally. Focus on people who excel at learning. The master student is not a vague or remote ideal. Rather, master students move freely among us.

In fact, there's one living inside your skin.

# masterstudentprofile

## Lalita Booth

Once homeless, and now a student at the University of Central Florida (UCF), accepted to Harvard University Business School.

Sitting in front of a classroom of LEAD Scholars, Lalita Booth looks like any other junior. The brown-eyed, freckle-faced student blends in with her peers in the University of Central Florida (UCF) leadership development program in every way.

That is, until she opens her mouth.

"You're looking at the face of a child abuse survivor, a perpetual runaway, a high school dropout," she says, as idle chitchat turns to complete silence.

"I was a teenage mother, a homeless parent, and a former welfare recipient."

Lalita's parents divorced when she was young; by age 12 she was a runaway pro—asking for permission to go somewhere and then simply not returning for a few days or a few weeks. . . .

She became proficient in "couch surfing" at friends' homes. When there was no couch to crash on, the teen would take her nightly refuge behind the closest dumpster and rest in the park during the day.

Furthering her quest to be a grownup, at 17 she married her long-time buddy and fellow high-school-dropout, Quinn. Three months later, she found out she was pregnant with her son, Kieren. What normally would be a joyful time was instead a stressful one while the new couple struggled in a prison of deep poverty. The miserable situation began to take its toll, and after just 2½ years of marriage, Quinn was ready to call it quits.

With her new boyfriend, Carl, and her most precious cargo, Kieren, in tow, Booth fled to Boulder, Colorado. Kieren lived with his paternal grandparents for 7 months while Lalita and Carl attempted to get back on their feet.

Being in Colorado proved to be fruitful for the 21-year-old Lalita. It started with an interesting job opportunity as an enrolled agent—an expert in U.S. taxation who can represent taxpayers before the Internal Revenue Service. Lalita could acquire the license without further schooling. Better yet, it would boost her income to

$32,000. She buckled down and read all 4,000 pages of the study guide, and, thanks to her nearly photographic memory, she aced the test.

But once again, she was in the wrong place at the wrong time. Carl's brother in Orlando was very ill, and he needed to move to Florida.

The only way to insure her independence was to do something that frightened her to the very core—go back to school. . . .

And soon after, she enrolled at Seminole Community College. . . .

In May 2005, Lalita was selected to attend the Salzburg Global Seminar, where she brainstormed ways to solve global problems with a group of international students. The thought-provoking trip led to her mission: to help others escape the choke hold of poverty.

Back in the states, Booth's world became even more dream-like when she won the Jack Kent Cooke Foundation Scholarship.

Lalita Booth strongly believes, and for good reason, that "things that are worth achieving are absolutely unreasonable." She advises, "Set unreasonable goals, and chase them unreasonably."

**LALITA BOOTH . . . is willing to work.**

**YOU . . . can work effectively by starting with a First Step.**

Adapted from Sarah Sekula, "Escape Artist," *Pegasus*, July/August 2008, *UCF Alumni Life*, 20–26. Reprinted with permission.

**You're One Click Away...**
*from learning more about Lalita Booth online at the Master Student Profiles. You can also visit the Master Student Hall of Fame to learn about other master students.*

# CHAPTER 1 QUIZ

1. The Power Process: "Ideas are tools" states that if you want to *use* an idea, you must *believe* in it. True or false? Explain your answer.

2. The First Step technique refers only to telling the truth about your areas for improvement. True or false? Explain your answer.

3. The four modes of learning are associated with certain questions. Give the appropriate question for each mode.

4. List the types of intelligence defined by Howard Gardner.

5. Describe three learning strategies related to one type of intelligence that you listed.

6. The word *kinesthetic* refers to:
   (a) Moving.
   (b) Hearing.
   (c) Seeing.
   (d) Listening.

7. List three strategies for getting the most from extracurricular activities.

8. Find an article in this book with suggestions that you could use in the workplace. List the title of that article, and summarize at least two of those suggestions here.

9. To get the most value from this course, the text suggests that you ask:
   (a) What's one new thing that you could do on a regular basis to make a significant, positive difference in your life?
   (b) How can you make a big change in your behavior within the next week?
   (c) How can you make several big changes in your behavior during this term?
   (d) None of the above.

10. List the 6 levels of thinking described by psychologist Benjamin Bloom.

# CHAPTER 1 SKILLS *Snapshot*

You'll find a Skills Snapshot at the end of each chapter in this book. Use these exercises to stay aware of your changing attitudes and behaviors—including your progress in developing the qualities of a Master Student.

The Discovery Wheel in this chapter includes a section labeled *Attitude*. For the next 10 to 15 minutes, go beyond your initial responses to that exercise. Take a snapshot of your skills as they exist today, after reading and doing this chapter.

Begin by reflecting on some recent experiences. Then take another step toward mastery by choosing to follow up on your reflections with a specific action.

## DISCOVERY

My score on the *Attitude* section of the Discovery Wheel was . . .

Three things I do well as a student are . . .

Three ways that I'd like to improve as a student are . . .

If asked to describe my learning style in one sentence, I would say that I am . . .

## INTENTION

To become a more flexible learner, I intend to . . .

To support my success in school, I intend to adopt the attitude that . . .

## NEXT ACTION

To show that I've adopted this attitude, the most important thing I can do right now is to . . .

At the end of this course, I would like my *Attitude* score on the Discovery Wheel to be . . .

# Time and Money

 Use this **Master Student Map** to ask yourself,

**WHY** THIS CHAPTER MATTERS . . .

- Procrastination, lack of planning, and money problems can quickly undermine your success in school.

 **WHAT** IS INCLUDED . . .

 **HOW** CAN I USE THIS CHAPTER . . .

- Discover the details about how you currently use time.
- Know exactly what to do today, this week, and this month to achieve your goals.
- Align your expenses with your income.
- Reduce credit card bills and other sources of debt.

 **WHAT** IF . . .

- I could meet my goals with time to spare?

**2**

**JOURNAL ENTRY 5**
*Intention Statement*

## Create value from this chapter

Take a few minutes to skim this chapter. Find at least three techniques that you intend to use. List them below, along with their associated page numbers.

| Strategy | Page number |
| --- | --- |
| | |
| | |
| | |
| | |
| | |
| | |
| | |
| | |
| | |
| | |
| | |
| | |
| | |
| | |

© Ruslan Ivantsov/Shutterstock.com

**B**eing right here, right now is such a simple idea. It seems obvious. Where else can you be but where you are? When else can you be there but when you are there?

The answer is that you can be somewhere else at any time—in your head. It's common for our thoughts to distract us from where we've chosen to be. When we let this happen, we lose the benefits of focusing our attention on what's important to us in the present moment.

To "be here now" means to do what you're doing when you're doing it. It means to be where you are when you're there. Students consistently report that focusing attention on the here and now is one of the most powerful tools in this book.

We all have a voice in our head that hardly ever shuts up. If you don't believe it, conduct this experiment: Close your eyes for 10 seconds, and pay attention to what is going on in your head. Please do this right now.

Notice something? Perhaps a voice in your head was saying, "Forget it. I'm in a hurry." Another might have said, "I wonder when 10 seconds is up?" Another could have been saying, "What little voice? I don't hear any little voice."

That's the voice.

This voice can take you anywhere at any time—especially when you are studying. When the voice takes you away, you might appear to be studying, but your brain is somewhere else.

All of us have experienced this voice, as well as the absence of it. When our inner voices are silent, time no longer seems to exist. We forget worries, aches, pains, reasons, excuses, and justifications. We fully experience the here and now. Life is magic.

Do not expect to be rid of the voice entirely. That is neither possible nor desirable. Inner voices serve a purpose. They enable us to analyze, predict, classify, and understand events out there in the "real" world. The trick is to consciously choose when to be with your inner voice and when to let it go.

Instead of trying to force a stray thought out of your head, simply notice it. Accept it. Tell yourself, "There's that thought again." Then gently return your attention to the task at hand. That thought, or another, will come back. Your mind will drift. Simply notice again where your thoughts take you, and gently bring yourself back to the here and now.

Also remember that planning supports this Power Process. Goals are tools that we create to guide our action in the present. Time management techniques—calendars, lists, and all the rest—have only one purpose. They reveal what's most important for you to focus on right *now*.

The idea behind this Power Process is simple. When you listen to a lecture, listen to a lecture. When you read this book, read this book. And when you choose to daydream, daydream. Do what you're doing when you're doing it. Be where you are when you're there.

Be here now . . . and now . . . and now.

**You're One Click Away...**
*from accessing Power Process Media online and finding out more about how to "be here now."*

# YOU'VE GOT THE TIME—
# *and the money*

The words *time management* may call forth images of restriction and control. You might visualize a prune-faced Scrooge hunched over your shoulder, stopwatch in hand, telling you what to do every minute. Bad news.

Good news: You do have enough time for the things you want to do. All it takes is thinking about the possibilities and making conscious choices.

........................................................

> ## Remember that time is an equal opportunity resource. All of us, regardless of gender, race, creed, or national origin, have exactly the same number of hours in a week. No matter how famous we are, no matter how rich or poor, we get 168 hours to spend each week—no more, no less.

........................................................

Time is an unusual commodity. There are several reasons for this. For one, it cannot really be saved. You can't stockpile time like wood for the stove or food for the winter.

Time also can't be seen, heard, touched, tasted, or smelled. Even scientists and philosophers find it hard to describe. And because time is so elusive, it is easy to ignore. That doesn't bother time at all. Time is perfectly content to remain hidden until you are nearly out of it. And when you are out of it, you are out of it.

In addition, time is a nonrenewable resource. If you're out of wood, you can chop some more. If you're out of money, you can earn a little extra. If you're out of love, there is still hope. If you're out of health, it can often be restored. But when you're out of time, that's it. When this minute is gone, it's gone.

Another challenge is that time seems hard to control. Sometimes it seems that your friends control your time; your boss controls your time; your teachers or your parents or your kids or somebody else controls your time.

This chapter invites you to test that idea. Approach time as if you *are* in control. When you say you don't have enough time, you

might really be saying that you are not spending the time you *do* have in the way that you want.

The same idea applies to money. When you say you don't have enough money, the real issue might be that you are not spending the money you *do* have in the way that you want.

Most money problems result from spending more than is available. It's that simple, even though we often do everything we can to make the problem much more complicated. The solution also is simple: Don't spend more than you have. If you are spending more than you have, then increase your income, decrease your spending, or do both. This idea has never won a Nobel Prize in Economics, but you won't go broke applying it.

Everything written about time and money management can be reduced to three main ideas:

1. **Know exactly *what* you want**. State your wants as clear, specific goals. And put them in writing.

2. **Know *how* to get what you want.** Take action to meet your goals, including financial goals. Determine what you'll do *today* to get what you want in the future. Put those actions in writing as well.

3. **Take action to *get* what you want.** When our lives lack this quality, we spend most of our time responding to interruptions, last-minute projects, and emergencies. Life feels like a scramble to just survive. We're so busy achieving someone else's goals that we forget about getting what *we* want.

........................................................

> ## When you say you don't have enough money, the real issue might be that you are not spending the money you *do* have in the way that you want.

........................................................

Useful strategies for managing time and money are not new. These strategies are all based on the cycle of discovery, intention, and action that you're already practicing in this book. Throw in the ability to add and subtract, and you have everything you need to take charge of your time and your money.

Use the strategies in this chapter to manage these valuable resources in ways that align with your values. ∎

2

# EXERCISE 7

## The Time Monitor

The purpose of this exercise is to transform time into a knowable and predictable resource. To do this, monitor your time in 15-minute intervals, 24 hours a day, for 7 days. Record how much time you spend sleeping, eating, studying, attending lectures, traveling to and from class, working, watching television, listening to music, taking care of the kids, running errands—everything.

If this sounds crazy, hang on for a minute. This exercise is not about keeping track of the rest of your life in 15-minute intervals. It is an opportunity to become conscious of how you spend your time—your life. Use the Time Monitor only for as long as it helps you do that.

When you know exactly how you spend your time, you can make choices with open eyes. You can plan to spend more time on the things that are most important to you and less time on the unimportant. Monitoring your time puts you in control of your life.

To do this exercise, complete the following steps:

1. **Look at Figure 2.1, a sample Time Monitor, on page 55.** On Monday, the student in this sample got up at 6:45 A.M., showered, and got dressed. He finished this activity and began breakfast at 7:15. He put this new activity in at the time he began, and drew a line just above it. He ate from 7:15 to 7:45. It took him 15 minutes to walk to class (7:45 to 8:00), and he attended classes from 8:00 to 11:00.

   You will list your activities in the same way. When you begin an activity, write it down next to the time you begin. Round off to the nearest 15 minutes. If, for example, you begin eating at 8:06, enter your starting time as 8:00.

2. **Fill out your Time Monitor.** Now it's your turn. Make copies of the blank Time Monitor (Figure 2.2 on page 56), or plan to do this exercise online. With your instructor, choose a day to begin monitoring your time. On that day, start filling out your Time Monitor. Keep it with you all day and use it for one full week. Take a few moments every couple of hours to record what you've done. Or, enter a note each time that you change activities.

3. **After you've monitored your time for one week, group your activities together into categories.** List them in the "Category" column in Figure 2.3 on page 58. This chart already includes the categories "sleep," "class," "study," and "meals." Think of other categories to add. "Grooming" might include showering, putting on makeup, brushing teeth, and getting dressed. "Travel" could include walking, driving, taking the bus, and riding your bike. Other categories might be "exercise," "entertainment," "work," "television," "domestic," and "children." Write in the categories that work for you.

4. **List your *estimated* hours for each category of activity.** Guess how many hours you *think* you spent on each category of activity. List these hours in the "Estimated" column in Figure 2.3.

5. **List your *actual* hours for each category of activity.** Now, add up the figures from your Time Monitor. List these hours in the "Actual" column in Figure 2.3. Make sure that the grand total of all categories is 168 hours.

6. **Reflect on the results of this exercise.** Compare the "Estimated" and "Actual" columns. Take a few minutes and let these numbers sink in. Notice your reactions. You might feel disappointed or even angry about where your time goes. Use those feelings as motivation to make different choices. Complete the following sentences:

   I was surprised at the amount of time I spent on . . .

   _____

   I want to spend more time on . . .

   _____

   I want to spend less time on . . .

   _____

7. **Repeat this exercise.** Do this exercise as many times as you want. The benefit is developing a constant awareness of your activities. With that awareness, you can make informed choices about how to spend the time of your life.

**You're One Click Away...**
*from doing this exercise online under Exercises.*

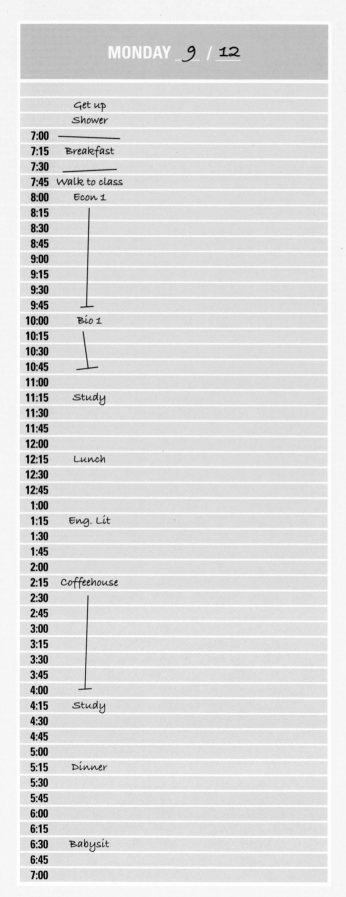

| MONDAY _9_ / _12_ | |
|---|---|
| | Get up |
| | Shower |
| **7:00** | ———— |
| **7:15** | Breakfast |
| **7:30** | ———— |
| **7:45** | Walk to class |
| **8:00** | Econ 1 |
| **8:15** | |
| **8:30** | |
| **8:45** | |
| **9:00** | |
| **9:15** | |
| **9:30** | |
| **9:45** | |
| **10:00** | Bio 1 |
| **10:15** | |
| **10:30** | |
| **10:45** | |
| **11:00** | |
| **11:15** | Study |
| **11:30** | |
| **11:45** | |
| **12:00** | |
| **12:15** | Lunch |
| **12:30** | |
| **12:45** | |
| **1:00** | |
| **1:15** | Eng. Lit |
| **1:30** | |
| **1:45** | |
| **2:00** | |
| **2:15** | Coffeehouse |
| **2:30** | |
| **2:45** | |
| **3:00** | |
| **3:15** | |
| **3:30** | |
| **3:45** | |
| **4:00** | |
| **4:15** | Study |
| **4:30** | |
| **4:45** | |
| **5:00** | |
| **5:15** | Dinner |
| **5:30** | |
| **5:45** | |
| **6:00** | |
| **6:15** | |
| **6:30** | Babysit |
| **6:45** | |
| **7:00** | |

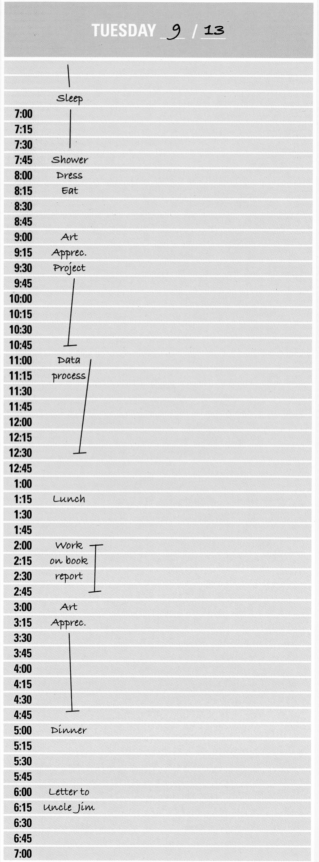

| TUESDAY _9_ / _13_ | |
|---|---|
| | Sleep |
| **7:00** | |
| **7:15** | |
| **7:30** | |
| **7:45** | Shower |
| **8:00** | Dress |
| **8:15** | Eat |
| **8:30** | |
| **8:45** | |
| **9:00** | Art |
| **9:15** | Apprec. |
| **9:30** | Project |
| **9:45** | |
| **10:00** | |
| **10:15** | |
| **10:30** | |
| **10:45** | |
| **11:00** | Data |
| **11:15** | process |
| **11:30** | |
| **11:45** | |
| **12:00** | |
| **12:15** | |
| **12:30** | |
| **12:45** | |
| **1:00** | |
| **1:15** | Lunch |
| **1:30** | |
| **1:45** | |
| **2:00** | Work |
| **2:15** | on book |
| **2:30** | report |
| **2:45** | |
| **3:00** | Art |
| **3:15** | Apprec. |
| **3:30** | |
| **3:45** | |
| **4:00** | |
| **4:15** | |
| **4:30** | |
| **4:45** | |
| **5:00** | Dinner |
| **5:15** | |
| **5:30** | |
| **5:45** | |
| **6:00** | Letter to |
| **6:15** | Uncle Jim |
| **6:30** | |
| **6:45** | |
| **7:00** | |

**Figure 2.1** Sample Time Monitor

| MONDAY ___ / ___ / ___ / | TUESDAY ___ / ___ / ___ / | WEDNESDAY ___ / ___ / ___ / | THURSDAY ___ / ___ / ___ / |
|---|---|---|---|
| 7:00 | 7:00 | 7:00 | 7:00 |
| 7:15 | 7:15 | 7:15 | 7:15 |
| 7:30 | 7:30 | 7:30 | 7:30 |
| 7:45 | 7:45 | 7:45 | 7:45 |
| 8:00 | 8:00 | 8:00 | 8:00 |
| 8:15 | 8:15 | 8:15 | 8:15 |
| 8:30 | 8:30 | 8:30 | 8:30 |
| 8:45 | 8:45 | 8:45 | 8:45 |
| 9:00 | 9:00 | 9:00 | 9:00 |
| 9:15 | 9:15 | 9:15 | 9:15 |
| 9:30 | 9:30 | 9:30 | 9:30 |
| 9:45 | 9:45 | 9:45 | 9:45 |
| 10:00 | 10:00 | 10:00 | 10:00 |
| 10:15 | 10:15 | 10:15 | 10:15 |
| 10:30 | 10:30 | 10:30 | 10:30 |
| 10:45 | 10:45 | 10:45 | 10:45 |
| 11:00 | 11:00 | 11:00 | 11:00 |
| 11:15 | 11:15 | 11:15 | 11:15 |
| 11:30 | 11:30 | 11:30 | 11:30 |
| 11:45 | 11:45 | 11:45 | 11:45 |
| 12:00 | 12:00 | 12:00 | 12:00 |
| 12:15 | 12:15 | 12:15 | 12:15 |
| 12:30 | 12:30 | 12:30 | 12:30 |
| 12:45 | 12:45 | 12:45 | 12:45 |
| 1:00 | 1:00 | 1:00 | 1:00 |
| 1:15 | 1:15 | 1:15 | 1:15 |
| 1:30 | 1:30 | 1:30 | 1:30 |
| 1:45 | 1:45 | 1:45 | 1:45 |
| 2:00 | 2:00 | 2:00 | 2:00 |
| 2:15 | 2:15 | 2:15 | 2:15 |
| 2:30 | 2:30 | 2:30 | 2:30 |
| 2:45 | 2:45 | 2:45 | 2:45 |
| 3:00 | 3:00 | 3:00 | 3:00 |
| 3:15 | 3:15 | 3:15 | 3:15 |
| 3:30 | 3:30 | 3:30 | 3:30 |
| 3:45 | 3:45 | 3:45 | 3:45 |
| 4:00 | 4:00 | 4:00 | 4:00 |
| 4:15 | 4:15 | 4:15 | 4:15 |
| 4:30 | 4:30 | 4:30 | 4:30 |
| 4:45 | 4:45 | 4:45 | 4:45 |
| 5:00 | 5:00 | 5:00 | 5:00 |
| 5:15 | 5:15 | 5:15 | 5:15 |
| 5:30 | 5:30 | 5:30 | 5:30 |
| 5:45 | 5:45 | 5:45 | 5:45 |
| 6:00 | 6:00 | 6:00 | 6:00 |
| 6:15 | 6:15 | 6:15 | 6:15 |
| 6:30 | 6:30 | 6:30 | 6:30 |
| 6:45 | 6:45 | 6:45 | 6:45 |
| 7:00 | 7:00 | 7:00 | 7:00 |
| 7:15 | 7:15 | 7:15 | 7:15 |
| 7:30 | 7:30 | 7:30 | 7:30 |
| 7:45 | 7:45 | 7:45 | 7:45 |
| 8:00 | 8:00 | 8:00 | 8:00 |
| 8:15 | 8:15 | 8:15 | 8:15 |
| 8:30 | 8:30 | 8:30 | 8:30 |
| 8:45 | 8:45 | 8:45 | 8:45 |
| 9:00 | 9:00 | 9:00 | 9:00 |
| 9:15 | 9:15 | 9:15 | 9:15 |
| 9:30 | 9:30 | 9:30 | 9:30 |
| 9:45 | 9:45 | 9:45 | 9:45 |
| 10:00 | 10:00 | 10:00 | 10:00 |
| 10:15 | 10:15 | 10:15 | 10:15 |
| 10:30 | 10:30 | 10:30 | 10:30 |
| 10:45 | 10:45 | 10:45 | 10:45 |
| 11:00 | 11:00 | 11:00 | 11:00 |
| 11:15 | 11:15 | 11:15 | 11:15 |
| 11:30 | 11:30 | 11:30 | 11:30 |
| 11:45 | 11:45 | 11:45 | 11:45 |
| 12:00 | 12:00 | 12:00 | 12:00 |

**Figure 2.2** Your Time Monitor

| FRIDAY ___ / ___ / ___ / | SATURDAY ___ / ___ / ___ / | SUNDAY ___ / ___ / ___ / |
|---|---|---|
| 7:00 | 7:00 | 7:00 |
| 7:15 | 7:15 | 7:15 |
| 7:30 | 7:30 | 7:30 |
| 7:45 | 7:45 | 7:45 |
| 8:00 | 8:00 | 8:00 |
| 8:15 | 8:15 | 8:15 |
| 8:30 | 8:30 | 8:30 |
| 8:45 | 8:45 | 8:45 |
| 9:00 | 9:00 | 9:00 |
| 9:15 | 9:15 | 9:15 |
| 9:30 | 9:30 | 9:30 |
| 9:45 | 9:45 | 9:45 |
| 10:00 | 10:00 | 10:00 |
| 10:15 | 10:15 | 10:15 |
| 10:30 | 10:30 | 10:30 |
| 10:45 | 10:45 | 10:45 |
| 11:00 | 11:00 | 11:00 |
| 11:15 | 11:15 | 11:15 |
| 11:30 | 11:30 | 11:30 |
| 11:45 | 11:45 | 11:45 |
| 12:00 | 12:00 | 12:00 |
| 12:15 | 12:15 | 12:15 |
| 12:30 | 12:30 | 12:30 |
| 12:45 | 12:45 | 12:45 |
| 1:00 | 1:00 | 1:00 |
| 1:15 | 1:15 | 1:15 |
| 1:30 | 1:30 | 1:30 |
| 1:45 | 1:45 | 1:45 |
| 2:00 | 2:00 | 2:00 |
| 2:15 | 2:15 | 2:15 |
| 2:30 | 2:30 | 2:30 |
| 2:45 | 2:45 | 2:45 |
| 3:00 | 3:00 | 3:00 |
| 3:15 | 3:15 | 3:15 |
| 3:30 | 3:30 | 3:30 |
| 3:45 | 3:45 | 3:45 |
| 4:00 | 4:00 | 4:00 |
| 4:15 | 4:15 | 4:15 |
| 4:30 | 4:30 | 4:30 |
| 4:45 | 4:45 | 4:45 |
| 5:00 | 5:00 | 5:00 |
| 5:15 | 5:15 | 5:15 |
| 5:30 | 5:30 | 5:30 |
| 5:45 | 5:45 | 5:45 |
| 6:00 | 6:00 | 6:00 |
| 6:15 | 6:15 | 6:15 |
| 6:30 | 6:30 | 6:30 |
| 6:45 | 6:45 | 6:45 |
| 7:00 | 7:00 | 7:00 |
| 7:15 | 7:15 | 7:15 |
| 7:30 | 7:30 | 7:30 |
| 7:45 | 7:45 | 7:45 |
| 8:00 | 8:00 | 8:00 |
| 8:15 | 8:15 | 8:15 |
| 8:30 | 8:30 | 8:30 |
| 8:45 | 8:45 | 8:45 |
| 9:00 | 9:00 | 9:00 |
| 9:15 | 9:15 | 9:15 |
| 9:30 | 9:30 | 9:30 |
| 9:45 | 9:45 | 9:45 |
| 10:00 | 10:00 | 10:00 |
| 10:15 | 10:15 | 10:15 |
| 10:30 | 10:30 | 10:30 |
| 10:45 | 10:45 | 10:45 |
| 11:00 | 11:00 | 11:00 |
| 11:15 | 11:15 | 11:15 |
| 11:30 | 11:30 | 11:30 |
| 11:45 | 11:45 | 11:45 |
| 12:00 | 12:00 | 12:00 |

2

| WEEK OF ___ / ___ / ___ / | | |
|---|---|---|
| Category | Estimated Hours | Actual Hours |
| Sleep | | |
| Class | | |
| Study | | |
| Meals | | |
| | | |
| | | |
| | | |
| | | |
| | | |
| | | |
| | | |
| | | |
| | | |
| | | |
| | | |
| | | |
| | | |
| | | |
| | | |

**Figure 2.3** Your Estimated and Actual Hours

# SETTING *and* ACHIEVING *goals*

Many people have no goals, or have only vague, idealized notions of what they want. These notions float among the clouds in their heads. They are wonderful, fuzzy, safe thoughts such as "I want to be a good person," "I want to be financially secure," or "I want to be happy."

Generalized outcomes have great potential as achievable goals. When we keep these goals in a nonspecific form, however, we may become confused about ways to actually achieve them.

Make your goal as real as a finely tuned engine. There is nothing vague or fuzzy about engines. You can see them, feel them, and hear them. You can take them apart and inspect the moving parts.

Goals can be every bit as real and useful. If you really want to meet a goal, then take it apart. Inspect the moving parts—the physical actions that you will take to make the goal happen and fine-tune your life.

There are many useful methods for setting goals. You're about to learn one of them. Experiment, and modify as you see fit.

**Write specific goals.** Writing down your goals greatly increases your chances of meeting them. Writing exposes undefined terms, unrealistic time frames, and other symptoms of fuzzy thinking.

To keep track of your goals, write each one on a separate 3 × 5 card, or type them all into a file on your computer. Update this file as your goals change.

Keep your goals specific. Make clear what actions are needed or what results are expected. Consider these examples:

| Vague goal | Specific goal |
|---|---|
| Get a good education. | Graduate with B.S. degree in engineering, with honors, by 2012. |
| Get good grades. | Earn a 3.5 grade point average next semester. |
| Enhance my spiritual life. | Meditate for 15 minutes daily. |
| Improve my appearance. | Lose 6 pounds during the next 6 months |
| Get control of my money. | Transfer $100 to my savings account each month. |

When stated specifically, a goal might look different to you. If you examine it closely, a goal you once thought you wanted might not be something you want after all. Or you might discover that you want to choose a new path to achieve a goal that you are sure you want.

**Write goals in several time frames.** To get a comprehensive vision of your future, write down the following:

- *Long-term goals.* Long-term goals represent major targets in your life. These goals can take 5 to 20 years to achieve. In some cases, they will take a lifetime. They can include goals in education, careers, personal relationships, travel, financial security—whatever is most important to you.
- *Midterm goals.* Midterm goals are objectives you can accomplish in 1 to 5 years. They include goals such as completing a course of education, paying off a car loan, or achieving a specific career level. These goals usually support your long-term goals.
- *Short-term goals.* Short-term goals are the ones you can accomplish in a year or less. These goals are specific achievements, such as completing a particular course or group of courses, hiking down the Appalachian Trail, or organizing a family reunion.

**Write goals in several areas of life.** People who set goals in only one area of life—such as their career—may find that their personal growth becomes one-sided. They might experience success at work while neglecting their health or relationships with family members and friends.

To avoid this outcome, set goals in a variety of categories. Consider what you want to experience in these areas:

- Education
- Career
- Financial life
- Family life or relationships
- Social life
- Spiritual life
- Level of health

Add goals in other areas as they occur to you.

**Move into action immediately.** To increase your odds of success, take immediate action. Decrease the gap between stating a goal and starting to achieve it. If you slip and forget about the goal, you can get back on track at any time by *doing* something about it. ■

# The ABC *daily to-do list*

One advantage of a daily to-do list is that you don't have to remember what to do next. It's on the list.

## STEP 1 BRAINSTORM TASKS

List all of the tasks you want to get done tomorrow. Each task will become an item on a to-do list. Don't worry about putting the entries in order or scheduling them yet. List everything you want to accomplish on a sheet of paper or in a notebook. You can also use 3 × 5 cards, writing one task on each card. Cards work well because you can slip them into your pocket or rearrange them, and you never have to copy to-do items from one list to another.

## STEP 2 ESTIMATE TIME

For each task you wrote down in Step 1, estimate how long it will take you to complete it. This can be tricky. If you allow too little time, you end up feeling rushed. If you allow too much time, you become less productive. For now, give it your best guess. If you are unsure, overestimate rather than underestimate how long it will take for each task.

Now pull out your calendar or Time Monitor/Time Plan. You've probably scheduled some hours for events such as classes or work. This leaves the unscheduled hours for tackling your to-do list.

Add up the time needed to complete all your to-do items. Also add up the number of unscheduled hours in your day. Then compare the two totals. The power of this step is that you can spot overload in advance. If you have 8 hours' worth of to-do items but only 4 unscheduled hours, that's a potential problem. To solve it, proceed to Step 3.

## STEP 3 RATE EACH TASK BY PRIORITY

To prevent overscheduling, decide which to-do items are the most important, given the time you have available. One suggestion for making this decision comes from the book *How to Get Control of Your Time and Your Life*, by Alan Lakein: Simply label each task A, B, or C.[1]

The A's on your list are those things that are the most critical. They include assignments that are coming due or jobs that need to be done immediately. Also included are activities that lead directly to your short-term goals.

The B's on your list are important, but less so than the A's. B's can be postponed, if necessary, for another day.

C's are often small, easy jobs with no set time line. They too can be postponed.

Once you've labeled the items on your to-do list, schedule time for all of the A's. The B's and C's can be done randomly during the day when you are in between tasks and are not yet ready to start the next A. Even if you only get only one or two of your A's done, you'll still be moving toward your goals.

## STEP 4 CROSS OFF TASKS

Keep your to-do list with you at all times. Cross off activities when you finish them, and add new ones when you think of them. If you're using 3 × 5 cards, you can toss away or recycle the cards with completed items. Crossing off tasks and releasing cards can be fun—a visible reward for your diligence. This step fosters a sense of accomplishment.

When using the ABC priority method, you might experience an ailment common to students: C fever. Symptoms include the uncontrollable urge to drop that A task and begin crossing C's off your to-do list. If your history paper is due tomorrow, you might feel compelled to vacuum the rug, call your third cousin in Tulsa, and make a trip to the store for shoelaces.

Use your to-do list to keep yourself on task, working on your A's. But don't panic or berate yourself when you realize that in the last six hours, you have completed eleven C's and not a single A. Just calmly return to the A's. ∎

**You're One Click Away...**
*from finding more strategies online for daily planning.*

## *Master Students* IN ACTION

"*Without my own planner, I would most likely draw a blank as to what I need to accomplish for the day, week, month, and beyond. I recommend that any student use it as a means of keeping organized.*"

—Deeanna Mosher,
Arizona State University

# Make choices about
# MULTITASKING

When we get busy, we get tempted to do several things at the same time. It seems like such a natural solution: Watch TV *and* read a textbook. Talk on the phone *and* outline a paper. Write an e-mail *and* listen to a lecture. These are examples of multitasking.

There's a problem with this strategy: Multitasking is much harder than it looks.

Despite the awe-inspiring complexity of the human brain, research reveals that we are basically wired to do one thing at a time.[2] One study found that people who interrupted work to check e-mail or surf the Internet took up to 25 minutes to get back to their original task.[3] In addition, people who use cell phones while driving have more accidents than anyone except drunk drivers.[4]

The solution is an old-fashioned one: Whenever possible, take life one task at a time. Develop a key quality of master students—focused attention. Start by reviewing and using the Power Process: "Be here now." Then add the following strategies to your toolbox.

## UNPLUG FROM TECHNOLOGY

To reduce the temptation of multitasking, turn off distracting devices. Shut off your TV and cell phone. Disconnect from the Internet unless it's required for your planned task. Later, you can take a break to make calls, send texts, check e-mail, and browse the Web.

## CAPTURE FAST-BREAKING IDEAS WITH MINIMAL INTERRUPTION

Your brain is an expert nagger. After you choose to focus on one task, it might issue urgent reminders about 10 more things you need to do. Keep $3 \times 5$ cards or paper and a pen handy to write down those reminders. You can take a break later and add them to your to-do list. Your mind can quiet down once it knows that a task has been captured in writing.

## MONITOR THE MOMENT-TO-MOMENT SHIFTS IN YOUR ATTENTION

Whenever you're studying and notice that you're distracted by thoughts of doing something else, make a tally mark on a sheet of paper. Simply being aware of your tendency to multitask can help you reclaim your attention.

## HANDLE INTERRUPTIONS WITH CARE

Some breaking events are so urgent that they call for your immediate attention. When this happens, note what you were doing when you were interrupted. For example, write down the number of the page you were reading, or the name of the computer file you were creating. When you return to the task, your notes can help you get up to speed again.

## MULTITASK BY CONSCIOUS CHOICE

If multitasking seems inevitable, then do it with skill. Pair one activity that requires concentration with another activity that you can do almost automatically. For example, studying for your psychology exam while downloading music is a way to reduce the disadvantages of multitasking. Pretending to listen to your children while watching TV is not.

## ALIGN YOUR ACTIVITIES WITH YOUR PASSIONS

Our attention naturally wanders when we find a task to be trivial, pointless, or irritating. At those times, switching attention to another activity becomes a way to reduce discomfort.

Handling routine tasks is a necessary part of daily life. But if you find that your attention frequently wanders throughout the day, ask yourself: Am I really doing what I want to do? Do my work and my classes connect to my interests?

If the answer is no, then the path beyond multitasking might call for a change in your academic and career plans. Determine what you want most in life. Then use the techniques in this chapter to set goals that inspire you. Whenever an activity aligns with your passion, the temptation to multitask loses power. ■

# BREAK IT DOWN, GET IT DONE
## Using a long-term planner

With a long-term planner, you can eliminate a lot of unpleasant surprises. Long-term planning allows you to avoid scheduling conflicts—the kind that obligate you to be in two places at the same time three weeks from now. You can also anticipate busy periods, such as finals week, and start preparing for them now. Good-bye, all-night cram sessions. Hello, serenity.

**Find a long-term planner, or make your own.** Many office supply stores carry academic planners in paper form that cover an entire school year. Computer software for three time management offers the same features. You can also be creative and make your own long-term planner. A big roll of newsprint pinned to a bulletin board or taped to a wall will do nicely. You can also search the Internet for a computer application or smartphone app that's designed for planning.

**Enter scheduled dates that extend into the future.** Use your long-term planner to list commitments that extend beyond the current month. Enter test dates, lab sessions, days that classes will be canceled, and other events that will take place over this term and next term.

**Create a master assignment list.** Find the syllabus for each course you're currently taking. Then, in your long-term planner, enter the due dates for all of the assignments in all of your courses. This step can be a powerful reality check.

The purpose of this technique is to not to make you feel overwhelmed with all the things you have to do. Rather, its aim is to help you take a First Step toward recognizing the demands on your time. Armed with the truth about how you use your time, you can make more accurate plans.

**Include nonacademic events.** In addition to tracking academic commitments, you can use your long-term planner to mark significant events in your life outside school. Include birthdays, doctors' appointments, concert dates, credit card payment due dates, and car maintenance schedules.

> Planning a day, a week, or a month ahead is a powerful practice. Using a long-term planner—one that displays an entire quarter, semester, or year at a glance—can yield even more benefits.

**Use your long-term planner to divide and conquer.** For some people, academic life is a series of last-minute crises punctuated by periods of exhaustion. You can avoid that fate. The trick is to break down big assignments and projects into smaller assignments and subprojects, each with their own due date.

When planning to write a paper, for instance, enter the final due date in your long-term planner. Then set individual due dates for each milestone in the writing process—creating an outline, completing your research, finishing a first draft, editing the draft, and preparing the final copy. By meeting these interim due dates, you make steady progress on the assignment throughout the term. That sure beats trying to crank out all those pages at the last minute. ∎

 **You're One Click Away...**
*from finding printable copies of this long-term planner online.*

| Week of | Monday | Tuesday | Wednesday | Thursday | Friday | Saturday | Sunday |
|---|---|---|---|---|---|---|---|
| 9 / 5 | | | | | | | |
| 9 / 12 | | English quiz | | | | | |
| 9 / 19 | | | English paper due | | Speech #1 | | |
| 9 / 26 | Chemistry test | | | | | Skiing at the lake | |
| 10 / 3 | | English quiz | | | Speech #2 | | |
| 10 / 10 | | | | Geography project due | | | |
| 10 / 17 | | | | --- No classes --- | | | |

# LONG-TERM PLANNER ___ / ___ / ___ to ___ / ___ / ___

| Week of | Monday | Tuesday | Wednesday | Thursday | Friday | Saturday | Sunday |
|---------|--------|---------|-----------|----------|--------|----------|--------|
| ___ / ___ | | | | | | | |
| ___ / ___ | | | | | | | |
| ___ / ___ | | | | | | | |
| ___ / ___ | | | | | | | |
| ___ / ___ | | | | | | | |
| ___ / ___ | | | | | | | |
| ___ / ___ | | | | | | | |
| ___ / ___ | | | | | | | |
| ___ / ___ | | | | | | | |
| ___ / ___ | | | | | | | |
| ___ / ___ | | | | | | | |
| ___ / ___ | | | | | | | |
| ___ / ___ | | | | | | | |
| ___ / ___ | | | | | | | |
| ___ / ___ | | | | | | | |
| ___ / ___ | | | | | | | |
| ___ / ___ | | | | | | | |
| ___ / ___ | | | | | | | |
| ___ / ___ | | | | | | | |
| ___ / ___ | | | | | | | |
| ___ / ___ | | | | | | | |
| ___ / ___ | | | | | | | |
| ___ / ___ | | | | | | | |
| ___ / ___ | | | | | | | |
| ___ / ___ | | | | | | | |
| ___ / ___ | | | | | | | |
| ___ / ___ | | | | | | | |
| ___ / ___ | | | | | | | |

# STOP Procrastination *Now*

Consider a bold idea: The way to stop procrastinating is to stop procrastinating. Giving up procrastination is actually a simple choice. People just make it complicated. Sound crazy? Well, test this idea for yourself.

Think of something that you've been putting off. Choose a small, specific task—one that you can complete in five minutes or less. Then do that task today.

Tomorrow, choose another task and do it. Repeat this strategy each day for one week. Notice what happens to your habit of procrastination.

If the above suggestion just doesn't work for you, then experiment with any strategy that follows.

## DISCOVER THE COSTS.
Think about whether procrastination keeps you from getting what you want. Clearly seeing the side effects of procrastination can help you kick the habit.

## TRICK YOURSELF INTO GETTING STARTED.
If you have a 50-page chapter to read, then grab the book and say to yourself, "I'm not really going to read this chapter right now. I'm just going to flip through the pages and scan the headings for 10 minutes." Tricks like these can get you started on a task you've been dreading.

## LET FEELINGS FOLLOW ACTION.
If you put off exercising until you feel energetic, you might wait for months. Instead, get moving now. Then watch your feelings change. After five minutes of brisk walking, you might be in the mood for a 20-minute run. This principle—action generates motivation—can apply to any task that you've put on the back burner.

## CHOOSE TO WORK UNDER PRESSURE.
Sometimes people thrive under pressure. As one writer puts it, "I don't do my *best* work under deadline. I do my *only* work under deadline." Used selectively, this strategy might also work for you.

## CREATE GOALS THAT DRAW YOU FORWARD.
A goal that grabs you by the heartstrings is an inspiration to act now. If you're procrastinating, then set some goals that excite you. You might wake up one day and discover that procrastination is part of your past. ■

 **You're One Click Away...**
*from finding more strategies online for ending procrastination.*

# THE 7-DAY *antiprocrastination plan*

Listed here are seven strategies you can use to reduce or eliminate many sources of procrastination. The suggestions are tied to the days of the week to help you remember them. Use this list to remind yourself that each day of your life presents an opportunity to stop the cycle of procrastination.

**MONDAY Make It Meaningful.** What is important about the task you've been putting off? List all the benefits of completing that task. To remember this strategy, keep in mind that it starts with the letter *M*, as in the word *Monday*.

**TUESDAY Take It Apart.** Break big jobs into a series of small ones you can do in 15 minutes or less. Even the biggest projects can be broken down into a series of small tasks. This strategy starts with the letter *T*, so mentally tie it to *Tuesday*.

**WEDNESDAY Write an Intention Statement.** If you can't get started on a term paper, you might write, "I intend to write a list of at least 10 possible topics by 9 p.m. I will reward myself with an hour of guilt-free recreational reading." In your memory, file the first word in this strategy—*write*—with *Wednesday*.

**THURSDAY Tell Everyone.** Publicly announce your intention to get a task done. Make the world your support group. Associate *tell* with *Thursday*.

**FRIDAY Find a Reward.** Construct rewards to yourself carefully. Be willing to withhold them if you do not complete the task. Remember that *Friday* is a fine day to *find* a reward.

**SATURDAY Settle It Now.** Do it now. The minute you notice yourself procrastinating, plunge into the task. Link *settle* with *Saturday*.

**SUNDAY Say No.** When you keep pushing a task into a low-priority category, reexamine your purpose for doing that task at all. If you realize that you really don't intend to do something, quit telling yourself that you will. *Sunday*—the last day of this 7-day plan—is a great day to finally let go and just *say* no.

# GET THE
## MOST
## OUT OF
## now

The following techniques are about getting the most from study time. Don't feel pressured to use all of the techniques or to tackle them in order. As you read, note the suggestions you think will be helpful. Pick one technique to use now. When it becomes a habit, come back to this article and select another one. Repeat this cycle, and enjoy the results as they unfold in your life.

**Study difficult (or boring) subjects first.** If your chemistry problems put you to sleep, then get to them first—while you are fresh. We tend to give top priority to what we enjoy studying, yet the courses that we find most difficult often require the most creative energy. Save your favorite subjects for later. If you find yourself avoiding a particular subject, get up an hour earlier to study it before breakfast. With that chore out of the way, the rest of the day can be a breeze.

**Be aware of your best time of day.** Many people learn best in daylight hours. If this is true for you, then schedule study time for your most difficult subjects or most difficult people before nightfall.

**Use waiting time.** Five minutes waiting for a subway, 20 minutes waiting for the dentist, 10 minutes in between classes—waiting time adds up fast. Have short study tasks ready to do during these periods, and keep your study materials handy. For example, carry 3 × 5 cards with facts, formulas, or definitions and pull them out anywhere. A mobile phone with an audio recording app can help you use commuting time to your advantage. Make a recording of yourself reading your notes. Play back the recording as you drive, or listen through headphones as you ride on the bus or subway.

**Study two hours for every hour you're in class.** Students in higher education are regularly advised to allow two hours of study time for every hour spent in class. If you are taking 15 credit hours, then plan to spend 30 hours a week studying. That adds up to 45 hours each week for school—more than a full-time job. The benefits of thinking in these terms will be apparent at exam time.

Keep in mind that the "2 hours for 1" rule doesn't distinguish between focused time and unfocused time. In one 4-hour block of study time, it's possible to use up two of those hours with phone calls, breaks, daydreaming, and doodling. With study time, quality counts as much as quantity.

# SETTING LIMITS ON screen time

Discover how much time you spend online. To get an accurate picture of your involvement in social networking and other online activity, use the Time Monitor/Time Plan exercise included earlier in this chapter. Then make conscious choices about how much time you want to spend online and on the phone. Don't let social networking distract you from meeting personal and academic goals.

Go offline to send the message that other people matter. It's hard to pay attention to the person who is right in front of you when you're hammering out text messages or updating your Twitter stream. You can also tell when someone else is doing these things and only half-listening to you. How engaged in your conversation do you think that person is?

An alternative is to ignore your devices and "be here now." When you're eating, stop answering the phone. Notice how the food tastes. When you're with a friend, close up your laptop. Hear every word he says. Rediscover where life actually takes place—in the present moment.

Developing emotional intelligence often requires being with people and away from a computer or cell phone. People who break up with a partner through text messaging are not developing that intelligence. True friends know when to go offline and head across campus to resolve a conflict. They know when to go back home and support a family member in crisis.

When it counts, your presence is your greatest present.

**Use a regular study area.** Your body and your mind know where you are. Using the same place to study, day after day, helps train your responses. When you arrive at that particular place, you can focus your attention more quickly.

Easy chairs and sofas are also dangerous places to study. Learning requires energy. Give your body a message that energy is needed. Put yourself in a posture that supports this message.

**Agree with living mates about study time.** This agreement includes roommates, spouses, and children. Make the rules about study time clear, and be sure to follow them yourself. Explicit agreements—even written contracts—work well. One student always wears a colorful hat when he wants to study. When his wife and children see the hat, they respect his wish to be left alone.

**Get off the phone.** The phone is the ultimate interrupter. People who wouldn't think of distracting you in person might call or text you at the worst times because they can't see that you are studying. You don't have to be a victim of your cell phone. If a simple "I can't talk; I'm studying" doesn't work, use dead silence. It's a conversation killer. Or short-circuit the whole problem by turning off your phone.

**Learn to say no.** Saying no is a time-saver and a valuable life skill for everyone. Some people feel it is rude to refuse a request. But you can say no effectively and courteously. Others want you to succeed as a student. When you tell them that you can't do what they ask because you are busy educating yourself, most people will understand.

**Get ready the night before.** Completing a few simple tasks just before you go to bed can help you get in gear the next day. If you need to make some phone calls first thing in the morning, then look up those numbers, write them on 3 × 5 cards, and set them near the phone. If you need to drive to a new location, make a note of the address and put it next to your car keys. If you plan to spend the next afternoon writing a paper, get your materials together: notes, outline, paper and pen or laptop—whatever you need. Pack your lunch or put gas in the car. Organize the baby's diaper bag and your briefcase or backpack.

**Ask: "Is this a piano?"** Carpenters who construct rough frames for buildings have a saying they use when they bend a nail or accidentally hack a chunk out of a two-by-four: "Well, this ain't no piano." It means that perfection is not necessary. Ask yourself whether what you are doing needs to be perfect. Perhaps you don't have to apply the same standards of grammar to lecture notes that you would apply to a term paper. If you can complete a job 95 percent perfectly in 2 hours and 100 percent perfectly in 4 hours, ask yourself whether the additional 5 percent improvement is worth doubling the amount of time you spend.

Remember that sometimes it *is* a piano. A tiny miscalculation can ruin an entire lab experiment. A misstep in solving a complex math problem can negate hours of work. Computers are notorious for turning little errors into nightmares. Accept lower standards only when appropriate.

**Ask: "Could I find the time if I really wanted to?"** The next time you're tempted to say, "I just don't have time," pause for a minute. Question the truth of this statement. Could you find 4 more hours this week for studying? Suppose that someone offered to pay you $10,000 to find those 4 hours. Suppose too that you will get paid only if you don't lose sleep, call in sick for work, or sacrifice anything important to you. Could you find the time if vast sums of money were involved? Remember that when it comes to school, vast sums of money *are* involved.

**Ask: "Am I willing to promise it?"** This time-management idea might be the most powerful of all: If you want to find time for a task, promise yourself—and others—that you'll get it done. Unleash one of the key qualities of master students and take responsibility for producing an outcome. ■

# ✔ EXERCISE 8

## The Money Monitor/Money Plan

Many of us find it easy to lose track of money. It likes to escape when no one is looking. And usually, no one is looking. That's why the simple act of noticing the details about money can be so useful—even if this is the only idea from the chapter that you ever apply.

Use this exercise as a chance to discover how money flows into and out of your life. The goal is to record all the money you receive and spend over the course of month. This sounds like a big task, but it's simpler than you might think. Besides, there's a big payoff for this action. With increased awareness of income and expenses, you can make choices about money that will change your life. Here's how to begin.

**STEP 1** **Tear out the Money Monitor/Money Plan form on page 70.** Make photocopies of this form to use each month. The form helps you do two things. One is to get a big picture of the money that flows in and out of your life. The other is to plan specific and immediate changes in how you earn and spend money.

**STEP 2** **Keep track of your income and expenses.** Use your creativity to figure out how you want to carry out this step. The goal is to create a record of exactly how much you earn and spend each month. Use any method that works for you. And keep it simple. Following are some options:

- **Carry 3 × 5 cards in your pocket, purse, backpack, or briefcase.** Every time you buy something or get paid, record a few details on a card. List the date. Add a description of what you bought or what you got paid. Note whether the item is a source of income (money coming in) or an expense (money going out). Be sure to use a separate card for each item. This makes it easier to sort your cards into categories at the end of the month and fill out your Money Monitor/Money Plan.

- **Save all receipts and file them.** This method does not require you to carry any 3 × 5 cards. But it does require that you faithfully hang on to every receipt and record of payment. Every time you buy something, ask for a receipt. Then stick it in your wallet, purse, or pocket. When you get home, make notes about the purchase on the receipt. Then file the receipts in a folder labeled with the current month and year (for example, January 2014). Every time you get a paycheck during that month, save the stub and add it to the folder. If you do not get a receipt or record of payment, whip out a 3 × 5 card and create one of your own. Detailed receipts will help you later on when you file taxes, categorize expenses (such as food and entertainment), and check your purchases against credit card statements.

- **Use personal finance software.** Learn to use Quicken or a similar product that allows you to record income and expenses on your computer and to sort them into categories. Also check out money management apps for your smart phone.

- **Use online banking services.** If you have a checking account that offers online services, take advantage of the records that the bank is already keeping for you. Every time you write a check, use a debit card, or make a deposit, the transaction will show up online. You can use a computer to log in to your account and view these transactions at any time. If you're unclear about how to use online banking, go in to your bank and ask for help.

- **Experiment with several of the above options.** Settle into one that feels most comfortable to you. Or create a method of your own. Anything will work, as long as you end each month with an *exact and accurate* record of your income and expenses.

**STEP 3** **On the last day of the month, fill out your Money Monitor/Money Plan.** Pull out a blank Money Monitor/Money Plan. Label it with the current month and year. Fill out this form using the records of your income and expenses for the month.

Notice that the far left column of the Money Monitor/Money Plan includes categories of income and expenses. (You can use the blank rows for categories of income and expenses that are not already included.) Write your total for each category in the middle column.

For example, if you spent $300 at the grocery store this month, write that amount in the middle column next to *Groceries*. If you work a part-time job and received two paychecks for the month, write the total in the middle column next to *Employment*. See the sample Money Monitor/Money Plan for more examples.

Remember to split expenses when necessary. For example, you might write one check each month to pay the balance due on your credit card. The purchases listed on your credit card bill might fall into several categories. Total up your expenses in each category, and list them separately.

Suppose that you used your credit card to buy music online, purchase a sweater, pay for three restaurant meals, and buy two tanks of gas for your car. Write the online music expense next to *Entertainment*. Write the amount you paid for the sweater next to *Clothes*. Write the total you spent at the restaurants next to *Eating Out*. Finally, write the total for your gas stops next to *Gas*.

Now look at the column on the far right of the Money Monitor/Money Plan. This column is where the magic happens. Review each category of income and expense. If you plan to reduce your spending in a certain category during the next month, write a minus sign (−) in the far right column. If you plan a spending increase in any category next month, write a plus sign (+) in the far right column. If you think that a category of income

or expense will remain the same next month, leave the column blank.

Look again at the sample Money Monitor/Money Plan on page 69. This student plans to reduce her spending for clothes, eating out, and entertainment (which for her includes movies and DVD rentals). She plans to increase the total she spends on groceries. She figures that even so, she'll save money by cooking more food at home and eating out less.

**STEP 4** After you've filled out your first Money Monitor/ Money Plan, take a moment to congratulate yourself. You have actively collected and analyzed the data needed to take charge of your financial life. No matter how the numbers add up, you are now in conscious control of your money. Repeat this exercise every month. It will keep you on a steady path to financial freedom.

**You're One Click Away...**
*from doing this exercise online.*

# Earn more, spend less

Increasing your income is definitely a way to build wealth. Ways to earn more money include:

- **Focus on your education.** Your most important assets are not your bank accounts, your car, or your house—they are your skills. Once you graduate and land a job in your chosen field, continue your education. Look for ways to gain additional skills or certifications that lead to higher earnings and more fulfilling work assignments.

- **Consider financial aid.** Student grants and loans can play a major role in your college success by freeing you up from having to work full-time or even part-time. Visit the financial aid office at your school to discover your options.

- **Work while you're in school.** You can use any job to gain experience, establish references, interact with a variety of people, and make contact with people who might hire you in the future.

- **Do your best at every job.** Excel as an employee. Suggest and implement ways to help your employer increase income and decrease expenses. A positive work experience can pay off for years by leading to other jobs, recommendations, and contacts.

For many people, finding a way to increase income is the most appealing way to fix a money problem. This approach has a potential problem: When their income increases, many people continue to spend more than they make. This means that money problems persist even at higher incomes. To avoid this problem, *manage your expenses—no matter how much money you make.*

Keep monitoring your income and expenses to discover the main drains on your finances. Then focus on one or two areas where you can reduce spending, increase income, or both.

## Sample Money Monitor/Money Plan

| Income | This Month | Next Month |
|---|---|---|
| Employment | 500 | |
| Grants | 100 | |
| Interest from Savings | | |
| Loans | 300 | |
| Scholarships | 100 | |
| | | |
| | | |
| | | |
| | | |
| | | |
| | | |
| | | |
| | | |
| | | |
| | | |
| | | |
| | | |
| | | |
| | | |
| | | |
| | | |
| | | |
| | | |
| | | |
| | | |
| | | |
| | | |
| | | |
| | | |
| | | |
| | | |
| | | |
| | | |
| Total Income | 1000 | |

| Expenses | This Month | Next Month |
|---|---|---|
| Books and Supplies | | |
| Car Maintenance | | |
| Car Payment | | |
| Clothes | | − |
| Deposits into Savings Account | | |
| Eating Out | 50 | − |
| Entertainment | 50 | − |
| Gas | 100 | |
| Groceries | 300 | + |
| Insurance (Car, Life, Health, Home) | | |
| Laundry | 20 | |
| Phone | 55 | |
| Rent/Mortgage Payment | 400 | |
| Tuition and Fees | | |
| Utilities | 50 | |
| | | |
| | | |
| | | |
| | | |
| | | |
| | | |
| | | |
| | | |
| | | |
| | | |
| | | |
| | | |
| | | |
| | | |
| | | |
| | | |
| | | |
| | | |
| Total Expenses | 1025 | − |

**Money Monitor/Money Plan**
**Month_____ Year_____**

| Income | This Month | Next Month | Expenses | This Month | Next Month |
|---|---|---|---|---|---|
| Employment | | | Books and Supplies | | |
| Grants | | | Car Maintenance | | |
| Interest from Savings | | | Car Payment | | |
| Loans | | | Clothes | | |
| Scholarships | | | Deposits into Savings Account | | |
| | | | Eating Out | | |
| | | | Entertainment | | |
| | | | Gas | | |
| | | | Groceries | | |
| | | | Insurance (Car, Life, Health, Home) | | |
| | | | Laundry | | |
| | | | Phone | | |
| | | | Rent/Mortgage Payment | | |
| | | | Tuition and Fees | | |
| | | | Utilities | | |
| | | | | | |
| | | | | | |
| | | | | | |
| | | | | | |
| | | | | | |
| | | | | | |
| | | | | | |
| | | | | | |
| | | | | | |
| | | | | | |
| | | | | | |
| | | | | | |
| | | | | | |
| | | | | | |
| Total Income | | | Total Expenses | | |

## Money Monitor/Money Plan
### Month_____ Year_____

| Income | This Month | Next Month | Expenses | This Month | Next Month |
|---|---|---|---|---|---|
| Employment | | | Books and Supplies | | |
| Grants | | | Car Maintenance | | |
| Interest from Savings | | | Car Payment | | |
| Loans | | | Clothes | | |
| Scholarships | | | Deposits into Savings Account | | |
| | | | Eating Out | | |
| | | | Entertainment | | |
| | | | Gas | | |
| | | | Groceries | | |
| | | | Insurance (Car, Life, Health, Home) | | |
| | | | Laundry | | |
| | | | Phone | | |
| | | | Rent/Mortgage Payment | | |
| | | | Tuition and Fees | | |
| | | | Utilities | | |
| | | | | | |
| | | | | | |
| | | | | | |
| | | | | | |
| | | | | | |
| | | | | | |
| | | | | | |
| | | | | | |
| | | | | | |
| | | | | | |
| | | | | | |
| | | | | | |
| | | | | | |
| Total Income | | | Total Expenses | | |

2

# Managing money during tough times

## TAKE A FIRST STEP

If the economy tanks, we can benefit by telling the truth about it. We can also tell the truth about ourselves. It's one thing to condemn the dishonesty of mortgage bankers and hedge-fund managers. It's another thing to have an unpaid balance on a credit card or wipe out a savings accounts and still believe that we are in charge of our money. The first step to changing such behaviors is simply to admit that they don't work.

## MAKE SURE THAT YOUR SAVINGS ARE PROTECTED

The Federal Deposit Insurance Corporation (FDIC) backs individual saving accounts. The National Credit Union Administration (NCUA) offers similar protection for credit union members. If your savings are protected by these programs, every penny you deposit is safe. Check your statements to find out, or go online to **www.myfdicinsurance.gov**.

## DO STELLAR WORK AT YOUR CURRENT JOB

The threat of layoffs increases during a recession. However, companies will hesitate to shed their star employees. If you're working right now, then think about ways to become indispensable. Gain skills and experience that will make you more valuable to your employer.

## THINK ABOUT YOUR NEXT JOB

Create a career plan that describes the next job you want, the skills that you'll develop to get it, and the next steps you'll take to gain those skills. Stay informed about the latest developments in your field. Find people who are already working in this area, and contact them for information interviews. See Chapter 10 of this book for more ideas about career planning and job hunting.

## RESEARCH UNEMPLOYMENT BENEFITS

Unemployment benefits have limits and may not replace your lost wages. However, they can cushion the blow of losing a job while you put other strategies in place. To learn about the benefits offered in your state, go online to **www.servicelocator.org**. Click "Unemployment Benefits." Then enter your state.

## GET HEALTH INSURANCE

A sudden illness or lengthy hospital stay can drain your savings. Health insurance can pick up all or most of the costs instead. If possible, get health insurance through your school or employer. Another option is private health insurance. This can be cheaper than extending an employer's policy if you lose your job. To find coverage, go online to the Web site of the National Association of Health Underwriters (**www.nahu.org**) and **www.ehealthinsurance.com**.

## GET HELP THAT YOU CAN TRUST

Avoid debt consolidators that offer schemes to wipe out your debt. What they don't tell you is that their fees are high, and that using them can lower your credit rating. Turn instead to the National Foundation for Credit Counseling (**www.nfcc.org**). Find a credit counselor that is accredited by this organization. Work with someone who is open about fees and willing to work with all your creditors. Don't pay any fees up front, before you actually get help.

## PUT YOUR FINANCIAL PLAN IN WRITING

List specific ways that you will reduce spending and increase income. If you have a family, consider posting this list for everyone to see.

## COPE WITH STRESS IN POSITIVE WAYS

When times get tough, some people are tempted to reduce stress with unhealthy behaviors like smoking, drinking, and overeating. Find better ways to cope. Exercise, meditation, sound sleep, and social support can do wonders. For specific suggestions, see Chapter 9: Health.

## CHOOSE YOUR MONEY CONVERSATION

Keep financial news in perspective. Yes, recessions are hard on people. At the same time, reporters tend to center the conversation on gloom and doom. Turn it around. If the official unemployment rate is 8 percent, for example, this means that 92 percent of people in the work force *are* employed. Our economy will continue to reward people who apply their skills to create valuable new products and services.

To manage stress, limit how much attention you pay to fear-based articles and programs. Avoid conversations that focus on problems. Instead, talk about solutions. Focus on what you can control, and forget about the rest. Even if the economy takes a nosedive, there is always at least one more thing you can do to manage stress and get on a firmer financial footing. ∎

**You're One Click Away...**
*from finding more ways online to thrive during tough times.*

# Take charge of *your credit*

A good credit rating will serve you for a lifetime. With this asset, you'll be able to borrow money any time you need it. A poor credit rating, however, can keep you from getting a car or a house in the future. You might also have to pay higher insurance rates, and you could even be turned down for a job.

To take charge of your credit, borrow money only when truly necessary. If you do borrow, make all of your payments, and make them on time. This is especially important for managing credit cards and student loans.

iStockphoto.com/Laurent davoust

## USE CREDIT CARDS WITH CAUTION

**Pay off the balance each month.** An unpaid credit card balance is a sure sign that you are spending more money than you have. To avoid this outcome, keep track of how much you spend with credit cards each month. Pay off the card balance each month, on time, and avoid finance or late charges.

**Scrutinize credit card offers.** Look carefully at credit card offers. Low rates might be temporary. After a few months, they could double or even triple. Also look for annual fees, late fees, and other charges buried in the fine print.

Be especially wary of credit card offers made to students. Remember that the companies who willingly dispense cards on campus are not there to offer an educational service. They are in business to make money by charging you interest.

**Avoid cash advances.** Due to their high interest rates and fees, credit cards are not a great source of spare cash. Even when you get cash advances on these cards from an ATM, it's still borrowed money. As an alternative, get a debit card tied to a checking account, and use that card when you need cash on the go.

**Use just one credit card.** To simplify your financial life and take charge of your credit, consider using only one card. Choose one with no annual fee and the lowest interest rate. Consider the bottom line, and be selective. If you do have more than one credit card, pay off the one with the highest interest rate first. Then consider cancelling that card.

**Get a copy of your credit report.** A credit report is a record of your payment history and other credit-related items. You are entitled to get a free copy each year. Go to your bank and ask someone there how to do this. You can also request a copy of your credit report online at **https://www.annualcreditreport.com**.

## MANAGE STUDENT LOANS

**Choose schools with costs in mind.** If you decide to transfer to another school, you can save thousands of dollars the moment you sign your application for admission. In addition to choosing schools on the basis of reputation, consider how much they cost and the financial aid packages that they offer.

**Avoid debt when possible.** The surest way to manage debt is to avoid it altogether. If you do take out loans, borrow only the amount that you cannot get from other sources—scholarships, grants, employment, gifts from relatives, and personal savings. Predict what your income will be when the first loan payments are due, and whether you'll make enough money to manage continuing payments.

Also set a target date for graduation, and stick to it. The fewer years you go to school, the lower your debt.

**Shop carefully for loans.** Go the financial aid office and ask whether you can get a Stafford loan. These are fixed-rate, low-interest loans from the federal government. If you qualify for a subsidized Stafford loan, the government pays the interest due while you're in school. Unsubsidized Stafford loans do not offer this benefit, but they are still one of the cheapest student loans you can get. Remember that *anyone* can apply for a Stafford loan. Take full advantage of this program before you look into other loans. For more information on the loans that are available to you, visit **www.studentaid.ed.gov**.

**Repay your loans.** If you take out student loans, find out exactly when the first payment is due on each of them. Don't assume that you can wait to start repayment until you find a job. Any bill payments that you miss will hammer your credit score.

Also ask your financial aid office about whether you can consolidate your loans—lump them all together and make just one payment every month. This can make it easier to stay on top of your payments and protect your credit score. ■

**You're One Click Away...**
*from finding more strategies online for credit mastery.*

# Education is worth it—
## and you can pay for it

Education is one of the few things you can buy that will last a lifetime. It can't rust, corrode, break down, or wear out. It can't be stolen, repossessed, or destroyed. Once you have a degree, no one can take it away. That makes your education a safer investment than real estate, gold, oil, diamonds, or stocks.

Higher levels of education are associated with the following:[5]

- Greater likelihood of being employed
- Greater likelihood of having health insurance
- Higher income
- Higher job satisfaction
- Higher tax revenues for governments, which fund libraries, schools, parks, and other public goods
- Lower dependence on income support services, such as food stamps
- Higher involvement in volunteer activities

In short, education is a good deal for you and for society. It's worth investing in it periodically to update your skills, reach your goals, and get more of what you want in life.

Millions of dollars are waiting for people who take part in higher education. The funds flow to students who know how to find them. There are many ways to pay for school. The kind of help you get depends on your financial need. In general, *financial need* equals the cost of your schooling minus what you can reasonably be expected to pay. A financial aid package includes three major types of assistance:

- Money you do not pay back (grants and scholarships)
- Money you *do* pay back (loans)
- Work-study programs

Many students who get financial aid receive a package that includes all of the above elements.

To find out more, visit your school's financial aid office on a regular basis. Also go online. Start with Student Aid on the Web at http://studentaid.ed.gov. ■

 **You're One Click Away...**
*from discovering more ways online to pay for school.*

 EXERCISE 9

## Education by the hour

Determine exactly what it costs you to go to school. Fill in the blanks, using totals for a semester, quarter, or whatever term system your school uses. **Note:** Include only the costs that relate directly to going to school. For example, under "Transportation," list only the amount that you pay for gas to drive back and forth to school—not the total amount you spend on gas for a semester.

| | |
|---|---|
| Tuition | $_____ |
| Books | $_____ |
| Fees | $_____ |
| Transportation | $_____ |
| Clothing | $_____ |
| Food | $_____ |
| Housing | $_____ |
| Entertainment | $_____ |
| Other expenses (such as insurance, medical costs, and child care) | $_____ |
| **Subtotal** | $_____ |
| Salary you could earn per term if you weren't in school | $_____ |
| **Total (A)** | $_____ |

Now figure out how many classes you attend in one term. This is the number of your scheduled class periods per week multiplied by the number of weeks in your school term. Put that figure below:

**Total (B)**      $_____

Divide the **Total (B)** into the **Total (A)**, and put that amount here:      $_____

This is what it costs you to go to one class one time.

On a separate sheet of paper, describe your responses to discovering this figure. Also list anything you will do differently as a result of knowing the hourly cost of your education.

 **You're One Click Away...**
*from completing this exercise online under Exercises.*

# critical thinking 2

Psychologist Benjamin Bloom described six kinds of thinking:

**Level 1: Remembering**—recalling an idea.

**Level 2: Understanding**—explaining an idea in your own words and giving examples from your own experience.

**Level 3: Applying**—using an idea to produce a desired result.

**Level 4: Analyzing**—dividing an idea into parts or steps.

**Level 5: Evaluating**—rating the truth, usefulness, or quality of an idea—and giving reasons for your rating.

**Level 6: Creating**—inventing something new based on an idea.

You can recall any suggestion from this book (**Level 1: Remembering**) and take that idea to a higher level of thinking.

Recall the suggestion to "take it apart" from the "The 7-day antiprocrastination plan" on page 64. Think about how you could use this suggestion to write a paper that's due October 30. Write notes on your calendar to:

- Choose a topic for the paper by October 1.
- Finish the first draft by October 15.
- Finish the final draft by October 28 (two days before the paper is due).

Creating a step-by-step plan is an example of **Level 3: Applying**. Thinking at this level often means answering questions such as: How can I actually use this idea? What is the very next action I would take? When? Where? Who else might be involved?

Now it's your turn. Choose another suggestion from this chapter (**Level 1: Remembering**) and think about it at **Level 3: Applying**. In the space provided here, state the suggestion and write a brief paragraph that summarizes your higher-level thinking. If you'd like to demonstrate your thinking in another way—such as by making a drawing, building a model, or even writing a song—then discuss this with your instructor.

*For more information on the six levels of thinking, see "Becoming a critical thinker" in Chapter 7.*

# masterstudentprofile

## Al Gore

(1948– ) Former vice president of the United States. Gore refocused his career on climate change, won a Nobel Peace Prize, and—in his film *An Inconvenient Truth*—invented a new type of documentary.

One hundred and nineteen years ago, a wealthy inventor read his own obituary, mistakenly published years before his death. Wrongly believing the inventor had just died, a newspaper printed a harsh judgment of his life's work, unfairly labeling him "The Merchant of Death" because of his invention—dynamite. Shaken by this condemnation, the inventor made a fateful choice to serve the cause of peace.

Seven years later, Alfred Nobel created this prize and the others that bear his name.

Seven years ago tomorrow, I read my own political obituary in a judgment that seemed to me harsh and mistaken—if not premature. But that unwelcome verdict also brought a precious if painful gift: an opportunity to search for fresh new ways to serve my purpose.

Unexpectedly, that quest has brought me here. Even though I fear my words cannot match this moment, I pray what I am feeling in my heart will be communicated clearly enough that those who hear me will say, "We must act." . . .

In the last few months, it has been harder and harder to misinterpret the signs that our world is spinning out of kilter. Major cities in North and South America, Asia, and Australia are nearly out of water due to massive droughts and melting glaciers. Desperate farmers are losing their livelihoods. Peoples in the frozen Arctic and on low-lying Pacific islands are planning evacuations of places they have long called home. Unprecedented wildfires have forced a half million people from their homes in one country and caused a national emergency that almost brought down the government in another. Climate refugees have migrated into areas already inhabited by people with different cultures, religions, and traditions, increasing the potential for conflict. Stronger storms in the Pacific and Atlantic have threatened whole cities. Millions have been displaced by massive flooding in South Asia, Mexico, and 18 countries in Africa. As temperature extremes have increased, tens of thousands have lost their lives. We are recklessly burning and clearing our forests and driving more and more species into extinction.

There is an African proverb that says, "If you want to go quickly, go alone. If you want to go far, go together." We need to go far, quickly. . . .

Fifteen years ago, I made that case at the "Earth Summit" in Rio de Janeiro. Ten years ago, I presented it in Kyoto. This week, I will urge the delegates in Bali to adopt a bold mandate for a treaty that establishes a universal global cap on emissions and uses the market in emissions trading to efficiently allocate resources to the most effective opportunities for speedy reductions.

This treaty should be ratified and brought into effect everywhere in the world by the beginning of 2010— 2 years sooner than presently contemplated. The pace of our response must be accelerated to match the accelerating pace of the crisis itself. . . .

Make no mistake, the next generation will ask us one of two questions. Either they will ask: "What were you thinking; why didn't you act?"

Or they will ask instead: "How did you find the moral courage to rise and successfully resolve a crisis that so many said was impossible to solve?"

**AL GORE . . .** is optimistic.

**YOU . . .** can be more optimistic by focusing on your goals.

**You're One Click Away...**
*from learning more about Al Gore online at the Master Student Profiles. You can also visit the Master Student Hall of Fame to learn about other master students.*

Name _____

Date _____

**2**

1. The Power Process: "Be here now" rules out planning. True or false? Explain your answer.

2. According to the text, everything written about time and money management can be reduced to three main ideas. What are they?

3. Rewrite the statement "I want to study harder" so that it becomes a specific goal.

4. Define *C fever* as it applies to the ABC priority method.

5. Define the term *multitasking* and explain one strategy for dealing with it.

6. What are three ways that you can avoid getting into financial trouble when you use credit cards?

7. Any student can apply for a Stafford loan. True or false? Explain your answer.

8. Describe two strategies for increasing your income.

9. According to the text, strategies for decreasing debt related to your education include the following:
   (a) Choose schools carefully.
   (b) Take out student loans only after considering other ways to pay for school.
   (c) Shop carefully for student loans.
   (d) Repay loans on time.
   (e) All of the above.

10. Describe two strategies for keeping track of your monthly expenses.

# 2 SKILLS *Snapshot*

CHAPTER

Take a snapshot of your current skills at working with time and money. Also think about the next step you'll take to develop more mastery in this area of life.

## DISCOVERY

My score on the *Time and Money* section of the Discovery Wheel on page 31 was . . .

I would describe my ability to set specific goals as . . .

When setting priorities for what to do each day, the first thing I consider is . . .

I keep track of my daily to-do items by . . .

Right now my main sources of income are . . .

My three biggest expenses each month are . . .

## INTENTION

One monthly expense that I intend to reduce is . . .

One source of procrastination that I intend to stop is . . .

## ACTION

To manage my time more effectively, the habit I will adopt next is . . .

To manage money more effectively, the habit I will adopt next is . . .

At the end of this course, I would like my *Time and Money* score on the Discovery Wheel to be . . .

# Memory

**3**

Use this **Master Student Map** to ask yourself,

## WHY THIS CHAPTER MATTERS . . .

- Learning memory techniques can boost your skills at test taking, reading, note taking, and many other tasks.

## WHAT IS INCLUDED . . .

## HOW CAN I USE THIS CHAPTER . . .

- Focus your attention.
- Make conscious choices about what to remember.
- Recall facts and ideas with more ease.

## WHAT IF . . .

- I could use my memory to its full potential?

**JOURNAL ENTRY 6**
*Intention Statement*

## Create value from this chapter

Think of a time when you struggled to remember something that was important. Perhaps you were trying to recall someone's name or recall some key information for a test. Then scan this chapter and find at least three strategies that you will use to prevent this problem in the future.

| Strategy | Page number |
| --- | --- |
|  |  |
|  |  |
|  |  |
|  |  |
|  |  |
|  |  |
|  |  |
|  |  |
|  |  |
|  |  |
|  |  |
|  |  |
|  |  |
|  |  |

© Ruslan Ivantsov/Shutterstock.com

# Love your problems
## (and experience your barriers)

We all have problems and barriers that block our progress or prevent us from moving into new areas. Often, the way we respond to our problems places limitations on what we can be, do, and have.

Problems often work like barriers. When we bump up against one of our problems, we usually turn away and start walking along a different path. And all of a sudden—bump!—we've struck another barrier. And we turn away again.

As we continue to bump into problems and turn away from them, our lives stay inside the same old boundaries. Inside these boundaries, we are unlikely to have new adventures. We are unlikely to keep learning.

If we respond to problems by loving them instead of resisting them, we can expand the boundaries in which we live our lives.

The word *love* might sound like an overstatement. In this Power Process, the word means to unconditionally accept the fact that your problems exist. The more we deny or resist a problem, the stronger it seems to become. When we accept the fact that we have a problem, we can find effective ways to deal with it.

Suppose one of your barriers is speaking in front of a group. You fear that you'll forget everything you planned to say.

One option for dealing with this barrier is denial. You could get up in front of a group and pretend that you're not afraid. You could tell yourself, "I'm not going to be scared," and then try to keep your knees from knocking.

A more effective approach is to love your fear. Go to the front of the room, look out into the audience, and say to yourself, "I am scared. I notice that my knees are shaking and my mouth feels dry, and I'm having a rush of thoughts about what might happen if I say the wrong thing. Yup, I'm scared, and I'm not going to fight it. I'm going to give this speech anyway."

The beauty of this Power Process is that you continue to take action—giving your speech, for example—no matter what you feel. You walk right up to the barrier and then *through* it. You might even find that if you totally accept and experience a barrier such as fear, it shrinks or disappears. When you relax, you reclaim your natural abilities. You can recall memories, learn something new, and even laugh a little. Even if this does not happen right away, you can still open up to a new experience.

Loving a problem does not mean *liking* it. Instead, loving a problem means admitting the truth about it. This helps us take effective action—which can free us of the problem once and for all.

**You're One Click Away...**
*from accessing Power Process Media online and finding out more ways to love your problems.*

iStockphoto.com/Miroslav Ferkuniak

# Take your memory
## *out of the closet*

Once upon a time, people talked about human memory as if it were a closet. You stored individual memories there as you would old shirts and stray socks. Remembering something was a matter of rummaging through all that stuff. If you were lucky, you found what you wanted.

This view of memory creates some problems. For one thing, closets can get crowded. Things too easily disappear. Even with the biggest closet, you eventually run out of space. If you want to pack some new memories in there—well, too bad. There's no room.

Brain researchers shattered this image to bits. Memory is not a closet. It's not a place or a thing. Instead, memory is a *process*.

On a conscious level, memories appear as distinct and unconnected mental events: words, sensations, images. They can include details from the distant past—the smell of cookies baking in your grandmother's kitchen or the feel of sunlight warming your face through the window of your first-grade classroom.

On a biological level, each of those memories involves millions of brain cells, or neurons, firing chemical messages to one another. If you could observe these exchanges in real time, you'd see regions of cells all over the brain glowing with electrical charges at speeds that would put a computer to shame.

When a series of brain cells connects several times in a similar pattern, the result is a memory. Psychologist Donald Hebb explains it this way: "Neurons which fire together, wire together."[1] It means that memories are not really stored. Instead, remembering is a process in which you *encode* information as links between active neurons that fire together. You also *decode*, or reactivate, neurons that wired together in the past.

There are critical moments in this process. Say that you're enjoying a lecture in introduction to psychology. It really makes sense. In fact, it's so interesting that you choose to just sit and listen—without taking notes. Two days later, you're studying for a test and wish you'd made a different choice. You remember that the lecture was interesting, but you don't recall much else. In technical terms, your decision to skip note taking was an *encoding error*.

So, you decide to change your behavior and take extensive notes during the next psychology lecture. Your goal is to capture everything the instructor says. This too has mixed results—a case of writer's cramp and 10 pages of dense, confusing scribbles. Oops. Another encoding error.

Effective encoding is finding a middle ground between these two extremes. As you listen and read, you make

> **Memory is the probability that certain patterns of brain activity will occur again in the future. In effect, you recreate a memory each time you recall it. In more practical terms, a good memory is not something you *have*. It's something you *do*.**

moment-to-moment choices about what you want to remember. You distinguish between key points, transitions, and minor details. You predict what material is likely to appear on a test. You also stay alert for ideas you can actively apply. These are things you capture in your notes.

Signs of memory mastery are making choices about *what* to remember and *how* to remember it. This in turn makes it easier for you to decode, or recall, the material at a crucial point in the future—such as during a test.

Whenever you efficiently encode and decode something new, your brain changes physically. You grow more connections between neurons. The more you learn, the greater the number of connections. For all practical purposes, there's no limit to how many memories your brain can process.

There's a lot you can do to wire those neural connections into place. That's where the memory techniques described in this chapter come into play. Use them to step out of your crowded mental closet into a world of infinite possibilities. ∎

# The *MEMORY JUNGLE*

Think of your memory as a vast, overgrown jungle. This memory jungle is thick with wild plants, exotic shrubs, twisted trees, and creeping vines. It spreads over thousands of square miles—dense, tangled, forbidding.

Imagine that the jungle is encompassed on all sides by towering mountains. There is only one entrance to the jungle, a small meadow that is reached by a narrow pass through the mountains.

In the jungle there are animals, millions of them. The animals represent all of the information in your memory. Imagine that every thought, mental picture, or perception you ever had is represented by an animal in this jungle. Every single event ever perceived by any of your five senses—sight, touch, hearing, smell, or taste—is a thought animal that has also passed through the meadow and entered the jungle. Some of the thought animals, such as the color of your seventh-grade teacher's favorite sweater, are well hidden. Other thoughts, such as your cell phone number or the position of the reverse gear in your car, are easier to find.

The memory jungle has two rules: Each thought animal must pass through the meadow at the entrance to the jungle. And once an animal enters the jungle, it never leaves.

The meadow represents short-term memory. You use this kind of memory when you look up a telephone number and hold it in your memory long enough to make a call. Short-term memory appears to have a limited capacity (the meadow is small) and disappears fast (animals pass through the meadow quickly).

The jungle itself represents long-term memory. This kind of memory allows you to recall information from day to day, week to week, and year to year. Remember that thought animals never leave the long-term memory jungle. The following visualizations can help you recall useful concepts about memory.

## VISUALIZATION #1: A WELL-WORN PATH

Imagine what happens as a thought—in this case, we'll call it an elephant—bounds across short-term memory and into the jungle. The elephant leaves a trail of broken twigs and hoof prints that you can follow.

Brain research suggests that thoughts can wear "paths" in the brain.[2] These paths consist of dendrites—string-like fibers that connect brain cells. The more these connections are activated, the easier it is to retrieve (recall) the thought. In other words, the more often the elephant retraces the path, the clearer the path becomes. The more often you recall information and the more often you put the same information into your memory, the easier it is to find.

When you buy a new car, for example, the first few times you try to find reverse, you have to think for a moment. After you have found reverse gear every day for a week, the path is worn into your memory. After a year, the path is so well-worn that when you dream about driving your car backward, you even dream the correct motion for putting the gear in reverse.

## VISUALIZATION #2: A HERD OF THOUGHTS

The second picture you can use to your advantage in recalling concepts about memory is the picture of many animals gathering at a clearing—like thoughts gathering at a central location in memory. It is easier to retrieve thoughts that are grouped together, just as it is easier to find a herd of animals than it is to find a single elephant.

Pieces of information are easier to recall if you can associate them with similar information. For example, you can more readily remember a particular player's batting average if you can associate it with other baseball statistics.

## VISUALIZATION #3: TURNING YOUR BACK

Imagine releasing the elephant into the jungle, turning your back, and counting to 10. When you turn around, the elephant is gone. This is exactly what happens to most of the information you receive.

Psychological research consistently shows that we start forgetting new material almost as soon as we learn it. The memory loss is steep, with most of it occurring within the first 24 hours.[3] This means that much of the material is not being encoded. It is wandering around, lost in the memory jungle.

The remedy is simple: Review quickly. Do not take your eyes off the thought animal as it crosses the short-term memory meadow. Look at it again (review it) soon after it enters the long-term memory jungle. Wear a path in your memory immediately.

## VISUALIZATION #4: DIRECTING THE ANIMAL TRAFFIC

The fourth picture is one you are in. You are standing at the entrance to the short-term memory meadow, directing herds of thought animals as they file through the pass, across the meadow, and into your long-term memory. You are taking an active role in the learning process. You are paying attention. You are doing more than sitting on a rock and watching the animals file past into your brain. You have become part of the process, and in doing so, you have taken control of your memory. ∎

**You're One Click Away...**
*from finding guided visualizations based on the memory jungle online.*

# Master Students
# IN ACTION

**You're One Click Away...**
*from a video about Master Students in Action.*

"*Before I read the Memory chapter, I had trouble remembering what I had studied when taking a test or quiz. Visualization is by far the most useful technique I have come across in this book. While I'm taking the test, I visualize the book or paper that I studied from. It also helps with names. I visualize something funny to go along with someone's name.*"

—*Tauni Aldinger,*
*Saddleback College*

# MEMORY *Techniques*

Experiment with these
techniques to develop a
flexible, custom-made
memory system that fits
your style of learning.

The techniques discussed here are divided into four categories, each of which represents a general principle for improving memory:

**Organize it.** Organized information is easier to find.

**Use your body.** Learning is an active process; get all of your senses involved.

**Use your brain.** Work *with* your memory, not *against* it.

**Recall it.** Regularly retrieve and apply key information.

## ORGANIZE IT

**1 Be selective.** There's a difference between gaining understanding and drowning in information. During your stay in higher education, you will be exposed to thousands of facts and ideas. No one expects you to memorize all of them. To a large degree, the art of memory is the art of selecting what to remember in the first place.

As you dig into your textbooks and notes, make choices about what is most important to learn. Imagine that you are going to create a test on the material. Then consider the questions you would ask.

When reading, look for chapter previews, summaries, and review questions. Pay attention to anything printed in bold type. Also notice visual elements—tables, charts, graphs, and illustrations. They are all clues pointing to what's important. During lectures, notice what the instructor emphasizes. Anything that's presented visually—on the board, in overheads, or with slides—is probably key.

**2 Make it meaningful.** You remember things better if they have meaning for you. One way to create meaning is to learn from the general to the specific. Before you begin your next reading assignment, skim the passage to locate the main ideas. If you're ever lost, step back and look at the big picture. The details then might make more sense.

Also, you can organize any list of items—even random items—in a meaningful way to make them easier to remember. Although there are probably an infinite number of facts, there are only a finite number of ways to organize them.

One option is to organize any group of items by *category*. You can apply this suggestion to long to-do lists. For example, write each item on a separate index card. Then create a pile of cards for calls to make, errands to run, and household chores to complete. These will become your working categories.

The same concept applies to the content of your courses. In chemistry, a common example of organizing by category is the periodic table of chemical elements. When reading a novel for a literature course, you can organize your notes in categories such as theme, setting, and plot. Then take any of these categories and divide them into subcategories such as major events and minor events in the story. Use index cards to describe each event.

Another option is to organize by *chronological order*. Any time that you create a numbered list of ideas, events, or steps, you are organizing by chronological order. To remember the events that led up to the stock market crash of 1929, for instance, create a timeline. List the key events on index cards. Then arrange the cards by the date of each event.

A third option is to organize by *spatial order*. In plain English, this means making a map. When studying for a history exam, for example, you can create a rough map of the major locations where events take place.

Fourth, there's an old standby for organizing lists—putting a list of items in *alphabetical* order. It's simple, and it works.

**3 Create associations.** The data already encoded in your neural networks are arranged according to a scheme that makes sense to you. When you introduce new data, you can remember them more effectively if you associate them with similar or related data.

Think about your favorite courses. They probably relate to subjects that you already know something about. If you have been interested in politics over the last few years, you'll find it easier to remember the facts in a modern history course. Even when you're tackling a new subject, you can build a mental store of basic background information—the raw material for creating associations. Preview reading assignments, and complete those readings before you attend lectures. Before taking upper-level courses, master the prerequisites.

## USE YOUR BODY

**4 Learn actively.** Action is a great memory enhancer. Test this theory by studying your assignments with the same energy that you bring to the dance floor or the basketball court.

You can use simple, direct methods to infuse your learning with action. When you sit at your desk, sit up straight. Sit on the edge of your chair as if you were about to spring out of it and sprint across the room.

Experiment with standing up when you study. It's harder to fall asleep in this position. Some people insist that their brains work better when they stand. Pace back and forth and gesture as you recite material out loud. Get your body moving.

**5 Relax.** When you're relaxed, you absorb new information quickly and recall it with greater ease and accuracy. Students who can't recall information under the stress of a final exam can often recite the same facts later when they are relaxed.

Relaxing might seem to contradict the idea of active learning, but it doesn't. Being relaxed is not the same as being drowsy, zoned out, or asleep. Relaxation is a state of alertness, free of tension, during which your mind can play with new information, roll it around, create associations with it, and apply many of the other memory techniques. You can be active *and* relaxed.

**6 Create pictures.** Draw diagrams. Make cartoons. Use these images to connect facts and illustrate relationships. You can "see" and recall associations within and among abstract concepts more easily when you visualize both the concepts and the associations. The key is to use your imagination. Creating pictures reinforces visual and kinesthetic learning styles.

For example, Boyle's law states that at a constant temperature the volume of a confined ideal gas varies inversely with its pressure. Simply put, cutting the volume in half doubles the pressure. To remember this concept, you might picture someone "doubled over," using a bicycle pump. As she increases the pressure in the pump by decreasing the volume in the pump cylinder, she seems to be getting angrier. By the time she has

| MEMORY TECHNIQUES | |
|---|---|
| **Point** | **Details** |
| 1. Be selective | Choose what not to remember. Look for clues to important material. |
| 2. Make it meaningful | Organize by time, location, category, continuum, or alphabet. |
| 3. Create associations | Link new facts with facts you already know. |
| 4. Learn actively | Sit straight. Stand while studying. Recite while walking. |
| 5. Relax | Release tension. Remain alert. |

**Figure 3.1** Topic-Point-Details Chart

doubled the pressure (and halved the volume), she is boiling ("Boyle-ing") mad.

You can also create pictures as you study by using *graphic organizers*. These preformatted charts prompt you to visualize relationships among facts and ideas.

One example is a *topic-point-details* chart. At the top of this chart, write the main topic of a lecture or reading assignment. In the left column, list the main points you want to remember. And in the right column, list key details related to each point. Figure 3.1 is the beginning of a chart based on this article.

You could use a similar chart to prompt critical thinking about an issue. Express that issue as a question, and write it at the top. In the left column, note the opinion about the issue. In the right column, list notable facts, expert opinions, reasons, and examples that support each opinion. Figure 3.2 is about tax cuts as a strategy for stimulating the economy.

Sometimes you'll want to remember the main actions in a story or historical event. Create a time line by drawing a straight line. Place points in order on that line to represent key events. Place earlier events toward the left end of the line and later events toward the right. Figure 3.3 shows the start of time line of events relating the U.S. war with Iraq.

When you want to compare or contrast two things, play with a Venn diagram. Represent each thing as a circle. Draw the circles so that they overlap. In the overlapping area, list characteristics that the two things share. In the outer parts of each circle, list the

Influx Productions/Getty Images

## STIMULATE THE ECONOMY WITH TAX CUTS?

| Opinion | Support |
|---|---|
| Yes | Savings from tax cuts allow businesses to invest money in new equipment.<br><br>Tax cuts encourage businesses to expand and hire new employees. |
| No | Years of tax cuts under the Bush administration failed to prevent the mortgage credit crisis.<br><br>Tax cuts create budget deficits. |
| Maybe | Tax cuts might work in some economic conditions.<br><br>Budget deficits might be only temporary. |

Figure 3.2  Question-Opinion-Support Chart

unique characteristics of each thing. Figure 3.4 compares the two types of journal entries included in this book—Discovery Statements and Intention Statements.

The graphic organizers described here are just a few of the many kinds available. To find more examples, do an Internet search. Have fun, and invent graphic organizers of your own.

**7 Recite and repeat.** When you repeat something out loud, you anchor the concept in two different senses. First, you get the physical sensation in your throat, tongue, and lips when voicing the concept. Second, you hear it. The combined result is synergistic, just as it is when you create pictures. That is, the effect of using two different senses is greater than the sum of their individual effects.

| ● 3/19/03<br>U.S.<br>invades<br>Iraq | ● 3/30/03<br>Rumsfeld<br>announces<br>location of<br>WMD | ● 4/9/03<br>Soldiers<br>topple<br>statue of<br>Saddam | ● 5/1/03<br>Bush<br>declares<br>mission<br>accomplished | ● 5/29/03<br>Bush:<br>"We found<br>WMD." |
|---|---|---|---|---|

Figure 3.3  Time Line

The "out loud" part is important. Reciting silently in your head can be useful—in the library, for example—but it is not as effective as making noise. Your mind can trick itself into thinking it knows something when it doesn't. Your ears are harder to fool.

The repetition part is important too. Repetition is a common memory device because it works. Also remember that recitation works best when you recite concepts in your own words.

**8 Write it down.** The technique of writing things down is obvious, yet easy to forget. Writing a note to yourself helps you remember an idea, even if you never look at the note again. Writing notes in the margins of your textbooks can help you remember what you read.

You can extend this technique by writing down an idea not just once, but many times. Let go of the old image of being forced to write "I will not throw paper wads" a hundred times on the chalkboard after school. When you choose to remember something, repetitive writing is a powerful tool.

## USE YOUR BRAIN

**9 Engage your emotions.** One powerful way to enhance your memory is to make friends with your amygdala. This area of your brain lights up with extra neural activity each time you feel a strong emotion. When a topic excites love, laughter, or fear, the amygdala sends a flurry of chemical messages that say, in effect, *This information is important and useful. Don't forget it.*

You're more likely to remember course material when you relate it to a goal—whether academic, personal, or career—that you feel strongly about. This is one reason why it pays to be specific about what you want. The more goals you have and the more clearly they are defined, the more channels you create for incoming information.

**10 Overlearn.** One way to fight mental fuzziness is to learn more than you need to know about a subject simply to pass a test. You can pick a subject apart, examine it, add to it, and go over it until it becomes second nature.

This technique is especially effective for problem solving. Do the assigned problems and then do more problems. Find another textbook and work similar problems. Then make up your own problems and solve them. When you pretest yourself in this way, the potential rewards are speed, accuracy, and greater confidence at exam time. Being well prepared can help you prevent test anxiety.

**11 Escape the short-term memory trap.** Short-term memory is different from the kind of memory you'll need during exam week. For example, most of us can look at an unfamiliar seven-digit phone number once and remember it long enough to dial it. See whether you can recall that number the next day.

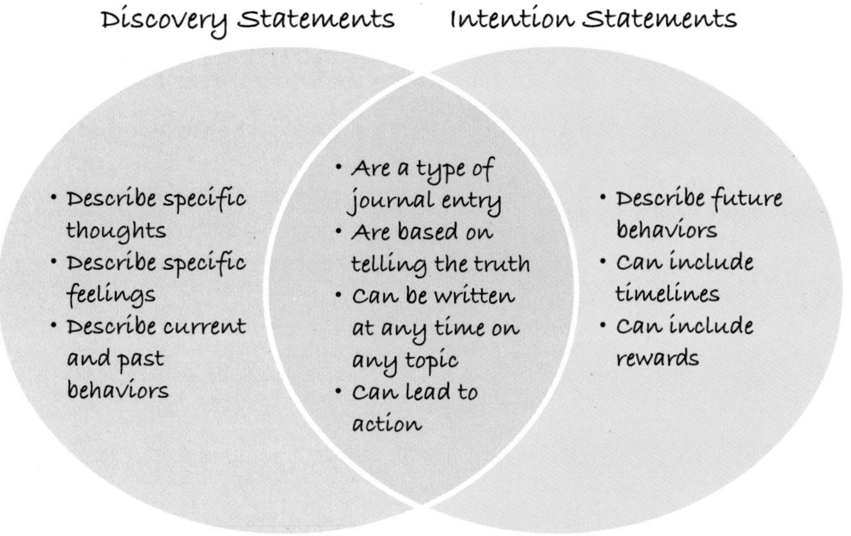

**Discovery Statements**     **Intention Statements**

- Describe specific thoughts
- Describe specific feelings
- Describe current and past behaviors

- Are a type of journal entry
- Are based on telling the truth
- Can be written at any time on any topic
- Can lead to action

- Describe future behaviors
- Can include timelines
- Can include rewards

**Figure 3.4** Venn Diagram

Short-term memory can fade after a few minutes, and it rarely lasts more than several hours. A short review within minutes or hours of a study session can move material from short-term memory into long-term memory. That quick mini-review can save you hours of study time when exams roll around.

**12 Use your times of peak energy.** Study your most difficult subjects during the times when your energy peaks. Some people can concentrate more effectively during daylight hours. Observe the peaks and valleys in your energy flow during the day, and adjust study times accordingly.

**13 Distribute learning.** As an alternative to marathon study sessions, experiment with several shorter sessions spaced out over time. You might find that you can get far more done in three 2-hour sessions than in one 6-hour session.

This suggestion does have an exception. When you are so engrossed in a textbook that you cannot put it down, when you are consumed by an idea for a term paper and cannot think of anything else—keep going. The master student within you has taken over. Enjoy the ride.

**14 Be aware of attitudes.** People who think history is boring tend to have trouble remembering dates and historical events. People who believe math is difficult often have a hard time recalling mathematical equations and formulas. All of us can forget information that contradicts our opinions.

If you think a subject is boring, remind yourself that everything is related to everything else. Look for connections that relate to your own interests.

Being aware of your attitudes is not the same as fighting them or struggling to give them up. Just notice your attitudes and be willing to put them on hold. For more ideas, see the Power Process: "Notice your pictures and let them go" on page 98.

**15 Elaborate.** According to Harvard psychologist Daniel Schacter, all courses in memory improvement are based on a single technique—elaboration. *Elaboration* means consciously encoding new information. Repetition is one basic way to elaborate. However, current brain research indicates that other types of elaboration are more effective for long-term memory.[4]

One way to elaborate is to ask yourself questions about incoming information: "Does this remind me of something or someone I already know?" "Is this similar to a technique that I already use?" and "Where and when can I use this information?"

The same idea applies to more complex material. When you meet someone new, for example, ask yourself, "Does she remind me of someone else?" Or when reading this book, preview the material using the Master Student Map that opens each chapter.

**16 Intend to remember.** To instantly enhance your memory, form the simple intention to *learn it now* rather than later. The intention to remember can be more powerful than any single memory technique.

You can build on your intention with simple tricks. During a lecture, for example, pretend that you'll be quizzed on the key points at the end of the period. Imagine that you'll get a $5 reward for every correct answer.

## RECALL IT

**17 Remember something else.** When you are stuck and can't remember something that you're sure you know, remember something else that is related to it.

If you can't remember your great-aunt's name, remember your great-uncle's name. During an economics exam, if you can't remember anything about the aggregate demand curve, recall what you do know about the aggregate supply curve. If you cannot recall specific facts, remember the example that the instructor used during her lecture. Any piece of information is encoded in the same area of the brain as a similar piece of information. You can unblock your recall by stimulating that area of your memory.

A brainstorm is a good memory jog. If you are stumped when taking a test, start writing down lots of answers to related questions, and—pop!—the answer you need may appear.

**18** **Notice when you do remember.** Everyone has a different memory style. Some people are best at recalling information they've read. Others have an easier time remembering what they've heard, seen, or done.

To develop your memory, notice when you recall information easily, and ask yourself what memory techniques you're using naturally. Also notice when you find it difficult to recall information. Be a reporter. Get the facts and then adjust your learning techniques. And remember to congratulate yourself when you remember.

**19** **Use it before you lose it.** Even information encoded in long-term memory becomes difficult to recall when we don't use it regularly. The pathways to the information become faint with disuse. For example, you can probably remember your current phone number. What was your phone number 10 years ago?

This example points to a powerful memory technique. To remember something, access it a lot. Read it, write it, speak it, listen to it, apply it—find some way to make contact with the material regularly. Each time you do so, you widen the neural pathway to the material and make it easier to recall the next time.

Another way to make contact with the material is to teach it. Teaching demands mastery. When you explain the function of the pancreas to a fellow student, you discover quickly whether you really understand it yourself. Study groups are especially effective because they put you on stage. The friendly pressure of knowing that you'll teach the group helps focus your attention.

**20** **Adopt the attitude that you never forget.** Instead of saying, "I don't remember," say, "It will come to me." The latter statement implies that the information you want is encoded in your brain and that you can retrieve it—just not right now. You might be surprised to find that the information obediently pops into mind. ■

- - - - - - - - - - - - - - - - - - - - - - - - - - - - - - - - - -

## If you think a subject is boring, remind yourself that everything is related to everything else. Look for connections that relate to your own interests.

- - - - - - - - - - - - - - - - - - - - - - - - - - - - - - - - - -

**You're One Click Away...**
*from finding more memory strategies online.*

# SET A TRAP FOR
## your memory

......................................

When you want to remind yourself to do something, link this activity to another event you know will take place. The key is to "trap" your memory by picking events that are certain to occur.

......................................

Say that you're walking to class and suddenly remember that your accounting assignment is due tomorrow. If you wear a ring, then switch it to a finger on the opposite hand. Now you're "trapped." Every time you glance at your hand and notice that you switched the ring, you get a reminder that you were supposed to remember something else. If you empty your pockets every night, put an unusual item in your pocket in the morning to remind yourself to do something before you go to bed. For example, to remember to call your younger sister on her birthday, pick an object that reminds you of her—a photograph, perhaps—and put it in your pocket. When you empty your pocket that evening and find the photo, you're more likely to make the call.

Everyday rituals that you seldom neglect, such as feeding a pet or unlacing your shoes, provide opportunities for setting traps. For example, tie a triple knot in your shoelace as a reminder to set the alarm for your early morning study group meeting.

You can even use imaginary traps. To remember to pay your phone bill, visualize a big, burly bill collector knocking on your front door to talk to you about how much you owe. The next time your arrive at your front door, you'll be glad that you got there before he did. You still have time to make your payment!

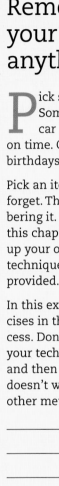

Mobile devices work well for setting memory traps. To remind yourself to bring your textbook to class, for example, set an alarm on your cell phone to go off 10 minutes before you leave the house. Visualize yourself picking up the book when the alarm goes off.

Link two activities together, and make the association unusual. ■

©Istockphoto.com/Tatiana Popova

✓ **EXERCISE** 10

## Remembering your car keys—or anything else

Pick something you frequently forget. Some people chronically lose their car keys or forget to pay their bills on time. Others let anniversaries and birthdays slip by.

Pick an item or a task you're prone to forget. Then design a strategy for remembering it. Use any of the techniques from this chapter, research others, or make up your own from scratch. Describe your technique and the results in the space provided.

In this exercise, as in most of the exercises in this book, a failure is also a success. Don't be concerned with whether your technique will work. Design it, and then find out whether it works. If it doesn't work for you this time, use another method.

**3**

_____

_____

_____

_____

_____

_____

_____

_____

_____

_____

_____

_____

_____

_____

_____

_____

_____

_____

# YOUR BRAIN—
## its care and feeding

When asked about brain-based learning, skeptics might say: "Well, obviously—how could learning be based anywhere other than the brain?"

That's a fair question. One answer is this: Although all learning involves the brain, some learning strategies use more of the brain's unique capacities.

## BRAINS THRIVE ON MEANINGFUL PATTERNS

Your brain is a pattern-making machine. It excels at taking random bits of information and translating them into meaningful wholes. Build on this capacity with *elaborative rehearsal*. For example:

- *Use your journal.* Write Discovery and Intention Statements like the ones in this book. Journal Entries prompt you to elaborate on what you hear in class and read in your textbooks. You can create your own writing prompts. For example: "In class today, I discovered that. . . ." "In order to overcome my confusion about this topic, I intend to. . . ."

- *Send yourself a message.* Imagine that an absent classmate has asked you to send her an e-mail about what happened in class today. Write up a reply and send this e-mail to yourself. You'll actively process your recent learning—and create a summary that you can use to review for tests.

- *Play with ideas.* Copy your notes on to 3 × 5 cards, one fact or idea per card. Then see whether you can arrange them into new patterns—chronological order, order of importance, or main ideas and supporting details.

## BRAINS THRIVE ON RICH SENSORY EXPERIENCE

Your brain's contact with the world comes through your five senses. So, anchor your learning in as many senses as possible. Beyond seeing and hearing, this can include touch, movement, smell, and taste:

- *Create images.* Draw mind map summaries of your readings and lecture notes. Include visual images. Put main ideas in larger letters and brighter colors.

- *Translate ideas into physical objects.* If one of your career goals is to work from a home office, for example, then create a model of your ideal workspace. Visit an art supplies store to find appropriate materials.

- *Immerse yourself in concrete experiences.* Say that you're in a music appreciation class and learning about jazz. Go to a local jazz club or concert to see and hear a live performance.

iStockphoto.com/sturti

## BRAINS THRIVE ON LONG-TERM CARE

Starting now, adopt habits to keep your brain lean and fit for life. Consider these research-based suggestions from the Alzheimer's Association.[5]

- *Stay mentally active.* If you sit at a desk most of the workday, take a hiking class or start a garden. If you seldom travel, start reading maps of new locations and plan a cross-country trip. Play challenging games and work crossword puzzles. Seek out museums, theaters, concerts, and other cultural events. Even after you graduate, consider learning another language or taking up a musical instrument. Learning gives your brain a workout, much like sit-ups condition your abs.

- *Stay socially active.* Having a network of supportive friends can reduce stress levels. In turn, stress management helps to maintain connections between brain cells. Stay socially active by working, volunteering, and joining clubs.

- *Stay physically active.* Physical activity promotes blood flow to the brain. It also reduces the risk of diabetes, cardiovascular disease, and other diseases that can impair brain function. Exercise that includes mental activity—such as planning a jogging route and watching for traffic signals—offers added benefits.

- *Adopt a brain-healthy diet.* A diet rich in dark-skinned fruits and vegetables boosts your supply of antioxidants—natural chemicals that nourish your brain. Examples of these foods are raisins, blueberries, blackberries, strawberries, raspberries, kale, spinach, brussels sprouts, alfalfa sprouts, and broccoli. Avoid foods that are high in saturated fat and cholesterol, which may increase the risk of Alzheimer's disease.

- *Protect your heart.* In general, what's good for your heart is good for your brain. Protect both organs by eating well, exercising regularly, managing your weight, staying tobacco-free, and getting plenty of sleep. These habits reduce your risk of heart attack, stroke, and other cardiovascular conditions that interfere with blood flow to the brain. ∎

90  *Chapter 3 • Memory*

# MNEMONIC DEVICES

It's pronounced "ne-MON-ik." The word refers to tricks that can increase your ability to recall everything from grocery lists to speeches.

Some entertainers use mnemonic devices to perform "impossible" feats of memory, such as recalling the names of everyone in a large audience after hearing them just once. Using mnemonic devices, speakers can go for hours without looking at their notes. The possibilities for students are endless.

There is a catch, though. Mnemonic devices have three serious limitations:

- They don't always help you understand or digest material. Mnemonics rely only on rote memorization.

- The mnemonic device itself is sometimes complicated to learn and time-consuming to develop.

- Mnemonic devices can be forgotten.

In spite of their limitations, mnemonic devices can be powerful. There are five general categories: new words, creative sentences, rhymes and songs, the loci system, and the peg system.

**Make up new words.** Acronyms are words created from the initial letters of a series of words. Examples include NASA (**N**ational **A**eronautics and **S**pace **A**dministration) and laser (**l**ight **a**mplification by **s**timulated **e**mission of **r**adiation).

You can make up your own acronyms to recall a series of facts. A common mnemonic acronym is Roy G. Biv, which has helped millions of students remember the colors of the visible spectrum (**r**ed, **o**range, **y**ellow, **g**reen, **b**lue, **i**ndigo, and **v**iolet). IPMAT helps biology students remember the stages of cell division (**i**nterphase, **p**rophase, **m**etaphase, **a**naphase, and **t**elophase). OCEAN helps psychology students recall the five major personality factors: **o**pen-mindedness, **c**onscientiousness, **e**xtraversion, **a**greeableness, and **n**euroticism.

**Use creative sentences.** Acrostics are sentences that help you remember a series of letters that stand for something. For example, the first letters of the words in the sentence *Every good boy does fine* (E, G, B, D, and F) are the music notes of the lines of the treble clef staff.

**Create rhymes and songs.** Madison Avenue advertising executives spend billions of dollars a year on advertisements designed to burn their messages into your memory. The song "It's the Real Thing" was used to market Coca-Cola, despite the soda's artificial ingredients.

Rhymes have been used for centuries to teach basic facts. "*I* before *e,* except after *c*" has helped many a student on spelling tests.

**Use the loci system.** The word *loci* is the plural of *locus,* a synonym for *place* or *location.* Use the loci system to create visual associations with familiar locations. Unusual associations are the easiest to remember.

The loci system is an old one. Ancient Greek orators used it to remember long speeches, and politicians use it today. For example, if a politician's position were that road taxes must be raised to pay for school equipment, his loci visualizations before a speech might look like the following.

First, as he walks in the door of his house, he imagines a large *porpoise* jumping through a hoop. This reminds him to begin by telling the audience the *purpose* of his speech.

Next, he visualizes his living room floor covered with paving stones, forming a road leading into the kitchen. In the kitchen, he pictures dozens of schoolchildren sitting on the floor because they have no desks.

Now it's the day of the big speech. The politician is nervous. He's perspiring so much that his clothes stick to his body. He stands up to give his speech and his mind goes blank. Then he starts thinking to himself:

*I can remember the rooms in my house. Let's see, I'm walking in the front door and—wow!—I see a porpoise. That reminds me to talk about the purpose of my speech. And then there's that road leading to the kitchen. Say, what are all those kids doing there on the floor? Oh, yeah, now I remember—they have no desks! We need to raise taxes on roads to pay for their desks and the other stuff they need in classrooms.*

**Use the peg system.** The peg system is a technique that employs key words that are paired with numbers. Each word forms a "peg" on which you can "hang" mental associations. To use this system effectively, learn the following peg words and their associated numbers well:

| | |
|---|---|
| *bun* goes with 1 | *sticks* goes with 6 |
| *shoe* goes with 2 | *heaven* goes with 7 |
| *tree* goes with 3 | *gate* goes with 8 |
| *door* goes with 4 | *wine* goes with 9 |
| *hive* goes with 5 | *hen* goes with 10 |

You can use the peg system to remember the Bill of Rights (the first ten amendments to the U.S. Constitution). For example, amendment number *four* is about protection from unlawful search and seizure. Imagine people knocking at your *door* who are demanding to search your home. This amendment means that you do not have to open your door unless those people have a proper search warrant. ■

Door: © Photospin, Bill of Rights: National Archives and Records Administration

# PRACTICING
# critical thinking 3

Memory skills connect to several qualities of a master student—being inquisitive, competent, and able to focus attention. Use this exercise as a way to further develop those qualities in yourself.

First, review the six levels of thinking described by Benjamin Bloom:

**Level 1: Remembering**—recalling an idea.

**Level 2: Understanding**—explaining an idea in your own words and giving examples from your own experience.

**Level 3: Applying**—using an idea to produce a desired result.

**Level 4: Analyzing**—dividing an idea into parts or steps.

**Level 5: Evaluating**—rating the truth, usefulness, or quality of an idea—and giving reasons for your rating.

**Level 6: Creating**—inventing something new based on an idea.

This exercise is about **Level 4: Analyzing**. For example, recall the "memory jungle" described in the article on pages 82–83. This is an idea with four parts. Each part includes a visualization and related feature about memory. These can all be summarized in a chart:

| Visualization #1: A well-worn path | Memory feature: Thoughts create "paths" of connected cell in the brain. |
| Visualization #2: A herd of thoughts | Memory feature: Thoughts that are grouped together ("herded") are easier to recall. |
| Visualization #3: Turning your back | Memory feature: We quickly forget ("turn our back") on new material unless we review it. |
| Visualization #4: Directing the animal traffic | Memory feature: You can direct new thoughts ("animals") into your long-term memory by actively using memory techniques. |

Creating a chart is one way to analyze an idea. This level of thinking can also involve making lists, drawing maps, and sorting things into groups or categories. On a test, questions that call for analysis might also ask you to *compare* (state how things are alike) and *contrast* (state how things differ).

Now it's your turn. Choose another idea from this chapter (**Level 1: Remembering**) and think about it at **Level 4: Analyzing**. In the space below, summarize the idea and then demonstrate your higher-level thinking. Continue on additional paper as needed.

_____

_____

_____

_____

_____

_____

_____

_____

_____

_____

_____

_____

_____

_____

_____

_____

_____

_____

_____

_____

_____

_____

*For more information on the six levels of thinking, see "Becoming a critical thinker" in Chapter 7.*

# EXERCISE 11

## Move from problems to solutions

Many students find it easy to complain about school and to dwell on problems. This exercise gives you an opportunity to change that habit and respond creatively to any problem you're currently experiencing—whether it be with memorizing or some other aspect of school or life.

The key is to dwell more on solutions than on problems. Do that by inventing as many solutions as possible for any given problem. See whether you can turn a problem into a *project* (a plan of action) or a *promise* to change some aspect of your life. Shifting the emphasis of your conversation from problems to solutions can raise your sense of possibility and unleash the master learner within you.

In the space below, describe at least three problems that could interfere with your success as a student. The problems can be related to courses, teachers, personal relationships, finances, or anything else that might get in the way of your success.

My problem is that . . .

_____

_____

My problem is that . . .

_____

_____

My problem is that . . .

_____

_____

Next, brainstorm at least five possible solutions to each of those problems. Ten solutions would be even better. (You can continue brainstorming on a separate piece of paper or on a computer.) You might find it hard to come up with that many ideas. That's okay. Stick with it. Stay in the inquiry, give yourself time, and ask other people for ideas.

I can solve my problem by . . .

_____

_____

I can solve my problem by . . .

_____

_____

I can solve my problem by . . .

_____

_____

**JOURNAL ENTRY 7**
*Discovery Statement*

## Revisit your memory skills

Take a minute to reflect on the memory techniques in this chapter. You probably use some of them already without being aware of it. In the space below, list at least three memory techniques you have used in the past, and describe how you have used them.

_____

_____

_____

_____

_____

_____

_____

_____

_____

_____

_____

_____

_____

_____

_____

_____

_____

_____

_____

_____

_____

_____

_____

3

# masterstudentprofile

# Pablo Alvarado

(1954– ) Executive Director of the National Day Laborer Organizing Network. Alvarado uses sports, music, and coalition building to foster humane conditions for day laborers.

Pablo Alvarado still remembers the sound of sirens from the five police cars that surrounded him one morning in 1992. He was an undocumented immigrant looking for work in Woodland Hills, California.

Eventually Alvarado managed to convince the police that he was not a criminal—only a person who'd heard about a job opening in the neighborhood. He hoped that his experience as a gardener, painter, driver, construction worker, and factory worker would help him to get hired.

When Alvarado came to Woodland Hills, he already carried a burden of memory. As a child walking to school in El Níspero, a farming village in El Salvador, he had stepped over dead bodies lying on the road sides. They were people killed by death squads during the country's civil war. Several of Alvarado's teachers were murdered; he watched them die.

Thousands of people fled from El Salvador during that twelve-year war—nearly a quarter of the country's population, according to one estimate. In 1990, Alvarado joined them by crossing the border into the United States.

By then Alvarado had already developed leadership skills. At age 12, he was a teaching assistant for a literacy class in El Níspero. At 16, he was a lay preacher who spoke about applying the Christian Gospels to political struggles. He also attended Universidad de El Salvador, where he earned a degree to teach high school.

Like many other immigrants, Alvarado eventually found himself waiting in store parking lots and on street corners, hoping to find work as a day laborer. This method of job hunting can be dangerous. Besides being targets of violence, day laborers live with fears of unsafe working conditions, underpayment, and being deported. Some cities pass ordinances that ban day laborers from gathering in public places, making jobs even harder to find.

Alvarado responded to these problems by using his skills as an organizer. He earned permanent resident status in the United States and became leader of the National Day Laborer Organizing Network (NDLON).

Alvarado noticed that immigrants looking for work often viewed each other as competitors. Conflicts arose between Mexicans and Central Americans, leading to verbal clashes and fights.

Alvarado's solution was unusual—using the arts and athletics as ways to reduce tensions. NDLON convinced day laborers to join soccer teams. The organization also sponsored marathon races, chess teams, and street theater. Alvarado found that friendships made during tournaments and performances carried over to the street corners where people gathered to find work.

The band Los Jornaleros del Norte (The Day Laborers of the North) is another of Alvarado's projects. The group has recorded three albums of music about conditions of day laborers.

In addition, Alvarado has stressed the importance of worker centers. These community-based, nonprofit organizations connect day laborers with jobs and help them file unpaid wage claims.

Writing his blog for *The Huffington Post*, Alvarado recalled the role of these organizations in his own life: "When I came to this country after escaping the war in my native El Salvador, it was a worker center where I was able to learn and practice English and begin to understand my rights and responsibilities in my new home."

Photo by Misha Erwit

**PABLO ALVARADO**...is caring.

**YOU** ... can care for people by helping them find common ground.

"The government should stop its immigrant witch hunt and start focusing on real solutions," he added. "What we need is verification of workplace safety and effective enforcement of wage and hour laws."

These are policies, Alvarado says, that would benefit any American who wants to work.

**You're One Click Away...**
*from finding more biographical information online about Pablo Alvarado at the Master Student Hall of Fame.*

1. Briefly define the word *love* as it is used in the Power Process: "Love your problems (and experience your barriers)."

2. According to the latest research, memory is:
   (a) A process rather than a thing.
   (b) A process of encoding and decoding.
   (c) A process that changes your brain physically.
   (d) All of the above..

3. In the article about the memory jungle, the meadow:
   (a) Is a place that every animal (thought or perception) must pass through.
   (b) Represents short-term memory.
   (c) Represents the idea that one type of memory has a limited capacity.
   (d) Is all of the above.

4. Give two examples of ways in which you can organize a long list of items.

5. Memorization on a deep level can take place if you:
   (a) Repeat the idea.
   (b) Repeat the idea.
   (c) Repeat the idea.
   (d) All of the above.

6. The article "Memory techniques" is divided into four categories. What are those categories?

7. Define the term *graphic organizer* and give two examples.

8. Define *acronym,* and give an example of one.

9. Even though mnemonic devices have limitations, they are the most efficient ways to memorize facts and ideas. True or false? Explain your answer.

10. List three ways to infuse your learning with action.

# 3 SKILLS *Snapshot*

Use this exercise to monitor the Master Student qualities that you're developing—especially those related to memory. Begin by reflecting on some recent experiences. Then take the next step toward memory mastery by committing to a specific action in the near future.

## DISCOVERY

My score on the *Memory* section of the Discovery Wheel on page 29 was . . .

Recalling key facts more quickly and accurately could help me be more effective in the following situations . . .

memory techniques that I already use include . . .

## INTENTION

I'll know that I've reached a new level of mastery with remembering ideas and information when . . .

Stated as a goal, my intention is . . .

## ACTION

To achieve the goal I just wrote, the most important thing I can do next is to . . .

At the end of this course, I would like my *Memory* score on the Discovery Wheel to be . . .

# Reading

Use this **Master Student Map** to ask yourself,

 **WHY** THIS CHAPTER MATTERS . . .

- Higher education requires extensive reading of complex material.

 **WHAT** IS INCLUDED . . .

 **HOW** CAN I USE THIS CHAPTER . . .

- Analyze what effective readers do, and experiment with new techniques.
- Increase your vocabulary and adjust your reading speed for different types of material.
- Comprehend difficult texts with more ease.

 **WHAT** IF . . .

- I could finish my reading with time to spare and easily recall the key points?

## JOURNAL ENTRY 8
*Intention Statement*

### Declare what you want from this chapter

R ecall a time when you encountered problems with reading, such as finding words you didn't understand or pausing to reread paragraphs more than once. Then list at least three specific reading skills you want to gain from this chapter.

I intend to . . .

_____

_____

_____

_____

_____

_____

_____

_____

_____

_____

_____

_____

_____

_____

_____

© Ruslan Ivantsov/Shutterstock.com

# POWER process

## Notice your pictures and let them go

One of the brain's primary jobs is to manufacture images. We use mental pictures to make predictions about the world, and we base much of our behavior on those predictions.

Pictures can sometimes get in our way. Take the student who plans to attend a school he hasn't visited. He chose this school for its strong curriculum and good academic standing, but his brain didn't stop there. In his mind, the campus has historic buildings with ivy-covered walls and tree-lined avenues. The professors, he imagines, will be as articulate as Barack Obama and as entertaining as Conan O'Brien. The cafeteria will be a cozy nook serving everything from delicate quiche to strong coffee. He will gather there with fellow students for hours of stimulating, intellectual conversation. The library will have every book, and the computer lab will boast the newest technology.

The school turns out to be four gray buildings downtown, next to the bus station. The first class he attends is taught by an overweight, balding professor wearing a purple and orange bird-of-paradise tie. The cafeteria is a nondescript hall with machine-dispensed food, and the student's apartment is barely large enough to accommodate his roommate's tuba. This hypothetical student gets depressed. He begins to think about dropping out of school.

The problem with pictures is that they can prevent us from seeing what is really there. That is what happened to the student in this story. His pictures prevented him from noticing that his school is in the heart of a culturally vital city—close to theaters, museums, government offices, clubs, and all kinds of stores. The professor with the weird tie is not only an expert in his field but also a superior teacher. The school cafeteria is skimpy because it can't compete with the variety of inexpensive restaurants in the area.

Our pictures often lead to our being angry or disappointed. We set up expectations of events before they occur. Sometimes we don't even realize that we have these expectations. The next time you discover you are angry, disappointed, or frustrated, look to see which of your pictures aren't being fulfilled.

When you notice that pictures are getting in your way, in the gentlest manner possible let your pictures go. Let them drift away like wisps of smoke picked up by a gentle wind.

This Power Process can be a lifesaver when it comes to reading. Some students enter higher education with pictures about all the reading they'll be required to do before they graduate. They see themselves feeling bored, confused, and worried about keeping up with assignments. If you have such pictures, be willing to let them go. This chapter can help you recreate your whole experience of reading, which is crucial to your success.

Sometimes when we let go of old pictures, it's helpful to replace them with new, positive pictures. These new images can help you take a fresh perspective. Your new pictures might not feel as comfortable and genuine as your old ones. That's okay. Give it time. It's your head, and you're ultimately in charge of the pictures that live there.

istockphoto.com/Tim Ashton

**You're One Click Away...**
*from accessing Power Process Media online and finding out more about how to "notice your pictures and let them go."*

Picture yourself sitting at a desk, a book in your hands. Your eyes are open, and it looks as if you're reading. Suddenly your head jerks up. You blink. You realize your eyes have been scanning the page for 10 minutes, and you can't remember a single thing you have read.

# MUSCLE READING

Or picture this: You've had a hard day. You were up at 6:00 A.M. to get the kids ready for school. A coworker called in sick, and you missed your lunch trying to do his job as well as your own. You picked up the kids, then had to shop for dinner. Dinner was late, of course, and the kids were grumpy.

Finally, you get to your books at 8:00 P.M. You begin a reading assignment on something called "the equity method of accounting for common stock investments." "I am preparing for the future," you tell yourself, as you plod through two paragraphs and begin the third. Suddenly, everything in the room looks different. Your head is resting on your elbow, which is resting on the equity method of accounting. The clock reads 11:00 P.M. Say good-bye to 3 hours.

Sometimes the only difference between a sleeping pill and a textbook is that the textbook doesn't have a warning on the label about operating heavy machinery.

Contrast this scenario with the image of an active reader, who exhibits the following behaviors:

- Stays alert, poses questions about what she reads, and searches for the answers

- Recognizes levels of information within the text, separating the main points and general principles from supporting details

- Quizzes herself about the material, makes written notes, and lists unanswered questions

- Instantly spots key terms and takes the time to find the definitions of unfamiliar words

- Thinks critically about the ideas in the text and looks for ways to apply them

That sounds like a lot to do. Yet skilled readers routinely accomplish all these things and more—while enjoying the process.

Master students engage actively with reading material. They're willing to grapple with even the most challenging texts. They wrestle meaning from each page. They fill the margins with handwritten questions. They underline, highlight, annotate, and nearly rewrite some books to make them their own.

Master students also commit to change their lives based on what they read. Of every chapter, they ask, "What's the point? And what's the payoff? How can I use this to live my purpose and achieve my goals?" These students are just as likely to create to-do lists as to take notes on their reading. And when they're done with a useful book, master students share it with others for continuing conversation. Reading becomes a creative act and a tool for building community.

One way to experience this kind of success is to approach reading with a system in mind. An example is Muscle Reading. You can use Muscle Reading to avoid mental minivacations and reduce the number of unscheduled naps during study time, even after a hard day. Muscle Reading is a way to decrease difficulty and struggle by increasing energy and skill. Once you learn this system, you might actually spend less time on your reading and get more out of it.

Boosting your reading skills will promote your success in school. It can also boost your income. According to a report from the National Endowment for the Arts, proficient readers earn more than people with only basic reading skills. In addition, better readers are more likely to work as managers or other professionals.[1]

This is not to say that Muscle Reading will make your job or education a breeze. Muscle Reading might even look like more work at first. Effective textbook reading is an active, energy-consuming, sit-on-the-edge-of-your-seat business. That's why this strategy is called Muscle Reading. ■

# How Muscle Reading WORKS

**M**uscle Reading is a three-phase technique you can use to extract the ideas and information you want.

- Phase 1 includes steps to take *before* you read.
- Phase 2 includes steps to take *while* you read.
- Phase 3 includes steps to take *after* you read.

Each phase has specific steps.

> **PHASE ONE:**
> **Before you read**
> Step 1: **Preview**
> Step 2: **Outline**
> Step 3: **Question**
>
> **PHASE TWO:**
> **While you read**
> Step 4: **Focus**
> Step 5: **Flag Answers**
>
> **PHASE THREE:**
> **After you read**
> Step 6: **Recite**
> Step 7: **Review**
> Step 8: **Review again**

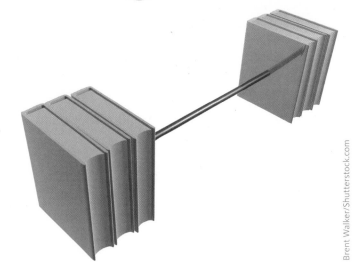

Brent Walker/Shutterstock.com

**To jog your memory, write the first letters of the Muscle Reading acrostic in a margin or at the top of your notes. Then check off the steps you intend to follow.**

To assist your recall of Muscle Reading strategies, memorize three short sentences:

**P**ry **O**ut **Q**uestions.
**F**ocus and **F**lag **A**nswers.
**R**ecite, **R**eview, and **R**eview again.

These three sentences correspond to the three phases of the Muscle Reading technique. Each sentence is an acrostic. The first letter of each word stands for one of the steps listed above.

Take a moment to invent images for each of those sentences.

For *Phase 1*, visualize or feel yourself prying out questions from a text. These questions are ones you want answered based on a brief survey of the assignment. Make a mental picture of yourself scanning the material, spotting a question, and reaching into the text to pry it out. Hear yourself saying, "I've got it. Here's my question."

Then for *Phase 2*, focus on finding answers to your questions. Feel free to underline, highlight, or mark up your text in other ways. Make the answers so obvious that they lift up from the page.

Finally, you enter *Phase 3*. Hear your voice reciting what you have learned. Listen to yourself making a speech or singing a song about the material as you review it.

To jog your memory, write the first letters of the Muscle Reading acrostic in a margin or at the top of your notes. Then check off the steps you intend to follow. Or write the Muscle Reading steps on 3 × 5 cards and then use them for bookmarks.

Muscle Reading might take a little time to learn. At first you might feel it's slowing you down. That's natural when you're gaining a new skill. Mastery comes with time and practice. ■

# PHASE 1 Before you read

## STEP 1 PREVIEW

Before you start reading, preview the entire assignment. You don't have to memorize what you preview to get value from this step. Previewing sets the stage for incoming information by warming up a space in your mental storage area.

If you are starting a new book, look over the table of contents and flip through the text page by page. If you're going to read one chapter, flip through the pages of that chapter. Even if your assignment is merely a few pages in a book, you can benefit from a brief preview of the table of contents.

Read all chapter headings and subheadings. Like the headlines in a newspaper, these are usually printed in large, bold type. Often headings are brief summaries in themselves.

Keep an eye out for summary statements. If the assignment is long or complex, read the summary first. Many textbooks have summaries in the introduction or at the end of each chapter.

When previewing, seek out familiar concepts, facts, or ideas. These items can help increase comprehension by linking new information to previously learned material. Take a few moments to reflect on what you already know about the subject—even if you think you know nothing. This technique prepares your brain to accept new information.

Look for ideas that spark your imagination or curiosity. Inspect drawings, diagrams, charts, tables, graphs, and photographs.

Imagine what kinds of questions will show up on a test. Previewing helps to clarify your purpose for reading. Ask yourself what you will do with this material and how it can relate to your long-term goals. Will you be reading just to get the main points? Key supporting details? Additional details? All of the above? Your answers will guide what you do with each step that follows.

Keep your preview short. If the entire reading assignment will take less than an hour, your preview might take 5 minutes. Previewing is also a way to get yourself started when an assignment looks too big to handle. It is an easy way to step into the material.

## STEP 2 OUTLINE

With complex material, take time to understand the structure of what you are about to read. Outlining actively organizes your thoughts about the assignment and can help make complex information easier to understand.

If your textbook provides chapter outlines, spend some time studying them. When an outline is not provided, sketch a brief one in the margin of your book or at the beginning of your notes on a separate sheet of paper. Later, as you read and take notes, you can add to your outline.

Headings in the text can serve as major and minor entries in your outline. For example, the heading for this article is "Phase 1: Before you read," and the subheadings list the three steps in this phase. When you outline, feel free to rewrite headings so that they are more meaningful to you.

The amount of time you spend on this outlining step will vary. For some assignments, a 10-second mental outline is all you might need. For other assignments (fiction and poetry, for example), you can skip this step altogether.

## STEP 3 QUESTION

Before you begin a careful reading, determine what you want from the assignment. Then write down a list of questions, including any questions that resulted from your preview of the materials.

Another useful technique is to turn chapter headings and sub-headings into questions. For example, if a heading is "Transference and Suggestion," you can ask yourself, "What are *transference* and *suggestion*? How does *transference* relate to *suggestion*?" Make up a quiz as if you were teaching this subject to your classmates.

If there are no headings, look for key sentences and turn them into questions. These sentences usually show up at the beginnings or ends of paragraphs and sections.

Have fun with this technique. Make the questions playful or creative. You don't need to answer every question that you ask. The purpose of making up questions is to get your brain involved in the assignment. Take your unanswered questions to class, where they can be springboards for class discussion.

Demand your money's worth from your textbook. If you do not understand a concept, write specific questions about it. The more detailed your questions, the more powerful this technique becomes.

> Have fun with this technique. Make the questions playful or creative. You don't need to answer every question that you ask. The purpose of making up questions is to get your brain involved in the assignment. Take your unanswered questions to class, where they can be springboards for class discussion.

**You're One Click Away...**
*from finding examples of Phase 1 strategies online.*

**4**

# PHASE 2 While you read

## STEP 4 FOCUS

You have previewed the reading assignment, organized it in your mind or on paper, and formulated questions. Now you are ready to begin reading.

It's easy to fool yourself about reading. Just having an open book in your hand and moving your eyes across a page doesn't mean that you are reading effectively. Reading takes mental focus.

As you read, be conscious of where you are and what you are doing. Use the Power Process: "Be here now" in Chapter 2. When you notice your attention wandering, gently bring it back to the present moment. There are many ways to do this.

To begin, get in a position to stay focused. If you observe chief executive officers, you'll find that some of them wear out the front of their chair first. They're literally on the edge of their seat. Approach your reading assignment in the same way. Sit up. Keep your spine straight. Avoid reading in bed, except for fun.

Avoid marathon reading sessions. Schedule breaks and set a reasonable goal for the entire session. Then reward yourself with an enjoyable activity for 10 or 15 minutes every hour or two.

# FIVE SMART WAYS to highlight a text

Step 5 in Muscle Reading mentions a powerful tool: highlighting. It also presents a danger—the ever-present temptation to highlight too much text. Excessive highlighting leads to wasted time during reviews. Get the most out of all that money you pay for books and the time you spend reading. Highlight in an efficient way that leaves texts readable for years to come and provides you with an easy reviewing method.

### Read carefully first.
Read an entire chapter or section at least once before you begin highlighting. Don't be in a hurry to mark up your book. Get to know the text first. Make two or three passes through difficult sections before you highlight.

### Make choices up front about what to highlight.
Perhaps you can accomplish your purposes by highlighting only certain chapters or sections of a text. When you highlight, remember to look for passages that directly answer the questions you posed during Step 3 of Muscle Reading. Within these passages, highlight individual words, phrases, or sentences rather than whole paragraphs. The important thing is to choose an overall strategy before you put highlighter to paper.

### Recite first.
You might want to apply Step 6 of Muscle Reading before you highlight. Talking about what you read—to yourself or with other people—can help you grasp the essence of a text. Recite first; then go back and highlight. You'll probably highlight more selectively.

### Underline, then highlight.
Underline key passages lightly in pencil. Then close your text and come back to it later. Assess your underlining. Perhaps you can highlight less than you underlined and still capture the key points.

### Use highlighting to monitor your comprehension.
Critical thinking plays a role in underlining and highlighting. When highlighting, you're making moment-by-moment decisions about what you want to remember from a text. You're also making inferences about what material might be included on a test. Take your critical thinking a step further by using highlighting to check your comprehension. Stop reading periodically and look back over the sentences you've highlighted. See whether you are making accurate distinctions between main points and supporting material. Highlighting too much—more than 10 percent of the text—can be a sign that you're not making this distinction and that you don't fully understand what you're reading. See the article "When Reading Is Tough" later in this chapter for suggestions that can help.

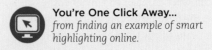

**You're One Click Away...**
*from finding an example of smart highlighting online.*

> **It's easy to fool yourself about reading. Just having an open book in your hand and moving your eyes across a page doesn't mean that you are reading effectively. Reading takes mental focus.**

For difficult reading, set more limited goals. Read for a half hour and then take a break. Most students find that shorter periods of reading distributed throughout the day and week can be more effective than long sessions.

Visualize the material. Form mental pictures of the concepts as they are presented. If you read that a voucher system can help control cash disbursements, picture a voucher handing out dollar bills. Using visual imagery in this way can help deepen your understanding of the text while allowing information to be transferred into your long-term memory.

Read material out loud, especially if it is complicated. Some of us remember better and understand more quickly when we hear an idea.

Get a "feel" for the subject. For example, let's say you are reading about a microorganism—a paramecium—in your biology text. Imagine what it would feel like to run your finger around the long, cigar-shaped body of the organism. Imagine feeling the large fold of its gullet on one side and the tickle of the hairy little cilia as they wiggle in your hand.

In addition, predict how the author will answer your key questions. Then read to find out if your predictions were accurate.

## STEP 5 FLAG ANSWERS

As you read, seek out the answers to your questions. You are a detective, watching for every clue. When you do find an answer, flag it so that it stands out on the page.

Deface your books. Have fun. Flag answers by highlighting, underlining, writing comments, filling in your outline, or marking up pages in any other way that helps you. Indulge yourself as you never could with your grade school books.

Marking up your books offers other benefits. When you read with a highlighter, pen, or pencil in your hand, you involve your kinesthetic senses of touch and motion. Being physical with your books can help build strong neural pathways in your memory.

You can mark up a text in many ways. For example:

- Place an asterisk (*) or an exclamation point (!) in the margin next to an especially important sentence or term.
- Circle key terms and words to look up later in a dictionary.
- Write short definitions of key terms in the margin.
- Write a *Q* in the margin to highlight possible test questions, passages you don't understand, and questions to ask in class.
- Write personal comments in the margin—points of agreement or disagreement with the author.
- Write mini-indexes in the margin—that is, the numbers of other pages in the book where the same topic is discussed.
- Write summaries in your own words.
- Rewrite chapter titles, headings, and subheadings so that they're more meaningful to you.
- Draw diagrams, pictures, tables, or maps that translate text into visual terms.
- Number each step in a list or series of related points.
- In the margins, write notes about the relationships between elements in your reading. For instance, note connections between an idea and examples of that idea.
- If you infer an answer to a question or come up with another idea of your own, write that down as well.

Avoid marking up a text too soon. Wait until you complete a chapter or section to make sure you know the key points. Then mark up the text. Sometimes, flagging answers after you read each paragraph works best.

Also remember that the purpose of making marks in a text is to call out important concepts or information that you will review later. Flagging key information can save lots of time when you are studying for tests. With this in mind, highlight or underline sparingly—usually less than 10 percent of the text. If you mark up too much on a page, you defeat the purpose: to flag the most important material for review.

Finally, jot down new questions, and note when you don't find the answers you are looking for. Ask these questions in class, or see your instructor personally. Demand that your textbooks give you what you want—answers.

**4**

 **You're One Click Away...**
*from finding examples of Phase 2 strategies online.*

# PHASE 3 After you read

## STEP 6 RECITE

Talk to yourself about what you've read. Or talk to someone else. When you finish a reading assignment, make a speech about it. When you recite, you practice an important aspect of metacognition—synthesis, or combining individual ideas and facts into a meaningful whole.

One way to recite is to look at each underlined point. Note what you marked; then put the book down and start talking out loud. Explain as much as you can about that particular point.

To make this technique more effective, do it in front of a mirror. It might seem silly, but the benefits can be enormous. Reap them at exam time.

A related technique is to stop reading periodically and write a short, free-form summary of what you just read. In one study, this informal "retrieval practice" helped students recall information better than other study techniques.[2]

Classmates are even better than mirrors. Form a group and practice teaching one another what you have read. One of the best ways to learn anything is to teach it to someone else.

In addition, talk about your reading whenever you can. Tell friends and family members what you're learning.

Talking about your reading reinforces a valuable skill—the ability to summarize. To practice this skill, pick one chapter (or one section of one chapter) from any of your textbooks. State the main topic covered in this chapter. Then state the main points that the author makes about this topic.

For example, the main topic up to this point in this chapter is Muscle Reading. The main point about this topic is that Muscle Reading includes three phases—steps to take before you read, while you read, and after you read. For a more detailed summary, you could name each of the steps.

**Note:** This topic-point method does not work so well when you want to summarize short stories, novels, plays, and other works of fiction. Instead, focus on action. In most stories, the main character confronts a major problem and takes a series of actions to solve it. Describe that problem and talk about the character's key actions—the turning points in the story.

## STEP 7 REVIEW

Plan to do your first complete review within 24 hours of reading the material. Sound the trumpets! This point is critical: A review within 24 hours moves information from your short-term memory to your long-term memory.

Review within 1 day. If you read it on Wednesday, review it on Thursday. During this review, look over your notes and clear up anything you don't understand. Recite some of the main points again.

This review can be short. You might spend as little as 15 minutes reviewing a difficult 2-hour reading assignment. Investing that time now can save you hours later when studying for exams.

# Muscle Reading—
# a leaner approach

Keep in mind that Muscle Reading is an overall approach, not a rigid, step-by-step procedure. Here's a shorter variation that students have found helpful. Practice it with any chapter in this book:

- **Preview and question.** Flip through the pages, looking at anything that catches your eye—headings, subheadings, illustrations, photographs. Turn the title of each article into a question. For example, "How Muscle Reading works" can become "How does Muscle Reading work?" List your questions on a separate sheet of paper, or write each question on a 3 × 5 card.

- **Read to answer your questions.** Read each article. Then go back over the text and underline or highlight answers to the appropriate questions on your list.

- **Recite and review.** When you're done with the chapter, close the book. Recite by reading each question—and answering it—out loud. Review the chapter by looking up the answers to your questions. (It's easy—they're already highlighted.) Review again by quizzing yourself one more time with your list of questions.

## STEP 8 REVIEW AGAIN

The final step in Muscle Reading is the weekly or monthly review. This step can be very short—perhaps only 4 or 5 minutes per assignment. Simply go over your notes. Read the highlighted parts of your text. Recite one or two of the more complicated points.

The purpose of these reviews is to keep the neural pathways to the information open and to make them more distinct. That way, the information can be easier to recall. You can accomplish these short reviews anytime, anywhere, if you are prepared.

Conduct a 5-minute review while you are waiting for a bus, for your socks to dry, or for the water to boil. Three-by-five cards are a handy review tool. Write ideas, formulas, concepts, and facts on cards, and carry them with you. These short review periods can be effortless and fun.

Sometimes longer review periods are appropriate. For example, if you found an assignment difficult, consider rereading it. Start over, as if you had never seen the material before. Sometimes a second reading will provide you with surprising insights.

Decades ago, psychologists identified the primacy-recency effect, which suggests that we most easily remember the first and last items in any presentation.[3] Previewing and reviewing your reading can put this theory to work for you. ■

**You're One Click Away...**
*from finding examples of Phase 3 strategies online.*

---

**JOURNAL ENTRY 9** *Discovery/Intention Statement*     **4**

# Experimenting with Muscle Reading

After reading the steps included in Muscle Reading, reflect on your reading skills. Are you a more effective reader than you thought you were? Less effective? Record your observations below.

I discovered that I . . .

_____

_____

_____

_____

_____

_____

_____

_____

_____

_____

_____

_____

_____

_____

_____

_____

_____

_____

Many students find that they only do the "read" step with their textbooks. You've just read about the advantages of eight additional steps you should perform. Depending on the text, reading assignment, your available time, and your commitment level to the material, you may discover through practice which additional steps work best for you. Right now, make a commitment to yourself to experiment with all or several of the additional Muscle Reading steps by completing the following Intention Statement.

I intend to use the following Muscle Reading steps for the next 2 weeks in my _____ class:

❏ Preview

❏ Outline

❏ Question

❏ Focus

❏ Flag answers

❏ Recite

❏ Review

❏ Review again

# Getting past ROADBLOCKS *to* READING

Even your favorite strategies for reading can fail when you're dealing with bigger issues. Those roadblocks to getting your reading done can come from three major sources:

- Finding enough time to keep up with your reading
- Getting interrupted by other people while you're reading
- Dealing with texts that are tough to read

For solutions to each of these problems, read on.

## FINDING TIME FOR READING

Planning dispels panic (*I've got 300 pages to read before tomorrow morning!*) and helps you finish off your entire reading load for a term. Creating a reading plan is relatively simple if you use the following steps.

**Step 1. Estimate the total number of pages that you'll read.** To arrive at this figure, check the course syllabus for each class that you're taking. Look for lists of reading assignments. Based on what you find, estimate the total number of pages that you'll read for all your classes.

**Step 2. Estimate how many pages you can read during 1 hour.** Remember that your reading speed will be different for various materials. It depends on everything from the layout of the pages to the difficulty of the text. To give your estimate some credibility, base it on actual experience. During your first reading assignment in each course, keep track of how many pages you read per hour.

**Step 3. Estimate your total number of reading hours.** Divide the total number of pages from Step 1 by your pages-per-hour from Step 2. For example, look at this calculation:

600 (total number of pages for all courses this term) ÷ 10 (pages read per hour)
= 60 (total reading hours needed for the term)

The result is the total number of hours you'll need to complete your reading assignments this term. Remember to give yourself some "wiggle room." Allow extra hours for rereading and unplanned events. Consider taking your initial number of projected hours and doubling it. You can always back off from there to an estimate that seems more reasonable.

**Step 4. Schedule reading time.** Take the total number of hours from Step 3 and divide it by the number of weeks in your current term. That will give you the number of hours to schedule for reading each week.

60 (total reading hours needed for the term) ÷ 16 (weeks in the term)
= 3.75 (hours per week to schedule for reading)

Now, go to your calendar or long-term planner and reflect on it for a few minutes. Look for ways to block out those hours next week. For ideas, review Chapter 2.

**Step 5. Refine your reading plan.** Scheduling your reading takes time. The potential benefits are beyond calculation. With a plan, you can be more confident that you'll actually get your reading done. Even if your estimates are off, you'll still go beyond blind guessing or leaving the whole thing to chance. Your reading matters too much for that.

## DEALING WITH INTERRUPTIONS

Sometimes the people you live with and care about the most—a friend, roommate, spouse, or child—can become a temporary roadblock to reading. The following strategies can help you stay focused on your reading:

**Attend to people first.** When you first come home from school, keep your books out of sight. Spend some time with your roommates or family members before you settle in to study. Make small talk and ask them about their day. Give the important people in your life a short period of full, focused attention rather than a longer period of partial attention. Then explain that you have some work to do. Set some ground rules for the amount of time you need to focus on studying. You could be rewarded with extra minutes or hours of quiet time.

**Plan for interruptions.** It's possible that you'll be interrupted even if you set up guidelines for your study time in advance. If so, schedule the kind of studying that can be interrupted. For instance, you could write out or review flash cards with key terms and definitions. Save the tasks that require sustained attention for more quiet times.

**Use "pockets" of time.** See whether you can arrange a study time in a quiet place at school before you come home. If you arrive at school 15 minutes earlier and stay 15 minutes later, you can squeeze in an extra half hour of reading that day. Also look for opportunities to study on campus between classes.

**Read with children underfoot.** It is possible to have both effective study time and quality time with your children. The following suggestions come mostly from students who are also parents. The specific strategies you use will depend on your schedule and the ages of your children.

- *Find a regular playmate for your child.* Some children can pair off with close friends and safely retreat to their rooms for hours of private play. You can check on them occasionally and still get lots of reading done.

- *Create a special space for your child.* Set aside one room or area of your home as a play space. Childproof this space. The goal is to create a place where children can roam freely and play with minimal supervision. Consider allowing your child in this area *only* when you study. Your homework time then becomes your child's reward. If you're cramped for space, just set aside some special toys for your child to play with during your study time.

- *Use television responsibly.* Whenever possible, select educational programs that keep your child's mind active and engaged. Also see whether your child can use headphones while watching television. That way, the house stays quiet while you study.

- *Schedule time to be with your children when you've finished studying.* Let your children in on the plan: "I'll be done reading at 7:30. That gives us a whole hour to play before you go to bed."

- *Ask other adults for help.* Getting help can be as simple as asking your spouse, partner, neighbor, or fellow student to take care of the children while you study. Offer to trade child care with a neighbor: You will take his kids and yours for two hours on Thursday night if he'll take them for two hours on Saturday morning.

- *Find community activities and services.* Ask whether your school provides a day care service. In some cases, these services are available to students at a reduced cost.

## DEALING WITH A TEXT THAT'S TOUGH TO READ

Successful readers monitor their understanding of reading material. They do not see confusion as a mistake or a personal shortcoming. Instead, they take it as a cue to change reading strategies and process ideas at a deeper level.

**Read it again.** Somehow, students get the idea that reading means opening a book and dutifully slogging through the text—line by line, page by page—moving in a straight line from the first word until the last. Feel free to shake up your routine. Make several passes through tough reading material. During a preview, for example, just scan the text to look for key words and highlighted material. Next, skim the entire chapter or article again, spending a little more time and taking in more than you did during your preview. Finally, read in more depth.

**Read it out loud.** Make noise. Read a passage out loud several times, each time using a different inflection and emphasizing a different part of the sentence. Be creative. Imagine that you are the author talking.

**Use another text.** Find a similar text in the library. Sometimes a concept is easier to understand if it is expressed another way. Children's books—especially children's encyclopedias—can provide useful overviews of baffling subjects.

**Talk to someone who can help.** Admit when you are stuck. Then bring questions about reading assignments to classmates and members of your study group. Also make an appointment with your instructor. Most teachers welcome the opportunity to work individually with students. Be specific about your confusion. Point out the paragraph that you found toughest to understand. ■

**4**

# Master Students
# **IN ACTION**

*One night when I was reading, I had so much on my mind, I reread the page probably five times. I finally just put the book down and cleared my mind. I put on some of my favorite music, and I took a fantasy trip by thinking about all my upcoming exciting things that I would be doing. When I was done, I got back to my reading with no trouble at all.*

—*Lindsey Giblin,*
*Central Piedmont Community College*

# Reading faster

One way to read faster is to read faster. This idea might sound like double-talk, but it is a serious suggestion. The fact is, you can probably read faster—without any loss in comprehension—simply by making a conscious effort to do so. Your comprehension might even improve.

Experiment with the "just do it" method right now. Read the rest of this article as fast as you can. After you finish, come back and reread the same paragraphs at your usual rate. Note how much you remember from your first sprint through the text. You might be surprised to find out how well you comprehend material even at dramatically increased speeds. Build on that success by experimenting with the following guidelines.

**Move your eyes faster.** When we read, our eyes leap across the page in short bursts called *saccades* (pronounced "să-käds"). A saccade is also a sharp jerk on the reins of a horse—a violent pull to stop the animal quickly. Our eyes stop like that too, in pauses called *fixations*.

Although we experience the illusion of continuously scanning each line, our eyes actually take in groups of words, usually about three at a time. For more than 90 percent of reading time, our eyes are at a dead stop, in those fixations.

One way to decrease saccades is to follow your finger as you read. The faster your finger moves, the faster your eyes move. You can also use a pen, pencil, or 3 × 5 card as a guide.

Your eyes can move faster if they take in more words with each burst—for example, six instead of three. To practice taking in more words between fixations, find a newspaper with narrow columns. Then read down one column at a time, and fixate only once per line.

In addition to using the above techniques, simply make a conscious effort to fixate less. You might feel a little uncomfortable at first. That's normal. Just practice often, for short periods of time.

**Notice and release ineffective habits.** Our eyes make regressions; that is, they back up and reread words. You can reduce regressions by paying attention to them. Use the handy 3 × 5 card to cover words and lines that you have just read. You can then note how often you stop and move the card back to reread the text. Don't be discouraged if you stop often at first. Being aware of it helps you regress less frequently.

Also notice vocalizing. You are more likely to read faster if you don't read out loud or move your lips. You can also increase your speed if you don't subvocalize—that is, if you don't mentally "hear" the words as you read them. To stop doing it, just be aware of it.

© Chris Pancewicz/Alamy

When you first attempt to release these habits, choose simpler reading material. That way, you can pay closer attention to your reading technique. Gradually work your way up to more complex material.

**Stay flexible.** Remember that speed isn't everything. Skillful readers vary their reading rate according to their purpose and the nature of the material. An advanced text in analytic geometry usually calls for a different reading rate than the Sunday comics.

You also can use different reading rates on the same material. For example, you might first sprint through an assignment for the key words and ideas, and then return to the difficult parts for a slower and more thorough reading.

Another option is to divide a large reading assignment into smaller sections and use different reading strategies for each one. You might choose to read the first and last sections in detail, for example, and skim the middle sections.

As a general guideline, slow down your reading pace for material that's technical and unfamiliar to you. Speed up for material that's familiar, staying alert for anything that seems new or significant.

Also remember that reading faster *without comprehension* can actually increase the amount of time that you study. Balance a desire for speed with the need for understanding what you read.

Finally, remember the first rule of reading fast: Just do it! ■

# WORD POWER—expanding your VOCABULARY

© Stockbyte

Having a large vocabulary makes reading more enjoyable and increases the range of materials you can explore. In addition, building your vocabulary gives you more options for self-expression when speaking or writing. With a larger vocabulary, you can think more precisely by making finer distinctions between ideas. And you won't have to stop to search for words at crucial times—such as a job interview.

Strengthen your vocabulary by taking delight in words. Look up unfamiliar terms. Pay special attention to words that arouse your curiosity.

Before the age of the Internet, students used two kinds of printed dictionaries: the desk dictionary and the unabridged dictionary. A desk dictionary is an easy-to-handle abridged dictionary that you can use many times in the course of a day. You can keep this book within easy reach (maybe in your lap) so you can look up unfamiliar words while reading.

In contrast, an unabridged dictionary is large and not made for you to carry around. It provides more complete information about words and definitions not included in your desk dictionary, as well as synonyms, usage notes, and word histories. Look for unabridged dictionaries in libraries and bookstores.

You might prefer using one of several online dictionaries, such as Dictionary.com. Another common option is to search for definitions by using a search engine such as Google.com. If you do this, inspect the results carefully. They can vary in quality and be less useful than the definitions you'd find in a good dictionary or thesaurus.

**Construct a word stack.** When you come across an unfamiliar word, write it down on a 3 × 5 card. Below the word, copy the sentence in which it was used, along with the page number. You can look up each word immediately, or you can accumulate a stack of these cards and look up the words later. Write the definition of each word on the back of the 3 × 5 card, adding the diacritics—marks that tell you how to pronounce it.

To expand your vocabulary and learn the history behind the words, take your stack of cards to an unabridged dictionary. As you find related words in the dictionary, add them to your stack. These cards become a portable study aid that you can review in your spare moments.

**Learn—even when your dictionary is across town.** When you are listening to a lecture and hear an unusual word or when you are reading on the bus and encounter a word you don't know, you can still build your word stack. Pull out a 3 × 5 card and write down the word and its sentence. Later, you can look up the definition and write it on the back of the card.

**Divide words into parts.** Another suggestion for building your vocabulary is to divide an unfamiliar word into syllables and look for familiar parts. This strategy works well if you make it a point to learn common prefixes (beginning syllables) and suffixes (ending syllables). For example, the suffix *-tude* usually refers to a condition or state of being. Knowing this makes it easier to conclude that *habitude* refers to a usual way of doing something and that *similitude* means being similar or having a quality of resemblance.

**Infer the meaning of words from their context.** You can often deduce the meaning of an unfamiliar word simply by paying attention to its context—the surrounding words, phrases, sentences, paragraphs, or images. Later, you can confirm your deduction by consulting a dictionary.

Practice looking for context clues such as these:

- *Definitions.* A key word might be defined right in the text. Look for phrases such as *defined as* or *in other words*.

- *Examples.* Authors often provide examples to clarify a word meaning. If the word is not explicitly defined, then study the examples. They're often preceded by the phrases *for example, for instance,* or *such as.*

- *Lists.* When a word is listed in a series, pay attention to the other items in the series. They might define the unfamiliar word through association.

- *Comparisons.* You might find a new word surrounded by synonyms—words with a similar meaning. Look for synonyms after words such as *like* and *as*.

- *Contrasts.* A writer might juxtapose a word with its antonym. Look for phrases such as *on the contrary* and *on the other hand.* ■

**4**

# Mastering the
# English
# LANGUAGE

| Errors | Corrections |
|---|---|
| Sun is bright. | The sun is bright. |
| He cheerful. | He is cheerful. |
| I enjoy to play chess. | I enjoy playing chess. |
| Good gifts received everyone. | Everyone received good gifts. |
| I knew what would present the teachers. | I knew what the teachers would present. |
| I like very much burritos. | I like burritos very much. |
| I want that you stay. | I want you to stay. |
| Is raining. | It is raining. |
| My mother, she lives in Iowa. | My mother lives in Iowa. |
| I gave the paper to she. | I gave the paper to her. |
| They felt safety in the car. | They felt safe in the car. |
| He has three car. | He has three cars. |
| I have helpfuls family members. | I have helpful family members. |
| She don't know nothing. | She knows nothing. |

## LEARN TO USE STANDARD ENGLISH WHEN IT COUNTS

Standard English is the form of the language used by educated speakers and writers. It is the form most likely to be understood by speakers and writers of English, no matter where they live.

Using non-standard English in the classroom or workplace might lead people to doubt your skills, your intentions, or your level of education. Non-standard English comes in many forms, including slang and dialects.

Save non-standard expressions for informal conversations with friends. If you're not sure whether a particular expression is standard English, then talk to an instructor.

## BUILD CONFIDENCE

Make it your intention to speak up in class. List several questions beforehand and plan to ask them. Also schedule a time to meet with your instructors during office hours to discuss any material that you find confusing. These strategies can help you build relationships while you develop English skills.

English is a complex language. Whenever you extend your vocabulary and range of expression, the likelihood of making mistakes increases. Do not look upon mistakes as a sign of weakness. Mistakes can be your best teachers—if you are willing to learn from them.

Remember that the terms *English as a Second Language* and *English Language Learner* describe a difference—not a deficiency. The fact that you've entered a new culture and are mastering another language gives you a broader perspective than people who speak only one language. And if you currently speak two or more languages, you've already demonstrated your ability to learn.

## ANALYZE ERRORS IN USING ENGLISH

To learn from your errors, make a list of those that are most common for you. Next to the error, write a corrected version. For examples, see the chart. Remember that native speakers of English also use this technique—for instance, by making lists of words they frequently misspell.

## LEARN BY SPEAKING AND LISTENING

You probably started your English studies by reading textbooks. To gain greater fluency and improve your pronunciation, also make it your goal to *hear* and *speak* standard English.

For example, listen to radio talk shows hosted by educated speakers with a wide audience. Imitate the speaker's pronunciation by repeating phrases and sentences that you hear. During TV shows and personal conversations, notice the facial expressions and gestures that accompany certain English words and phrases.

Take advantage of opportunities to read and hear English at the same time. For instance, turn on English subtitles when watching a film. Also, check your library for audio books. Check out the printed book, and follow along as you listen.

## CREATE A COMMUNITY OF ENGLISH LEARNERS

Learning as part of a community can increase your mastery. For example, when completing a writing assignment in English, get together with other people who are learning the language. Read each other's papers and suggest revisions. Plan on revising your paper a number of times based on feedback from your peers.

## CELEBRATE YOUR GAINS

Every time you analyze and correct an error in English, you make a small gain. Celebrate those gains. Taken together over time, they add up to major progress in mastering English as a second language. ■

# Developing information literacy

An important quality of master students is curiosity. To answer questions, these students find information from appropriate sources, evaluate the information, organize it, and use it to achieve a purpose. The ability to do this in a world where data is literally at your fingertips is called information literacy.

## DISCOVER YOUR QUESTIONS

Start with your *main question*. This is the thing that sparked your curiosity in the first place. Answering it is your purpose for doing research.

Your main question will raise a number of smaller, related questions. These are *supporting questions*. They also call for answers.

Suppose that your main question is this: "During the mortgage credit crisis of 2007 to 2010, what led banks to lend money to people with poor credit histories?" Your list of supporting questions might include the following:

- What banks were involved in the mortgage credit crisis?
- How do banks discover a person's credit history?
- What are the signs of a poor credit history?

## CONSIDER PRIMARY AND SECONDARY SOURCES OF INFORMATION

Consider the variety of information sources that are available to you: billions of Web pages, books, magazines, newspapers, and audio and video recordings. You can reduce this vast range of materials to a few manageable categories. Start with the distinction between primary and secondary sources.

**Primary sources.** These can lead to information treasures. Primary sources are firsthand materials—personal journals, letters, speeches, government documents, scientific experiments, field observations, interviews with recognized experts, archeological digs, artifacts, and original works of art.

Primary sources can also include scholarly publications such as the *New England Journal of Medicine*, *Contemporary Literary Criticism*, and similar publications. One clue that you're dealing with a

primary source is the title. If it includes the word *journal*, then you're probably reading a primary source.

Following are some signs of scholarly articles:

- Names of authors with their credentials and academic affiliations
- A brief abstract (summary) of the article, along with a section on research methods (how the authors tested their ideas and reached their conclusions)
- Lengthy articles with detailed treatment of the main topic and definitions of key terms
- Conclusions based on an extensive review of relevant publications, survey research, data collected in a laboratory experiment, or a combination of these
- Extensive bibliographies and references to the work of other scholars in the form of footnotes (at the bottom of each page) or endnotes (at the end of the article)

If you pick up a magazine with pages of full-color advertisements and photos of celebrities, you're not reading a scholarly journal. Though some scholarly articles run just a few pages, many run to 10, 20, or even more. Although that's a lot to read, you get more information to use for your assignment or to answer your questions.

**Secondary sources.** These sources summarize, explain, and comment on primary sources:

- Popular magazines such as *Time* and *Newsweek*
- Magazines—such as the *Atlantic Monthly* and *Scientific American*—with wide circulation and long articles
- Nationally circulated newspapers such as the *Washington Post*, *New York Times*, and *Los Angeles Times*
- General reference works such as the *Encyclopaedia Britannica* and the *Oxford Companion to English Literature*

Secondary sources are useful places to start your research. Use them to get an overview of your topic. Depending on the assignment, these may be all you need for informal research.

## GET TO KNOW YOUR LIBRARY

Remember that many published materials are available in print as well as online. For a full range of sources, head to your campus library.

One reason for a trip to the library is to find a reference librarian. Tell this person about the questions you want answered, and ask for good sources of information. Remember that a librarian can help you apply the suggestions in this article, including those that relate to using technology.

## SEARCH FOR INFORMATION WITH KEY WORDS

One crucial skill for information literacy is using key words. Key words are the main terms in your main and supporting questions. These are the words that you enter into a search box. Your choice of key words determines the quality of results that you get from Internet search engines such as google.com, and from library catalogs. For better search results:

- *Use specific key words.* Entering *Firefox* or *Safari* will give you more focused results than entering *Web browser. Reading strategies* or *note-taking strategies* will get more specific results than *study strategies.* Do not type in your whole research question as a sentence. The search engine will look for each word and give you a lot of useless results.

- *Use unique key words.* Whenever possible, use proper names. Enter *Beatles* or *Radiohead* rather than *British rock bands.* If you're looking for nearby restaurants, enter *restaurant* and your zip code rather than the name of your city.

- *Use quotation marks if you're looking for certain words in a certain order.* "Audacity of hope" will return a list of pages with that exact phrase.

- *Search within a site.* If you're looking only for articles about college tuition from the *New York Times,* then add *new york times* or *nytimes.com* to the search box.

- *Remember to think of synonyms.* For example, "hypertension" is often called "high blood pressure."

- *When you're not sure of a key word, add a wild card character.* In most search engines, that character is the asterisk (*). If you're looking for the title of a film directed by Clint Eastwood and just can't remember the name, enter *clint eastwood directed\**.

- *Look for more search options.* Many search engines also offer advanced search features and explain how to use them. Look for the word *advanced* or *more* on the site's home page, and click on the link.

## TURN TO PEOPLE AS SOURCES OF INFORMATION

Making direct contact with people can offer a welcome relief from hours of solitary research time and give you valuable hands-on involvement. Your initial research will uncover the names of experts on your chosen topic. Consider doing an interview with one of these people—in person, over the phone, or via e-mail.

## EVALUATE INFORMATION

Some students assume that anything that's published in print or on the Internet is true. Unfortunately, that's not the case. Some sources of information are more reliable than others, and some published information is misleading or mistaken.

Before evaluating any source of information, make sure that you understand what it says. Use the techniques of Muscle Reading to comprehend an author's message. Then think critically about the information. Chapter 7 offers many suggestions for doing this. Here are some essential things to look for:

- *Currency.* Notice the published date of your source material. If your topic is time sensitive, then set some guidelines about how current you want your sources to be—for example, that they were published during the last 5 years.

- *Credibility.* Scan the source for biographical information about the author. Look for educational degrees, training, and work experience that qualify this person to publish on the topic of your research.

- *Bias.* Determine what the Web site or other source is "selling"—the product, service, or point of view it promotes. Political affiliations or funding sources might color the author's point of view. For instance, you can predict that a pamphlet on gun control policies that's printed with funding from the National Rifle Association will promote certain points of view. Round out your research with other sources on the topic.

## USE INFORMATION

Many students use information to write a paper or create a presentation. See Chapter 8 of this book for suggestions. In addition, take careful notes on your sources, using the techniques explained in Chapter 5. Remember to keep a list of all your sources of information, and avoid plagiarism. Be prepared to cite your sources in footnotes or endnotes, and a bibliography.

Also make time to digest all the information you gather. Ask yourself:

- Do I have answers to my main question?

- Do I have answers to my supporting questions?

- What are the main ideas from my sources?

- Do I have personal experiences that can help me answer these questions?

- If a television talk show host asked me these questions, how would I answer?

- On what points do my sources agree?

- On what points do my sources disagree?

- Do I have statistics and other facts that I can use to support my ideas?

- What new questions do I have?

The beauty of these questions is that they stimulate *your* thinking. Discover the pleasures of emerging insights and sudden inspiration. You just might get hooked on the adventure of information literacy. ■

# PRACTICING
# critical thinking 4

By thinking deeply about your reading, you can make an immediate difference in your ability to learn anything.

Psychologist Benjamin Bloom described six levels of thinking.

**Level 1: Remembering**—recalling an idea.

**Level 2: Understanding**—explaining an idea in your own words and giving examples from your own experience.

**Level 3: Applying**—using an idea to produce a desired result.

**Level 4: Analyzing**—dividing an idea into parts or steps.

**Level 5: Evaluating**—rating the truth, usefulness, or quality of an idea—and giving reasons for your rating.

**Level 6: Creating**—inventing something new based on an idea.

The purpose of this exercise is to practice thinking at **Level 5: Evaluating**. This means rating the truth, usefulness, or quality of an idea—and giving reasons for your rating.

Following is a sample evaluation of the method of Muscle Reading:

*The steps of Muscle Reading are useful. Applying all the steps of this method does lead me to actively preview and review as well as read. Doing this consistently would help me stay on top of material throughout the whole term rather than relying on cramming during the night before a test. The disadvantage is that eight steps are a lot to remember. For this reason, I prefer the three-step "leaner approach" to Muscle Reading (see page 104). This approach is easier to remember. Because it only includes three major steps, I am also more likely to use it.*

Evaluating often means answering questions such as these:

- Do you agree? If not, why?
- How effective is this idea?
- Would you recommend a different options?
- What makes this option better than the others?

Now it's your turn. Recall any idea from this chapter (**Level 1: Remembering**) and think about it at **Level 5: Evaluating**. In the space below, summarize the idea and then demonstrate your higher-level thinking. Continue on additional paper as needed.

_____

_____

_____

_____

_____

_____

_____

_____

_____

_____

_____

_____

_____

_____

_____

_____

_____

_____

_____

_____

_____

_____

_____

*For more information on the six levels of thinking, see "Becoming a critical thinker" in Chapter 7.*

# masterstudentprofile

## Matias Manzano

(1985– ) One of five finalists for Rookie Teacher of the Year in Miami-Dade County, Florida, the fourth largest school district in America.

I struggled early on with reading. In fourth grade, I scored a 23 percent on a reading proficiency assessment. Many people would have written me off at that young age—a poor, Latino, illegal immigrant who ended up in New York and was destined to fail.

I remember thinking in elementary school that it wasn't fair that the other kids spoke English at home and for that reason, they were better readers than I was. There were times when I would try to read something, and the words would float around the page as if they didn't want to be understood.

I had a teacher in fifth grade, Ms. Leventhaul, who really made me want to improve my reading. She was inspirational. There was something about her demeanor, the way that she carried herself, which was both intimidating and motivational at the same time. She treated me as if she knew that I could achieve greatness.

My brother also challenged me to just read more books. I read at least 20 R. L. Stine *Goosebumps* books in a competition that I had one year with him. We used to have conversations after reading the books. I didn't realize it at the time, but having those conversations allowed me to develop reading skills like making comparisons, identifying main ideas, describing settings, and identifying foreshadowing. By sixth grade, I had scored a 99 percent on the reading assessment.

After high school, I decided to follow in my brother's footsteps and attend Stony Brook University in New York. Money was tight. We would roam around the college, staying with different friends who allowed us to sleep on their floor for the night. I guess I was, in a way, homeless.

Toward the end of my sophomore year, the letter came that our application for legal residence was accepted. I was able to receive financial aid. I no longer had to work 40 hours a week to pay for tuition. I could focus my energy on academics.

The reading skills that I started developing in elementary school became the foundation for my success in college. As a history major and Latin American Caribbean studies minor, I found that my assignments were based on reading scholarly journals and books. My vocabulary improved exponentially. I learned to read entire books in just a few hours.

I can tell you first-hand what research says is true: The greatest factor impacting the education of our nation's poorest children is the quality of the teacher that they get. I joined Teach for America and the staff at Jose De Diego Middle School in Miami because I know that the children living in poverty can achieve at the highest rates. All of my students have talents. All of my students have a spark.

If I had taken certain tests in Florida when I was in fourth grade, the state would have projected me as a future prison inmate. My apologies to the statisticians who use elementary student achievement scores to predict future prison needs. Soon I will finish my master's degree in educational leadership. I am driven by a desire to be the best and to achieve greatness in all aspects of my life, because I believe that no task is insurmountable.

Courtesy of Matias Manzano

**MATIAS MANZANO . . .** is self-directed.

**YOU . . .** can be self-directed by focusing your energy on what matters most to you.

**You're One Click Away...**
*from learning more about Matias Manzano online at the Master Student Profiles. You can also visit the Master Student Hall of Fame to learn about other master students.*

# CHAPTER 4 QUIZ

Name _____

Date _____

1. Briefly explain a problem with holding on to mental pictures, as suggested by the Power Process in this chapter.

2. Name the acrostic that can help you remember the steps of Muscle Reading.

3. You must complete all the steps of Muscle Reading to get the most out of any reading assignment. True or false? Explain your answer.

4. Give three examples of what to look for when previewing a reading assignment.

**4**

5. Briefly explain how to use headings in a text to create an outline.

6. In addition to underlining and highlighting, there are other ways to mark up a text. List three possibilities.

7. To get the most benefit from marking a book, underline at least 20 percent of the text. True or False? Explain your answer.

8. Compare the steps of Muscle Reading with the approach described in "Muscle Reading—a leaner approach." How do these two methods differ?

9. Explain at least three strategies you can use when dealing with a text that's hard to read.

10. Define the term *information literacy*.

# 4 SKILLS *Snapshot*

After studying this chapter, you might want to make some changes in the way you read. First, take a snapshot of your current reading habits and reflect on the reading skills you've already developed. Complete the following sentences.

## DISCOVERY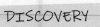

My score on the *Reading* section of the Discovery Wheel on page 29 was . . .

If someone asked me how well I keep up with my assigned reading, I would say that . . .

To get the most out of a long reading assignment, I start by . . .

When I take notes on my reading, my usual method is to . . .

When it's important for me to remember what I read, I . . .

When I don't understand something that I've read, I overcome confusion by . . .

## INTENTION

I'll know that I've reached a new level of mastery with reading when . . .

Stated as a goal, my intention is to . . .

## ACTION

To reach my goal, the most important thing I can do next is to . . .

At the end of this course, I would like my *Reading* score on the Discovery Wheel to be . . .

# Notes

Use this **Master Student Map**
to ask yourself,

## WHY THIS CHAPTER MATTERS . . .

- Note taking helps you remember information and influences how well you do on tests.

## WHAT IS INCLUDED . . .

## HOW CAN I USE THIS CHAPTER . . .

- Experiment with several formats for note taking.
- Create a note-taking format that works especially well for you.
- Take effective notes in special situations—such as while reading, and when instructors talk quickly.

## WHAT IF . . .

- You could take notes that remain informative and useful for weeks, months, or even years to come?

**JOURNAL ENTRY 10**
*Intention Statement*

## Get what you want from this chapter

Recall a recent incident in which you had difficulty taking notes. Perhaps you were listening to an instructor who talked fast, or you got confused and stopped taking notes altogether. Then preview this chapter to find at least three strategies that you can use right away to help you take better notes.

| Strategy | Page number |
|---|---|
| _____ | _____ |
| _____ | _____ |
| _____ | _____ |
| _____ | _____ |
| _____ | _____ |
| _____ | _____ |
| _____ | _____ |
| _____ | _____ |
| _____ | _____ |
| _____ | _____ |
| _____ | _____ |

© Ruslan Ivantsov/Shutterstock.com

# POWER process

# I create it all

This article describes a powerful tool for times of trouble. In a crisis, "I create it all" can lead the way to solutions. The main point of this Power Process is to treat experiences, events, and circumstances in your life *as if* you created them.

"I create it all" is one of the most unusual and bizarre suggestions in this book. It certainly is not a belief. Use it when it works. Don't when it doesn't.

Keeping that in mind, consider how powerful this Power Process can be. It is really about the difference between two distinct positions in life: being a victim or being responsible.

A victim of circumstances is controlled by outside forces. We've all felt like victims at one time or another. Sometimes we felt helpless.

In contrast, we can take responsibility. Responsibility is "response-ability"—the ability to choose a *response* to any event. You can choose your *response* to any event, even when the event itself is beyond your control.

Many students approach grades from the position of being victims. When the student who sees the world this way gets an "F," she reacts something like this:

"Another 'F'! That teacher couldn't teach her way out of a wet paper bag. She can't teach English for anything. There's no way to take notes in that class. And that textbook—what a bore!"

The problem with this viewpoint is that in looking for excuses, the student is robbing herself of the power to get any grade other than an "F." She's giving all of her power to a bad teacher and a boring textbook.

There is another way, called *taking responsibility*. You can recognize that you choose your grades by choosing your actions. Then you are the source, rather than the result, of the grades you get. The student who got an "F" could react like this:

"Another 'F'! Oh, shoot! Well, hmmm . . . What did I do to create it?"

Now, that's power. By asking, "How did I contribute to this outcome?" you are no longer the victim. This student might continue by saying, "Well, let's see. I didn't review my notes after class. That might have done it." Or "I went out with my friends the night before the test. Well, that probably helped me fulfill some of the requirements for getting an 'F.'"

The point is this: When the "F" is the result of your friends, the book, or the teacher, you probably can't do anything about it. However, if you *chose* the "F," you can choose a different grade next time. You are in charge.

**You're One Click Away...**
*from accessing Power Process Media online and finding out more about how to "create it all."*

# The Note-Taking Process FLOWS

One way to understand note taking is to realize that taking notes is just one part of the process. Effective note taking consists of three parts: observing, recording, and reviewing. First, you **observe** an "event." This can be a statement by an instructor, a lab experiment, a slide show of an artist's works, or a chapter of required reading.

Then you **record** your observations of that event. That is, you "take notes."

Finally, you **review** what you have recorded. You memorize, reflect, apply, and rehearse what you're learning. This step lifts ideas off the page and turns them into a working part of your mind.

Each part of the note-taking process is essential, and each depends on the other. Your observations determine what you record. What you record determines what you review. And the quality of your review can determine how effective your next observations will be. If you review your notes on the Sino-Japanese War of 1894, for example, the next day's lecture on the Boxer Rebellion of 1900 will make more sense.

Legible and speedy handwriting is also useful in taking notes. Knowledge of outlining is handy too. A nifty pen, a new notebook, and a laptop computer are all great note-taking devices.

And they're all worthless—unless you participate as an energetic observer *in* class and regularly review your notes *after* class. If you take those two steps, you can turn even the most disorganized chicken scratches into a powerful tool.

This is a well-researched aspect of student success in higher education. Study after study points to the benefits of taking notes. The value is added in two ways. First, you create a set of materials that refreshes your memory and helps you prepare for tests. Second, taking notes prompts you to listen effectively during class. You translate new ideas into your own words and images. You impose a personal and meaningful structure on what you see, read, and hear. You move from passive observer to active participant.[1] It's not that you take notes so that you can learn from them later. Instead, you learn *while* taking notes.

Computer technology takes traditional note taking to a whole new level. You can capture key notes with word-processing, outlining, database, and publishing software. Your notes become living documents that you can search, bookmark, tag, and archive like other digital files.

Sometimes note taking looks like a passive affair, especially in large lecture classes. One person at the front of the room does most of the talking. Everyone else is seated and silent, taking notes. The lecturer seems to be doing all of the work.

Don't be deceived.

Look more closely. You'll see some students taking notes in a way that radiates energy. They're awake and alert, poised on the edge of their seats. They're writing—a physical activity that expresses mental engagement. These students listen for levels of ideas and information, make choices about what to record, and compile materials to review.

In higher education, you might spend hundreds of hours taking notes. Making them more effective is a direct investment in your success.

Think of your notes as a textbook that *you* create—one that's more current and more in tune with your learning preferences than any textbook you could buy. ∎

iStockphoto.com/Chad McDermott

5

# OBSERVE

## The note-taking process flows

OBSERVE

Woman in red: © Getty/Frame: Shutterstock

Sherlock Holmes, a fictional master detective and student of the obvious, could track down a villain by observing the fold of his scarf and the mud on his shoes. In real life, a doctor can save a life by observing a mole—one a patient has always had—that undergoes a rapid change.

Keen observers see facts and relationships. They know ways to focus their attention on the details and then tap their creative energy to discover patterns. To sharpen your classroom observation skills, experiment with the following techniques.

### SET THE STAGE

**Complete outside assignments.** The more familiar you are with a subject, the more easily you can absorb important information during class lectures. Instructors usually assume that students complete assignments, and they construct their lectures accordingly.

**Sit front and center.** Students who get as close as possible to the front and center of the classroom often do better on tests for several reasons. The closer you sit to the lecturer, the harder it is to fall asleep. The closer you sit to the front, the fewer interesting or distracting classmates are situated between you and the instructor. Material on the board is easier to read from up front. Also, the instructor can see you more easily when you have a question.

Sitting close to the front is a way to commit yourself to getting what you want out of school. One reason students gravitate to the back of the classroom is that they think the instructor is less likely to call on them. Sitting in back can signal a lack of commitment. When you sit up front, you are declaring your willingness to take a risk and participate.

**Conduct a short preclass review.** Arrive early, and then put your brain in gear by reviewing your notes from the previous class. Scan your reading assignment. Look at the sections you have underlined or highlighted. Review assigned problems and exercises. Note questions you intend to ask.

### "BE HERE NOW" IN CLASS

**Accept your wandering mind.** The techniques in Chapter 2's Power Process: "Be here now" can be especially useful when your head soars into the clouds. Don't fight daydreaming. When you notice your mind wandering during class, look at it as an opportunity to refocus your attention. If thermodynamics is losing out to beach parties, let go of the beach.

**Be with the instructor.** In your mind, put yourself right up front with the instructor. Imagine that you and the instructor are the only ones in the room and that the lecture is a personal conversation between the two of you. Pay attention to the instructor's body language and facial expressions. Look the instructor in the eye.

Remember that the power of this suggestion is immediately reduced by digital distractions—Web surfing, e-mail checking, or text messaging. Taking notes is a way to stay focused. The physical act of taking notes signals your mind to stay in the same room as the instructor.

**Postpone debate.** When you hear something you disagree with, note your disagreement and let it go. Don't allow your internal dialogue to drown out subsequent material. If your disagreement is persistent and strong, make note of it and then move on. Internal debate can prevent you from absorbing new information. It's okay to absorb information you don't agree with. Just absorb it with the mental tag "My instructor says, . . . and I don't agree with it."

**Let go of judgments about lecture styles.** Human beings are judgment machines. We evaluate everything, especially other people. If another person's eyebrows are too close together (or too far apart), if she walks a certain way or speaks with an unusual accent, we instantly make up a story about her. We do this so quickly that the process is usually not a conscious one.

Don't let your attitude about an instructor's lecture style, habits, or appearance get in the way of your education. You can decrease the power of your judgments if you pay attention to them and let them go.

You can even let go of judgments about rambling, unorganized lectures. Turn them to your advantage. Take the initiative and organize the material yourself. While taking notes, separate the key points from the examples and supporting evidence. Note the places where you got confused, and make a list of questions to ask.

**Participate in class activities.** Ask questions. Volunteer for demonstrations. Join in class discussions. Be willing to take a risk or look foolish, if that's what it takes for you to learn. Chances are, the question you think is dumb is also on the minds of several of your classmates.

**Relate the class to your goals.** If you have trouble staying awake in a particular class, write at the top of your notes how that class relates to a specific goal. Identify the reward or payoff for reaching that goal.

**Think critically about what you hear.** This suggestion might seem contrary to the previously mentioned technique "postpone debate." It's not. You might choose not to think critically about the instructor's ideas during the lecture. That's fine. Do it later, as you review and edit your notes. This is the time to list questions or write down your agreements and disagreements.

## WATCH FOR CLUES ABOUT IMPORTANT MATERIAL

**Be alert to repetition.** When an instructor repeats a phrase or an idea, make a note of it. Repetition is a signal that the instructor thinks the information is important.

**Listen for introductory, concluding, and transition words and phrases.** Examples include phrases such as *the following three factors, in conclusion, the most important consideration, in addition to,* and *on the other hand.* These phrases and others signal relationships, definitions, new subjects, conclusions, cause and effect, and examples. They reveal the structure of the lecture. You can use these phrases to organize your notes.

**Watch the board or PowerPoint presentation.** If an instructor takes the time to write something down on the board or show a PowerPoint presentation, consider the material to be important. Copy all diagrams and drawings, equations, names, places, dates, statistics, and definitions.

**Watch the instructor's eyes.** If an instructor glances at her notes and then makes a point, it is probably a signal that the information is especially important. Anything she reads from her notes is a potential test question.

**Highlight the obvious clues.** Instructors often hint strongly or tell students point-blank that certain information is likely to appear on an exam. Make stars or other special marks in your notes next to this information. Instructors are not trying to hide what's important.

**Notice the instructor's interest level.** If the instructor is excited about a topic, it is more likely to appear on an exam. Pay attention when she seems more animated than usual.

**You're One Click Away...**
*from finding more strategies for observing online.*

# What to do when you miss a class

For most courses, you'll benefit by attending every class session. This allows you to observe and actively participate. If you miss a class, then catch up as quickly as possible. Find additional ways to observe class content.

## Clarify policies on missed classes.
On the first day of classes, find out about your instructors' policies on absences. See whether you will be allowed to make up assignments, quizzes, and tests. Also inquire about doing extra-credit assignments.

## Contact a classmate.
Early in the semester, identify a student in each class who seems responsible and dependable. Exchange e-mail addresses and phone numbers. If you know you won't be in class, contact this student ahead of time. When you notice that your classmate is absent, pick up extra copies of handouts, make assignments lists, and offer copies of your notes.

## Contact your instructor.
If you miss a class, e-mail or call your instructor, or put a note in his mailbox. Ask whether he has another section of the same course that you can attend so you won't miss the lecture information. Also ask about getting handouts you might need before the next class meeting.

## Consider technology.
If there is a Web site for your class, check it for assignments and the availability of handouts you missed. Free online services such as NoteMesh allow students to share notes with one another. These services use wiki software, which allows you to create and edit Web pages using any browser. Before using such tools, however, check with instructors for their policies on note sharing.

**5**

# RECORD

## The note-taking process flows

© Getty/Frame: Shutterstock

The format and structure of your notes are more important than how fast you write or how elegant your handwriting is. The following techniques can improve the effectiveness of your notes.

### GENERAL TECHNIQUES FOR NOTE TAKING

**Use key words.** An easy way to sort the extraneous material from the important points is to take notes using key words. Key words or phrases contain the essence of communication. They include these:

- Concepts, technical terms, names, and numbers

- Linking words, including words that describe action, relationship, and degree (for example, *most, least,* and *faster*)

Key words evoke images and associations with other words and ideas. They trigger your memory. That characteristic makes them powerful review tools. One key word can initiate the recall of a whole cluster of ideas. A few key words can form a chain from which you can reconstruct an entire lecture.

To see how key words work, take yourself to an imaginary classroom. You are now in the middle of an anatomy lecture. Picture what the room looks like, what it feels like, how it smells. You hear the instructor say:

*Okay, what happens when we look directly over our heads and see a piano falling out of the sky? How do we take that signal and translate it into the action of getting out of the way? The first thing that happens is that a stimulus is generated in the neurons—receptor neurons—of the eye. Light reflected from the piano reaches our eyes. In other words, we see the piano.*

*The receptor neurons in the eye transmit that sensory signal—the sight of the piano—to the body's nervous system. That's all they can do—pass on information. So we've got a sensory signal coming into the nervous system. But the neurons that initiate movement in our legs are effector neurons. The information from the sensory neurons must be transmitted to effector neurons, or we will get squashed by the piano. There must be some kind of interconnection between receptor and effector neurons. What happens between the two? What is the connection?*

Key words you might note in this example include *stimulus, generated, receptor neurons, transmit, sensory signals, nervous system, effector neurons,* and *connection.* You can reduce the instructor's 163 words to these 12 key words. With a few transitional words, your notes might look like this:

> Stimulus (piano) generated in receptor neurons (eye)
>
> Sensory signals transmitted by nervous system to effector neurons (legs)
>
> What connects receptor to effector?

Note the last key word of the lecture: *connection.* This word is part of the instructor's question and leads to the next point in the lecture. Be on the lookout for questions like this. They can help you organize your notes and are often clues for test questions.

**Use pictures and diagrams.** Make relationships visual. Copy all diagrams from the board, and invent your own. A drawing of a piano falling on someone who is looking up, for example, might be used to demonstrate the relationship of receptor neurons to effector neurons. Label the eyes "receptor" and the feet "effector." This picture implies that the sight of the piano must be translated into a motor response. By connecting the explanation of the process with the unusual picture of the piano falling, you can link the elements of the process together.

**Write notes in paragraphs.** When it is difficult to follow the organization of a lecture or put information into outline form, create a series of informal paragraphs. These paragraphs should contain few complete sentences. Reserve complete sentences for precise definitions, direct quotations, and important points that the instructor emphasizes by repetition or other signals—such as the phrase "This is an important point."

**Copy material from the board or a PowerPoint presentation.** Record key formulas, diagrams, and problems that the teacher presents on the board or in a PowerPoint presentation. Copy dates, numbers, names, places, and other facts. You can even use your own signal or code to flag important material.

**Use a three-ring binder.** Three-ring binders have several advantages over other kinds of notebooks. First, pages can be removed and spread out when you review. This way, you can get the whole picture of a lecture. Second, the three-ring-binder format allows you to insert handouts right into your notes. Third, you can insert your own out-of-class notes in the correct order.

**Use only one side of a piece of paper.** When you use one side of a page, you can review and organize all your notes by spreading them out side by side. Most students find the benefit well worth the cost of the paper. Perhaps you're concerned about the environmental impact of consuming more paper. If so, you can use the blank side of old notes and use recycled paper.

**Use 3 × 5 cards.** As an alternative to using notebook paper, use 3 × 5 cards to take lecture notes. Copy each new concept onto a separate 3 × 5 card.

**Keep your own thoughts separate.** For the most part, avoid making editorial comments in your lecture notes. The danger is that when you return to your notes, you might mistake your own ideas for those of the instructor. If you want to make a comment, clearly label it as your own.

**Use an "I'm lost" signal.** No matter how attentive and alert you are, you might get lost and confused in a lecture. If it is inappropriate to ask a question, record in your notes that you were lost. Invent your own signal—for example, a circled question mark. When you write down your code for "I'm lost," leave space for the explanation or clarification that you will get later. The space will also be a signal that you missed something. Later, you can speak to your instructor or ask to see a fellow student's notes.

**Label, number, and date all notes.** Develop the habit of labeling and dating your notes at the beginning of each class. Number the page too. Sometimes the sequence of material in a lecture is important. Write your name and phone number in each notebook in case you lose it.

**Use standard abbreviations.** Be consistent with your abbreviations. If you make up your own abbreviations or symbols, write a key explaining them in your notes. Avoid vague abbreviations. When you use an abbreviation such as *comm.* for *committee,* you run the risk of not being able to remember whether you meant *committee, commission, common,* or *commit.* One way to abbreviate is to leave out vowels. For example, *talk* becomes *tlk, said* becomes *sd, American* becomes *Amrcn.*

**Leave blank space.** Notes tightly crammed into every corner of the page are hard to read and difficult to use for review. Give your eyes a break by leaving plenty of space.

Later, when you review, you can use the blank spaces in your notes to clarify points, write questions, or add other material.

**Take notes in different colors.** You can use colors as highly visible organizers. For example, you can signal important points with red. Or use one color of ink for notes about the text and another color for lecture notes.

**Use graphic signals.** The following ideas can be used with any note-taking format:

- Use brackets, parentheses, circles, and squares to group information that belongs together.
- Use stars, arrows, and underlining to indicate important points. Flag the most important points with double stars, double arrows, or double underlines.
- Use arrows and connecting lines to link related groups.
- Use equal signs and greater-than and less-than signs to indicate compared quantities.

To avoid creating confusion with graphic symbols, write a "dictionary" of your symbols in the front of your notebooks; an example is shown on the next page.

5

[ ], ( ), ◯, ▢ = info
      that belongs together

∗, ↘, ═ = important

∗∗, ↘↘, ≡, !!! = extra important

> = greater than    < = less than
═ = equal to

⟶ = leads to, becomes
  Ex: school → job → money

? = huh?, lost

?? = big trouble, clear up
     immediately

**Use recorders effectively.** Some students record lectures with audio or digital recorders, but there are persuasive arguments against doing so. When you record a lecture, there is a strong temptation to daydream. After all, you can always listen to the lecture again later on. Unfortunately, if you let the recorder do all of the work, you are skipping a valuable part of the learning process.

There are other potential problems as well. Listening to recorded lectures can take a lot of time—more time than reviewing written notes. Recorders can't answer the questions you didn't ask in class. Also, recording devices malfunction. In fact, the unscientific Hypothesis of Recording Glitches states that the tendency of recorders to malfunction is directly proportional to the importance of the material. With those warnings in mind, you can use a recorder effectively if you choose. For example, you can use recordings as backups to written notes. (Check with your instructor first. Some prefer not to be recorded.) Turn the recorder on; then take notes as if it weren't there. Recordings can be especially useful if an instructor speaks fast.

## THE CORNELL METHOD

A note-taking system that has worked for students around the world is the *Cornell method*.[2] Originally developed by Walter Pauk at Cornell University during the 1950s, this approach continues to be taught across the United States and in other countries as well.

The cornerstone of this method is what Pauk calls the *cue column*—a wide margin on the left-hand side of the paper. The cue column is the key to the Cornell method's many benefits. Here's how to use it.

**Format your paper.** On each sheet of your notepaper, draw a vertical line, top to bottom, about 2 inches from the left edge of the paper. This line creates the cue column—the space to the left of the line. You can also find Web sites that allow you to print out pages in this format. Just do an Internet search using the key words *cornell method pdf*.

**Take notes, leaving the cue column blank.** As you read an assignment or listen to a lecture, take notes on the right-hand side of the paper. Fill up this column with sentences, paragraphs, outlines, charts, or drawings. Do not write in the cue column. You'll use this space later, as you do the next steps.

**Condense your notes in the cue column.** Think of the notes you took on the right-hand side of the paper as a set of answers. In the cue column, list potential test questions that correspond to your notes. Write one question for each major term or point.

As an alternative to questions, you can list key words from your notes. Another option is to pretend that your notes are a series of articles on different topics. In the cue column, write a newspaper-style headline for each "article." In any case, be brief. Cramming the cue column full of words defeats its purpose—to reduce the number and length of your notes.

**Write a summary.** Pauk recommends reducing your notes even more by writing a brief summary at the bottom of each page. This step offers you another way to engage actively with the material.

| Cue column | Notes |
|---|---|
| What are the 3 phases of Muscle Reading? | Phase 1: Before you read<br>Phase 2: While you read<br>Phase 3: After you read |
| What are the steps in phase 1? | 1. Preview<br>2. Outline<br>3. Question |
| What are the steps in phase 2? | 4. Focus<br>5. Flag answers |
| What are the steps in phase 3? | 6. Recite<br>7. Review<br>8. Review again |
| What is an acronym for Muscle Reading? | Pry = preview<br>Out = outline<br>Questions = question<br>Focus<br>Flag Answers<br>Recite<br>Review<br>Review again |

| Summary |
|---|
| Muscle Reading includes 3 phases: before, during, and after reading. Each phase includes specific steps. Use the acronym to recall all the steps. |

**Use the cue column to recite.** Cover the right-hand side of your notes with a blank sheet of paper. Leave only the cue column showing. Then look at each item you wrote in the cue column and talk about it. If you wrote questions, answer each question. If you wrote key words, define each word and talk about why it's important. If you wrote headlines in the cue column, explain what each one means and offer supporting details. After reciting, uncover your notes and look for any important points you missed.

## MIND MAPPING

Mind mapping, a system developed by Tony Buzan,[3] can be used in conjunction with the Cornell method to take notes. In some circumstances, you might want to use mind maps exclusively.

To understand mind maps, first review the features of traditional note taking. Outlines (explained in the next section) divide major topics into minor topics, which in turn are subdivided further. They organize information in a sequential, linear way.

The traditional outline reflects only a limited range of brain function—a point that is often made in discussions about "left-brain" and "right-brain" activities. People often use the term *right brain* when referring to creative, pattern-making, visual, intuitive brain activity. They use the term *left brain* when talking about orderly, logical, step-by-step characteristics of thought. Writing teacher Gabrielle Rico uses another metaphor. She refers to the left-brain mode as our "sign mind" (concerned with words) and the right-brain mode as our "design mind" (concerned with visuals).[4] A mind map uses both kinds of brain functions. Mind maps can contain lists and sequences and show relationships. They can also provide a picture of a subject. They work on both verbal and nonverbal levels.

One benefit of mind maps is that they quickly, vividly, and accurately show the relationships between ideas. Also, mind mapping helps you think from general to specific. By choosing a main topic, you focus first on the big picture, then zero in on subordinate details. And by using only key words, you can condense a large subject into a small area on a mind map. You can review more quickly by looking at the key words on a mind map than by reading notes word for word.

**Give yourself plenty of room.** To create a mind map, use blank paper that measures at least 11 by 17 inches. If that's not available, turn regular notebook paper on its side so that you can take notes in a horizontal (instead of vertical) format. If you use a computer in class to take notes, consider

software that allows you to create digital mind maps that can include graphics, photos, and URL links.

**Determine the main concept of the lecture, article, or chapter.** As you listen to a lecture or read, figure out the main concept. Write it in the center of the paper and circle it, underline it, or highlight it with color. You can also write the concept in large letters. Record concepts related to the main concept on lines that radiate outward from the center. An alternative is to circle or box in these concepts.

**Use key words only.** Whenever possible, reduce each concept to a single word per line or circle or box in your mind map. Although this reduction might seem awkward at first, it prompts you to summarize and to condense ideas to their essence. That means fewer words for you to write now and fewer to review when it's time to prepare for tests. (Using shorthand symbols and abbreviations can help.) Key words are usually nouns and verbs that communicate the bulk of the speaker's ideas. Choose words that are rich in associations and that can help you recreate the lecture.

**Create links.** A single mind map doesn't have to include all of the ideas in a lecture, book, or article. Instead, you can link mind maps. For example, draw a mind map that sums up the five key points in a chapter, and then make a separate, more detailed mind map for each of those key points. Within each mind map, include references to the other mind maps. This technique helps explain and reinforce the relationships among many ideas. Some students pin several mind maps next to one another on a bulletin board or tape them to a wall. This allows for a dramatic—and effective—look at the big picture.

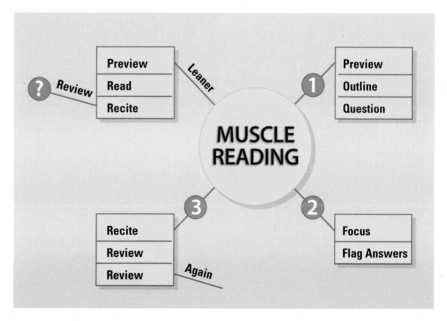

**5**

## OUTLINING

A traditional outline shows the relationships among major points and supporting ideas. One benefit of taking notes in the outline format is that doing so can totally occupy your attention. You are recording ideas and also organizing them. This process can be an advantage if the material has been presented in a disorganized way. By playing with variations, you can discover the power of outlining to reveal relationships among ideas. Technically, each word, phrase, or sentence that appears in an outline is called a *heading*. Headings are arranged in different levels:

* In the first, or top, level of headings, note the major topics presented in a lecture or reading assignment.

* In the second level of headings, record the key points that relate to each topic in the first-level headings.

* In the third level of headings, record specific facts and details that support or explain each of your second-level headings. Each additional level of subordinate heading supports the ideas in the previous level of heading.

Roman numerals offer one way to illustrate the difference between levels of headings. See the following examples.

**First-level heading**

**Second-level heading**

**Third-level heading**

I. Muscle Reading includes 3 phases.
  A. Phase 1: Before you read
    1. Preview
    2. Outline
    3. Question
  B. Phase 2: While you read
    4. Focus
    5. Flag answers
  C. Phase 3: After you read
    6. Recite
    7. Review
    8. Review again

## COMBINING FORMATS

Feel free to use different note-taking systems for different subjects and to combine formats. Do what works for you.

**Distinguish levels with indentations only:**

Muscle Reading includes 3 phases
  Phase 1: Before you read
    Preview

**Distinguish levels with bullets and dashes:**

MUSCLE READING INCLUDES 3 PHASES
  • Phase 1: Before you read
    – Preview

**Distinguish headings by size:**

MUSCLE READING INCLUDES 3 PHASES
Phase 1: Before you read
Preview

For example, combine mind maps along with the Cornell method. You can modify the Cornell format by dividing your notepaper in half. Reserve one half for mind maps and the other for linear information such as lists, graphs, and outlines, as well as equations, long explanations, and word-for-word definitions. You can incorporate a mind map into your paragraph-style notes whenever you feel one is appropriate. Minds maps are also useful for summarizing notes taken in the Cornell format.

John Sperry, a teacher at Utah Valley State College, developed a note-taking system that can include all of the formats discussed in this article:

* Fill up a three-ring binder with fresh paper. Open your notebook so that you see two blank pages—one on the left and one on the right. Plan to take notes across this entire two-page spread.

* During class or while reading, write your notes only on the left-hand page. Place a large dash next to each main topic or point. If your instructor skips a step or switches topics unexpectedly, just keep writing.

* Later, use the right-hand page to review and elaborate on the notes that you took earlier. This page is for anything you want. For example, add visuals such as mind maps. Write review questions, headlines, possible test questions, summaries, outlines, mnemonics, or analogies that link new concepts to your current knowledge.

* To keep ideas in sequence, place appropriate numbers on top of the dashes in your notes on the left-hand page. Even if concepts are presented out of order during class, they'll still be numbered correctly in your notes. ■

**You're One Click Away...**
*from seeing more examples of notes in various formats online*

# REVIEW

## The note-taking process flows

Think of reviewing as an integral part of note taking rather than an added task. To make new information useful, encode it in a way that connects it to your long-term memory. The key is reviewing.

**Review within 24 hours.** The sooner you review your notes, the better, especially if the content is difficult. In fact, you can start reviewing during class. When your instructor pauses to set up the overhead display or erase the board, scan your notes. Dot the *i*'s, cross the *t*'s, and write out unclear abbreviations. Another way to use this technique is to get to your next class as quickly as you can. Then use the 4 or 5 minutes before the lecture begins to review the notes you just took in the previous class. If you do not get to your notes immediately after class, you can still benefit by reviewing them later in the day. A review right before you go to sleep can also be valuable.

Think of the day's unreviewed notes as leaky faucets, constantly dripping and losing precious information until you shut them off with a quick review. Remember, it's possible to forget most of the material within 24 hours—unless you review.

**Edit your notes.** During your first review, fix words that are illegible. Write out abbreviated words that might be unclear to you later. Make sure you can read everything. If you can't read something or don't understand something you *can* read, mark it, and make a note to ask your instructor or another student about it. Check to see that your notes are labeled with the date and class and that the pages are numbered.

**Fill in key words.** As you review your notes, focus on extracting important concepts. Using the key word principles described earlier in this chapter, go through your notes and make a list of key words or phrases. These key words will speed up the review process later. Also experiment with the Cornell method for taking notes, which centers on organizing your notes based on key words.

**Use your key words as cues to recite.** Cover your notes with a blank sheet of paper so that you can see only the key words in the left-hand margin. Take each key word in order, and recite as much as you can about the point. Then uncover your notes and look for any important points you missed.

**Conduct short weekly review periods.** Once a week, review all of your notes again. These review sessions don't need to take a lot of time. Even a 20-minute weekly review period is valuable. Some students find that a weekend review—say, on Sunday afternoon—helps them stay in continuous touch with the material. Scheduling regular review sessions on your calendar helps develop the habit.

**Consider typing your notes.** Some students type up their handwritten notes on the computer. The argument for doing so is threefold. First, typed notes are easier to read. Second, they take up less space. Third, the process of typing them forces you to review the material.

**Create summaries.** Mind mapping is an excellent way to summarize large sections of your course notes or reading assignments. Create one map that shows all the main topics you want to remember. Then create another map about each main topic. After drawing your maps, look at your original notes, and fill in anything you missed. This system is fun and quick.

Another option is to create a "cheat sheet." There's only one guideline: Fit all your review notes on a single sheet of paper. Use any note-taking format that you want—mind map, outline, Cornell method, or a combination of all of them. The beauty of this technique is that it forces you to pick out main ideas and key details. There's not enough room for anything else!

Some instructors might let you use a summary sheet during an exam. But even if you can't use it, you'll benefit from creating one while you study for the test. Summarizing is a powerful way to review. ■

**You're One Click Away...**
*from finding more strategies for reviewing online.*

# Turn POWERPOINTS into POWERFUL NOTES

PowerPoint presentations are common. They can also be lethal for students who want to master course content or those who simply want to stay awake.

Some students stop taking notes during a PowerPoint presentation. This choice can be hazardous to your academic health for several reasons. For one thing, PowerPoint presentations don't always include all the key material. Depending on them can leave large gaps in your notes. When you stop taking notes, you might also stop being an active participant in class.

To create value from PowerPoint presentations, take notes on them. Continue to observe, record, and review. See PowerPoint as a way to *guide* rather than to *replace* your own note taking. Even the slickest, smartest presentation is no substitute for your own thinking.

Experiment with the following suggestions. They include ideas about what to do before, during, and after a PowerPoint presentation.

## BEFORE THE PRESENTATION

Sometimes instructors make PowerPoint slides available before a lecture. If you have computer access, download these files. Scan the slides, just as you would preview a reading assignment.

Consider printing out the slides and bringing them along to class. (If you own a copy of PowerPoint, then choose the "handouts" option when printing. This will save paper and ink.) You can take notes directly on the pages that you print out. Be sure to add the slide numbers if they are missing.

If you use a laptop computer for taking notes during class, then you might not want to bother with printing. Just open up the PowerPoint file and type your notes in the window that appears at the bottom of each slide. After class, you can print out the slides in note view. This will show the original slides plus any text that you added.

## DURING THE PRESENTATION

In many cases, PowerPoint slides are presented visually by the instructor *only during class*. The slides are not provided as handouts, and they are not available online for students to print out.

This makes it even more important to take effective notes in class. Capture the main points and key details as you normally would. Use your preferred note-taking strategies.

Be selective in what you write down. Determine what kind of material is on each slide. Stay alert for new topics, main points, and important details. Taking too many notes makes it hard to keep up with a speaker and separate main points from minor details.

In any case, go *beyond* the slides. Record valuable questions and answers that come up during a discussion, even if they are not a planned part of the presentation.

## AFTER THE PRESENTATION

If you printed out slides before class and took notes on those pages, then find a way to integrate them with the rest of your notes. For example, add references in your notebook to specific slides. Or create summary notes that include the major topics and points from readings, class meetings, and PowerPoint presentations.

Printouts of slides can make review tools. Use them as cues to recite. Cover up your notes so that only the main image or words on each slide are visible. See whether you can remember what else appears on the slide, along with the key points from any notes you added.

Also consider "editing" the presentation. If you have the PowerPoint file on your computer, make another copy of it. Open up this copy, and see whether you can condense the presentation. Cut slides that don't include anything you want to remember. Also rearrange slides so that the order makes more sense to you. Remember that you can open up the original file later if you want to see exactly what your instructor presented. ■

# Note taking 2.0

Taking notes? There's an app for that. Lots of apps, as a matter of fact. Many of them allow you to synchronize notes between a laptop or desktop computer, smart phone, and iPad or other tablet device.

Some apps store only text-based notes. Check out simplenote (simplenoteapp.com), Notational Velocity (notational.net), and ResophNotes (www.resoph.com). Other apps allow you to store images and audio recordings as well. Evernote (evernote.com) and Microsoft OneNote (office.microsoft.com/onenote/) are popular examples.

The beauty of these tools is that your notes are stored online (in "the cloud"). This means that you can access and edit your notes from any digital device with Internet access.

# When your instructor talks QUICKLY

**Take more time to prepare for class.** Familiarity with a subject increases your ability to pick up on key points. If an instructor lectures quickly or is difficult to understand, conduct a thorough preview of the material to be covered.

**Be willing to make choices.** Focus your attention on key points. Instead of trying to write everything down, choose what you think is important. Occasionally, you will make a less than perfect choice or even neglect an important point. Worse things could happen. Stay with the lecture, write down key words, and revise your notes immediately after class.

**Exchange photocopies of notes with classmates.** Your fellow students might write down something you missed. At the same time, your notes might help them. Exchanging photocopies can fill in the gaps.

**Leave large empty spaces in your notes.** Leave plenty of room for filling in information you missed. Use a symbol that signals you've missed something, so you can remember to come back to it.

**See the instructor after class.** Take your class notes with you, and show the instructor what you missed.

**Use an audio recorder.** Recording a lecture gives you a chance to hear it again whenever you choose. Some audio recording software allows you to vary the speed of the recording. With this feature, you can perform magic and actually slow down the instructor's speech.

**Before class, take notes on your reading assignment.** You can take detailed notes on the text before class. Leave plenty of blank space. Take these notes with you to class, and simply add your lecture notes to them.

**Go to the lecture again.** Many classes are taught in multiple sections. That gives you the chance to hear a lecture at least twice—once in your regular class and again in another section of the class.

**Learn shorthand.** Some note-taking systems, known as shorthand, are specifically designed for getting ideas down fast. Books and courses are available to help you learn these systems. You can also devise your own shorthand method by inventing one- or two-letter symbols for common words and phrases.

**Ask questions—even if you're totally lost.** Many instructors allow a question session. This is the time to ask about the points you missed.

At times you might feel so lost that you can't even formulate a question. That's okay. One option is to report this fact to the instructor. He can often guide you to a clear question. Another option is to ask a related question. Doing so might lead you to the question you really wanted to ask.

**Ask the instructor to slow down.** This solution is the most obvious. If asking the instructor to slow down doesn't work, ask her to repeat what you missed. ■

## ✓ EXERCISE 12

## Taking notes under pressure

With note taking, as with other skills, the more you practice, the better you become. You can use TV programs and videos to practice listening for key words, writing quickly, focusing your attention, and reviewing. Programs that feature speeches and panel discussions work well for this purpose. So do documentary films.

The next time you watch such a program, use pen and paper to jot down key words and information. If you fall behind, relax. Just leave a space in your notes and return your attention to the program. If a program includes commercial breaks, use them to review and revise your notes.

At the end of the program, spend 5 minutes reviewing all of your notes. Create a mind map based on your notes. Then sum up the main points of the program for a friend.

This exercise will help you develop an ear for key words. Because you can't ask questions or request that speakers slow down, you train yourself to stay totally in the moment.

Don't be discouraged if you miss a lot the first time around. Do this exercise several times, and observe how your mind works.

Another option is to record a program and then take notes. You can stop the recording at any point to review what you've written.

Ask a classmate to do this exercise with you. Compare your notes and look for any points that either of you missed.

5

# Taking notes
# WHILE READING

Taking notes while reading requires the same skills that apply to taking class notes: observing, recording, and reviewing. Use these skills to take notes for review and for research.

## REVIEW NOTES

Review notes will look like the notes you take in class. Take review notes when you want more detailed notes than writing in the margin of your text allows. You might want to single out a particularly difficult section of a text and make separate notes. Or make summaries of overlapping lecture and text material. Because you can't underline or make notes in library books, these sources will require separate notes, too. To take more effective review notes, use the following suggestions.

**Set priorities.** Single out a particularly difficult section of a text and make separate notes. Or make summaries of overlapping lecture and text material.

**Use a variety of formats.** Translate text into Cornell notes, mind maps, or outlines. Combine these formats to create your own. Translate diagrams, charts, and other visual elements into words. Then reverse the process by translating straight text into visual elements.

However, don't let the creation of formats get in your way. Even a simple list of key points and examples can become a powerful review tool. Another option is to close your book and just start writing. Write quickly about what you intend to remember from the text, and don't worry about following any format.

**Condense a passage to key quotes.** Authors embed their essential ideas in key sentences. As you read, continually ask yourself, "What's the point?" Then see whether you can point to a specific sentence on the page to answer your question. Look especially at headings, subheadings, and topic sentences of paragraphs. Write these key sentences word for word in your notes, and put them within quotation marks. Copy as few sentences as you can and still retain the core meaning of the passage.

**Condense by paraphrasing.** Pretend that you have to summarize a chapter, article, or book on a postcard. Limit yourself to a single paragraph—or a single sentence—and use your own words. This is a great way to test your understanding of the material.

**Take a cue from the table of contents.** Look at the table of contents in your book. Write each major heading on a piece of paper, or key those headings into a word-processing file on your computer. Include page numbers. Next, see whether you can improve on the table of contents. Substitute your own headings for those that appear in the book. Turn single words or phrases into complete sentences, and use words that are meaningful to you.

**Adapt to special cases.** The style of your notes can vary according to the nature of the reading material. If you are assigned a short story or poem, for example, then read the entire work once without taking any notes. On your first reading, simply enjoy the piece. When you finish, write down your immediate impressions. Then go over the piece again. Make brief notes on characters, images, symbols, settings, plot, point of view, or other aspects of the work.

**Note key concepts in math and science.** When you read mathematical, scientific, or other technical materials, copy important formulas or equations. Recreate important diagrams, and draw your own visual representations of concepts. Also write down data that might appear on an exam.

## RESEARCH NOTES

Take research notes when preparing to write a paper or deliver a speech. One traditional method of research is to take notes on index cards. You write *one* idea, fact, or quotation per card, along with a note about the source (where you found it). The advantage of limiting each card to one item is that you can easily arrange cards according to the sequence of ideas in your outline. If you change your outline, no problem. Just resort your cards.

Taking notes on a computer offers the same flexibility as index cards. Just include one idea, fact, or quotation per paragraph along with the source. Think of each paragraph as a separate "card." When you're ready to create the first draft of your paper or presentation, just move paragraphs around so that they fit your outline.

**Include your sources.** No matter whether you use cards or a computer, be sure to *include a source for each note that you take.*

Say, for example, that you find a useful quotation from a book. You want to include that quotation in your paper. Copy the quotation word for word onto a card, or key the quotation into a computer file. Along with the quotation, note the book's author, title, date and place of publication, and publisher. You'll need such information later when you create a formal list of your sources—a bibliography, or a list of endnotes or footnotes.

For guidelines on what information to record about each type of source, see the sidebar to this article as a place to start. Your instructors might have different preferences, so ask them for guidance as well.

**Avoid plagiarism.** When people take material from a source and fail to acknowledge that source, they are committing plagiarism. Even when plagiarism is accidental, the consequences can be harsh. For essential information on this topic, see "Academic integrity: avoiding plagiarism" on page 190.

Many cases of plagiarism occur during the process of taking research notes. To prevent this problem, remember that a major goal of taking research notes is to *clearly separate your own words and images from words and images created by someone else.* To meet this goal, develop the following habits:

- If you take a direct quote from one of your sources, then enclose those words in quotation marks, and note information about that source.

- If you take an image (photo, illustration, chart, or diagram) from one of your sources, then note information about that source.

- If you summarize or paraphrase *a specific passage* from one of your sources, then use your own words, and note information about that source.

- If your notes include any idea that is closely identified with a particular person, then note information about the source.

- When you include one of your own ideas in your notes, then simply note the source as "me."

If you're taking notes on a computer and using Internet sources, be especially careful to avoid plagiarism. When you copy text or images from a Web site, separate those notes from your own ideas. Use a different font for copied material, or enclose it in quotation marks.

You do *not* need to note a source for these:

- Facts that are considered common knowledge ("The history of the twentieth century includes two world wars").

- Facts that can be easily verified ("The United States Constitution includes a group of amendments known as the Bill of Rights").

- Your own opinion ("Hip-hop artists are the most important poets of our age").

The bottom line: Always present your own work—not materials that have been created or revised by someone else. If you're ever in doubt about what to do, then take the safest course: Cite a source. Give credit where credit is due. ■

**You're One Click Away...**
*from finding examples of effective research and review notes online.*

# Note key information about
# YOUR SOURCES

**5**

Whenever possible, print out or make photocopies of each source. For books, include a copy of the title page and copyright page, both of which are found in the front matter. For magazines and scholarly journals, copy the table of contents.

## For each *book* you consult, record the following:
- Author
- Editor (if listed)
- Translator (if listed)
- Edition number (if listed)
- Full title, including the subtitle
- Name and location of the publisher
- Copyright date
- Page numbers for passages that you quote, summarize, or paraphrase

## For each *article* you consult, record the following:
- Author
- Editor (if listed)
- Translator (if listed)
- Full title, including the subtitle
- Name of the periodical
- Volume number
- Issue number
- Issue date
- Page numbers for passages that you quote, summarize, or paraphrase

For other types of sources, ask your instructor for guidelines about what information to record.

# Taking *effective notes* for *online coursework*

**Do a trial run with technology.** Verify your access to course Web sites, including online tutorials, PowerPoint presentations, readings, quizzes, tests, assignments, bulletin boards, and chat rooms. Ask your instructors for Web site addresses, e-mail addresses, and passwords. Work out any bugs when you start the course and well before that first assignment is due.

**Develop a contingency plan.** Murphy's Law of Computer Crashes states that technology tends to break down at the moment of greatest inconvenience. You might not believe this piece of folklore, but it's still wise to prepare for it:

- Find a "technology buddy" in each of your classes—someone who can contact the instructor if you lose Internet access or experience other computer problems.

- Every day, make backup copies of files created for your courses.

- Keep extra printer supplies—paper and toner or ink cartridges—on hand at all times. Don't run out of necessary supplies on the day a paper is due.

**Take notes on course material.** You can print out anything that appears on a computer screen. This includes online course materials—articles, books, manuscripts, e-mail messages, chat room sessions, and more.

The potential problem is that you might skip the note-taking process altogether. ("I can just print out everything!") You would then miss the chance to internalize a new idea by restating it in your own words—a principal benefit of note taking. Result: Material passes from computer to printer without ever intersecting with your brain. To prevent this problem, take notes on your online course material.

Of course, it's fine to print out online material. If you do, treat your printouts like mini-textbooks. Apply the steps of Muscle Reading as explained in Chapter 4.

**Ask for help.** If you feel confused about anything you're learning online, ask for help right away. This is especially important when you don't see the instructor face-to-face in class. Some students simply drop online courses rather than seek help. E-mail or call the instructor before you make that choice. If the instructor is on campus, you might be able to arrange for a meeting during office hours.

**Manage time and tasks carefully.** Courses that take place mostly or totally online can become invisible in your weekly academic schedule. This reinforces the temptation to put off dealing with these courses until late in the term.

Avoid this mistake! Consider the real possibility that an online course can take *more* time than a traditional, face-to-face lecture class.

iStockphoto.com/Andrew Rich

One key to keeping up with the course is frequent contact and careful time management:

- Early in the term, create a detailed schedule for online courses. In your calendar, list a due date for each assignment. Break big assignments into smaller steps, and schedule a due date for each step.

- Schedule times in your calendar to complete online course work. Give these scheduled sessions the same priority as regular classroom meetings. At these times, check for online announcements relating to assignments, tests, and other course events. Check for course-related e-mails daily.

- If the class includes discussion forums, check those daily as well. Look for new posts and add your replies. The point of these tools is to create a lively conversation that starts early and continues throughout the term.

- When you receive an online assignment, e-mail any questions immediately. If you want to meet with an instructor in person, request an appointment several days in advance.

- Give online instructors plenty of time to respond. They are not always online. Many online instructors have traditional courses to teach, along with administration and research duties.

- Download or print out online course materials as soon as they're posted on the class Web site. These materials might not be available later in the term.

**Focus your attention.** Some students are used to visiting Web sites while watching television, listening to loud music, or using instant messaging software. When applied to online learning, these habits can reduce your learning and imperil your grades. To succeed with technology, turn off the television, quit online chat sessions, and turn down the music. Whenever you go online, stay in charge of your attention. ■

The purpose of this exercise is to practice thinking about note taking at **Level 6: Creating**. This means inventing something new based on an idea or strategy that you've learned.

According to psychologist Benjamin Bloom, creating is the highest level of thinking. At the same time, you can set the stage for creativity by thinking at any of the other levels—remembering, understanding, applying, analyzing, and evaluating.

**Level 1: Remembering**—recalling an idea.

**Level 2: Understanding**—explaining an idea in your own words and giving examples from your own experience.

**Level 3: Applying**—using an idea to produce a desired result.

**Level 4: Analyzing**—dividing an idea into parts or steps.

**Level 5: Evaluating**—rating the truth, usefulness, or quality of an idea—and giving reasons for your rating.

**Level 6: Creating**—inventing something new based on an idea.

This chapter presents three major formats for taking notes: the Cornell method, mind mapping, and outlining. These formats can be modified and combined. For example, you could take notes during class with the Cornell method. After class, you could expand on your notes by capturing some of the main points in mind maps and outlines. Combining all three formats is an example of creative thinking.

Now, based on your experience with this chapter, create a note-taking format of your own. Describe this format in the space provided to the right. Or, use additional paper and other materials to create a detailed example or model of your format.

_For more information on the six levels of thinking, see "Becoming a critical thinker" in Chapter 7._

**5**

# masterstudentprofile

## Harvey Milk

(1930–1978) One of America's first openly gay men to win political office, Harvey Milk was assassinated by a former San Francisco city supervisor.

People told Harvey Milk that no openly gay man could win political office. Fortunately, he ignored them.

There was a time when it was impossible for people—straight or gay—even to imagine a Harvey Milk. The funny thing about Milk is that he didn't seem to care that he lived in such a time. After he defied the governing class of San Francisco in 1977 to become a member of its board of supervisors, many people—straight and gay—had to adjust to a new reality he embodied: that a gay person could live an honest life and succeed. That laborious adjustment plods on—now forward, now backward—though with every gay character to emerge on TV and with every presidential speech to a gay group, its eventual outcome favoring equality seems clear.

The few gays who had scratched their way into the city's [San Francisco's] establishment blanched when Milk announced his first run for supervisor in 1973, but Milk had a powerful idea: he would reach downward, not upward, for support. He convinced the growing gay masses of "Sodom by the Sea" that they could have a role in city leadership, and they turned out to form "human billboards" for him along major thoroughfares. In doing so, they outed themselves in a way once unthinkable. It was invigorating.

While his first three tries for office failed, they lent Milk the credibility and positive media focus that probably no openly gay person ever had. Not everyone cheered, of course, and death threats multiplied. Milk spoke often of his ineluctable assassination, even recording a will naming acceptable successors to his seat and containing the famous line: "If a bullet should enter my brain, let that bullet destroy every closet door."

Two bullets actually entered his brain. It was Nov. 27, 1978, in city hall, and Mayor George Moscone was also killed. Fellow supervisor Daniel White, a troubled anti-gay conservative, had left the board, and he became unhinged when Moscone denied his request to return. White admitted the murders within hours. . . .

A jury gave him just five years with parole. Defense lawyers had barred anyone remotely pro-gay from the jury and brought a psychologist to testify that junk food had exacerbated White's depression. (The so-called Twinkie defense was later banned.) Milk's words had averted gay riots before, but after the verdict, the city erupted. More than 160 people ended up in the hospital.

Milk's killing probably awakened as many gay people as his election had. His death inspired many associates—most notably Cleve Jones, who later envisioned the greatest work of American folk art, the AIDS quilt. But while assassination offered Milk something then rare for openly gay men—mainstream empathy—it would have been thrilling to see how far he could have gone as a leader. He had sworn off gay bathhouses when he entered public life, and he may have eluded the virus that killed so many of his contemporaries. He could have guided gay America through the confused start of the AIDS horror. Instead, he remains frozen in time, a symbol of what gays can accomplish and the dangers they face in doing so.

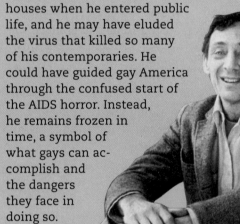

© Bettmann/CORBIS

**HARVEY MILK . . . was courageous.**

**YOU . . . can demonstrate courage by choosing your response to any event.**

*Source:* John Cloud, "The Pioneer," *Time,* June 14, 1999, Copyright © 1999, Time Inc. All rights reserved. Reprinted by permission.

**You're One Click Away...**
*from learning more about Harvey Milk online at the Master Student Profiles. You can also visit the Master Student Hall of Fame to learn about other master students.*

## CHAPTER 5

# QUIZ

Name _____

Date _____

1. Define the word *responsibility* as it is used in the Power Process: "I create it all."

2. What are the three major parts of effective note taking as explained in this chapter? Summarize each step in one sentence.

3. According to the text, neat handwriting and a knowledge of outlining are the only requirements for effective notes. True or false? Explain your answer.

4. What are some advantages of sitting in the front and center of the classroom?

5. Describe a way to apply the Power Process: "Be here now" to the job of taking notes in class.

6. Instructors sometimes give clues that the material they are presenting is important. List at least three of these clues.

7. Postponing debate while taking notes means that you have to agree with everything that the instructor says. True or False? Explain your answer.

8. Describe the two main types of key words. Then write down five key words from this chapter.

9. Graphic signals include which of the following?
   (a)  Brackets and parentheses
   (b)  Stars and arrows
   (c)  Connecting lines
   (d)  Equal signs and greater-than and less-than signs
   (e)  All of the above.

10. Describe three strategies for reviewing notes.

# 5 SKILLS Snapshot

Take a snapshot of your note-taking skills as they exist today, after reading and doing this chapter. Begin by reflecting on some of your recent experiences with note taking. Then take the next step toward mastery by committing to a specific action in the near future.

## DISCOVERY

My score on the *Notes* section of the Discovery Wheel on page 29 was . . .

If my attention wanders while taking notes, I refocus by . . .

When I strongly disagree with the opinion of a speaker or author, I respond by . . .

If asked to rate the overall quality of the notes that I've taken in the last week, I would say that . . .

In general, I find my notes to be most useful when they . . .

## INTENTION

I'll know that I've reached a new level of mastery with note taking when . . .

My main goal for note taking is . . .

## ACTION

The most important thing I can do next to meet my goal is . . .

By the time I finish this course, I would like my *Notes* score on the Discovery Wheel to be . . .

**136** *Chapter 5 • Notes*

# Tests

Use this **Master Student Map** to ask yourself,

## HOW CAN I USE THIS CHAPTER . . .

- Predict test questions and use your study time more effectively.
- Harness the power of cooperative learning by studying with other people.
- Gain strategies for raising your scores on tests.
- Separate your self-image from your test scores.

## WHAT IF . . .

- I could let go of anxiety about tests—or anything else?

**JOURNAL ENTRY 11**
*Intention Statement*

## Use this chapter to transform your experience with tests

Think about how you want your experience of test taking to change. For example, you might want to walk into every test feeling well rested and thoroughly prepared. Next, preview this chapter to find at least three strategies to accomplish your goal. List those strategies below, and note the page numbers where you can find out more about each one.

| Strategy | Page number |
| --- | --- |
| _____ | _____ |
| _____ | _____ |
| _____ | _____ |
| _____ | _____ |
| _____ | _____ |
| _____ | _____ |
| _____ | _____ |
| _____ | _____ |
| _____ | _____ |
| _____ | _____ |
| _____ | _____ |
| _____ | _____ |

© Ruslan Ivantsov/Shutterstock.com

# POWER process

# DETACH

This Power Process helps you release the powerful, natural student within you. It is especially useful whenever negative emotions are getting in your way.

Attachments are addictions. When we are attached to something, we think we cannot live without it, just as a drug addict feels he cannot live without drugs. We believe our well-being depends on maintaining our attachments.

We can be attached to just about anything: beliefs, emotions, people, roles, objects. The list is endless.

One person, for example, might be so attached to his car that he takes an accident as a personal attack. Pity the poor unfortunate who backs into this person's car. He might as well have backed into the owner himself.

Another person might be attached to her job. Her identity and sense of well-being depend on it. She could become depressed if she got fired.

When we are attached and things don't go our way, we can feel angry, sad, afraid, or confused.

Suppose you are attached to getting an "A" on your physics test. You feel as though your success in life depends on getting that "A." As the clock ticks away, you work harder on the test, getting more stuck. That voice in your head gets louder: "I must get an 'A.' I MUST get an 'A.' I MUST GET AN 'A!'"

Now is a time to detach. See whether you can just *observe* what's going on, letting go of all your judgments. When you just observe, you reach a quiet state above and beyond your usual thoughts. This is a place where you can be aware of being aware. It's a tranquil spot, apart from your emotions. From here, you can see yourself objectively, as if you were watching someone else.

That place of detachment might sound far away and hard to reach. You can get there in three ways.

First, pay attention to your thoughts and physical sensations. If you are confused and feeling stuck, tell yourself, "Here I am, confused and stuck." If your palms are sweaty and your stomach is one big knot, admit it.

Second, practice relaxation. Start by simply noticing your breathing. Then breathe more slowly and more deeply. See whether you can breathe the relaxing feeling into your whole body.

Third, practice seeing current events from a broader perspective. In your mind, zoom out to a bigger picture. Ask yourself how much today's test score will matter to you in one week, one month, one year, or one decade from today. You can apply this technique to any challenge in life.

*Caution:* Giving up an *attachment* to being an "A" student does not mean giving up *being* an "A" student. Giving up an attachment to a job doesn't mean giving up the job. When you detach, you get to keep your values and goals. However, you know that you will be okay even if you fail to achieve a goal.

Remember that you are more than your goals. You are more than your thoughts and feelings. These things come and go. Meanwhile, the part of you that can *just observe* is always there and always safe, no matter what happens.

Behind your attachments is a master student. Release that mastery. Detach.

**You're One Click Away...**
*from accessing Power Process Media online and finding out more about how to "detach."*

# DISARM TESTS

On the surface, tests don't look dangerous. Maybe that's why we sometimes treat them as if they were land mines. Suppose a stranger walked up to you on the street and asked, "Does a finite abelian P-group have a basis?" Would you break out in a cold sweat? Would your muscles tense up? Would your breathing become shallow?

Probably not. Even if you had never heard of a finite abelian P-group, you probably would remain coolly detached. However, if you find the same question on a test and you have never heard of a finite abelian P-group, your hands might get clammy.

Grades ("A" to "F") are what we use to give power to tests. And there are lots of misconceptions about what grades are. Grades are not a measure of intelligence or creativity. They are not an indication of our ability to contribute to society. Grades are simply a measure of how well we do on tests.

Some people think that a test score measures what a student has accomplished in a course. This idea is false. A test score is a measure of what a student scored on a test. If you are anxious about a test and blank out, the grade cannot measure what you've learned. The reverse is also true: If you are good at taking tests and you are a lucky guesser, the score won't be an accurate reflection of what you know.

Grades are not a measure of self-worth. Yet we tend to give test scores the power to determine how we feel about ourselves. Common thoughts include "If I fail a test, I am a failure" or "If I do badly on a test, I am a bad person." The truth is that if you do badly on a test, you are a person who did badly on a test. That's all.

If you experience test anxiety, then you might find this line of reasoning hard to swallow. Test anxiety is a common problem among students. And it can surface in many ways, masquerading as a variety of emotions. Here are some examples:

- *Anger:* "The teacher never wanted me to pass this stupid course anyway."
- *Blame:* "If only the class were not so boring."
- *Fear:* "I'll never have enough time to study."

Believing in any of these statements leaves us powerless. We become victims of things that we don't control—the teacher, the textbook, or the wording of the test questions.

Another option is to ask: "What can *I* do to experience my next test differently? How can I prepare more effectively? How can I manage stress before, during, and after the test?" When you answer such questions, you take back your power.

Carrying around misconceptions about tests and grades can put undue pressure on your performance. It's like balancing on a railroad track. Many people can walk along the rail and stay balanced for long periods. Yet the task seems entirely different if the rail is placed between two buildings, 52 stories up.

It is easier to do well on exams if you don't put too much pressure on yourself. Don't give the test some magical power over your own worth as a human being. Academic tests are not a matter of life and death. Scoring low on important tests—standardized tests or medical school exams, bar exams, CPA exams—usually means only a delay.

Whether the chance of doing poorly is real or exaggerated, worrying about it can become paralyzing. The way to deal with tests is to keep them in perspective. Keep the railroad track on the ground. ■

## PRACTICING
# critical thinking 6

You might find the Power Process: "Detach" to be one of the more challenging ideas in *Becoming a Master Student*. Use your thinking skills to unlock the power in this Power Process.

One way to demonstrate an understanding of this Power Process is to give an example of it:

*A man dying from lung cancer spent his last days celebrating his long life. One day his son asked him how he was feeling.*

*"Oh, I'm great," said the man with cancer. "Your mom and I have been having a wonderful time just rejoicing in the life that we have had together."*

*"Oh, I'm glad you're doing well," said the man's son. "The prednisone you have been taking must have kicked in again and helped your breathing."*

*"Well, not exactly. Actually, my body is in terrible shape. My breathing has been a struggle these last few days.*

*I guess what I'm saying is that my body is not working well at all, but I am still great."*

This dying man was painfully aware of his body. He also thought of himself as *more* than his body. Above all, he celebrated his marriage. He saw the most important fact about himself to be love, not cancer. This man gave his son—who just happens to be the author of this book—an unforgettable lesson in detachment.

Now do your own thinking about detachment. First, think at **Level 1: Remembering**. Review the Power Process on page 138. You might want to underline or highlight key words or sentences.

Next, move up to **Level 2: Understanding**. Imagine that you are going to explain this Power Process to someone who has not read this book. What would you say? Answer this question by writing a short paragraph. Be sure to use your own words rather than quoting the article directly. Include an example of how you practiced detachment in the past or could practice it in the future.

## JOURNAL ENTRY 12
*Discovery Statement*

# Explore your feelings about tests

Complete the following sentences:

As exam time gets closer, one thing I notice that I do is . . .

_____

_____

_____

When it comes to taking tests, I have trouble . . .

_____

_____

_____

The night before a test, I usually feel . . .

_____

_____

_____

The morning of a test, I usually feel . . .

_____

_____

_____

During a test, I usually feel . . .

_____

_____

_____

After a test, I usually feel . . .

_____

_____

_____

When I learn a test score, I usually feel . . .

_____

_____

_____

 **You're One Click Away...**
*from accessing and completing this Journal Entry online under Success Tools in Becoming a Master Student's College Success CourseMate.*

## JOURNAL ENTRY 13
*Discovery/Intention Statement*

# Notice your excuses and let them go

Do a timed, 4-minute brainstorm of all the reasons, rationalizations, justifications, and excuses you have used to avoid studying. Be creative. Write your list of excuses in the space below. Use additional paper as needed.

Review your list. Then write a Discovery Statement about patterns that you see in your excuses.

I discovered that I . . .

Next, review your list, pick the excuse that you use the most, and circle it. In the space below, write an Intention Statement about what you will do to begin eliminating your favorite excuse. Make this Intention Statement one that you can keep, with a time line and a reward.

I intend to . . .

_____

_____

_____

_____

_____

_____

_____

_____

_____

_____

_____

_____

_____

_____

_____

_____

_____

_____

_____

# WHAT TO DO BEFORE THE TEST

**Do daily reviews.** Daily reviews include short preclass and post-class reviews of lecture notes. Also conduct brief daily reviews with textbooks: Before reading a new assignment, scan your notes and the sections you underlined or highlighted in the previous assignment. In addition, use the time you spend waiting for the bus or doing the laundry to conduct short reviews.

Concentrate daily reviews on two kinds of material. One is material you have just learned, either in class or in your reading. Second is material that involves simple memorization—equations, formulas, dates, definitions.

Begin to review on the first day of class. Most instructors outline the whole course at that time. You can even start reviewing within seconds after learning. During a lull in class, go over the notes you just took. Immediately after class, review your notes again.

**Do weekly reviews.** Review each subject at least once a week, allowing about 1 hour per subject. Include reviews of assigned reading and lecture notes. Look over any mind map summaries or flash cards you have created. Also practice working on sample problems.

**Do major reviews.** Major reviews are usually most helpful when conducted the week before finals or other critical exams. They help you integrate concepts and deepen your understanding of material presented throughout the term. These are longer review periods—2 to 5 hours at a stretch, with sufficient breaks. Remember that the effectiveness of your review begins to drop after an hour or so unless you give yourself a short rest.

After a certain point, short breaks every hour might not be enough to refresh you. That's when it's time to quit. Learn your limits by being conscious of the quality of your concentration.

During long sessions, study the most difficult subjects when you are the most alert: at the beginning of the session.

**Schedule reviews.** Schedule specific times in your calendar for reviews. Start reviewing key topics at least 5 days before you'll be tested on them. This allows plenty of time to find the answers to questions and close any gaps in your understanding.

**Create study checklists.** You can use study checklists the way a pilot uses a preflight checklist. Pilots go through a standard routine before they take off. They physically mark off each item: test flaps, check magnetos, check fuel tanks, adjust instruments, check rudder. A written list helps them to be sure they don't miss anything. Once they are in the air, it's too late. Taking an exam is like flying a plane. Once the test begins, it's too late to memorize that one equation you forgot to include in your review.

Make a checklist for each subject. List reading assignments by chapters or page numbers. List dates of lecture notes. Write down various types of problems you will need to solve. Write down other skills to master. Include major ideas, definitions, theories, formulas, and equations. For math and science tests, choose some problems and do them over again as a way to review for the test.

**"'How To Do Well In School Without Studying' is over there in the fiction section."**

6

Remember that a study checklist is not a review sheet; it is a to-do list. Checklists contain the briefest possible description of each item to study.

Instead of a checklist, you may want to use a test prep plan. This written plan goes beyond a study checklist to include the following:

- The date and time of each test, along with the name of the course and instructor.

- The type of items—such as essay or multiple choice—that are likely to appear on each test.

- Specific dates and times that you intend to study for each test (which you then enter on your calendar).

- Specific strategies that you intend to use while studying for each test.

**Create mind map summary sheets.**  There are several ways to make a mind map as you study for tests. Start by creating a map totally from memory. You might be surprised by how much you already know. After you have gone as far as you can using recall alone, go over your notes and text, and fill in the rest of the map. Another option is to go through your notes and write down key words as you pick them out. Then, without looking at your notes, create a mind map of everything you can recall about each key word. Finally, go back to your notes, and fill in material you left out.

**Create flash cards.**  Flash cards are like portable test questions. On one side of some $3 \times 5$ cards, write questions. On the other side, write the answers. It's that simple. Always carry a pack of flash cards with you, and review them whenever you have a minute to spare. Use flash cards for formulas, definitions, theories, key words from your notes, axioms, dates, foreign language phrases, hypotheses, and sample problems. Create flash cards regularly as the term progresses. Buy an inexpensive card file to keep your flash cards arranged by subject.

**Monitor your reviews.**  Each day that you prepare for a test, assess what you have learned and what you still want to learn. See how many items you've covered from your study checklist. Look at the tables of contents in your textbooks, and mark an X next to the sections that you've summarized. This helps you gauge the thoroughness of your reviews and alerts you to areas that still need attention.

**Take a practice test.**  Write up your own questions based on course material—a good activity for study groups. Take your practice test several times before the actual exam. You might type this "test" so that it looks like the real thing. If possible, take your practice test in the same room where you will take the actual test.

Also meet with your instructor to go over your practice test. Ask whether your questions focus on appropriate topics and represent the kind of items you can expect to see. The instructor might decline to give you any of this information. More often, though, instructors will answer some or all of your questions about an upcoming test.

**Get copies of old exams.**  Copies of previous exams for the class might be available from the instructor, the instructor's department, the library, or the counseling office. Old tests can help you plan a review strategy. One caution: If you rely on old tests exclusively, you might gloss over material the instructor has added since the last test. Also, check your school's policy about making past tests available to students. Some schools might not allow it. ■

**You're One Click Away...**
*from seeing examples of mind map summary sheets and other review tools online.*

# How to cram (even though you "shouldn't")

Know the limitations of cramming, and be aware of its costs. Cramming won't work if you've neglected all of the reading assignments or if you've skipped most of the lectures and daydreamed through the rest. The more courses you have to cram for, the less effective cramming will be. Also, cramming is not the same as learning: You won't remember what you cram.

If you are going to cram, however, then avoid telling yourself that you *should* have studied earlier, you *should* have read the assignments, or you *should* have been more conscientious. All those *shoulds* get you nowhere. Instead, write an Intention Statement about how you will change your study habits. Give yourself permission to be the fallible human being you are. Then make the best of the situation.

Make choices Pick out a *few* of the most important elements of the course and learn them backward, forward, and upside down. For example, devote most of your attention to the topic sentences, tables, and charts in a long reading assignment.

Make a plan After you've chosen what elements you want to study, determine how much time to spend on each one.

Recite and recite again The key to cramming is repetition. Go over your material again and again.

# Ways to
# PREDICT TEST QUESTIONS

Predicting test questions can do more than get you a better grade. It can also keep you focused on the purpose of a course and help you design your learning strategies. Making predictions can be fun too—especially when they turn out to be accurate.

**Ask about the nature of the test.** Eliminate as much guesswork as possible. Ask your instructor to describe upcoming tests. Do this early in the term so you can be alert for possible test questions throughout the course. Here are some questions to ask:

- What course material will the test cover—readings, lectures, lab sessions, or a combination?

- Will the test be cumulative, or will it cover just the most recent material you've studied?

- Will the test focus on facts and details or major themes and relationships?

- Will the test call on you to solve problems or apply concepts?

- Will you have choices about which questions to answer?

- What types of questions will be on the test—true/false, multiple choice, short answer, essay?

*Note:* In order to study appropriately for essay tests, find out how much detail the instructor wants in your answers. Ask how much time you'll be allowed for the test and about the length of essay answers (number of pages, blue books, or word limit). Having that information before you begin studying will help you gauge your depth for learning the material.

**Put yourself in your instructor's shoes.** If you were teaching the course, what kinds of questions would you put on an exam? You can also brainstorm test questions with other students—a great activity for study groups.

**Look for possible test questions in your notes and readings.** Have a separate section in your notebook labeled "Test questions." Add several questions to this section after every lecture and assignment. You can also create your own code or graphic signal—such as a "*T!*" in a circle—to flag possible test questions in your notes. Use the same symbol to flag review questions and problems in your textbooks that could appear on a test.

Remember that textbook authors have many ways of pointing you to potential test items. Look for clues in chapter overviews and summaries, headings, lists of key words, and review questions. Some textbooks have related Web sites where you can take practice tests.

**Look for clues to possible questions during class.** During lectures, you can predict test questions by observing what an instructor says and how he says it. Instructors often give clues. They might repeat important points several times, write them on the board, or return to them in later classes.

Gestures can indicate critical points. For example, your instructor might pause, look at notes, or read passages word for word.

Notice whether your teacher has any strong points of view on certain issues. Questions on those issues are likely to appear on a test. Also pay attention to questions the instructor poses to students, and note questions that other students ask.

When material from reading assignments is covered extensively in class, it is likely to be on a test. For science courses and other courses involving problem solving, work on sample problems using different variables.

**Save all quizzes, papers, lab sheets, and graded materials of any kind.** Quiz questions have a way of reappearing, in slightly altered form, on final exams. If copies of previous exams and other graded materials are available, use them to predict test questions.

**Apply your predictions.** To get the most value from your predictions, use them to guide your review sessions.

**Remember the obvious.** Be on the lookout for these words: *This material will be on the test.* ◼

6

# COOPERATIVE LEARNING:
## Studying in groups

Study groups can lift your mood on days when you just don't feel like working. If you skip a solo study session, no one else will know. If you declare your intention to study with others who are depending on you, your intention gains strength.

Study groups are especially important if going to school has thrown you into a new culture. Joining a study group with people you already know can help ease the transition. To multiply the benefits of working with study groups, seek out people of other backgrounds, cultures, races, and ethnic groups. You can get a whole new perspective on the world, along with some new friends.

Joining a study group also helps you to develop a number of skills for working on teams in the workplace. Effective teams consist of people who know how to resolve conflict, give each other constructive feedback, collaborate to reach a common goal, and build consensus based on creative and critical thinking. None of us is born with these skills. You can start learning them now and use them to advance your career in the future.

**Look for dedicated students.** Find people you are comfortable with and who share your academic goals. Look for students who pay attention, participate in class, and actively take notes. Invite them to join your group.

Limit groups to four people. Larger groups can be unwieldy. Studying with friends is fine, but if your common interests are pizza and jokes, you might find it hard to focus.

**Do a trial run.** Test the group first by planning a one-time session. If that session works, plan another. After a few successful sessions, you can schedule regular meetings.

**Ask your instructor for guidelines on study group activity.** Many instructors welcome and encourage study groups. However, they have different ideas about what kinds of collaboration are acceptable. Some activities—such as sharing test items or writing papers from a shared outline—are considered cheating. Let your instructor know that you're forming a group, and ask for clear guidelines.

**Set an agenda for each meeting.** At the beginning of each meeting, reach agreement on what you intend to do. Set a time limit for each agenda item, and determine a quitting time. End each meeting with assignments for all members to complete before the next meeting.

**Assign roles.** To make the most of your time, ask one member to lead each group meeting. The leader's role is to keep the discussion focused on the agenda and ask for contributions from all members. Assign another person to act as recorder. This person will take notes on the meeting, recording possible test questions, answers, and main points from group discussions. Rotate both of these roles so that every group member takes a turn.

**Teach each other.** Teaching is a great way to learn something. Turn the material you're studying into a list of topics and assign a specific topic to each person, who will then teach it to the group.

**Test one another.** During your meeting, take a practice test created from questions contributed by group members. When you're finished, compare answers. Or turn testing into a game by pretending you're on a television game show. Use sample test questions to quiz one another.

**Compare notes.** Make sure that all the group's members heard the same thing in class and that you all recorded the important information. Ask others to help explain material in your notes that is confusing to you.

**Create wall-size mind maps or concept maps to summarize a textbook or series of lectures.** Work on large sheets of butcher paper, or tape together pieces of construction paper. When creating a mind map, assign one branch to each member of the study group. Use a different colored pen or marker for each branch of the mind map. (For more information on concept maps and mind maps, see Chapter 5: Notes.)

**Use technology to collaborate.** Web-based applications allow you to create virtual study groups and collaborate online. For example, create and revise documents with sites such as Google Docs (www.docs.google.com) and Zoho Writer (http://www.writer.zoho.com). For more options, do an Internet search with the key words *collaborate online*. ■

## Master Students
# IN ACTION

*When studying for a test, the first thing I usually do is to read over my notes. Sometimes I reread the chapter just to make sure I comprehend what the chapter is saying. I find it very helpful to go online to the publisher's Web site and do the practice exams. By doing the practice exams, I get a better perspective of what the critical points are in the chapters. I like to go through the chapter outline because sometimes the answers are in the outlines.*

*Photo courtesy of Lea Dean*

*—Lea Dean, Central Michigan University*

# What to do during the test

Prepare yourself for the test by arriving early. Being early often leaves time to do a relaxation exercise. While you're waiting for the test to begin and talking with classmates, avoid asking the question "How much did you study for the test?" This question might fuel anxious thoughts that you didn't study enough.

## AS YOU BEGIN

Ask the teacher or test administrator if you can use scratch paper during the test. (If you use a separate sheet of paper without permission, you might appear to be cheating.) If you *do* get permission, use this paper to jot down memory aids, formulas, equations, definitions, facts, or other material you know you'll need and might forget. An alternative is to make quick notes in the margins of the test sheet.

Pay attention to verbal directions given as a test is distributed. Then scan the whole test immediately. Evaluate the importance of each section. Notice how many points each part of the test is worth; then estimate how much time you'll need for each section, using its point value as your guide. For example, don't budget 20 percent of your time for a section that is worth only 10 percent of the points.

Read the directions slowly. Then reread them. It can be agonizing to discover that you lost points on a test merely because you failed to follow the directions. When the directions are confusing, ask to have them clarified.

Now you are ready to begin the test. If necessary, allow yourself a minute or two of "panic" time. Notice any tension you feel, and apply one of the techniques explained in the article "Let Go of Test Anxiety" later in this chapter.

Answer the easiest, shortest questions first. This gives you the experience of success. It also stimulates associations and prepares you for more difficult questions. Pace yourself, and watch the time. If you can't think of an answer, move on. Follow your time plan.

If you are unable to determine the answer to a test question, keep an eye out throughout the test for context clues that may remind you of the correct answer or provide you with evidence to eliminate wrong answers.

## MULTIPLE-CHOICE QUESTIONS

- **Answer each question in your head first.** Do this step before you look at the possible answers. If you come up with an answer that you're confident is right, look for that answer in the list of choices.

- **Read all possible answers before selecting one.** Sometimes two answers will be similar and only one will be correct.

- **Test each possible answer.** Remember that multiple-choice questions consist of two parts: the stem (an incomplete statement or question at the beginning) and a list of possible answers. Each answer, when combined with the stem, makes a complete statement or question-and-answer pair that is either true or false. When you combine the stem with each possible answer, you are turning each multiple-choice question into a small series of true/false questions. Choose the answer that makes a true statement.

- **Eliminate incorrect answers.** Cross off the answers that are clearly not correct. The answer you cannot eliminate is probably the best choice.

## TRUE/FALSE QUESTIONS

- **Read the entire question.** Separate the statement into its grammatical parts—individual clauses and phrases—and then test each part. If any part is false, the entire statement is false.

- **Look for qualifiers.** Qualifiers include words such as *all, most, sometimes,* or *rarely.* Absolute qualifiers such as *always* or *never* generally indicate a false statement.

- **Find the devil in the details.** Double-check each number, fact, and date in a true/false statement. Look for numbers that have been transposed or facts that have been slightly altered. These are signals of a false statement.

- **Watch for negatives.** Look for words such as *not* and *cannot.* Read the sentence without these words and see whether you come up with a true/false statement. Then reinsert the negative words and see whether the statement makes more sense. Watch especially for sentences with two negative words. As in math operations, two negatives cancel each

**6**

other out: *We cannot say that Chekhov never succeeded at short-story writing* means the same as *Chekhov succeeded at short-story writing.*

## COMPUTER-GRADED TESTS

- Make sure that the answer you mark corresponds to the question you are answering.
- Check the test booklet against the answer sheet whenever you switch sections and whenever you come to the top of a column.
- Watch for stray marks on the answer sheet; they can look like answers.
- If you change an answer, be sure to erase the wrong answer thoroughly, removing all pencil marks completely.

## OPEN-BOOK TEST

- Carefully organize your notes, readings, and any other materials you plan to consult when writing answers.
- Write down any formulas you will need on a separate sheet of paper.
- Bookmark the table of contents and index in each of your textbooks. Place sticky notes and stick-on tabs or paper clips on other important pages of books (pages with tables, for instance).
- Create an informal table of contents or index for the notes you took in class.
- Predict which material will be covered on the test, and highlight relevant sections in your readings and notes.

## SHORT-ANSWER/FILL-IN-THE-BLANK TESTS

- Concentrate on key words and facts. Be brief.
- Overlearning material can really pay off. When you know a subject backward and forward, you can answer this type of question almost as fast as you can write.

## MATCHING TESTS

- Begin by reading through each column, starting with the one with fewer items. Check the number of items in each column to see whether they're equal. If they're not, look for an item in one column that you can match with two or more items in the other column.
- Look for any items with similar wording, and make special note of the differences between these items.
- Match words that are similar grammatically. For example, match verbs with verbs and nouns with nouns.

- When matching individual words with phrases, first read a phrase. Then look for the word that logically completes the phrase.
- Cross out items in each column when you are through with them.

## ESSAY QUESTIONS

Managing your time is crucial in answering essay questions. Note how many questions you have to answer, and monitor your progress during the test period. Writing shorter answers and completing all of the questions on an essay test will probably yield a better score than leaving some questions blank.

**Find out what an essay question is asking—precisely.** If a question asks you to *compare* the ideas of Sigmund Freud and Karl Marx, no matter how eloquently you *explain* them, you are on a one-way trip to No Credit City.

**Before you write, make a quick outline.** An outline can help speed up the writing of your detailed answer; you're less likely to leave out important facts; and if you don't have time to finish your answer, your outline could win you some points. To use test time efficiently, keep your outline brief. Focus on key words to use in your answer.

**Introduce your answer by getting to the point.** General statements such as "There are many interesting facets to this difficult question" can cause irritation to teachers grading dozens of tests.

One way to get to the point is to begin your answer with part of the question. Suppose the question is "Discuss how increasing the city police budget might or might not contribute to a decrease in street crime." Your first sentence might be this: "An increase in police expenditures will not have a significant effect on street crime for the following reasons." Your position is clear. You are on your way to an answer.

Then expand your answer with supporting ideas and facts. Start out with the most solid points. Be brief and avoid filler sentences.

**Write legibly.** Grading essay questions is in large part a subjective process. Sloppy, difficult-to-read handwriting might actually lower your grade.

**Write on one side of the paper only.** If you write on both sides of the paper, writing may show through and obscure the words on the other side. If necessary, use the blank side to add points you missed. Leave a generous left-hand margin and plenty of space between your answers, in case you want to add points that you missed later on.

Finally, if you have time, review your answers for grammar and spelling errors, clarity, and legibility. ■

# Words to watch for in
# ESSAY QUESTIONS

The following words are commonly found in essay test questions. They give you precise directions about what to include in your answer. Get to know these words well. When you see them on a test, underline them. Also look for them in your notes. Locating such key words can help you predict test questions.

**Analyze:** Break into separate parts and discuss, examine, or interpret each part. Then give your opinion.

**Compare:** Examine two or more items. Identify similarities and differences.

**Contrast:** Show differences. Set in opposition.

**Criticize:** Make judgments about accuracy, quality, or both. Evaluate comparative worth. Criticism often involves analysis.

**Define:** Explain the exact meaning—usually, a meaning specific to the course or subject. Definitions are usually short.

**Describe:** Give a detailed account. Make a picture with words. List characteristics, qualities, and parts.

**Diagram:** Create a drawing, chart, or other visual element. Label and explain key parts.

**Discuss:** Consider and debate or argue the pros and cons of an issue. Write about any conflict. Compare and contrast.

**Enumerate:** List the main parts or features in a meaningful order and briefly describe each one.

**Evaluate:** Make judgments about accuracy, quality, or both (similar to *criticize*).

**Explain:** Make an idea clear. Show logically how a concept is developed. Give the reasons for an event.

**Illustrate:** Clarify an idea by giving examples of it. Illustration often involves comparison and contrast. Read the test directions to see whether the question calls for actually drawing a diagram as well.

**Interpret:** Explain the meaning of a new idea or event by showing how it relates to more familiar ideas or events. Interpretation can involve evaluation.

**List:** Write a series of concise statements (similar to *enumerate*).

**Outline:** List the main topics, points, features, or events and briefly describe each one. (This does not necessarily mean creating a traditional outline with Roman numerals, numbers, and letters.)

**Prove:** Support with facts, examples, and quotations from credible sources (especially those presented in class or in the text).

**Relate:** Show the connections between ideas or events. Provide a larger context for seeing the big picture.

**State:** Explain precisely and clearly.

**Summarize:** Give a brief, condensed account. Include main ideas and conclusions. Avoid supporting details, or include only significant details.

**Trace:** Show the order of events or the progress of a subject or event.

Notice how these words differ. For example, *compare* asks you to do something different from *contrast*. Likewise, *criticize* and *explain* call for different responses.

If any of these terms are still unclear to you, look them up in an unabridged dictionary.

During a test, you might be allowed to ask for an explanation of a key word. Check with instructors for policies.

**You're One Click Away...**
*from reviewing these key words and other helpful vocabulary terms by using online flash cards.*

6

# The test isn't over *UNTIL* . . .

**M**any students believe that a test is over as soon as they turn in the answer sheet. Consider another point of view: You're not done with a test until you know the answer to any question that you missed—and why you missed it.

This point of view offers major benefits. Tests in many courses are cumulative. In other words, the content included on the first test is assumed to be working knowledge for the second test, midterm, or final exam. When you discover what questions you missed and understand the reasons for lost points, you learn something—and you greatly increase your odds of achieving better scores later in the course.

To get the most value from any test, take control of what you do at two critical points: the time immediately following the test and the time when the test is returned to you.

**Immediately following the test.** After finishing a test, your first thought might be to nap, snack, or go out with friends to celebrate. Restrain those impulses for a short while so that you can reflect on the test. The time you invest now carries the potential to raise your grades in the future.

To begin with, sit down in a quiet place. Take a few minutes to write some Discovery Statements related to your experience of taking the test. Describe how you felt about taking the test, how effective your review strategies were, and whether you accurately predicted the questions that appeared on the test.

Follow up with an Intention Statement or two. State what, if anything, you will do differently to prepare for the next test. The more specific you are, the better.

**When the test is returned.** When a returned test includes a teacher's comments, view this document as a treasure trove of intellectual gold.

First, make sure that the point totals add up correctly, and double-check for any other errors in grading. Even the best teachers make an occasional mistake.

Next, look at the test items that you missed. Ask these questions:

- On what material did the teacher base test questions—readings, lectures, discussions, or other class activities?
- What types of questions appeared in the test—objective (such as matching items, true/false questions, or multiple choice), short answer, or essay?
- What types of questions did you miss?
- Can you learn anything from the instructor's comments that will help you prepare for the next test?
- What strategies did you use to prepare for this test? What would you do differently to prepare for your next test?

Also see whether you can correct any answers that lost points. To do this, carefully analyze the source of your errors, and find a solution. Consult the chart below for help. ∎

| Source of test error | Possible solutions |
|---|---|
| Study errors—studying material that was not included on the test, or spending too little time on material that did appear on the test | • Ask your teacher about specific topics that will be included on a test.<br>• Practice predicting test questions.<br>• Form a study group with class members to create mock tests. |
| Careless errors, such as skipping or misreading directions | • Read and follow directions more carefully—especially when tests are divided into several sections with different directions.<br>• Set aside time during the next test to proofread your answers. |
| Concept errors—mistakes made when you do not understand the underlying principles needed to answer a question or solve a problem | • Look for patterns in the questions you missed.<br>• Make sure that you complete all assigned readings, attend all lectures, and show up for laboratory sessions.<br>• Ask your teacher for help with specific questions. |
| Application errors—mistakes made when you understand underlying principles but fail to apply them correctly | • Rewrite your answers correctly.<br>• When studying, spend more time on solving sample problems.<br>• Predict application questions that will appear on future tests, and practice answering them. |
| Test mechanics errors—missing more questions in certain parts of the test than others, changing correct answers to incorrect ones at the last minute, leaving items blank, miscopying answers from scratch paper to the answer sheet | • Set time limits for taking each section of a test, and stick to them.<br>• Proofread your test answers carefully.<br>• Look for patterns in the kind of answers you change at the last minute.<br>• Change answers only if you can state a clear and compelling reason to do so. |

# The HIGH COSTS of cheating

• • • • • • • • • • • • • • • • • • • • •

Cheating on tests can be a tempting strategy. It offers the chance to get a good grade without having to study.

• • • • • • • • • • • • • • • • • • • • •

Instead of studying, you could spend more time watching TV, partying, sleeping, or doing anything that seems like more fun. Another benefit is that you could avoid the risk of doing poorly on a test—which could happen even if you *do* study.

Remember that cheating carries costs. Here are some consequences to consider.

**You risk failing the course or getting expelled from college.** The consequences for cheating are serious. Cheating can result in failing the assignment, failing the entire course, getting suspended, or getting expelled from college entirely. Documentation of cheating may also prevent you from being accepted to other colleges.

**You learn less.** Although you might think that some courses offer little or no value, you can create value from any course. If you look deeply enough, you can discover some idea or acquire some skill to prepare you for future courses or a career after graduation.

**You lose time and money.** Getting an education costs a lot of money. It also calls for years of sustained effort. Cheating sabotages your purchase. You pay full tuition and invest your energy without getting full value for it. You shortchange yourself and possibly your future coworkers, customers, and clients. Think about it: You probably don't want a surgeon who cheated in medical school to operate on you.

**Fear of getting caught promotes stress.** When you're fully aware of your emotions about cheating, you might discover intense stress. Even if you're not fully aware of your emotions, you're likely to feel some level of discomfort about getting caught.

**Violating your values promotes stress.** Even if you don't get caught cheating, you can feel stress about violating your own ethical standards. Stress can compromise your physical health and overall quality of life.

**Cheating on tests can make it easier to violate your integrity again.** Human beings become comfortable with behaviors that they repeat. Cheating is no exception.

Think about the first time you drove a car. You might have felt excited—even a little frightened. Now driving is probably second nature, and you don't give it much thought. Repeated experience with driving creates familiarity, which lessens the intense feelings you had during your first time at the wheel.

You can experience the same process with almost any behavior. Cheating once will make it easier to cheat again. And if you become comfortable with compromising your integrity in one area of life, you might find it easier to compromise in other areas.

**Cheating lowers your self-concept.** Whether or not you are fully aware of it, cheating sends the message that you are not smart enough or responsible enough to make it on your own. You deny yourself the celebration and satisfaction of authentic success.

An alternative to cheating is to become a master student. Ways to do this are described on every page of this book. ■

## Perils of high-tech CHEATING

Digital technology offers many blessings, but it also expands the options for cheating during a test. For example, one student loaded class notes onto a smartphone and tried to read them. Another student dictated his class notes into files stored on his iPod and tried to listen to them. At one school, students used cell phones to take photos of test questions. They sent the photos to classmates outside the testing room, who responded by text-messaging the answers.[1]

All of these students were caught. Schools are becoming sophisticated about detecting high-tech cheating. Some install cameras in exam rooms. Others use software that monitors the programs running on students' computers during tests. And some schools simply ban all digital devices during tests.

The bottom line: If you cheat on a test, you are more likely than ever before to get caught.

There's no need to learn the hard way—through painful consequences—about the high costs of high-tech cheating. Using the suggestions in this chapter can help you succeed on tests *and* preserve your academic integrity.

6

> **If you freeze during tests and flub questions when you know the answers, you might be dealing with test anxiety.**

# Let go of
# TEST ANXIETY

Masterfile (Royalty-Free Div.)

A little tension before a test is fine. That tingly, butterflies-in-the-stomach feeling you get from extra adrenaline can sharpen your awareness and keep you alert. You can enjoy the benefits of a little tension while you stay confident and relaxed.

**Yell "Stop!"** If you notice that your mind is consumed with worries and fears—that your thoughts are spinning out of control—mentally yell, "Stop!" If you're in a situation that allows it, yell it out loud. This action can allow you to redirect your thoughts. Once you've broken the cycle of worry or panic, you can use any of the following techniques.

**Describe your thoughts in writing.** Certain thoughts tend to increase test anxiety. One way to defuse them is to simply acknowledge them. To get the full benefit of this technique, take the time to make a list. Write down what you think and feel about an upcoming test. Capture everything that's on your mind, and don't stop to edit. One study indicates that this technique can relieve anxiety and potentially raise your test score.[2]

**Dispute your thoughts.** You can take the above technique one step further. Do some critical thinking. Remember that anxiety-creating thoughts about tests often boil down to this statement: *Getting a low grade on a test is a disaster.* Do the math, however: A 4-year degree often involves taking about 32 courses (8 courses per year over 4 years for a full-time student). This means that your final grade on any one course amounts to about only 3 percent of your total grade point average. This is *not* an excuse to avoid studying. It is simply a reason to keep tests in perspective.

**Praise yourself.** Many of us take the first opportunity to belittle ourselves: "Way to go, dummy! You don't even know the answer to the first question on the test." We wouldn't dream of treating a friend this way, yet we do it to ourselves. An alternative is to give yourself some encouragement. Treat yourself as if you were your own best friend. Prepare carefully for each test. Then remind yourself, "I am ready. I can do a great job on this test."

**Consider the worst.** Rather than trying to put a stop to your worrying, consider the very worst thing that could happen. Take your fear to the limit of absurdity. Imagine the catastrophic problems that might occur if you were to fail the test. You might say to yourself, "Well, if I fail this test, I might fail the course, lose my financial aid, and get kicked out of school. Then I won't be able to get a job, so the bank will repossess my car, and I'll start drinking." Keep going until you see the absurdity of your predictions. After you stop chuckling, you can backtrack to discover a reasonable level of concern.

**Breathe.** You can calm physical sensations within your body by focusing your attention on your breathing. Concentrate on the air going in and out of your lungs. Experience it as it passes through your nose and mouth. Do this exercise for 2 to 5 minutes. If you notice that you are taking short, shallow breaths, begin to take longer and deeper breaths. Imagine your lungs to be a pair of bagpipes. Expand your chest to bring in as much air as possible. Then listen to the plaintive chords as you slowly release the air. ■

# Have some FUN!

Contrary to popular belief, finals week does not have to be a drag. In fact, if you have used techniques in this chapter, exam week can be fun. You will have done most of your studying long before finals arrive.

When you are well prepared for tests, you can even use fun as a technique to enhance your performance. The day before a final, go for a run or play a game of basketball. Take in a movie or a concert. A relaxed brain is a more effective brain. If you have studied for a test, your mind will continue to prepare itself even while you're at the movies. Get plenty of rest too. There's no need to cram until 3:00 A.M. when you have reviewed material throughout the term.

# Getting ready for math tests

Consider a three-part program for math success. Begin with strategies for overcoming math anxiety. Next, boost your study skills. Finally, let your knowledge shine during tests.

## OVERCOME MATH ANXIETY

**Connect math to life.** Think of the benefits of mastering math courses. You'll have more options for choosing a major and a career. Math skills can also put you at ease in everyday situations—calculating the tip for a waiter, balancing your checkbook, working with a spreadsheet on a computer. If you follow baseball statistics, cook, do construction work, or snap pictures with a camera, you'll use math. And speaking the language of math can help you feel at home in a world driven by technology.

Pause occasionally to get an overview of the branch of math that you're studying. What's it all about? What basic problems is it designed to solve? How do people apply this knowledge in daily life? For example, many architects, engineers, and scientists use calculus daily.

**Take a First Step.** To ensure that you have an adequate base of knowledge, tell the truth about your current level of knowledge and skill. Before you register for a math course, locate assigned texts for the prerequisite courses. If the material in those books seems new or difficult for you, see the instructor. Ask for suggestions on ways to prepare for the course.

**Notice your pictures about math.** Succeeding in math won't turn you into a nerd. Actually, you'll be able to enjoy school more, and your friends will still like you.

Mental pictures about math can be funny, but they can have serious effects. If math is seen as a field for white males, then women and people of color are likely to get excluded. Promoting math success for all students helps to overcome racism and sexism.

**Change your conversation about math.** When students fear math, they often say negative things to themselves about their abilities in this subject. Many times this self-talk includes statements such as *I'll never be fast enough at solving math problems* or *I'm good with words, so I can't be good with numbers.*

Get such statements out in the open, and apply some emergency critical thinking. You'll find two self-defeating assumptions lurking there: *Everybody else is better at math and science than I am*

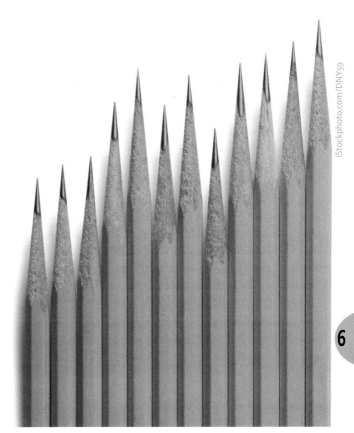

iStockphoto.com/DNY59

**6**

and *Since I don't understand a math concept right now, I'll never understand it.* Both of these statements are illogical.

Replace negative beliefs with logical, realistic statements that affirm your ability to succeed in math: *Any confusion I feel now can be resolved. I learn math without comparing myself to others.* And *I ask whatever questions are needed to aid my understanding.*

**Choose your response to stress.** Math anxiety is seldom just "in your head." It can also register as sweaty palms, shallow breathing, tightness in the chest, or a mild headache. Instead of trying to ignore these sensations, just notice them without judgment. Over time, simple awareness decreases their power.

In addition, use stress management techniques. "Let Go of Test Anxiety" on page 150 offers a bundle of them.

Many schools offer courses in overcoming math anxiety. Ask your advisor about resources on your campus.

# BOOST STUDY SKILLS FOR MATH

**Choose teachers with care.** Whenever possible, find a math teacher whose approach to math matches your learning style. Talk with several teachers until you find one you enjoy. Another option is to ask around. Maybe your academic advisor can recommend math teachers. Also ask classmates to name their favorite math teachers—and to explain the reasons for their choices.

**Take math courses back to back.** Approach math in the same way that you learn a foreign language. If you take a year off in between Spanish I and Spanish II, you won't gain much fluency. To master a language, you take courses back to back. It works the same way with math, which is a language in itself.

**Avoid short courses.** Courses that you take during summer school or another shortened term are condensed. You might find yourself doing far more reading and homework each week than you do in longer courses. If you enjoy math, the extra intensity can provide a stimulus to learn. But if math is not your favorite subject, give yourself extra time. Enroll in courses spread out over more calendar days.

**Form a study group.** During the first week of each math course, organize a study group. Ask each member to bring five problems to group meetings, along with solutions. Also exchange contact information so that you can stay in touch via e-mail, phone, and text messaging.

**Make your text top priority.** Math courses are often text driven. Budget for math textbooks and buy them as early as possible. Class activities closely follow the book. This fact underscores the importance of completing your reading assignments. Master one concept before going on to the next, and stay current with your reading. Be willing to read slowly and reread sections as needed.

**Do homework consistently.** Students who succeed in math do their homework daily—from beginning to end, and from the easy problems all the way through the hard problems. If you do homework consistently, you're not likely to be surprised on a test.

**Take notes that promote success in math.** Though math courses are often text-driven, you might find that the content and organization of your notes makes a big difference as well. Take notes during every class and organize them by date. Also number the pages of your notes. Create a table of contents or index for them so that you can locate key concepts quickly.

**Participate in class.** Success in math depends on your active involvement. Attend class regularly. Complete homework assignments *when they're due*—not just before the test. If you're confused, get help right away from an instructor, tutor, or study group. Instructors' office hours, free on-campus tutoring, and classmates are just a few of the resources available to you. Also support class participation with time for homework. Make daily contact with math.

**Ask questions fearlessly.** It's a cliché, and it's true: In math, there are no dumb questions. Ask whatever questions will aid your understanding. Keep a running list of them, and bring the list to class.

**Read actively.** To get the most out of your math texts, read with paper and pencil in hand. Work out examples. Copy diagrams, formulas, and equations. Use chapter summaries and introductory outlines to organize your learning. From time to time, stop, close your book, and mentally reconstruct the steps in solving a problem. Before you memorize a formula, understand the basic concepts behind it.

# USE TESTS TO SHOW WHAT YOU KNOW

**Practice problem solving.** To get ready for math tests, work *lots* of problems. Find out whether practice problems or previous tests are on file in the library, in the math department, or with your math teacher.

Isolate the types of problems that you find the most difficult. Practice them more often. Be sure to get help with these kinds of problems *before* exhaustion or frustration sets in.

To prepare for tests, practice working problems fast. Time yourself. This activity is a great one for math study groups.

**Ask appropriate questions.** If you don't understand a test item, ask for clarification. The worst that can happen is that an instructor or proctor will politely decline to answer your question.

**Write legibly.** Put yourself in the instructor's place. Imagine the prospect of grading stacks of illegible answer sheets. Make your answers easy to read. If you show your work, underline key sections and circle your answer.

**Do your best.** There are no secrets involved in getting ready for math tests. Master some stress management techniques, do your homework, get answers to your questions, and work sample problems. If you've done those things, you're ready for the test and deserve to do well. If you haven't done all those things, just do the best you can.

Remember that your personal best can vary from test to test, and even from day to day. Even if you don't answer all test questions correctly, you can demonstrate what you *do* know right now.

During the test, notice when solutions come easily. Savor the times when you feel relaxed and confident. If you ever feel math anxiety in the future, these are the times to remember.[3] ∎

# Celebrate mistakes

The title of this article is no mistake. And, it is not a suggestion that you purposely set out to *make* mistakes. Rather, the goal is to shine a light on mistakes so that we can examine them and fix them. Mistakes that are hidden cannot be corrected and are often worth celebrating for the following reasons.

**Mistakes are valuable feedback.** Mistakes are part of the learning process. In fact, mistakes are often more interesting and more instructive than are successes.

**Mistakes demonstrate that we're taking risks.** People who play it safe make few

mistakes. Making mistakes can be evidence that we're stretching to the limit of our abilities—growing, risking, and learning.

**Celebrating mistakes gets them out into the open.** When we celebrate a mistake, we remind ourselves that the person who made the mistake is not bad—just human. Everyone makes mistakes. And hiding mistakes takes a lot of energy that could be channeled into correcting errors. This is not a recommendation that you purposely set out to make mistakes. Mistakes are not an end in themselves. Rather, their value lies in what we learn from them. When we make a mistake, we can admit it and correct it.

**Mistakes happen only when we're committed to making things work.** Imagine a school where teachers usually come to class late. Residence halls are never cleaned, and scholarship checks are always late. The administration is in chronic debt, students seldom pay tuition on time, and no one cares. In this school, the word *mistake* would have little meaning. Mistakes become apparent only when people are committed to quality. ■

**6**

# "F" is for feedback

When some students get an "F" on an assignment, they interpret that letter as a message: "You are a failure." That interpretation is not accurate. Getting an "F" means only that you failed a test—not that you failed your life.

From now on, imagine that the letter "F" when used as a grade represents another word: *feedback*. An "F" is an indication that you didn't understand the material well enough. It's a message to do something differently before the next test or assignment. If you interpret "F" as *failure*, you don't get to change anything. But if you

interpret "F" as *feedback,* you can change your thinking and behavior in ways that promote your success. You can choose a new learning strategy, or let go of an excuse about not having the time to study.

Getting prompt and meaningful feedback on your performance is a powerful strategy for learning *anything*. Tests are not the only source of feedback. Make a habit of asking for feedback from your instructors, advisors, classmates, coworkers, friends, family members, and anyone else who knows you. Just determine what you want to improve and ask, "How am I doing?"

# Bert and John Jacobs

Bert Jacobs (1965– ) and John Jacobs (1968– ), whose job titles are "chief executive optimist" and "chief creative optimist," started their business by selling T-shirts out of the back of a van.

"Life is good" says the T-shirt, the hoodie, the baseball cap, and the onesie, to which one might reasonably respond in these days of doom and gloom, "Really?"

When Bert and John Jacobs launched their self-described optimistic apparel company out of a Boston apartment 15 years ago, we were smack in the middle of the go-go '90s, and those three little words—part lifestyle, part mantra, part last ditch effort by a pair of struggling T-shirt entrepreneurs to make rent money—seemed to mirror the national mood.

Today, not so much. Which oddly enough might make this something of a golden moment for the Life is good company.

"It is generally people who face the greatest adversity who embrace this message the most," says Bert Jacobs, whose company Web site features a section of "inspiring letters that fuel us all to keep spreading good vibes." The letters include testimonials from survivors of a grizzly bear attack, a young amputee, and a soldier stationed in Iraq. "People have a higher sense and appreciation of the simple things when they've been through something difficult. It's our job to see the glass half full."

Life is good doesn't have a demographic, the brothers like to say, but rather a psychographic: the optimists. And while one might imagine that their numbers are dwindling at roughly the same rate as their retirement accounts, some observers suggest otherwise.

That's not to say Life is good is immune to the downturn, but in this company's case it's all relative.

Until last year, the company, whose annual sales top $100 million, had never had a year with less than 30 percent growth. In 2008, it grew only 10 percent, a slowdown that Jacobs notes (in apropos parlance) is "not exactly something you bum out about." Especially since the company hasn't spent a dime on advertising.

Life is good was tested once before, not by the company's customers, but its employees. In the days following 9/11, a number of managers approached Bert Jacobs and said that they weren't feeling right about spreading the company's signature tidings. Some had lost friends in the attacks. The news was all about anthrax and terrorism and tips on turning your basement into a bunker. Maybe life wasn't so good, and maybe this was not the message the American people wanted to hear.

But the company forged ahead, launching its first (wildly successful) nationwide fund-raiser. Jacobs calls it the pivotal moment in his business life.

"Our company has this fantastic positive energy, and our brand is capable of bringing people together," he says. "We know there's trauma and violence and hardship. Life is good isn't the land of Willy Wonka. We're not throwing Frisbees all day. We live in the real world. But you can look around you and find good things any time."

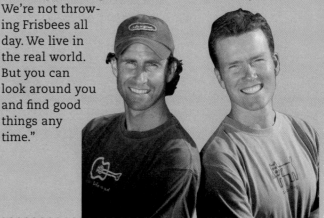

© John Rich Photography

## BERT AND JOHN JACOBS . . .
### are positive.

## YOU . . . can detach from negative thoughts and open up to other perspectives.

**You're One Click Away...**
*from learning more about Bert and John Jacobs online at the Master Student Profiles. You can also visit the Master Student Hall of Fame to learn about other master students.*

**CHAPTER 6 QUIZ**

Name _____

Date _____

1. Describe how using the Power Process: "Detach" differs from giving up.

2. According to the text, test scores measure your accomplishments in a course. True or false? Explain your answer.

3. Briefly explain the difference between a daily review and a major review.

4. Define the term *study checklist,* and give three examples of what to include on such checklists.

5. Study groups can focus on which of the following?
   (a) Comparing and editing class notes.
   (b) Creating mind maps and concept maps
   (c) Letting members teach specific course topics
   (d) Creating and taking practice tests.
   (e) All of the above.

6. When answering multiple-choice questions, the recommended strategy is to read all of the possible answers before answering the question in your head. True or false? Explain your answer.

7. The presence of absolute qualifiers, such as *always* or *never*, generally indicates a false statement. True or false? Explain your answer.

8. Describe three techniques for dealing with test anxiety.

9. Summarize three strategies for boosting your math study skills.

10. According to the text, learning from mistakes is so powerful that we should deliberately set out to *make* mistakes. True or false? Explain your answer.

6

# CHAPTER 6 SKILLS Snapshot

Take a minute to reflect on your responses to the "Tests" section of the Discovery Wheel on page 29. Then take your discoveries and intentions about tests to the next level by completing the following sentences:

## DISCOVERY

My score on the *Tests* section of the Discovery Wheel on page 29 was . . .

To study for a test, what I usually do is . . .

One strategy that really helps me with taking tests is . . .

If I feel stressed about a test, I respond by . . .

## INTENTION

I'll know that I've reached a new level of mastery with tests when . . .

By the time I finish this course, I would like my *Tests* score on the Discovery Wheel to be . . .

My main goal related to test taking is . . .

## NEXT ACTION

To reach my goal, the most important thing I can do next is . . .

# Thinking

Use this **Master Student Map** to ask yourself,

## WHY THIS CHAPTER MATTERS . . .

- The ability to think creatively and critically helps you succeed in any course.

## WHAT IS INCLUDED . . .

## HOW CAN I USE THIS CHAPTER . . .

- Read, write, speak, and listen more effectively.
- Learn strategies to enhance your success in problem solving.
- Apply thinking skills to practical decisions, such as choosing a major.

## WHAT IF . . .

- I could solve problems more creatively and make decisions in every area of life with more confidence?

© Ruslan Ivantsov/Shutterstock.com

**JOURNAL ENTRY 14**
*Intention Statement*

## Choose to create value from this chapter

Remember a time in your life when you felt unable to choose among several different solutions to a problem or struggled with making a decision. Then scan this chapter to find useful suggestions for decision making, problem solving, and critical thinking. Below, note three techniques that you definitely intend to use.

| Strategy | Page number |
|---|---|
| _____ | _____ |
| _____ | _____ |
| _____ | _____ |
| _____ | _____ |
| _____ | _____ |
| _____ | _____ |
| _____ | _____ |
| _____ | _____ |
| _____ | _____ |
| _____ | _____ |
| _____ | _____ |
| _____ | _____ |

# POWER process

# Find a bigger problem

It is impossible to live a life that's free of problems. Besides, problems serve a purpose. They provide opportunities to participate in life. Problems stimulate us and pull us forward.

Seen from this perspective, our goal becomes not to eliminate problems, but to find problems that are worthy of us. Worthy problems are those that challenge us to think, consider our values, and define our goals. Solving the biggest problems offers the greatest potential benefits for others and ourselves. Engaging with big problems changes us for the better. Bigger problems give more meaning to our lives.

Problems expand to fill whatever space is available. Suppose that your only problem for today is to write a thank-you letter to a job interview. You could spend the entire day thinking about what you're going to say, writing the letter, finding a stamp, going to the post office—and then thinking about all of the things you forgot to say.

Now suppose that you get a phone call with an urgent message: A close friend has been admitted to the hospital and wants you to come right away. It's amazing how quickly and easily that letter can get finished when there's a bigger problem on your plate.

True, the smaller problems that enter our lives still need to be solved. The goal is simply to solve them in less time and with less energy.

Bigger problems are easy to find—world hunger, child abuse, environmental pollution, terrorism, human rights violations, drug abuse, street crime, energy shortages, poverty, and wars. These problems await your attention and involvement.

Tackling a bigger problem does not have to be depressing. In fact, it can be energizing—a reason for getting up in the morning. A huge project can channel your passion and purpose.

When we take on a bigger problem, we play full out. We do justice to our potentials. We start to love what we do and do what we love. We're awake, alert, and engaged. Playing full out means living our lives as if our lives depended on it.

Perhaps a little voice in your mind is saying, "That's crazy. I can't do anything about global problems." In the spirit of critical thinking, put that idea to the test. Get involved in solving a bigger problem. Then notice the difference that you *can* make. And just as important, notice how your other problems dwindle—or even vanish.

 **You're One Click Away...**
*from accessing Power Process Media online and finding out more about how to "find bigger problems."*

# CRITICAL THINKING: a survival skill

Society depends on persuasion. We are flooded with content from TV, radio, magazines, books, billboards and the Internet. This leaves us with hundreds of choices about what to buy, where to go, and who to be. It's easy to lose our heads in the crosscurrent of competing ideas—unless we develop skills in critical thinking. When we think critically, we can make choices with open eyes.

It has been said that human beings are rational creatures. Yet no one is born as an effective thinker. Critical thinking is a learned skill. This is one reason that you study so many subjects in higher education—math, science, history, psychology, literature, and more. A broad base of courses helps you develop as a thinker. You see how people with different viewpoints arrive at conclusions, make decisions, and solve problems. This gives you a foundation for dealing with complex challenges in your career, your relationships, and your community.

**Critical thinking frees us from nonsense.** Novelist Ernest Hemingway once said that anyone who wants to be a great writer must have a built-in, shockproof "crap" detector.[1] That inelegant comment points to a basic truth: As critical thinkers, we are constantly on the lookout for thinking that's inaccurate, sloppy, or misleading.

Critical thinking is a skill that will never go out of style. At various times in human history, nonsense has been taken for the truth. For example, people have believed the following:

- Illness results from an imbalance in the four vital fluids: blood, phlegm, water, and bile.
- Racial integration of the armed forces will lead to destruction of soldiers' morale.
- Women are incapable of voting intelligently.
- We will never invent anything smaller than a transistor. (This was before the computer chip.)

The critical thinkers of history arose to challenge short-sighted ideas such as those above. These courageous men and women held their peers to higher standards of critical thinking.

**Critical thinking frees us from self-deception.** Critical thinking is a path to freedom from half-truths and deception. You have the right to question everything that you see, hear, and read. Acquiring this ability is a major goal of a college education.

One of the reasons that critical thinking is so challenging—and so rewarding—is that we have a remarkable capacity to fool ourselves. Some of our ill-formed thoughts and half-truths have a source that hits a little close to home. That source is ourselves.

Master students are willing to admit the truth when they discover that their thinking is fuzzy, lazy, based on a false assumption, or dishonest. These students value facts. When a solid fact contradicts a cherished belief, they are willing to change the belief.

**Critical thinking as thorough thinking.** For some people, the term *critical thinking* has negative connotations. If you prefer, use *thorough thinking* instead. Both terms point to the same activities: sorting out conflicting claims, weighing the evidence, letting go of personal biases, and arriving at reasonable conclusions. These activities add up to an ongoing conversation—a constant process, not a final product.

We live in a culture that values quick answers and certainty. These concepts are often at odds with effective thinking. Thorough thinking is the ability to examine and reexamine ideas that might seem obvious. This kind of thinking takes time and the willingness to say three subversive words: *I don't know.*

Thorough thinking is the basis for much of what you do in school—reading, writing, speaking, listening, note taking, test taking, problem solving, and other forms of decision making. Skilled students have strategies for accomplishing all these tasks. They distinguish between opinion and fact. They ask probing questions and make detailed observations. They uncover assumptions and define their terms. They make assertions carefully, basing them on sound logic and solid evidence. Almost everything that we call *knowledge* is a result of these activities. This means that critical thinking and learning are intimately linked.

Use the suggestions in this chapter to claim the thinking powers that are your birthright. The critical thinker is one aspect of the master student who lives inside you. ■

7

# Becoming a
# CRITICAL THINKER

Thinking is a path to intellectual adventure. Although there are dozens of possible approaches to thinking well, the process boils down to asking and answering questions.

Steve Cole/Getty Images

One quality of a master student is the ability to ask questions that lead to deeper learning. Your mind is an obedient servant. It will deliver answers at the same level as your questions. Becoming a critical thinker means being flexible and asking a wide range of questions.

## GETTING READY FOR CRITICAL THINKING

A psychologist named Benjamin Bloom named six levels of thinking. (He called them *educational objectives*, or goals for learning). Each level of thinking calls for asking and answering different kinds of questions.

**LEVEL 1: Remembering.** At this level of thinking, the key question is *Can I recall the key terms, facts, or events?* To prompt level 1 thinking, an instructor might ask you to do the following:

- List the nine steps of Muscle Reading.
- State the primary features of a mind map.
- Name the master student profiled in Chapter 6 of this book.

To study for a test with level 1 questions, you could create flash cards to review ideas from your readings and class notes. You could also read a book with a set of questions in mind and underline the answers to those questions in the text. Or, you could memorize a list of definitions so that you can recite them exactly. These are just a few examples.

Although remembering is important, this is a relatively low level of learning. No critical or creative thinking is involved. You simply recognize or recall something that you've observed in the past.

**LEVEL 2: Understanding.** At this level, the main question is *Can I explain this idea in my own words?* Often this means giving examples of an idea based on your own experience.

Suppose that your instructor asks you to do the following:

- Explain the main point of the Power Process: "I create it all."
- Summarize the steps involved in creating a concept map.
- Compare mind mapping with concept mapping, stating how they're alike and how they differ.

Other key words in level 2 questions are *discuss, estimate,* and *restate.* All of these are cues to go one step beyond remembering and to show that you truly *comprehend* an idea.

**LEVEL 3: Applying.** Learning at level 3 means asking: *Can I use this idea to produce a desired result?* That result might include completing a task, meeting a goal, making a decision, or solving a problem.

Some examples of level 3 thinking are listed here:

- Write an affirmation about succeeding in school, based on the guidelines in this text.
- Write an effective goal statement.
- Choose a mnemonic to remember the names of the Great Lakes.

Some key words in level 3 questions include *apply, solve, construct, plan, predict,* and *produce.*

**LEVEL 4: Analyzing.** Questions at this level boil down to this: *Can I divide this idea into parts or steps?* For example, you could do the following:

- Divide the steps of Muscle Reading into three major phases.
- Take a list of key events in the Vietnam War and arrange them in chronological order.
- Organize the memory techniques from Chapter 3 into different categories.

Other key words in level 4 questions are *classify, separate, distinguish,* and *outline.*

**LEVEL 5: Evaluating.** Learning at level 5 means asking, *Can I rate the truth, usefulness, or quality of this idea—and give reasons for my rating?* This is the level of thinking you would use to do the following:

- Judge the effectiveness of an Intention Statement.
- Recommend a method for taking lecture notes when an instructor talks fast.
- Rank the Power Processes in order of importance to you—from most useful to least useful.

Level 5 involves genuine critical thinking. At this level you agree with an idea, disagree with it, or suspend judgment until you get more information. In addition, you give reasons for your opinion and offer supporting evidence.

Some key words in level 5 questions are *critique, defend,* and *comment.*

**LEVEL 6: Creating.** To think at this level, ask, *Can I invent something new based on this idea?* For instance, you might do the following:

- Invent your own format for taking lecture notes.
- Prepare a list of topics that you would cover if you were teaching a student success course.

- Imagine that you now have enough money to retire and then write goals you would like to accomplish with your extra time.
- Create a Power Point presentation based on ideas found in this chapter. Put the material in your own words, and use visual elements to enhance the points.

Creative thinking often involves analyzing an idea into parts and then combining those parts in a new way. Another source of creativity is taking several ideas and finding an unexpected connection among them. In either case, you are thinking at a very high level. You are going beyond agreement and disagreement to offer something unique—an original contribution of your own.

Questions for creative thinking often start with words such as *adapt, change, collaborate, compose, construct, create, design,* and *develop.* You might also notice phrases such as *What changes would you make . . . ? How could you improve . . . ? Can you think of another way to . . . ? What would happen if . . . ?*

## GAINING SKILL AS A CRITICAL THINKER

Critical and creative thinking are exciting. The potential rewards are many, and the stakes are high. Your major decisions in life—from choosing a major to choosing a spouse—depend on your skills at critical and creative thinking.

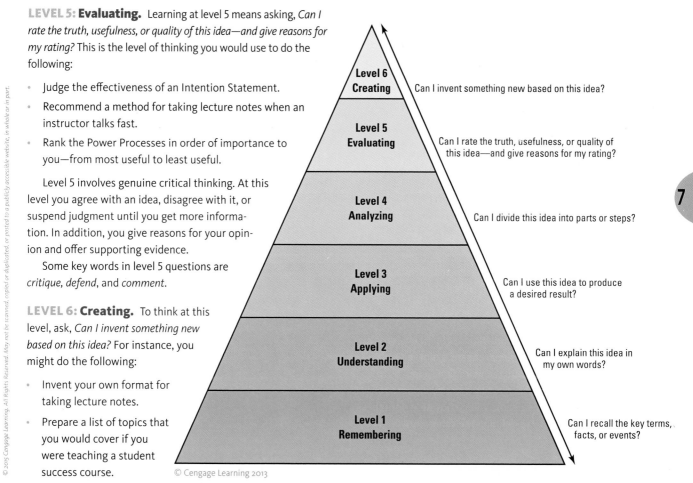

© Cengage Learning 2013

All levels of thinking are useful. Notice that the lower levels of thinking (1 to 3) give you fewer options than the highest levels (4 to 6). Lower levels of thinking are sometimes about finding the "right" answer to a question. At levels 4, 5, and 6, you might discover several valid answers or create several workable solutions.

Also notice that the levels build on each other. Before you agree or disagree with an idea, make sure that you *remember* it accurately and truly *understand* it. Your understanding will go deeper if you can *apply* and *analyze* the idea as well. Master students stay aware of their current level of thinking. They can also move to other levels with a clear intention.

Remember that the highest levels of thinking call for the highest investments of time and energy. Also, moving from a lower level of thinking to a higher level often requires courage, along with an ability to tolerate discomfort. Give yourself permission to experiment, practice, and learn from mistakes.

The suggestions here will help you to deepen your skills at critical thinking. To learn more about creative thinking, see "Ways to create ideas" on page 164.

**Find various points of view on any issue.** Imagine George Bush, Cesar Chavez, and Barack Obama assembled in one room to debate the most desirable way to reshape our government. Picture Madonna, Oprah Winfrey, and Mark Zuckerberg leading a workshop on how to plan your career. When seeking out alternative points of view, let scenes like these unfold in your mind.

Dozens of viewpoints exist on every important issue—reducing crime, ending world hunger, preventing war, educating our children, and countless other concerns. In fact, few problems have any single, permanent solution. Each generation produces its own answers to critical questions, based on current conditions. Our search for answers is a conversation that spans centuries. On each question, many voices are waiting to be heard.

You can take advantage of this diversity by seeking out alternative views with an open mind. When talking to another person, be willing to walk away with a new point of view—even if it's the one you brought to the table, supported with new evidence.

Examining different points of view is an exercise in analysis, which you can do with the suggestions that follow.

**Define terms.** Imagine two people arguing about whether an employer should limit health care benefits to members of a family. To one person, the word *family* means a mother, father, and children; to the other person, the word *family* applies to any individuals who live together in a long-term, supportive relationship. Chances are the debate will go nowhere until these two people realize that they're defining the same word in different ways.

Conflicts of opinion can often be resolved—or at least clarified—when we define our key terms up front. This is especially true with abstract, emotion-laden terms such as *freedom*, *peace*, *progress*, or *justice*. Blood has been shed over the meaning of those words. Define terms with care.

**Look for assertions.** Speakers and writers present their key terms in a larger context called an *assertion*. An assertion is a complete sentence that directly answers a key question. For example, consider this sentence from the article "Master student qualities" in the Introduction to this book: "Mastery means attaining a level of skill that goes beyond technique." This sentence is an assertion that answers an important question: How do we recognize mastery?

**Look for at least three viewpoints.** When asking questions, let go of the temptation to settle for just a single answer. Once you have come up with an answer, say to yourself, "Yes, that is one answer. Now what's another?" Using this approach can sustain honest inquiry, fuel creativity, and lead to conceptual breakthroughs. Be prepared: The world is complicated, and critical thinking is a complex business. Some of your answers might contradict others. Resist the temptation to have all of your ideas in a neat, orderly bundle.

**Practice tolerance.** One path to critical thinking is tolerance for a wide range of opinions. Taking a position on important issues is natural. When we stop having an opinion on things, we've probably stopped breathing.

Problems occur when we become so attached to our current viewpoints that we refuse to consider alternatives. Likewise, it can be disastrous when we blindly follow everything any person or group believes without questioning its validity.

> Each generation produces its own answers to critical questions, based on current conditions. Our search for answers is a conversation that spans centuries. On each question, many voices are waiting to be heard.

Many ideas that are widely accepted in Western cultures—for example, civil liberties for people of color and the right of women to vote—were once considered dangerous. Viewpoints that seem outlandish today might become widely accepted a century, a decade, or even a year from now. Remembering this idea can help us practice tolerance for differing beliefs and, in doing so, make room for new ideas that might alter our lives.

**Look for logic and evidence.** Uncritical thinkers shield themselves from new information and ideas. As an alternative, you can follow the example of scientists, who constantly search for evidence that contradicts their theories. The following suggestions can help you do so.

The aim of using logic is to make statements that are clear, consistent, and coherent. As you examine a speaker's or writer's assertions, you might find errors in logic—assertions that contradict each other or assumptions that are unfounded.

Also assess the evidence used to support points of view. Evidence comes in several forms, including facts, expert testimony, and examples. To think critically about evidence, ask questions such as these:

- Are all or most of the relevant facts presented?
- Are the facts consistent with one another?
- Are facts presented accurately—or in a misleading way?
- Are opinions mistakenly being presented as facts?
- Are enough examples included to make a solid case for the viewpoint?
- Do the examples truly support the viewpoint?
- Are the examples typical? That is, could the author or speaker support the assertion with other examples that are similar?
- Is the expert credible—truly knowledgeable about the topic?
- Does this evidence affirm or contradict something that I already know?

**Consider the source.** Look again at that article on the problems of manufacturing cars powered by natural gas. It might have been written by an executive from an oil company. Check out the expert who disputes the connection between smoking and lung cancer. That "expert" might be the president of a tobacco company.

This is not to say that we should dismiss the ideas of people who have a vested interest in stating their opinions. Rather, we should take their self-interest into account as we consider their ideas.

**Understand before criticizing.** Polished debaters are good at summing up their opponents' viewpoints—often better than the people who support those viewpoints themselves. Likewise, critical thinkers take the time to understand a statement of opinion before agreeing or disagreeing with it.

Effective understanding calls for listening without judgment. Enter another person's world by expressing her viewpoint in your own words. If you're conversing with that person, keep revising your summary until she agrees that you've stated her position accurately. If you're reading an article, write a short summary of it. Then scan the article again, checking to see whether your synopsis is on target.

**Watch for hot spots.** Many people have mental "hot spots"—topics that provoke strong opinions and feelings. Examples are abortion, homosexuality, gun control, and the death penalty.

To become more skilled at examining various points of view, notice your own particular hot spots. Make a clear intention to accept your feelings about these topics and to continue using critical thinking techniques in relation to them.

One way to cool down our hot spots is to remember that we can change or even give up our current opinions without giving up ourselves. That's a key message behind the Power Processes: "Ideas are tools" and "Detach." These articles remind us that human beings are much more than the sum of their current opinions.

**Be willing to be uncertain.** Some of the most profound thinkers have practiced the art of thinking by using a magic sentence: "I'm not sure yet."

Those are words that many people do not like to hear. Our society rewards quick answers and quotable sound bites. We're under considerable pressure to utter the truth in 10 seconds or less.

In such a society, it is courageous and unusual to take the time to pause, to look, to examine, to be thoughtful, to consider many points of view—and to be unsure. When a society adopts half-truths in a blind rush for certainty, a willingness to embrace uncertainty can move us forward.

**Write about it.** Thoughts can move at blinding speed. Writing slows down that process. Gaps in logic that slip by us in thought or speech are often exposed when we commit the same ideas to paper. Writing down our thoughts allows us to compare, contrast, and combine points of view more clearly—and therefore to think more thoroughly.

**Notice your changing perspectives.** Researcher William Perry found that students in higher education move through stages of intellectual development.[4] In earlier stages, students tend to think there is only one correct viewpoint on each issue, and they look to their instructors to reveal that truth. Later, students acknowledge a variety of opinions on issues and construct their own viewpoints.

Remember that the process of becoming a critical thinker will take you through a variety of stages. Give yourself time, and celebrate your growing mastery. ■

7

# WAYS TO CREATE IDEAS

Anyone can think creatively. Use the following techniques to generate ideas about anything—whether you're studying math problems, remodeling a house, or writing a best seller.

**Conduct a brainstorm.** Brainstorming is a technique for creating plans, finding solutions, and discovering new ideas. When you are stuck on a problem, brainstorming can break the logjam. For example, if you run out of money 2 days before payday every week, you can brainstorm ways to make your money last longer. You can brainstorm ways to pay for your education. You can brainstorm ways to find a job.

The overall purpose of brainstorming is to generate as many solutions as possible. Sometimes the craziest, most outlandish ideas, while unworkable in themselves, can lead to new ways to solve problems. Use the following steps:

- *Focus on a single problem or issue.* State your focus as a question. Open-ended questions that start with the words *what, how, who, where,* and *when* often make effective focusing questions. For example, What is my ideal career? What is my ideal major? How can I raise the quality of relationships? What is the single most important change I can make in my life right now?

- *Relax.* Creativity is enhanced by a state of relaxed alertness.

- *Set a quota or goal for the number of solutions you want to generate.* Goals give your subconscious mind something to aim for.

- *Set a time limit.* Use a clock to time it to the minute. Digital sports watches with built-in stopwatches work well. Experiment with various lengths of time. Both short and long brainstorms can be powerful.

- *Allow all answers.* Brainstorming is based on attitudes of permissiveness and patience. Accept every idea. At this stage, there are no wrong answers. If it pops into your head, put it down on paper. Quantity, not quality, is the goal.

- *Brainstorm with others.* Group brainstorming is a powerful technique. Group brainstorms take on lives of their own.

*Sitting woman: Floresco Productions/Getty Images, Word bubbles: maigi/Shutterstock.com*

Assign one member of the group to write down solutions. Feed off the ideas of others, and remember to avoid evaluating or judging anyone's ideas during the brainstorm.

After your brainstorming session, evaluate the results. Toss out any truly nutty ideas, but not before you give them a chance.

**Focus and let go.** Focusing and letting go are alternating parts of the same process. Intense focus taps the resources of your conscious mind. Letting go gives your subconscious mind time to work. When you focus on solving a problem for intense periods and then let go for a while, the conscious and subconscious parts of your brain work in harmony.

You might not be focused all of the time. Periods of inspiration might last only seconds. Be gentle with yourself when you notice that your concentration has lapsed. In fact, that might be a time to let go. *Letting go* means not forcing yourself to be creative. Practice focusing for short periods at first, and then give yourself a break. Play a board game. Go outside and look for shapes in the clouds. Switch to a new location. Take a nap when you are tired. Thomas Edison, the inventor, took frequent naps. Then the lightbulb clicked on.

**Cultivate creative serendipity.** The word *serendipity* was coined by the English author Horace Walpole, from the title of an ancient Persian fairy tale, "The Three Princes of Serendip." The princes had a knack for making lucky discoveries. Serendipity is that knack, and it involves more than luck. It is the ability to see something valuable that you weren't looking for.

History is full of people who make serendipitous discoveries. Country doctor Edward Jenner noticed "by accident" that milkmaids seldom got smallpox. The result was his discovery that mild cases of cowpox immunized them. Penicillin was also discovered "by accident." Scottish scientist Alexander Fleming was growing bacteria in a laboratory petri dish. A spore of *Penicillium notatum,* a kind of mold, blew in the window and landed in the dish, killing the bacteria. Fleming isolated the active ingredient. A few years later, during World War II, it saved thousands of lives. Had Fleming not been alert to the possibility, the discovery might never have been made.

Keep your eyes open. You might find a solution to an accounting problem in a Saturday morning cartoon. You might discover a topic for your term paper at the corner convenience store. Multiply your contacts with the world. Resolve to meet new people. Join a study or discussion group. Read. Go to plays, concerts, art shows, lectures, and movies. Watch television programs you normally wouldn't watch.

**Keep idea files.** We all have ideas. People who treat their ideas with care are often labeled "creative." They not only recognize ideas but also record them and follow up on them.

One way to keep track of ideas is to write them down on $3 \times 5$ cards. Collect powerful quotations, random insights, notes on your reading, and useful ideas that you encounter in class. Collect jokes too. Include this material in a personal journal, and fuel your discoveries with voracious reading.

Review your files regularly. Some amusing thought that came to you in November might be the perfect solution to a problem in March.

**Collect and play with data.** Look from all sides at the data you collect. Switch your attention from one aspect to another. Examine each fact, and avoid getting stuck on one particular part of a problem. Turn a problem upside down by picking a solution first and then working backward. Ask other people to look at the data. Solicit opinions.

Living with the problem invites a solution. Write down data, possible solutions, or a formulation of the problem on $3 \times 5$ cards,

and carry them with you. Look at them before you go to bed at night. Review them when you are waiting for the bus. Make them part of your life, and think about them frequently.

Look for the obvious solutions or the obvious "truths" about the problem—then toss them out. Ask yourself, "Well, I know X is true, but if X were *not* true, what would happen?" Or ask the reverse: "If that *were* true, what would follow next?"

It has been said that there are no new ideas—only new ways to combine old ideas. Creativity is the ability to discover those new combinations.

**Refine ideas and follow through.** Many of us ignore the part of the creative process that involves refining ideas and following through. How many great moneymaking schemes have we had that we never pursued? How many good ideas have we had for short stories that we never wrote? How many times have we said to ourselves, "You know, what they ought to do is attach two handles to one of those things, paint it orange, and sell it to police departments. They'd make a fortune." And we never realize that we are "they." Genius resides in the follow-through—the application of perspiration to inspiration.

**Trust the process.** Learn to trust the creative process—even when no answers are in sight. We are often reluctant to look at problems if no immediate solution is at hand. Trust that a solution will show up. Frustration and a feeling of being stuck are often signals that a solution is imminent. ◼

**You're One Click Away...**
*from finding more strategies online for creative thinking.*

# EXERCISE 13

## Fix-the-world brainstorm

This exercise works well with four to six people. Pick a major world problem, such as hunger, poverty, terrorism, overpopulation, or pollution. Then conduct a 10-minute brainstorm about the steps an individual could take to contribute to solving the problem.

Use the brainstorming techniques explained in the article "Ways to create ideas." Remember not to

evaluate or judge the solutions during the process. The purpose of a brainstorm is to generate a flow of ideas and record them all.

After the brainstorming session, discuss the process and the solutions that it generated. Did you feel any energy from the group? Was a long list of ideas generated? Are several of them worth pursuing? Write your responses below or on a separate piece of paper.

_____

_____

_____

_____

# DON'T FOOL YOURSELF: common mistakes IN LOGIC

Rich Reid/National Geographic/Getty Images

Logic is a branch of philosophy that seeks to distinguish between effective and ineffective reasoning. This is not just an idle pastime for unemployed philosophers. Learning to think logically offers many benefits: When you think logically, you take your reading, writing, speaking, and listening skills to a higher level. You avoid costly mistakes in decision making. You can join discussions and debates with more confidence, cast your election votes with a clear head, and become a better-informed citizen. People have even improved their mental health by learning to dispute illogical beliefs.[2]

Over the last 2,500 years, specialists have listed some classic land mines in the field of logic—common mistakes in thinking that are called *fallacies*. The study of fallacies could fill a yearlong course. Following are some examples to get you started. Knowing about them before you string together a bunch of assertions can help you avoid getting fooled.

**Jumping to conclusions.** Jumping to conclusions is the only exercise that some lazy thinkers get. This fallacy involves drawing conclusions without sufficient evidence. Take the bank officer who hears about a student's failing to pay back an education loan. After that, the officer turns down all loan applications from students. This person has formed a rigid opinion on the basis of hearsay. Jumping to conclusions—also called *hasty generalization*—is at work here.

**Attacking the person.** The mistake of attacking the person is common at election time. An example is the candidate who claims that her opponent has failed to attend church regularly during the campaign. People who indulge in personal attacks are attempting an intellectual sleight of hand to divert our attention away from the truly relevant issues.

**Pointing to a false cause.** The fact that one event follows another does not necessarily mean that the two events have a cause-and-effect relationship. All we can actually say is that the events might be correlated. For example, as children's vocabularies improve, they can get more cavities. This does not mean that cavities are the result of an improved vocabulary. Instead, the increase in cavities is due to other factors, such as physical maturation and changes in diet or personal care.

**Thinking in all-or-nothing terms.** Consider these statements: *Doctors are greedy. You can't trust politicians. Students these days are in school just to get high-paying jobs; they lack idealism. Homeless people don't want to work.*

These opinions imply the word *all.* They gloss over individual differences, claiming that all members of a group are exactly alike. They also ignore key facts—for instance, that some doctors volunteer their time at free medical clinics and that many homeless people are children who are too young to work.

All-or-nothing thinking is one of the most common errors in logic. To avoid this fallacy, watch out for words such as *all, everyone, no one, none, always,* and *never.* Statements that include these words often make sweeping claims that require a lot of evidence. See whether words such as *usually, some, many, few,* and *sometimes* lead to more accurate statements. Sometimes the words are implied. For example, the implication in the claim "Doctors are greedy" is that *all* doctors are greedy.

**Basing arguments on emotion.** The politician who ends every campaign speech with flag waving and slides of his mother eating apple pie is staking his future on appeals to emotion. So is the candidate who paints a grim scenario of the disaster and ruination that will transpire unless she is elected. Get past the fluff to see whether you can uncover any worthwhile ideas.

**The bottom line—finding fallacies before they bite you.**
Consider this statement: "My mother and father have a happy marriage—after all, they're still together after 35 years." Behind this statement is a big assumption: *Happy marriages are those that last a long time.* And there's a possible fallacy here: You might know of married couples who've stayed together for decades even though they confess to be unhappy in the relationship.

Uncovering assumptions and looking for exceptions can help you detect many errors in logic. This is a tool you can pull out any time you want to experience the benefits of critical thinking. ■

**You're One Click Away...**
*from practicing hunting for fallacies online.*

# THINK CRITICALLY about
# information on the *INTERNET*

Sources of information on the Internet range from the reputable (such as the Library of Congress) to the flamboyant (such as the *National Enquirer*). People are free to post *anything* on the Internet, including outdated facts as well as intentional misinformation.

Newspaper, magazine, and book publishers often employ fact checkers, editors, and lawyers to screen out errors and scrutinize questionable material before publication. Authors of Web pages and other Internet sources might not have these resources or choose to use them.

Taking a few simple precautions when you surf the Internet can keep you from crashing onto the rocky shore of misinformation.

**Distinguish between *ideas* and *information*.** To think more powerfully about what you find on the Internet, remember the difference between information and ideas. For example, consider the following sentence: *Nelson Mandela became president of South Africa in 1994.* That statement provides information about South Africa. In contrast, the following sentence states an idea: *Nelson Mandela's presidency means that apartheid has no future in South Africa.*

*Information* refers to facts that can be verified by independent observers. *Ideas* are interpretations or opinions based on facts. These include statements of opinion and value judgments. Several people with the same information might adopt different ideas based on that information.

People who speak of the Internet as the "information superhighway" often forget to make the distinction between information and ideas. Don't assume that an idea is more current, reasonable,

> People who speak of the Internet as the "information superhighway" often forget to make the distinction between information and ideas. Don't assume that an idea is more current, reasonable, or accurate just because you find it on the Internet.

or accurate just because you find it on the Internet. Apply your critical thinking skills to all published material—print and online.

**Look for overall quality.** Examine the features of a Web site in general. Notice the effectiveness of the text and visuals as a whole. Also note how well the site is organized and whether you can navigate the site's features with ease. Look for the date that crucial information was posted, and determine how often the site is updated.

Next, get an overview of the site's content. Examine several of the site's pages, and look for consistency of facts, quality of information, and competency with grammar and spelling. Are the links within the site easy to navigate?

Also evaluate the site's links to related Web pages. Look for links to pages of reputable organizations. Click on a few of those links. If they lead you to dead ends, it might indicate that the site you're evaluating is not updated often—a clue that it's not a reliable source for late-breaking information.

**Look at the source.** Find a clear description of the person or organization responsible for the Web site. Many sites include this information in an "About" link.

The domain in the uniform resource locator (URL) for a Web site gives you clues about sources of information and possible bias. For example, distinguish among information from a for-profit commercial enterprise (URL ending in .com); a nonprofit organization (.org); a government agency (.gov); and a school, college, or university (.edu).

If the site asks you to subscribe or become a member, then find out what it does with the personal information that you provide. Look for a way to contact the site's publisher with questions and comments.

**Look for documentation.** When you encounter an assertion on a Web page or some other Internet resource, note the types and quality of the evidence offered. Look for credible examples, quotations from authorities in the field, documented statistics, or summaries of scientific studies.

Remember that wikis (peer-edited sites) such as Wikipedia do not employ editors to screen out errors or scrutinize questionable material before publication. Do not rely on these sites when researching a paper or presentation. Also, be cautious about citing blogs, which often are not reviewed for accuracy. Such sources may, however, provide you with key words and concepts that help lead you to scholarly research on your topic.

**Set an example.** In the midst of the Internet's chaotic growth, you can light a path of rationality. Whether you're sending a short e-mail message or building a massive Web site, bring your own critical thinking skills into play. Every word and image that you send down the wires to the Web can display the hallmarks of critical thinking— sound logic, credible evidence, and respect for your audience. ■

7

# Gaining skill at
# DECISION MAKING

© Mike Baldwin / Cornered

© Mike Baldwin. Reproduction rights available from
www.CartoonStock.com

**W**e make decisions all the time, whether we realize it or not. Even avoiding decisions is a form of decision making. The student who puts off studying for a test until the last minute might really be saying, "I've decided this course is not important" or "I've decided not to give this course much time." In order to escape such a fate, decide right now to experiment with the following suggestions.

**Recognize decisions.** Decisions are more than wishes or desires. There's a world of difference between "I wish I could be a better student" and "I will take more powerful notes, read with greater retention, and review my class notes daily." Decisions are specific and lead to focused action. When we decide, we narrow down. We give up actions that are inconsistent with our decision. Deciding to eat fruit for dessert instead of ice cream rules out the next trip to the ice cream store.

**Establish priorities.** Some decisions are trivial. No matter what the outcome, your life is not affected much. Other decisions can shape your circumstances for years. Devote more time and energy to the decisions with big outcomes.

**Base your decisions on a life plan.** The benefit of having long-term goals for our lives is that they provide a basis for many of our daily decisions. Being certain about what we want to accomplish this year and this month makes today's choices more clear.

**Balance learning styles in decision making.** To make decisions more effectively, use all four modes of learning explained in Chapter 1: First Steps. The key is to balance reflection with action, and thinking with experience. First, take the time to think creatively, and generate many options. Then think critically about the possible consequences of each option before choosing one. Remember, however, that thinking is no substitute for experience. Act on your chosen option, and notice what happens. If you're not getting the results that you want, then quickly return to creative thinking to invent new options.

**Choose an overall strategy.** Every time you make a decision, you choose a strategy—even when you're not aware of it. Effective decision makers can articulate and choose from among several strategies. For example:

- *Find all of the available options, and choose one deliberately.* Save this strategy for times when you have a relatively small number of options, each of which leads to noticeably different results.

- *Find all of the available options, and choose one randomly.* This strategy can be risky. Save it for times when your options are basically similar and fairness is the main issue.

- *Limit the options, and then choose.* When deciding which search engine to use on the World Wide Web, visit many sites and then narrow the list down to two or three that you choose.

**Use time as an ally.** Sometimes we face dilemmas—situations in which any course of action leads to undesirable consequences. In such cases, consider putting a decision on hold. Wait it out. Do nothing until the circumstances change, making one alternative clearly preferable to another.

**Use intuition.** Some decisions seem to make themselves. A solution pops into your mind, and you gain newfound clarity. Using intuition is not the same as forgetting about the decision or refusing to make it. Intuitive decisions usually arrive after we've gathered the relevant facts and faced a problem for some time.

**Evaluate your decision.** Hindsight is a source of insight. After you act on a decision, observe the consequences over time. Reflect on how well your decision worked and what you might have done differently.

**Think choices.** This final suggestion involves some creative thinking. Consider that the word *decide* derives from the same roots as *suicide* and *homicide*. In the spirit of those words, a decision forever "kills" all other options. That's kind of heavy. Instead, use the word *choice,* and see whether it frees up your thinking. When you *choose,* you express a preference for one option over others. However, those options remain live possibilities for the future. Choose for today, knowing that as you gain more wisdom and experience, you can choose again. ■

**You're One Click Away...**
*from finding more strategies online
for making decisions.*

# Four ways to solve problems

Think of problem solving as a process with four P's: Define the *problem*, generate *possibilities*, create a *plan*, and *perform* your plan.

**1 Define the problem.** To define a problem effectively, understand what a problem is—a mismatch between what you want and what you have. Problem solving is all about reducing the gap between these two factors.

Tell the truth about what's present in your life right now, without shame or blame. For example: "I often get sleepy while reading my physics assignments, and after closing the book I cannot remember what I just read."

Next, describe in detail what you want. Go for specifics: "I want to remain alert as I read about physics. I also want to accurately summarize each chapter I read."

Remember that when we define a problem in limiting ways, our solutions merely generate new problems. As Albert Einstein said, "The world we have made is a result of the level of thinking we have done thus far. We cannot solve problems at the same level at which we created them."[3]

| Define the **problem** |
|---|
| Generate **possibilities** |
| Create a **plan** |
| **Perform** your plan |

| **What** is the problem? |
|---|
| **What if** there are several possible solutions? |
| **How** would this possible solution work? |
| **Why** is one solution more workable than another? |

This idea has many applications for success in school. An example is the student who struggles with note taking. The problem, she thinks, is that her notes are too sketchy. The logical solution, she decides, is to take more notes, and her new goal is to write down almost everything her instructors say. No matter how fast and furiously she writes, she cannot capture all of the instructors' comments.

Consider what happens when this student defines the problem in a new way. After more thought, she decides that her dilemma is not the *quantity* of her notes but their *quality*. She adopts a new format for taking notes, dividing her notepaper into two columns. In the right-hand column, she writes down only the main points of each lecture. And in the left-hand column, she notes two or three supporting details for each point.

Over time, this student makes the joyous discovery that there are usually just three or four core ideas to remember from each lecture. She originally thought the solution was to take more notes. What really worked was taking notes in a new way.

**2 Generate possibilities.** Now put on your creative thinking hat. Open up. Brainstorm as many possible solutions to the problem as you can. At this stage, quantity counts. As you generate possibilities, gather relevant facts. For example, when you're faced with a dilemma about what courses to take next term, get information on class times, locations, and instructors. If you haven't decided which summer job offer to accept, gather information on salary, benefits, and working conditions.

**3 Create a plan.** After rereading your problem definition and list of possible solutions, choose the solution that seems most workable. Think about specific actions that will reduce the gap between what you have and what you want. Visualize the steps you will take to make this solution a reality, and arrange them in chronological order. To make your plan even more powerful, put it in writing.

**4 Perform your plan.** This step gets you off your chair and out into the world. Now you actually *do* what you have planned.

Ultimately, your skill in solving problems lies in how well you perform your plan. Through the quality of your actions, you become the architect of your own success.

When facing problems, experiment with these four P's, and remember that the order of steps is not absolute. Also remember that any solution has the potential to create new problems. If that happens, cycle through the four P's of problem solving again. ∎

**You're One Click Away...**
*from finding more strategies online for problem solving.*

7

# Asking questions— learning through inquiry

Thinking is born of questions. Questions wake us up. Questions alert us to hidden assumptions. Questions promote curiosity and create new distinctions. Questions open up options that otherwise go unexplored. Besides, teachers love questions.

Questions have practical power. Asking for directions can shave hours off a trip. Asking a librarian for help can save hours of research time. Asking how to address an instructor, whether by first name or formal title, can change your relationship with that person. Asking your academic advisor a question can alter your entire education. Asking people about their career plans can alter *your* career plans.

**Ask questions that create possibilities.** At any moment you can ask a question that opens up a new possibility for someone. Suppose a friend walks up to you and says, "People just never listen to me."

You listen carefully. Then you say, "Let me make sure I understand. Who, specifically, doesn't listen to you? And how do you know they're not listening?"

Another friend comes up to you and says, "I just lost my job to someone who has less experience. That should never happen."

"Wow, that's hard," you say. "I'm sorry you lost your job. Who can help you find another job?"

Then a relative seeks your advice. "My mother-in-law makes me mad," she says.

"You're having a hard time with this person," you say. "What does she say and do when you feel mad at her? And are there times when you *don't* get mad at her?"

These kinds of questions—asked with compassion and a sense of timing—can help people move from complaining about problems to solving them.

**Discover new questions.** Students sometimes say, "I don't know what questions to ask." Consider the following ways to create questions about any subject you want to study, or about any area of your life that you want to change.

*Let your pen start moving.* Sometimes you can access a deeper level of knowledge by taking out your pen, putting it on a piece of paper, and writing down questions—even before you know what to write. Don't think. Just watch the pen move across the paper. Notice what appears. The results might be surprising.

*Ask about what's missing.* Another way to invent useful questions is to notice what's missing from your life and then ask how to supply it. For example, if you want to take better notes, you can write, "What's missing is skill in note taking. How can I gain more skill in taking notes?" If you always feel rushed, you can write, "What's missing is time. How do I create enough time in my day to actually do the things that I say I want to do?"

*Pretend to be someone else.* Another way to invent questions is first to think of someone you greatly respect. Then pretend you're that person. Ask the questions you think she would ask.

*Begin a general question; then brainstorm endings.* By starting with a general question and then brainstorming a long list of endings, you can invent a question that you've never asked before. For example:

- *What can I do when* . . . an instructor calls on me in class and I have no idea what to say? When a teacher doesn't show up for class on time? When I feel overwhelmed with assignments?

- *How can I* . . . take the kind of courses that I want? Expand my career options? Become much more effective as a student, starting today?

- *When do I* . . . decide on a major? Transfer to another school? Meet with an instructor to discuss an upcoming term paper?

- *What else do I want to know about* . . . my academic plan? My career plan? My options for job hunting? My friends? My relatives? My spouse?

- *Who can I ask about* . . . my career options? My major? My love life? My values and purpose in life?

Many times you can quickly generate questions by simply asking yourself, "What else do I want to know?" Ask this question immediately after you read a paragraph in a book or listen to someone speak.

Start from the assumption that you are brilliant. Then ask questions to unlock your brilliance. ■

# Thinking about your major

One decision that troubles many students in higher education is the choice of a major. Weighing the benefits, costs, and outcomes of a possible major is an intellectual challenge. This choice is an opportunity to apply your critical thinking, decision making, and problem solving skills. The following suggestions will guide you through this seemingly overwhelming process.

## 1. DISCOVER OPTIONS

**Follow the fun.** Perhaps you look forward to attending one of your classes and even like completing the assignments. This is a clue to your choice of major.

See whether you can find lasting patterns in the subjects and extracurricular activities that you've enjoyed over the years. Look for a major that allows you to continue and expand on these experiences.

Also, sit down with a stack of 3 × 5 cards and brainstorm answers to the following questions:

- What do you enjoy doing most with your unscheduled time?

- Imagine that you're at a party and having a fascinating conversation. What is this conversation about?

- What kind of problems do you enjoy solving—those that involve people? Products? Ideas?

- What interests are revealed by your choices of reading material, television shows, and other entertainment?

- What would an ideal day look like for you? Describe where you'd live, who would be with you, and what you'd do throughout the day. Do any of these visions suggest a possible major?

Questions like these can uncover a "fun factor" that energizes you to finish the work of completing a major.

**Consider your abilities.** In choosing a major, ability counts as much as interest. In addition to considering what you enjoy, think about times and places when you excelled. List the courses that you aced, the work assignments that you mastered, and the hobbies that led to rewards or recognition. Let your choice of a major reflect a discovery of your passions *and* potentials.

**Use formal techniques for self-discovery.** Explore questionnaires and inventories that are designed to correlate your interests with specific majors. Examples include the Strong Interest Inventory and the Self-Directed Search. Your academic advisor or someone in your school's career planning office can give you more details about these and related inventories. For some fun, take several of them and meet with an advisor to interpret the results. Remember inventories can help you gain self-knowledge, and other people can offer valuable perspectives. However, what you *do* with all this input is entirely up to you.

**Link to long-term goals.** Your choice of a major can fall into place once you determine what you want in life. Before you choose a major, back up to a bigger picture. List your core values, such as contributing to society, achieving financial security and professional recognition, enjoying good health, or making time for fun. Also write down specific goals that you want to accomplish 5 years, 10 years, or even 50 years from today.

Many students find that the prospect of getting what they want in life justifies all of the time, money, and day-to-day effort invested in going to school. Having a major gives you a powerful incentive for attending classes, taking part in discussions, reading textbooks, writing papers, and completing other assignments. When you see a clear connection between finishing school and creating the life of your dreams, the daily tasks of higher education become charged with meaning.

**Ask other people.** Key people in your life might have valuable suggestions about your choice of major. Ask for their ideas, and listen with an open mind. At the same time, distance yourself from any pressure to choose a major or career that fails to interest you. If you make a choice based solely on the expectations of other people, you could end up with a major or even a career you don't enjoy.

**Gather information.** Check your school's catalog or Web site for a list of available majors. Here is a gold mine of information. Take a quick glance, and highlight all the majors that interest you. Then talk to students who have declared them. Also read descriptions of courses required for these majors. Do you get excited about the chance to enroll in them? Pay attention to your "gut feelings."

Also chat with instructors who teach courses in a specific major. Ask for copies of their class syllabi. Go the bookstore and browse the required texts. Based on all this information, write a list of prospective majors. Discuss them with an academic advisor and someone at your school's career-planning center.

**Invent a major.** When choosing a major, you might not need to limit yourself to those listed in your school catalog. Many schools now have flexible programs that allow for independent study. Through such programs you might be able to combine two existing majors or invent an entirely new one of your own.

**Consider a complementary minor.** You can add flexibility to your academic program by choosing a minor to complement or contrast with your major. The student who wants to be a minister could opt for a minor in English; all of those courses in composition can help in writing sermons. Or the student with a major in psychology might choose a minor in business administration, with the idea of managing a counseling service some day. An effective choice of a minor can expand your skills and career options.

7

**Think critically about the link between your major and your career.** Your career goals might have a significant impact on your choice of major. For an overview of career planning and an immediate chance to put ideas down on paper, see Chapter 10: What's Next?

You could pursue a rewarding career by choosing among *several* different majors. Even students planning to apply for law school or medical school have flexibility in their choice of majors. In addition, after graduation, many people are employed in jobs with little relationship to their major. And you might choose a career in the future that is unrelated to any currently available major.

## 2. MAKE A TRIAL CHOICE

Pretend that you have to choose a major today. Based on the options for a major that you've already discovered, write down the first three ideas that come to mind. Review the list for a few minutes, and then just choose one.

## 3. EVALUATE YOUR TRIAL CHOICE

When you've made a trial choice of major, take on the role of a scientist. Treat your choice as a hypothesis, and then design a series of experiments to evaluate and test it. For example:

- Schedule office meetings with instructors who teach courses in the major. Ask about required course work and career options in the field.

- Discuss your trial choice with an academic advisor or career counselor.

- Enroll in a course related to your possible major. Remember that introductory courses might not give you a realistic picture of the workloads involved in advanced courses. Also, you might not be able to register for certain courses until you've actually declared a related major.

- Find a volunteer experience, internship, part-time job, or service-learning experience related to the major.

- Interview students who have declared the same major. Ask them in detail about their experiences and suggestions for success.

- Interview people who work in a field related to the major and "shadow" them—that is, spend time with those people during their workday.

- Think about whether you can complete your major given the amount of time and money that you plan to invest in higher education.

- Consider whether declaring this major would require a transfer to another program or even another school.

If your "experiments" confirm your choice of major, celebrate that fact. If they result in choosing a new major, celebrate that outcome as well.

Also remember that higher education represents a safe place to test your choice of major—and to change your mind. As you sort through your options, help is always available from administrators, instructors, advisors, and peers.

## 4. CHOOSE AGAIN

Keep your choice of a major in perspective. There is probably no single "correct" choice. Your unique collection of skills is likely to provide the basis for majoring in several fields.

Odds are that you'll change your major at least once—and that you'll change careers several times during your life. One benefit of higher education is mobility. You gain the general skills and knowledge that can help you move into a new major or career field at any time.

Viewing a major as a one-time choice that determines your entire future can raise your stress levels. Instead, look at choosing a major as the start of a continuing path that involves discovery, choice, and passionate action. ■

 **You're One Click Away...**
*from finding more strategies online for choosing a major.*

# *Master Students*
# IN ACTION

"*I think critical thinking is when you're presented with a problem or a scenario and you just don't go with your gut reaction. You have to look at the problem from many different angles and weigh different options before you decide what is the right answer.*"

—*Lauren Swidler,*
*Providence College*

# ✔ EXERCISE 14

## Translating goals into action

Goal setting is an exercise in decision making and problem solving. Choose one long-range goal, such as a personal project or a social change you'd like to help bring about. Examples include learning to scuba dive, eating a more healthful diet, studying to be an astronaut, improving health care for chronically ill children, inventing an energy-saving technology, increasing the effectiveness of American schools, and becoming a better parent.

Review the suggestions for writing and setting goals in Chapter 2. Then write one long-range goal here:

_____

_____

Next, ask yourself, "What specific actions are needed in the short term to meet my long-range goal?" Brainstorm a list of actions below:

_____

_____

_____

_____

_____

Finally, from the above list, choose at least one action that you can take during the next 24 hours. Add that action to your to-do list or calendar.

 **PRACTICING**
# critical thinking 7

Recall an idea or suggestion from the chapter that you'd like to explore in more detail. Summarize it, and include the page number where it appears:

_____

_____

You've just done some thinking at **Level 1: Remembering**. Now, take your thinking about this idea or suggestion to **one** of the higher levels:

**Level 2: Understanding**—Explain this idea in your own words and give examples from your own experience.

**Level 3: Applying**—Use the idea to produce a desired result.

**Level 4: Analyzing**—Divide this idea into parts or steps.

**Level 5: Evaluating**—Rate the truth, usefulness or quality of the idea—and give reasons for your rating.

**Level 6: Creating**—Invent something new based on the idea.

Demonstrate your higher-level thinking by writing a brief paragraph below. If you want to show your thinking in another way, then check with your instructor. In either case, clearly state your intended level of thinking (For example, "To *apply* this idea, I would . . .")

_____

_____

_____

_____

_____

_____

_____

_____

_____

_____

_____

7

# masterstudentprofile

## Twyla Tharp

(1941– ) A choreographer who has worked with her own company, the Joffrey Ballet, the Paris Opera Ballet, London's Royal Ballet, and the American Ballet Theatre, she also created dances for the films *Hair*, *Ragtime*, and *Amadeus*.

Every creative person has to learn to deal with failure, because failure, like death and taxes, is inescapable. If Leonardo and Beethoven and Goethe failed on occasion, what makes you think you'll be the exception?

I don't mean to romanticize failure. . . . Believe me, success is preferable to failure. But there is a therapeutic power to failure. It cleanses. It helps you put aside who you aren't and reminds you of who you are. Failure humbles. . . .

When I tape a 3-hour improvisational session with a dancer and find only 30 seconds of useful material in the tape, I am earning straight A's in failure. Do the math: I have rejected 99.7 percent of my work that day. It would be like a writer knocking out a 2,000-word chapter and upon rereading deciding that only three words were worth keeping. Painful, yes, but for me absolutely necessary.

What's so wonderful about wasting that kind of time? It's simple: The more you fail in private, the less you will fail in public. In many ways, the creative act is editing. You're editing out all the lame ideas that won't resonate with the public. It's not pandering. It's exercising your judgment. It's setting the bar a little higher for yourself, and therefore for your audience. . . .

Some of my favorite dancers at New York City Ballet were the ones who fell the most. I always loved watching Mimi Paul; she took big risks onstage and went down often. Her falls reminded you that the dancers were doing superhuman things onstage, and when she fell, I would realize, "Damn, she's human." And hitting the ground seemed to transform Mimi: It was as though the stage absorbed the energy of her fall and injected it back into her with an extra dose of fearlessness. Mimi would bounce back up, ignore the fall, and right before my eyes would become superhuman again. I thought, "Go, Mimi!" She became greater because she had fallen. Failure enlarged her dancing.

That should be your model for dealing with failure.

When you fail in public, you are forcing yourself to learn a whole new set of skills, skills that have nothing to do with creating and everything to do with surviving.

Jerome Robbins liked to say that you do your best work after your biggest disasters. For one thing, it's so painful that it almost guarantees that you won't make those mistakes again. Also, you have nothing to lose; you've hit bottom and the only place to go is up. A fiasco compels you to change dramatically. The golfer Bobby Jones said, "I never learned anything from a match I won." He respected defeat and profited from it. . . .

My heroes in *The Odyssey* are the older warriors who have been through many wars. They don't hide their scars, they wear them proudly as a kind of armor. When you fail—when your short film induces yawns or your photographs inspire people to say, "That's nice" (ouch!), or your novel is trashed in a journal of opinion that matters to you—the best thing to do is acknowledge your battle scars and gird yourself for the next round. Tell yourself, "This is a deep wound. But it's going to heal and I will remember the wound. When I go back into the fray, it will serve me well."

© Petre Buzoianu/Corbis

**TWYLA THARP** . . . is creative.

**YOU** . . . can be more creative by seeing failure as a chance to learn.

**You're One Click Away...**
*from learning more about Twyla Tharp online at the Master Student Profiles. You can also visit the Master Student Hall of Fame to learn about other master students.*

# QUIZ

Name _____

Date _____

1. List the six levels of thinking described by Benjamin Bloom.

2. List the key question associated with each level of thinking of Bloom's taxonomy.

3. According to the text, the highest levels of thinking are the most useful. True or false? Explain your answer.

4. List three questions that you can ask when thinking about the evidence offered for a point of view.

5. Briefly describe three strategies for creative thinking.

6. List three types of logical fallacies, and give an example of each type.

7. Name at least one logical fallacy involved in this statement: "Everyone who's ever visited this school agrees that it's the best in the state."

8. Describe two techniques for discovering questions.

9. According to the text, the words *choose* and *decide* have the same meaning. True or false? Explain your answer.

10. Summarize the four steps in the process of choosing a major, as explained in this chapter.

7

# CHAPTER 7 SKILLS Snapshot

Take a minute to reflect on your responses to the "Thinking" section of the Discovery Wheel on page 30. Then take your discoveries and intentions about creative and critical thinking to the next level by completing the following sentences:

## DISCOVERY

When I'm asked to come up with a topic for a paper or speech, the first thing I do is . . .

When I get involved in a conversation and hear an idea I disagree with, my first response is often to . . .

When I face a major choice in my life, the way that I usually make a decision is . . .

In declaring my major, the steps I plan to take include . . .

## INTENTION

One of the biggest problems I face right now is . . .

To come up with a solution for this problem, I will . . .

By the time I finish this course, I would like my *Thinking* score on the Discovery Wheel to be . . .

I'll know that I've reached a new level of mastery with critical and creative thinking skills when . . .

## ACTION

To reach that level of mastery, the most important thing I can do next is to . . .

# Communicating

Use this **Master Student Map** to ask yourself,

## WHY THIS CHAPTER MATTERS . . .

- Your communication abilities—including your skills in listening, speaking, and writing—are as important to your success as your technical skills.

## WHAT IS INCLUDED . . .

## HOW CAN I USE THIS CHAPTER . . .

- Listen, speak, and write in ways that promote your success.
- Prevent and resolve conflict with other people.
- Make and keep agreements as a tool for creating your future.

## WHAT IF . . .

- I could consistently create the kind of relationships that I've always wanted?

### JOURNAL **ENTRY 15**
*Intention Statement*

## Commit to create value from this chapter

Think of a time when you experienced an emotionally charged conflict with another person.

Then scan this chapter for ideas that can help you get your feelings and ideas across more skillfully in similar situations. List at least three ideas below, along with the page numbers where you intend to read more about them.

| Strategy | Page number |
|---|---|
| _____ | _____ |
| _____ | _____ |
| _____ | _____ |
| _____ | _____ |
| _____ | _____ |
| _____ | _____ |
| _____ | _____ |
| _____ | _____ |
| _____ | _____ |
| _____ | _____ |
| _____ | _____ |
| _____ | _____ |

© Ruslan Ivantsov/Shutterstock.com

# POWER process

# Employ your word

When you give your word, you are creating—literally. The person you are is, for the most part, a result of the agreements you make. Others know who you are by your words and your commitments. And you can learn who you are by observing which commitments you choose to keep and which ones you choose to avoid.

Relationships are built on agreements. When we break a promise to be faithful to a spouse, to help a friend move to a new apartment, or to pay a bill on time, relationships are strained.

The words we use to make agreements can be placed into six different levels. We can think of each level as one rung on a ladder—the ladder of powerful speaking. As we move up the ladder, our speaking becomes more effective.

The first and lowest rung on the ladder is *obligation*. Words used at this level include *I should, he ought to, someone had better, they need to, I must,* and *I had to.* Speaking this way implies that something other than ourselves is in control of our lives. When we live at the level of obligation, we speak as if we are victims.

The second rung is *possibility*. At this level, we examine new options. We play with new ideas, possible solutions, and alternative courses of action. As we do, we learn that we can make choices that dramatically affect the quality of our lives. We are not the victims of circumstance. Phrases that signal this level include *I might, I could, I'll consider, I hope to,* and *maybe.*

From possibility, we can move up to the third level—*preference*. Here we begin the process of choice. The words *I prefer* signal that we're moving toward one set of possibilities over another, perhaps setting the stage for eventual action.

Above preference is a fourth rung called *passion*. Again, certain words signal this level: *I want to, I'm really excited to do that,* and *I can't wait.*

Action comes with the fifth rung—*planning*. When people use phrases such as *I intend to, my goal is to, I plan to,* and *I'll try like mad to,* they're at the level of planning. The Intention Statements you write in this book are examples of planning.

The sixth and highest rung on the ladder is *promising*. This is where the power of your word really comes into play. At this level, it's common to use phrases such as these: *I will, I promise to, I am committed,* and *you can count on it.* Promising is where we bridge from possibility and planning to action. Promising brings with it all of the rewards of employing your word.

**You're One Click Away...**
*from accessing Power Process Media online and finding out more about how to "employ your word.".*

In our daily contact with other people and the mass media, we are exposed to hundreds of messages. Yet the obstacles to receiving those messages accurately are numerous.

# Communication— keeping the channels open

For one thing, only a small percentage of communication is verbal. We also send messages with our bodies and with the tone of our voices. Throw in a few other factors, such as a hot room or background noise, and it's a wonder we can communicate at all.

Written communication adds a whole other set of variables. When you speak, you supplement the meaning of your words with the power of body language and voice inflection. When you write, those nonverbal elements are absent. Instead, you depend on your skills at word choice, sentence construction, and punctuation to get your message across. The choices that you make in these areas can aid—or hinder—communication.

In communication theory, the term *noise* refers to any factor that distorts meaning. When noise is present, the channels of communication start to close. Noise can be external (a lawn mower outside a classroom) or internal (the emotions of the sender or receiver, such as speech anxiety). To a large extent, skillful communication means reducing noise and keeping channels open.

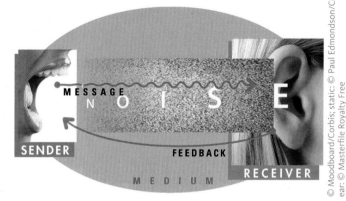

One powerful technique for doing these crucial things is to separate the roles of sending and receiving. Communication channels get blocked when we try to send and receive messages at the same time. Instead, be aware of when you are the receiver and when you are the sender. If you are receiving (listening or reading), just receive; avoid switching into the sending (speaking or writing) mode. When you are sending, stick with it until you are finished.

Communication works best when each of us has plenty of time to receive what others send *and* the opportunity to send a complete message when it's our turn. Communication is a two-way street. When someone else talks, just listen. Then switch roles so that you can be the sender for a while. Keep this up until you do a reasonably complete job of creating shared meaning. ■

**8**

# ✓ EXERCISE 15

## Practice sending or receiving

The purpose of this exercise is to help you slow down the pace of communication and clearly separate the roles of sending and receiving. Begin by applying the following steps to conversations on neutral topics. With some practice, you'll be ready to use this technique in situations that could escalate into an argument.

First, find a partner, and choose a topic for a conversation. Also set a time limit for doing this exercise. Then complete the following steps:

1. Get two 3 × 5 cards. Label one of them *sender*. Label the other *receiver*. Choose one card, and give the other one to your partner.

2. If you chose the *sender* card, then start speaking. If you chose the *receiver* card, then listen to your partner without saying a word.

3. When the sender is done speaking, exchange cards and switch roles. The person who listened in Step 2 now gets to speak. However, *do not exchange cards until the sender in Step 2 declares that she has expressed everything she wants to say.*

4. Keep switching cards and roles until your time is up.

After completing these steps, reflect on the experience. What has this exercise taught you about your current skills as a speaker and listener?

# Choosing to LISTEN

Effective listening calls for concentration and energy. But it's worth the trouble. People love a good listener. The best salespeople, managers, coworkers, teachers, parents, and friends are the best listeners.

To listen well, begin from a clear intention. *Choose* to listen well. Once you've made this choice, use the following techniques to be even more effective at listening.

## NONVERBAL LISTENING

**Be quiet.** Allowing several seconds to pass before you begin to talk gives the speaker time to catch her breath and gather her thoughts. Someone who talks nonstop might fear she will lose the floor if she pauses.

If the message being sent is complete, this short break gives you time to form your response. If you make up a response before the person is finished, you might miss the end of the message, which is often the main point.

In some circumstances, pausing for several seconds might be inappropriate. Ignore this suggestion completely where immediate action is usually necessary.

**Maintain eye contact.** Maintaining eye contact demonstrates your attentiveness and keeps your mind from wandering.

However, this idea is not an absolute. Maintaining eye contact is valued more in some cultures than others.

**Display openness.** You can display openness through your facial expression and body position. Uncross your arms and legs. Sit up straight. Face the other person, and remove any physical barriers between you.

**Send acknowledgments.** Words and nonverbal gestures of acknowledgment convey to the speaker that you are receiving his message. These words and gestures include "Okay," "Yes," and head nods.

**Release distractions.** Even when your intention is to listen, you might find your mind wandering. There's a simple solution: Notice your wandering mind without judgment. Then bring your attention back to the act of listening.

Set up your immediate environment to release distractions. Turn off or silence your cell phone and other digital devices. Send the message that your intention is to listen.

**Suspend judgments.** As listeners, our goal is to fully receive another person's message. This does not mean that we must agree with the message. Once you're confident that you accurately understand a speaker's point of view, you are free to agree or disagree with it. The key to effective listening is understanding *before* evaluating.

## VERBAL LISTENING

**Choose when to speak.** When we listen to another person, we often interrupt with our own stories, opinions, suggestions, and comments.

To avoid this kind of one-sided conversation, delay your verbal responses and wait for an *appropriate* moment to respond.

**Feed back meaning.** Sometimes you can help a speaker clarify her message by paraphrasing it. This does not mean parroting what she says. Instead, briefly summarize.

There will be no doubt when you get it right. The sender will say, "Yeah, that's it."

**Notice verbal *and* nonverbal messages.** Sometimes a speaker's body language seems to convey the opposite of her words.

Keep in mind that the same nonverbal behavior can have various meanings across cultures. Someone who looks bored might simply be listening in a different way.

**Listen for requests and intentions.** An effective way to listen to complaints is to look for the request hidden in them. "The instructor talks too fast" might be asking "What strategies can I use to take notes when the instructor covers material rapidly?"

Viewing complaints as requests gives us more choices. We can decide whether to grant the request or help the person translate his own complaint into an action plan.

**Allow emotion.** In the presence of full listening, some people will share things that they feel deeply about. If you feel uncomfortable when this happens, try to accept the discomfort for a little while longer. Emotional release can bring relief and trigger unexpected insights.

**Be careful with questions and advice.** Questions can take conversations in a new direction, which may not be where the speaker wants to go. Ask questions only to clarify the speaker's message. When it's your turn to speak, you can introduce any topic that you want.

Also be cautious about giving advice. Unsolicited advice can be taken as condescending or even insulting. Skilled listeners do not assume that they know what's best for someone else.

**Take care of yourself.** Be honest. Don't pretend to listen. You can say, "What you're telling me is important, but I'm pressed for time right now. Can we set aside another time to talk about this?"

**Stay open to the adventure of listening.** Listening fully, and opening yourself to how others see the world, means taking risks and challenging your own opinions.

Listening in an unguarded way can take your relationships to a new depth and level of honesty. This kind of listening can open up new possibilities for thinking, feeling, and behaving. ■

**You're One Click Away...**
*from finding more strategies online for full listening.*

# Choosing to SPEAK

We all have this problem. Sometimes we feel wonderful or rotten or sad or scared, and we want to express it. Emotions, though, can get in the way of the message. And although you can send almost any message through tears, laughter, fist pounding, or hugging, sometimes words are better. Begin with a sincere intention to reach common ground with your listener. Then experiment with the suggestions that follow.

**Replace "you" messages with "I" messages.** It can be difficult to disagree with someone without the person becoming angry or your becoming upset. When conflict occurs, we often make statements about the other person, or "you" messages:

"You are rude."
"You make me mad."
"You must be crazy."
"You don't love me anymore."

This kind of communication results in defensiveness. The responses might be similar to these:

"I am not rude."
"I don't care."
"No, *you* are crazy."
"No, *you* don't love *me!*"

"You" messages are hard to listen to. They label, judge, blame, and assume things that may or may not be true. They demand rebuttal. Even praise can sometimes be an ineffective "you" message. "You" messages don't work.

Psychologist Thomas Gordon suggests that when communication is emotionally charged, consider limiting your statements to descriptions about yourself.[1] Replace "you" messages with "I" messages:

"You are rude" might become "I feel upset."
"You make me mad" could be "I feel angry."
"You must be crazy" can be "I don't understand."
"You don't love me anymore" could become "I'm afraid we're drifting apart."

Suppose a friend asks you to pick him up at the airport. You drive 20 miles and wait for the plane. No friend. You decide your friend missed her plane, so you wait 3 hours for the next flight. No friend. Perplexed and worried, you drive home. The next day, you see your friend downtown.

"What happened?" you ask.
"Oh, I caught an earlier flight."
"You are a rude person," you reply.

Look for and talk about the facts—the observable behavior. Everyone will agree that your friend asked you to pick her up, that she did take an earlier flight, and that you did not receive a call from her. But the idea that she is rude is not a fact—it's a judgment.

She might go on to say, "I called your home, and no one answered. My mom had a stroke and was rushed to Valley View. I caught the earliest flight I could get." Your judgment no longer fits.

When you saw your friend, you might have said, "I waited and waited at the airport. I was worried about you. I didn't get a call. I feel angry and hurt. I don't want to waste my time. Next time, you can call me when your flight arrives, and I'll be happy to pick you up."

"I" messages don't judge, blame, criticize, or insult. They don't invite the other person to counterattack with more of the same. "I" messages are also more accurate. They report our own thoughts and feelings.

At first, "I" messages might feel uncomfortable or seem forced. That's okay. Use the five ways to say "I" explained on page 182.

**Remember that questions are not always questions.** You've heard these "questions" before. A parent asks, "Don't you want to look nice?" Translation: "I wish you'd cut your hair, lose the blue jeans, and put on a tie." Or how about this question from a spouse: "Honey, wouldn't you love to go to an exciting hockey game tonight?" Translation: "I've already bought tickets."

We use questions that aren't questions to sneak our opinions and requests into conversations. "Doesn't it upset you?" means "It upsets me," and "Shouldn't we hang the picture over here?" means "I want to hang the picture over here."

Communication improves when we say, "I'm upset" and "Let's hang the picture over here." ■

**You're One Click Away...**
*from finding more strategies online for speaking your mind.*

## Master Students
## IN ACTION

*Dealing with conflict online is totally different from dealing with it in person. I find that even if something is "resolved" online, it will probably come up in person anyway, so why not just talk face-to-face?*

—Cat Salerno, University of New Hampshire

Cat Salerno

8

# FIVE WAYS to say "I"

An "I" message can include any or all of the following five elements. Be careful when including the last two elements, though, because they can contain hidden judgments or threats.

**Observations.** Describe the facts—the indisputable, observable realities. Talk about what you—or anyone else—can see, hear, smell, taste, or touch. Avoid judgments, interpretations, or opinions. Instead of saying, "You're a slob," say, "Last night's lasagna pan was still on the stove this morning."

**Feelings.** Describe your own feelings. It is easier to listen to "I feel frustrated" than to "You never help me." Stating how you feel about another's actions can be valuable feedback for that person.

**Wants.** You are far more likely to get what you want if you say what you want. If someone doesn't know what you want, she doesn't have a chance to help you get it. Ask clearly. Avoid demanding or using the word *need*. Most people like to feel helpful, not obligated. Instead of saying, "Do the dishes when it's your turn, or else!" say, "I want to divide the housework fairly."

**Thoughts.** Communicate your thoughts, and use caution. Beginning your statement with the word "I" doesn't automatically make it an "I" message. "I think you are a slob" is a "you" judgment in disguise. Instead, say, "I'd have more time to study if I didn't have to clean up so often."

**Intentions.** The last part of an "I" message is a statement about what you intend to do. Have a plan that doesn't depend on the other person. For example, instead of "From now on, we're going to split the dishwashing evenly," you could say, "I intend to do my share of the housework and leave the rest."

 # EXERCISE 16

## Write an "I" message

First, pick something about school that irritates you. Then pretend that you are talking to a person who is associated with this irritation. In the space below, write down what you would say to this person as a "you" message.

_____

_____

_____

_____

_____

_____

_____

_____

Now write the same complaint as an "I" message. Include at least the first three elements suggested in "Five Ways to Say 'I.'"

_____

_____

_____

_____

_____

_____

_____

_____

# Developing
# EMOTIONAL INTELLIGENCE

In his book *Working with Emotional Intelligence*, Daniel Goleman defines emotional intelligence as a cluster of traits: self-awareness, self-regulation, motivation, empathy, and skill in relationships.[2]

Your emotional intelligence skills will serve you in school and in the workplace, especially when you collaborate on project teams. You can deepen your skills with the following strategies.

## RECOGNIZE THREE ELEMENTS OF EMOTION

Even the strongest emotion consists of just three elements: physical sensations, thoughts, and urges to take action. Usually they happen so fast that you can barely distinguish them. Separating them out is a first step toward emotional intelligence.

Imagine that you suddenly perceive a threat—such as a supervisor who's screaming at you. Immediately your heart starts beating in double-time and your stomach muscles clench (physical sensations). Then thoughts race through your head: *This is a disaster. She hates me. And everyone's watching.* Finally, you feel like doing something, such as staring at her, yelling back, or running away.

## NAME YOUR EMOTIONS

Naming your emotions is a first step to going beyond the "fight or flight" reaction to any emotion. Naming gives you power. The second that you attach a word to an emotion, you start to gain perspective. People with emotional intelligence have a rich vocabulary to describe a wide range of emotions. For examples, do an Internet search with the key words *feeling list*. Read through the lists you find for examples of ways that you can name your feelings in the future.

## ACCEPT YOUR EMOTIONS

Another step toward emotional intelligence is accepting your emotions—*all* of them. This can be challenging if you've been taught that some emotions are "good," whereas others are "bad." Experiment with another viewpoint: You do not choose your emotional reactions. However, you can choose what you *do* in response to any emotion.

## EXPRESS YOUR EMOTIONS

One possible response to any emotion is expressing it. The key is to speak without blaming others for the way you feel. The basic tool for doing so is using "I" messages, as described on page 182.

## RESPOND RATHER THAN REACT

The heart of emotional intelligence is moving from mindless reaction to mindful action. See whether you can introduce an intentional gap between sensations and thoughts on the one hand and your next action on the other hand. To do this more often, use Discovery Statements. In your journal, write about situations in daily life that trigger strong emotions. Describe these events—and your usual responses to them—in detail. Follow up with Intention Statements. After seeing patterns in your emotions, you can consciously choose to behave in new ways. Instead of yelling back at the angry supervisor, for example, make it your intention to simply remain silent and breathe deeply until he finishes. Then say, "I'll wait to respond until we've both had a chance to cool down."

## MAKE DECISIONS WITH EMOTIONAL INTELLIGENCE

When considering a possible choice, ask yourself, "How am I likely to feel if I do this? And how will other people feel?" You can use "gut feelings" to tell when an action might violate your values or hurt someone.

## TRANSLATE DECISIONS INTO EFFECTIVE ACTION

Emotional intelligence will help you succeed on project teams in the workplace. Two questions recommended by consultant David Allen can lead to team meetings that actually produce results.[3]

First: "What's the successful outcome?" If no one on your team can visualize a successful outcome for a meeting, then save everybody some frustration. Ask that the meeting be postponed until your team can create a clear agenda.

Second: "What's the next action to make it happen?" Too many meetings end with no clear agreement about the next actions to be taken, who will take them, and by what date. To get clarity and accountability, ask each team member to state what he or she will do before the next meeting.

Think of emotions as energy. Anger, sadness, and fear send currents of sensation through your whole body. Ask yourself how you can channel that energy into constructive action. ■

**You're One Click Away...**
*from learning more ways online to develop emotional intelligence.*

© 2015 Cengage Learning. All Rights Reserved. May not be scanned, copied or duplicated, or posted to a publicly accessible website, in whole or in part.

8

# MANAGING CONFLICT

Conflict management is one of the most practical skills you'll ever learn. Here are strategies that can help.

**Back up to common ground.** As a first step in managing conflict, back up to common ground. List all of the points on which you are *not* in conflict: "I know that we disagree about how much to spend on a new car, but we do agree that the old one needs to be replaced." Often, such comments put the problem in perspective and pave the way for a solution.

**State the problem.** Using "I" messages, as explained earlier in this chapter, state the problem. Tell people what you observe, feel, think, want, and intend to do. Allow the other people in a particular conflict to do the same.

Each person might have a different perception of the problem. That's fine. Let the conflict come into clear focus. It's hard to fix something unless people agree on what's broken.

Remember that the way you state the problem largely determines the solution. Defining the problem in a new way can open up a world of possibilities. For example, "I need a new roommate" is a problem statement that dictates one solution. "We could use some agreements about who cleans the apartment" opens up more options, such as resolving a conflict about who will wash the dishes tonight.

**State all points of view.** If you want to defuse tension or defensiveness, set aside your opinions for a moment. Take the time to understand the other points of view. Sum up those viewpoints in words that the other parties can accept. When people feel that they've been heard, they're often more willing to listen.

**Ask for complete communication.** In times of conflict, we often say one thing and mean another. So before responding to what the other person says, use active listening. Check to see whether you have correctly received that person's message by saying, "What I'm hearing you say is . . . Did I get it correctly?"

**Focus on solutions.** After stating the problem, dream up as many solutions as you can. Be outrageous. Don't hold back. Quantity—not quality—is the key. If you get stuck, restate the problem and continue brainstorming.

Next, evaluate the solutions you brainstormed. Discard the unacceptable ones. Talk about which solutions will work and how difficult they will be to implement. You might hit upon a totally new solution.

**Focus on the future.** Instead of rehashing the past, talk about new possibilities. Think about what you can do to prevent problems in the future. State how you intend to change, and ask others for their contributions to the solution.

**Commit to the relationship.** The thorniest conflicts usually arise between people who genuinely care for each other. Begin by affirming your commitment to the other person: "I care about you, and I want this relationship to last. So I'm willing to do whatever it takes to resolve this problem." Also ask the other person for a similar commitment.

**Allow strong feelings.** Permitting conflict can also mean permitting emotion. Being upset is all right. Feeling angry is often appropriate.

Crying is okay. Allowing other people to see the strength of our feelings can help resolve the conflict. This suggestion can be especially useful during times when differences are so extreme that reaching common ground seems impossible.

Expressing the full range of your feelings can transform the conflict. Often what's on the far side of anger is love. When we express and release resentment, we might discover genuine compassion in its place.

**Notice your need to be "right."** Some people approach conflict as a situation where only one person wins. That person has the "right" point of view. Everyone else loses.

When this happens, step back. See whether you can approach the situation in a neutral way. Define the conflict as a problem to be solved, not as a contest to be won. Explore the possibility that you might be mistaken. There might be more than one acceptable solution. The other person might simply have a different learning style than yours. Let go of being "right," and aim for being effective at resolving conflict instead.

Sometimes this means apologizing. Conflict sometimes arises from our own errors. Others might move quickly to end the conflict when we acknowledge this fact and ask for forgiveness.

**Slow down the communication.** In times of great conflict, people often talk all at once. Words fly like speeding bullets, and no one listens. Chances for resolving the conflict take a nosedive.

When everyone is talking at once, choose either to listen or to talk—not both at the same time. Just send your message. Or just receive the other person's message. Usually, this technique slows down the pace and allows everyone to become more levelheaded.

To slow down the communication even more, take a break. Depending on the level of conflict, this might mean anything from a few minutes to a few days.

A related suggestion is to do something nonthreatening together. Share an activity with the others involved that's not a source of conflict.

**Allow for cultural differences.** People respond to conflict in different ways, depending on their cultural background. Some stand close, speak loudly, and make direct eye contact. Other people avert their eyes, mute their voices, and increase physical distance.

When it seems to you that other people are sidestepping or escalating a conflict, consider whether your reaction is based on cultural bias.

**Agree to disagree.** Sometimes we say all we have to say on an issue. We do all of the problem solving we can do. We get all points of view across. And the conflict still remains, staring us right in the face.

What's left is to recognize that honest disagreement is a fact of life. We can peacefully coexist with other people—and respect them—even though we don't agree on fundamental issues. Conflict can be accepted even when it is not resolved.

**Take on leadership roles.** There's a useful motto for leaders: "Be the change you want to see." If you want the people around you to demonstrate skill in speaking, listening, and resolving conflict, then begin by modeling these qualities yourself.

No one is born knowing how to lead. We acquire the skills over time. Begin now, while you are in higher education. Campuses offer continual opportunities to gain leadership skills. Volunteer for clubs, organizations, and student government. Look for opportunities to tutor or to become a peer advisor or mentor. No matter what you do, take on big projects—those that are worthy of your time and talents.

These projects will put you in direct contact with human diversity. Your next boss or coworker could be a person whose life experiences and views of the world differ radically from yours. Use this fact as an opportunity to take the ideas in this article and put them into practice. ■

**You're One Click Away...**
*from discovering more ways online to manage conflict.*

Pete Saloutos/Shutterstock.com

# Three ways to say no . . .
## RESPECTFULLY

Students in higher education tend to have many commitments. Saying no helps you to prevent an overloaded schedule that compromises your health and grade point average. You can use three strategies to say no in a respectful way—gracefully.

### Think critically about your assumptions.
An inability to say no can spring from the assumption that you'll lose friends if you state what you really want. But consider this: If you cannot say no, then you are not in charge of your time. You've given that right to whoever wants to interrupt you. This is not a friendship based on equality. True friends will respect your wishes.

### Plan your refusal.
You might find it easier to say no when you don't have to grasp for words. Choose some key words and phrases in advance—for example, "Thanks for asking. I have a huge test tomorrow and want to study rather than party."

### Avoid apologies or qualifiers.
People give away their power when they couch their no's in phrases such as "I'm sorry, but I just don't know whether I want to," or "Would you get upset if I said no?" You don't have to apologize for being in charge of your life. It's okay to say no.

8

**You're One Click Away...**
*from discovering more online about the power of saying no.*

# Communicating
# across cultures

Techniques for communicating across cultures are valuable. And what gives them power is a sincere desire and commitment to create understanding. If you truly value cultural diversity, then you can discover ways to build bridges between people. Use the following suggestions and invent more of your own.

**Start with self-discovery.** One step to developing diversity skills is to learn about yourself and understand the lenses through which you see the world. One way to do this is to intentionally switch lenses—that is, to consciously perceive familiar events in a new way.

For example, think of a situation in your life that involved an emotionally charged conflict among several people. Now mentally put yourself inside the skin of another person in that conflict. Ask yourself, "How would I view this situation if I were that person?"

You can also learn by asking, "What if I were a person of the opposite gender? Or if I were member of a different racial or ethnic group? Or if I were older or younger?" Do this exercise consistently, and you'll discover that we live in a world of multiple realities. There are many different ways to interpret any event—and just as many ways to respond, given our individual differences.

**Look for differences between individualist and collectivist cultures.** Individualist cultures flourish in the United States, Canada, and Western Europe. If your family has deep roots in one of these areas, you were probably raised to value personal fulfillment and personal success. You received recognition or rewards when you stood out from your peers by earning the highest grades in your class, scoring the most points during a basketball season, or demonstrating another form of individual achievement.

In contrast, collectivist cultures value cooperation over competition. Group progress is more important than individual success. Credit for an achievement is widely shared. If you were raised in such a culture, you probably place a high value on your family and were taught to respect your elders. Collectivist cultures dominate Asia, Africa, and Latin America.

In short, individualist cultures often emphasize "I." Collectivist cultures tend to emphasize "we." Forgetting about the differences between them can strain a friendship or wreck an international business deal.

If you were raised in an individualist culture:

- *Remember that someone from a collectivist culture may place a high value on "saving face."* This idea involves more than simply avoiding embarrassment. This person may *not* want to be singled out from other members of a group, even for a positive achievement. If you have a direct request for this person or want to share something that could be taken as a personal criticism, save it for a private conversation.

- *Respect titles and last names.* Although Americans often like to use first names immediately after meeting someone, in some cultures this practice is acceptable only among family members. Especially in work settings, use last names and job titles during your first meetings. Allow time for informal relationships to develop.

- *Put messages in context.* For members of collectivist cultures, words convey only part of an intended message. Notice gestures and other nonverbal communication as well.

If you were raised in a collectivist culture, you can creatively "reverse" the preceding list. Keep in mind that direct questions from an American student or coworker are meant not to offend, but only to clarify, an idea. Don't be surprised if you are called by a nickname, if no one asks about your family, or if you are rewarded for a personal achievement. In social situations, remember that indirect cues might not get another person's attention. Practice asking clearly and directly for what you want.

**Look for common ground.** Students in higher education often find that they worry about many of the same things—including tuition bills, the quality of dormitory food, and the shortage of on-campus parking spaces. More important, our fundamental goals as human beings—such as health, physical safety, and economic security—cross culture lines.

**Speak and listen with cultural sensitivity.** After first speaking with someone from another culture, don't assume that you've been understood or that you fully understand the other person. The same action can have different meanings at different times, even for members of the same culture. Check it out. Verify what you think you have heard. Listen to see whether what you spoke is what the other person received.

If you're speaking with someone who doesn't understand English well, keep the following ideas in mind:

- Speak slowly, distinctly, and patiently.
- To clarify your statement, don't repeat individual words over and over again. Restate your entire message with simple, direct language and short sentences.
- Avoid slang and figures of speech.
- Use gestures to accompany your words.
- English courses for nonnative speakers often emphasize written English, so write down what you're saying. Print your message in capital letters.
- Stay calm, and avoid sending nonverbal messages that you're frustrated.

If you're unsure about how well you're communicating, ask questions: "I don't know how to make this idea clear to you. How might I communicate better?" "When you look away from me during our conversation, I feel uneasy. Is there something else we need to talk about?" "When you don't ask questions, I wonder whether I am being clear. Do you want any more explanation?" Questions such as these can get cultural differences out in the open in a constructive way.

**Look for individuals, not group representatives.** Sometimes the way we speak glosses over differences among individuals and reinforces stereotypes. For example, a student worried about her grade in math expresses concern over "all those Asian students who are skewing the class curve." Or a white music major assumes that her black classmate knows a lot about jazz or hip-hop music. We can avoid such errors by seeing people as individuals—not spokespersons for an entire group.

**Find a translator, mediator, or model.** People who move with ease in two or more cultures can help us greatly. Diane de Anda, a professor at the University of California, Los Angeles, speaks of three kinds of people who can communicate across cultures. She calls them *translators, mediators,* and *models.*[4]

A *translator* is someone who is truly bicultural—a person who relates naturally to both people in a mainstream culture and people from a contrasting culture. This person can share her own experiences in overcoming discrimination, learning another language or dialect, and coping with stress.

*Mediators* are people who belong to the dominant or mainstream culture. Unlike translators, they might not be bicultural. However, mediators value diversity and are committed to cultural understanding. Often they are teachers, counselors, tutors, mentors, or social workers.

*Models* are members of a culture who are positive examples. Models include students from any racial or cultural group who participate in class and demonstrate effective study habits. Models can also include entertainers, athletes, and community leaders.

Your school might have people who serve these functions, even if they're not labeled translators, mediators, or models. Some schools have mentor or "bridge" programs that pair new students with teachers of the same race or culture. Ask your student counseling service about such programs.

**Develop support systems.** Many students find that their social adjustment affects their academic performance. Students with strong support systems—such as families, friends, churches, self-help groups, and mentors—are using a powerful strategy for success in school. As an exercise, list the support systems that you rely on right now. Also list new support systems you could develop.

Support systems can help you bridge culture gaps. With a strong base of support in your own group, you can feel more confident in meeting people outside that group.

**Be willing to accept feedback.** Members of another culture might let you know that some of your words or actions had a meaning other than what you intended. For example, perhaps a comment that seems harmless to you is offensive to them. And they may tell you directly about it.

Avoid responding to such feedback with comments such as "Don't get me wrong," "You're taking this way too seriously," or "You're too sensitive." Instead, listen without resistance. Open yourself to what others have to say. Remember to distinguish between the *intention* of your behavior and its actual *impact* on other people. Then take the feedback you receive and ask yourself how you can use it to communicate more effectively in the future.

You can also interpret such feedback positively—a sign that others believe you can change and that they see the possibility of a better relationship with you.

If you are new at responding to diversity, expect to make some mistakes along the way. As long as you approach people in a spirit of tolerance, your words and actions can always be changed.

- - - - - - - - - - - - - - - - - - - - - - - - - - - - - - -

**In social situations, remember that indirect cues might not get another person's attention. Practice asking clearly and directly for what you want.**

8

- - - - - - - - - - - - - - - - - - - - - - - - - - - - - - -

**Speak up against discrimination.** You might find yourself in the presence of someone who tells a racist joke, makes a homophobic comment, or utters an ethnic slur. When this happens, you have a right to state what you observe, share what you think, and communicate how you feel. Depending on the circumstance, you might say:

- "That's a stereotype, and we don't have to fall for it."
- "Other people are going to take offense at that. Let's tell jokes that don't put people down."
- "I realize that you don't mean to offend anybody, but I feel hurt and angry by what you just said."
- "I know that an African American person told you that story, but I still think it's racist and creates an atmosphere that I don't want to be in."

This kind of speaking may be the most difficult communicating you ever do. However, if you *don't* do it, you give the impression that you agree with biased speech.

In response to your candid comments, many people will apologize and express their willingness to change. Even if they don't, you can still know that you practiced integrity by aligning your words with your values.

**Change the institution.** None of us lives in isolation. We all live in systems, and these systems do not always tolerate diversity. As a student, you might see people of color ignored in class. You might see people of a certain ethnic group passed over in job hiring or underrepresented in school organizations. And you might see gay and lesbian students ridiculed or even threatened with violence. One way to stop these actions is to point them out.

Federal civil rights laws, as well as the written policies of most schools, ban racial and ethnic discrimination. If your school receives federal aid, it must set up procedures that protect students against such discrimination.

When it comes to ending discrimination, you are in an environment where you can make a difference. Express your viewpoint. This is training for citizenship in a multicultural world. ■

**You're One Click Away...**
*from gaining more strategies online for building relationships across cultures.*

# Strategies for
# NONSEXIST COMMUNICATION

Following are tools you can use to speak and write in ways that are gender fair—without twisting yourself into verbal knots.

## Use gender-neutral terms.
Instead of writing *policeman* or *chairman*, for example, use *police officer* or *chairperson*. In many cases there's no need to identify the gender or marital status of a person. This allows us to dispose of expressions such as *female driver* and *lady doctor*.

## Use examples that include both men and women.
Good writing thrives on examples and illustrations. As you search for details to support the main points in your paper, include the stories and accomplishments of women as well as men.

## Alternate pronoun gender.
In an attempt to be gender fair, some writers make a point of mentioning both sexes whenever they refer to gender. Another method is to alternate the gender of pronouns throughout your writing. Still another option is to alternate male and female pronouns—the strategy used in this book. This allows you to avoid using awkward wording such as "He/she should open his/her book."

## Switch to plural.
Because plural pronouns in English are not gender specific, a sentence such as *The writer has many tools at her disposal* becomes *Writers have many tools at their disposal.*

© 2015 Cengage Learning. All Rights Reserved. May not be scanned, copied or duplicated, or posted to a publicly accessible website, in whole or in part.

Strategies for

Effective writing is essential to your success. Papers, presentations, essay tests, e-mail, social networking sites—and even the occasional text message—call for your ability to communicate ideas with force and clarity.

# EFFECTIVE WRITING

**Schedule and list writing tasks.** You can divide the ultimate goal—a finished paper—into smaller steps that you can tackle right away. Estimate how long it will take to complete each step. Start with the date your paper is due and work backward to the present. Say that the due date is December 1, and you have about 3 months to write the paper. To give yourself a cushion, schedule November 20 as your targeted completion date. Plan what you want to get done by November 1, and then list what you want to get done by October 1.

**Narrow your topic.** The most common pitfall is selecting a topic that's too broad. "Harriet Tubman" is not a useful topic for your American history paper because it's too broad. Covering that topic would take hundreds of pages. Instead, consider "Harriet Tubman's activities as a Union spy during the Civil War." Your topic statement can function as a working title.

**Write a thesis statement.** Clarify what you want to say by summarizing it in one concise sentence. This sentence, called a *thesis statement,* refines your working title. It also helps in making a preliminary outline.

You might write a thesis statement such as "Harriet Tubman's activities with the Underground Railroad led to a relationship with the Union army during the Civil War." A thesis statement that's clear and to the point can make your paper easier to write. Remember, you can always rewrite your thesis statement as you learn more about your topic.

A thesis statement is different from a topic. Like newspaper headlines, a thesis statement makes an assertion or describes an action. It is expressed in a complete sentence, including a verb. "Diversity" is a topic. "Cultural diversity is valuable" is a thesis statement.

**Consider your purpose.** Effective writing flows from a purpose. Discuss the purpose of your assignment with your instructor. Also think about how you'd like your reader or listener to respond after considering your ideas. Do you want your audience to think differently, to feel differently, or to take a certain action?

How you answer these questions greatly affects your writing strategy. If you want someone to think differently, make your writing clear and logical. Support your assertions with evidence. If you want someone to feel differently, consider crafting a story. Write about a character your audience can empathize with, and tell how that character resolves a problem that the audience can relate to. And if your purpose is to move the reader into action, explain exactly what steps to take, and offer solid benefits for doing so.

To clarify your purpose, state it in one sentence. For example, "I will define the term *success* in such a clear and convincing way that I win a scholarship from the publisher of this textbook."

**Do research.** Research happens in two phases. First, you gain an overview of the subject. Discover the structure of your topic—its major divisions and branches. Say that you want to persuade the reader to vote for a certain candidate. You must first learn enough about this person to summarize his background and state his stands on key issues.

During the second phase, you uncover specific facts about your topic and take detailed notes. For suggested strategies, see Chapter 4: Reading and Chapter 5: Notes.

**Outline.** An outline is a kind of map. When you follow a map, you avoid getting lost. Likewise, an outline keeps you from wandering off the topic.

To start an outline, gather a stack of 3 × 5 cards. Brainstorm ideas you want to include in your paper. Write one phrase or sentence per card. Then experiment with the cards. Group them into separate stacks, each stack representing one major category. After that, arrange the stacks in order. Finally, arrange the cards within each stack in a logical order. Rearrange them until you discover an organization that you like. If you write on a computer, consider using the outlining feature of your word-processing software.

8

**Gather your notes and outline.** If you've planned your writing project and completed your research, you've already done much of the hard work. Now you can relax into writing your first draft. To create your draft, gather your notes and arrange them to follow your outline. Then write about the ideas in your notes. Write in paragraphs, with one idea per paragraph. If you have organized your notes logically, related facts will appear close to one another.

**Plan to revise a paper two or three times.** Make a clean copy of each revision, and then let the last revised draft sit for at least 3 or 4 days.

During each revision, look for the following:

- A clear thesis statement

- Sentences that introduce your topic, guide the reader through the major sections of your paper, and summarize your conclusions

- Details—such as quotations, examples, and statistics—that support your conclusions.

- Lean sentences that have been purged of needless words

- Plenty of action verbs and concrete, specific nouns

Finally, look over your paper with an eye for spelling and grammar mistakes. If you're writing with software that checks for such errors, take advantage of this feature. Also keep in mind that even the best software will miss some mistakes. Computers still cannot replace a skilled human proofreader.

When you're through proofreading, take a minute to savor the result. You've just witnessed something of a miracle—the mind attaining clarity and resolution. That's the *aha!* in writing. ■

 **You're One Click Away...** *from finding more paths online to effective writing.*

# ACADEMIC INTEGRITY:
## Avoid plagiarism

Using another person's words, images, or other original creations without giving proper credit is called *plagiarism*. Plagiarism amounts to taking someone else's work and presenting it as your own—the equivalent of cheating on a test.

To avoid plagiarism, ask an instructor where you can find your school's written policy on this issue. Also review the following suggestions whenever you write.

### Know the perils of "paper mills." A
quick Web search will uncover hundreds of online businesses that sell term papers, essays, and book reports. These businesses are often called "paper mills." Some of them offer to customize their products for an additional fee. Even so, these services are based on plagiarism.

### Don't recycle papers. Also remember that
plagiarism includes turning in a paper—or portions of a paper—that you have already written for another class. If you want to draw on prior research, talk to your instructor first.

### Identify direct quotes. If you use a direct
quote from another writer or speaker, put that person's words in quotation marks. If you do research online, you might find yourself copying words or images from a Web page and pasting them directly into your notes. *This is the same as taking direct quotes from your source.* To avoid plagiarism, identify such passages in an obvious way. Besides enclosing them in quotation marks, you could format them in a different font or color.

### Paraphrase carefully. Instead of using a direct quote, you might choose to paraphrase an author's words. Paraphrasing means restating the original passage in your own words, usually making it shorter and simpler. Students who copy a passage word for word and then just rearrange or delete a few phrases are running a serious risk of plagiarism.

### Summarize carefully. For some of your
notes, you may simply want to summarize your source in a few sentences or paragraphs. Be sure to write the summary in your own words.

### List your sources. Remember to list a source
for any material that you quote, paraphrase, or summarize. Your list of sources will appear as footnotes or endnotes in your paper. Ask your instructor about which format to use.

### Identify distinctive terms and
### phrases. Some ideas are closely identified with
their individual creators. Students who present such ideas without mentioning the individual are plagiarizing. This is true even if they do not copy words, sentence structure, or overall organization of ideas.

### Submit only your own work. Turning in
materials that have been written or revised by someone else puts your education at risk.

 **You're One Click Away...** *from finding examples online of the suggestions in this article.*

Some people tune out during a speech. Just think of all the times you have listened to instructors, lecturers, and politicians. Remember all the wonderful daydreams you had during their speeches. The way you plan and present your speech can determine the number of audience members who will stay with you until the end.

James Steidl/Shutterstock.com

# Strategies for PUBLIC SPEAKING

**Start from your passions.** If your instructor allows you to choose the topic of presentation, then choose one that you find interesting. Imagine that the first words in your presentation will be: "I'm here to talk to you because I feel passionately about . . ." How would you complete the sentence? Turn your answer into your main topic.

**Analyze your audience.** Remember that audiences want to know that your presentation relates to their needs and desires. To convince people that you have something worthwhile to say, think of your main topic or point. Then see whether you can complete this sentence: *I'm telling you this because . . .*

**Organize your presentation.** List three to five questions that your audience members are likely to ask about your topic. Put those questions in logical order. Organize your presentation so that it directly answers those questions.

Aim for a lean presentation—enough words to make your point but not so many as to make your audience restless. Leave your listeners wanting more. When you speak, be brief and then be seated.

Speeches are usually organized in three main parts: the introduction, the main body, and the conclusion.

**Write the introduction.** Rambling speeches with no clear point or organization put audiences to sleep. Solve this problem with your introduction. The following introduction, for example, reveals the thesis and exactly what's coming. It reveals that the speech will have three distinct parts, each in logical order:

> *Dog fighting is a cruel sport. I intend to describe exactly what happens to the animals, tell you who is doing this, and show you how you can stop this inhumane practice.*

Whenever possible, talk about things that hold your interest. Include your personal experiences and start with a bang. Consider this introduction to a speech on the subject of world hunger:

> *I'm very honored to be here with you today. I intend to talk about malnutrition and starvation. First, I want to outline the extent of these problems, then I will discuss some basic assumptions concerning world hunger, and finally I will propose some solutions.*

You can almost hear the snores from the audience. Following is a rewrite:

> *More people have died from hunger in the past 5 years than have been killed in all of the wars, revolutions, and murders in the past 150 years. Yet there is enough food to go around. I'm honored to be here with you today to discuss solutions to this problem.*

8

**Write the main body.**  The main body of your speech is the content, which accounts for 70 to 90 percent of most speeches. In the main body, you develop your ideas in much the same way that you develop a written paper. If you raised questions in your introduction, be sure to directly answer them.

Transitions are especially important. Give your audience a signal when you change points. Do so by using meaningful pauses and verbal emphasis as well as transitional phrases: "On the other hand, until the public realizes what is happening to children in these countries . . ." or "The second reason hunger persists is . . ."

In long speeches, recap from time to time. Also preview what's to come. Hold your audience's attention by using facts, descriptions, expert opinions, and statistics.

**Write the conclusion.**  At the end of the speech, summarize your points and draw your conclusion. You started with a bang; now finish with drama. The first and last parts of a speech are the most important. Make it clear to your audience when you've reached the end. Avoid endings such as "This is the end of my speech." A simple standby is "So in conclusion, I want to reiterate three points: First, . . ." When you are finished, stop talking.

**Create speaking notes.**  Some professional speakers recommend writing out your speech in full, and then putting key words or main points on a few 3 × 5 cards. Number the cards so that if you drop them, you can quickly put them in order again. As you finish the information on each card, move it to the back of the pile. Write information clearly and in letters large enough to be seen from a distance.

The disadvantage of the 3 × 5 card system is that it involves card shuffling. Some speakers prefer to use standard outlined notes. Another option is mind mapping. Even an hour-long speech can be mapped on one sheet of paper. You can also use memory techniques to memorize the outline of your speech.

**Create supporting visuals.**  Presentations often include visuals such as PowerPoint slides and posters. With PowerPoint, you can also add video clips from your computer or cell phone. These visuals can reinforce your main points and help your audience understand how your presentation is organized.

Use visuals to *complement* rather than *replace* your speaking. If you use too many visuals—or visuals that are too complex—your audience might focus on them and forget about you.

**Overcome fear of public speaking.**  You may not be able to eliminate fear of public speaking entirely, but you can take steps to reduce and manage it.

First, prepare thoroughly. Research your topic thoroughly. Knowing your topic inside and out can create a baseline of confidence. To make a strong start, memorize the first four sentences that you plan to deliver, and practice them many times. Delivering them flawlessly when you're in front of an audience can build your confidence for the rest of your speech.

Second, accept any physical sensations associated with stage fright: dry mouth, a pounding heart, sweaty hands, muscle jitters, shortness of breath, and a shaky voice. When you fully accept sensations, they start to lose power.

**Practice your presentation.**  The key to successful public speaking is practice. Do this with your "speaker's voice." Your voice sounds different when you talk loudly, and this fact can be unnerving. Get used to it early on. If possible, practice in the room in which you will deliver your speech. Keep an eye on the time to make sure that you stay within the limit.

Keep practicing. Avoid speaking word for word, as if you were reading a script. When you know your material well, you can deliver it in a natural way. Practice your presentation until you could deliver it in your sleep. Then run through it a few more times.

**Deliver your presentation.**  Before you begin, get the audience's attention. If people are still filing into the room or adjusting their seats, they're not ready to listen. When all eyes are on you, then begin.

**Project your voice.**  When you speak, talk loudly enough to be heard. Avoid leaning over your notes or the podium.

**Maintain eye contact.**  When you look at people, they become less frightening. Also, remember that it is easier for the audience to listen to someone when that person is looking at them.

**Notice your nonverbal communication.**  Be aware of what your body is telling your audience. Contrived or staged gestures will look dishonest. Be natural. If you don't know what to do with your hands, notice that. Then don't do anything with them.

**Pause when appropriate.**  Beginners sometimes feel that they have to fill every moment with the sound of their voice. Release that expectation. Give your listeners a chance to make notes and absorb what you say.

**Have fun.**  Chances are that if you lighten up and enjoy your presentation, so will your listeners.

**Make the grade in group presentations.**  When preparing group presentations, you can use three strategies for making a memorable impression. First, get organized. As soon as you get the assignment, select a group leader and exchange contact information. Find out how your presentation will be graded. Then write a to-do list that includes all of the tasks involved in completing the assignment. Distribute tasks fairly, paying attention to the strengths of individuals in your group.

Second, practice your presentation before giving it in class. Develop smooth, short transitions between individual speakers. Keep track of the time so that you stay within the guidelines for the assignment.

Finally, communicate with group members in an open and sensitive way. Contribute your ideas, and be responsive to the viewpoints of other members. When you cooperate, your group is on the way to an effective presentation. ■

**You're One Click Away...**
*from finding more strategies online
for stunning speaking.*

# PRACTICING
# critical thinking 8

Throughout this book, you've practiced the six levels of thinking described in "Becoming a critical thinker" on page 160. Doing this exercise will give you additional practice with **Level 2: Understanding**.

At this level of thinking, you comprehend information and ideas well enough to explain them in your own words. Test questions that call for understanding begin with terms such as these:

- Compare
- Contrast
- Discuss
- Estimate
- Explain
- Give an example
- Illustrate
- Infer
- Interpret
- Paraphrase
- Predict
- Summarize
- Translate

You can do this level of thinking in any of your courses. In a science class, for example, an instructor might ask you to name the various types of clouds and then **explain** the factors that cause each kind of cloud to form. In a literature class, the instructor might ask you to **summarize** the plot of a short story.

This level of thinking is especially useful when you want to clarify your intentions. In the space below, list one of your personal values or goals. Then demonstrate how well you understand it. **Give an example** of how you put the value into action. Or **explain** how you will know when you've reached the goal.

_____

_____

_____

_____

_____

_____

_____

_____

_____

_____

_____

_____

_____

_____

_____

_____

_____

8

# masterstudentprofile

# Sampson Davis

(1973– ) As a teenager growing up in Newark, New Jersey, Davis made a pact with two of his friends to "beat the street," attend college, and become a physician.

Medical school was one of the roughest periods of my life. Something unexpected was always threatening to knock me out of the game: family distractions, the results of my first state board exam, the outcome of my initial search for a residency. But through determination, discipline, and dedication, I was able to persevere.

I call them my three "D's", and I believe that they are the perfect formula for survival, no matter what you are going through.

Determination is simply fixing your mind on a desired outcome, and I believe it is the first step to a successful end in practically any situation. When I made the pact with George and Rameck at the age of 17, I was desperate to change my life. Going to college and medical school with my friends seemed the best way to make that happen.

But, of course, I had no idea of the challenges awaiting me, and many times over the years I felt like giving up. Trust me, even if you're the most dedicated person, you can get weary when setbacks halt or interfere with your progress. But determination means nothing without the discipline to go through the steps necessary to reach your goal—whether you're trying to lose weight or finish college—and the dedication to stick with it.

When I failed the state board exam, the light in the tunnel disappeared. But I just kept crawling toward my goal. I sought counseling when I needed it, and I found at least one person with whom I could share the range of emotions I was experiencing. If you're going through a difficult time and can't see your way out alone, you should consider asking for help. I know how difficult that is for most guys . . . . But reaching out to counselors I had come to trust over the years and talking to my roommate Camille helped me unload some of the weight I was carrying. Only then was I able to focus clearly on what I needed to do to change my circumstances.

I'm grateful that I took kung fu lessons as a kid, because the discipline I learned back then really helped me to stay consistent once I started meditating, working out, and studying every single day. . . .

Another important ingredient of perseverance is surrounding yourself with friends who support your endeavor. I can't tell you how much it helped me to have George and Rameck in my life to help me reach my goal. Even though things were awkward between us for a while after I failed the state boards, just knowing they were there and that they expected me to succeed motivated me.

I found motivation wherever I could. One of my college professors once told me that I didn't have what it takes to be a doctor, and I even used that to motivate me. I love being the underdog. I love it when someone expects me to fail. That, like nothing else, can ignite my three "D's."

And when success comes, I'm the one who's not surprised.

© Michael Didyoung/Retna Ltd./Corbis

**SAMPSON DAVIS . . .** is determined.

**YOU . . .** can be determined by defining goals that make a huge difference in your life.

"Sam on Perseverance," from *The Pact* by Sampson Davis, George Jenkins, and Rameck Hunt, with Liza Frazier Page. Copyright © 2002 by Three Doctors LLC. Used by permission of Riverhead Books, an imprint of Penguin Group (USA), Inc.

**You're One Click Away...**
*from learning more about Sampson Davis online at the Master Student Profiles. You can also visit the Master Student Hall of Fame to learn about other master students.*

# QUIZ

Name _____

Date _____

1. Name the six rungs on the ladder of powerful speaking from the Power Process: "Employ your word."

2. Write one example of a statement on the lowest rung of the ladder of powerful speaking—and another example of a statement on the highest rung.

3. One strategy for effective communication is to separate the roles of sending and receiving. Briefly explain how to do this.

4. According to the text, a big barrier to communication is "listening with your answer running." Briefly explain what this means.

5. You can send acknowledgments to a speaker even when you disagree with that person's viewpoint. True or false? Explain your Answer.

6. Reword the following complaint as a request: "You always interrupt when I talk!"

7. List the five parts of an "I" message (the five ways to say "I").

8. According to the text, emotions consist of:
   (a) Physical sensations        (b) Thoughts        (c) Urges to take action        (d) All of the above

9. Briefly explain the difference between individualist and collectivist cultures.

8

10. Describe at least three techniques for practicing and delivering a speech.

# 8 SKILLS Snapshot

Take a minute to reflect on your responses to the *Communicating* section of the Discovery Wheel on page 30. Reflect on the progress you've made, and clarify your intentions to develop further mastery. Complete the following sentences:

## DISCOVERY

My self-score on the *Communicating* section of the Discovery Wheel was . . .

The technique that has made the biggest difference in my skill at listening is . . .

When I feel angry with people, the way I usually express it is to . . .

When I'm effective at managing conflict, I remember to . . .

When I hear an accomplished public speaker, the skill that I would most like to acquire is . . .

## INTENTION

By the time I finish the course, I visualize giving myself a score of _____ on the *Communicating* section of the Discovery Wheel.

I'll know that I've reached a new level of mastery with my communication skills when . . .

## ACTION

To reach that level of mastery, the most important thing I can do next is to . . .

# Health

 Use this **Master Student Map** to ask yourself,

 ## WHY THIS CHAPTER MATTERS . . .

- Succeeding in higher education calls for a baseline of physical and emotional well-being.

 ## WHAT IS INCLUDED . . .

 ## HOW CAN I USE THIS CHAPTER . . .

- Maintain your physical and mental energy.
- Enhance your self-esteem.
- Make decisions about alcohol and other drugs in a way that supports your success.

 ## WHAT IF . . .

- I could meet the demands of daily life with energy and optimism to spare?

**JOURNAL ENTRY 16**
*Discovery Statement*

## Take a First Step about your health

This chapter allows you to look closely at your health. Aim to change your behavior in specific ways that make a dramatic, positive difference in your life. Start with a one-sentence First Step:

What concerns me more than anything else about my health right now is . . .

_____

_____

_____

_____

_____

_____

_____

_____

_____

_____

_____

_____

_____

_____

_____

*Note:* You can expand on your response—and keep it private—by writing it on a separate piece of paper.

© Ruslan Ivantsov/Shutterstock.com

© 2015 Cengage Learning. All Rights Reserved. May not be scanned, copied or duplicated, or posted to a publicly accessible website, in whole or in part.

# Surrender

Life can be magnificent and satisfying. It can also be devastating. Sometimes there is too much pain or confusion. Problems can be too big and too numerous. Life can bring us to our knees in a pitiful, helpless, and hopeless state. A broken relationship, a sudden diagnosis of cancer, a dependence on drugs, or a stress-filled job can leave us feeling overwhelmed—powerless.

In these troubling situations, the first thing we can do is to admit that we don't have the resources to handle the problem. No matter how hard we try and no matter what skills we bring to bear, some problems remain out of our control. When this is the case, we can tell the truth: "It's too big and too mean. I can't handle it." In that moment, we take a step toward greater health.

Desperately struggling to control a problem can easily result in the problem controlling us. Surrender is letting go of being the master in order to avoid becoming the slave.

Many traditions make note of this idea. Western religions speak of surrendering to God. Hindus say surrender to the Self. Members of Alcoholics Anonymous talk about turning their lives over to a Higher Power. Agnostics might suggest surrendering to their intellect, their intuition, or their conscience.

In any case, surrender means being receptive. Once we admit that we're at the end of our rope, we open ourselves up to help. We learn that we don't have to go it alone. We find out that other people have faced similar problems and survived. We give up our old habits of thinking and behaving as if we have to be in control of everything. We stop acting as general manager of the universe. We surrender. And that creates a space for something new in our lives.

Surrender is not "giving up." It is not a suggestion to quit and do nothing about your problems. Giving up is fatalistic and accomplishes nothing. You have many skills and resources. Use them. You can apply all of your energy to handling a situation and still surrender at the same time. You can surrender to weight gain even as you step up your exercise program. You can surrender to a toothache even as you go to the dentist. You can surrender to the past while adopting new habits for a healthy future.

Surrender includes doing whatever you can in a positive, trusting spirit. Let go, keep going, and know when a source of help lies beyond you.

**You're One Click Away...**
*from accessing Power Process Media online and finding out more about how to "surrender."*

Hannamariah/Shutterstock.com

# Wake up TO HEALTH

Some people see health as just a matter of common sense. These people might see little value in reading a health chapter. After all, they already know how to take care of themselves.

Yet *knowing* and *doing* are two different things. Health information does not always translate into healthy habits.

We expect to experience health challenges as we age. Even youth, though, is no guarantee of good health. Over the last 3 decades, obesity among young adults has tripled. Twenty-nine percent of young men smoke. And 70 percent of deaths among adults ages 18 to 29 result from unintentional injuries, accidents, homicide, and suicide.[1]

As a student, your success in school is directly tied to your health. Lack of sleep and exercise have been associated with lower grade point averages among undergraduate students. So have alcohol use, tobacco use, gambling, and chronic health conditions.[2] And any health habit that undermines your success in school can also undermine your success in later life.

On the other hand, we can adopt habits that sustain our well-being. One study found that people lengthened their lives an average of 14 years by adopting just four habits: staying tobacco-free, eating more fruits and vegetables, exercising regularly, and drinking alcohol in moderation if at all.[3]

Health also hinges on a habit of exercising some tissue that lies between your ears—the organ called your brain. One path to greater health starts not with new food or a new form of exercise, but with new ideas.

Olena Pivnenko/Shutterstock.com

Consider the power of beliefs. Some of them create barriers to higher levels of health: "Your health is programmed by your heredity." "Some people are just low on energy." "Healthy food doesn't taste very good." "Over the long run, people just don't change their habits." Be willing to test these ideas and change them when it serves you.

People often misunderstand what the word *health* means. Remember that this word is similar in origin to *whole, hale, hardy,* and even *holy*. Implied in these words are qualities that most of

us associate with healthy people: alertness, vitality, vigor. Healthy people meet the demands of daily life with energy to spare. Illness or stress might slow them down for a while, but then they bounce back. They know how to relax, create loving relationships, and find satisfaction in their work.

To open up your inquiry into health—and to open up new possibilities for your life—consider three ideas.

First, health is a continuum. On one end of that continuum is a death that comes too early. On the other end is a long life filled with satisfying work and fulfilling relationships. Many of us exist between those extremes at a point we might call average. Most of the time we're not sick. And most of the time we're not truly thriving either.

Second, health changes. Health is not a fixed state. In fact, health fluctuates from year to year, day to day, and moment to moment. Those changes can occur largely by chance. Or they can occur more often by choice, as we take conscious control of our thinking and behavior.

Third, even when faced with health challenges, we have choices. We can choose attitudes and habits that promote a higher quality of life. For example, people with diabetes can often manage the disease by exercising more and changing their diet.

*Health* is one of those rich, multilayered concepts that we can never define completely. In the end, your definition of *health* comes from your own experience. The proof lies not on these pages but in your life—in the level of health that you create, starting now.

You have choices. You can remain unaware of habits that have major consequences for your health. Or you can become aware of current habits (discovery), choose new habits (intention), and take appropriate action.

Health is a choice you make every moment, with each thought and behavior. Wake up to this possibility by experimenting with the suggestions in this chapter. ■

9

# Choose Your FUEL

Food is your primary fuel for body and mind. And even though you've been eating all your life, entering higher education is bound to change the way that you fuel yourself.

There have been hundreds of books written about nutrition. One says don't drink milk. Another says the calcium provided by milk is an essential nutrient we need daily. Although such debate seems confusing, take comfort. There is actually wide agreement about how to fuel yourself for health.

Today, federal nutrition guidelines are summarized visually as a *dinner plate.* The idea is to eat more of the foods shown in the bigger sections of the dinner plate. To see an example and build your personal food pyramid, go online to www.choosemyplate.gov.

The various food guidelines available agree on several core principles:[4]

- Emphasize fruits, vegetables, whole grains, and fat-free or low-fat milk and milk products.

- Include lean meats, poultry, fish, beans, eggs, and nuts.

- Choose foods that are low in saturated fats, trans fats, cholesterol, salt (sodium), and added sugars.

Michael Pollan, a writer for the *New York Times Magazine,* spent several years sorting out the scientific literature on nutrition.[5] He boiled the key guidelines down to seven words in three sentences:

- *Eat food.* In other words, choose whole, fresh foods over processed products with a lot of ingredients.

- *Not too much.* If you want to manage your weight, then control how much you eat. Notice portion sizes. Pass on snacks, seconds, and desserts—or indulge just occasionally.

- *Mostly plants.* Fruits, vegetables, and grains are loaded with chemicals that help to prevent disease. Plant-based foods, on the whole, are also lower in calories than foods from animals (meat and dairy products).

Finally, forget diets. *How* you eat can matter more than *what* you eat. If you want to eat less, then eat slowly. Savor each bite. Stop when you're satisfied instead of when you feel full. Use meal times as a chance to relax, reduce stress, and connect with people. ■

iStockphoto.com/james steidl

**You're One Click Away...**
*from discovering more strategies online for fueling your body.*

# Prevent and treat eating disorders

Eating disorders affect many students. These disorders involve serious disturbances in eating behavior. Examples are overeating or extreme reduction of food intake, as well as irrational concern about body shape or weight. Women are much more likely to develop these disorders than are men, though cases are on the rise among males.

*Bulimia* involves cycles of excessive eating and forced purges. A person with this disorder might gorge on a pizza, doughnuts, and ice cream and then force herself to vomit. Or she might compensate for overeating with excessive use of laxatives, enemas, or diuretics.

*Anorexia nervosa* is a potentially fatal illness marked by self-starvation. People with anorexia may practice extended fasting or eat only one kind of food for weeks at a time.

These disorders are not due to a failure of willpower. They are real illnesses in which harmful patterns of eating take on a life of their own.

Eating disorders can lead to many complications, including life-threatening heart conditions and kidney failure. Many people with eating disorders also struggle with depression, substance abuse, and anxiety. They need immediate treatment to stabilize their health. This is usually followed by continuing medical care, counseling, and medication to promote a full recovery.

If you're worried you might have an eating disorder, visit a doctor, campus health service, or local public health clinic. If you see signs of an eating disorder in someone else, express your concern with "I" messages, as explained in Chapter 8: Communicating.

For more information, contact the National Eating Disorders Association at 1-800-931-2237 or online at www.nationaleatingdisorders.org.

# Choose to EXERCISE

Our bodies need to be exercised. The world ran on muscle power back in the era when we had to hunt down a woolly mammoth every few weeks and drag it back to the cave. Now we can grab a burger at a drive-up window. Today we need to make a special effort to exercise.

Exercise promotes weight control and reduces the symptoms of depression. It also helps to prevent heart attack, diabetes, and several forms of cancer.[6] Exercise also refreshes your body and your mind. If you're stuck on a math problem or blocked on writing a paper, take an exercise break. Chances are that you'll come back with a fresh perspective and some new ideas.

If you get moving, you'll create lean muscles, a strong heart, and an alert brain. If the word *exercise* turns you off, think *physical activity* instead. Here are some things you can do:

**Stay active throughout the day.** Park a little farther from work or school. Do your heart a favor by walking some extra blocks. Take the stairs instead of riding elevators. For an extra workout, climb two stairs at a time.

An hour of daily activity is ideal, but do whatever you can. Some activity is better than none.

No matter what you do, ease into it. For example, start by walking briskly for at least 15 minutes every day. Increase that time gradually, and add a little jogging.

**Adapt to your campus environment.** Look for exercise facilities on campus. Search for classes in aerobics, swimming, volleyball, basketball, golf, tennis, and other sports. Intramural sports are another option. School can be a great place to get in shape.

**Do what you enjoy.** Stay active with aerobic activities that you enjoy. You might like martial arts, kickboxing, yoga, ballroom dance classes, stage combat classes, or mountain climbing. Check your school catalog for such courses.

**Vary your routine.** Find several activities that you like to do, and rotate them throughout the year. Your main form of activity during winter might be ballroom dancing, riding an exercise bike, or skiing. In summer, you could switch to outdoor sports. Whenever possible, choose weight-bearing activities such as walking, running, or stair climbing.

**Get active early.** Work out first thing in the morning. Then it's done for the day. Make it part of your daily routine, just like brushing your teeth.

**Exercise with other people.** Making exercise a social affair can add a fun factor and raise your level of commitment.

**Join a gym without fear.** Many health clubs welcome people who are just starting to get in shape.

**Look for gradual results.** If your goal is to lose weight, be patient. Because 1 pound equals 3,500 calories, you might feel tempted to reduce weight loss to a simple formula: *Let's see … if I burn away just 100 calories each day through exercise, I should lose 1 pound every 35 days.*

Actually, the relationship between exercise and weight loss is complex. Many factors—including individual differences in metabolism and the type of exercise you do—affect the amount of weight you actually lose.[7]

When you step on the bathroom scale, look for small changes over time rather than sudden, dramatic losses. Gradual weight loss is more healthy, anyway—and easier to sustain over the long term.

Weight loss is just one potential benefit of exercise. Choosing to exercise can lift your mood, increase your stamina, strengthen your bones, stabilize your joints, and help prevent heart disease. It can also reduce your risk of high blood pressure, diabetes, and several forms of cancer. If you do resistance training—such as weight machines or elastic-band workouts—you'll strengthen your muscles as well. For a complete fitness program, add stretching exercises to enjoy increased flexibility.[8]

*Before beginning any vigorous exercise program, consult a health care professional. This is critical if you are overweight, over age 60, in poor condition, or a heavy smoker, or if you have a history of health problems.* ■

**You're One Click Away...**
*from discovering more ways online to follow through on your exercise goals.*

9

iStockphoto.com/AlbanyPictures

# CHOOSE EMOTIONAL HEALTH

The number of students in higher education who have emotional health problems is steadily increasing.[9] According to the American College Health Association, 31 percent of college students report that they have felt so depressed that it was difficult to function. Almost half of students say that they've felt overwhelming anxiety, and 60 percent report that they've felt very lonely.[10]

Emotional health includes many factors. Your skill at managing stress and ability to build loving relationships are key. So are your capacity to meet the demands of school and work, and your beliefs about your ability to succeed. People with mental illness have thoughts, emotions, or behaviors that consistently interfere with these skills.

You can take simple and immediate steps to prevent emotional health problems—and cope with them if they do occur. Remember that strategies for managing test-related stress can help you manage *any* form of stress. (See "Let go of test anxiety" on page 150.) Here are some other suggestions to promote your emotional health.

**Take care of your body.** Your thoughts and emotions can get scrambled if you go too long feeling hungry or tired. Follow the suggestions in this chapter for eating, exercise, and sleep.

**Solve problems.** Although you can't "fix" a bad feeling in the same way that you can fix a machine, you can choose to change a situation associated with that feeling. There might be a problem that needs a solution. You can use feelings as your motivation to solve that problem.

If you feel intense sadness, anger, or fear, think about whether it is related to a specific situation in your life. Describe the problem in a Discovery Statement. Then brainstorm solutions, choose one to implement, and write an Intention Statement to describe the next action you'll take. Reducing your course load, cutting back on hours at work, getting more financial aid, delegating a task, or taking some other concrete action might solve the problem—and help you feel better.

**Stay active.** A related strategy is to do something—*anything* that's constructive, even if it's not a solution to a specific problem. For example, mop the kitchen floor. Clean out your dresser drawers. Iron your shirts. This sounds silly, but it works.

The basic principle is that you can separate emotions from actions. It is appropriate to feel miserable when you do. It's normal to cry and express your feelings. It is also possible to go to class, study, work, eat, and feel miserable at the same time. Unless you have a diagnosable problem with anxiety or depression, you can continue your normal activities until the misery passes.

Japanese psychiatrist Morita Masatake, a contemporary of Sigmund Freud, based his whole approach to treatment on this insight: We can face our emotional pain directly and still take constructive action. One of Masatake's favorite suggestions for people who felt depressed was that they tend a garden.[11]

**Focus on one task at a time.** It's easy to feel stressed if you dwell on how much you have to accomplish this year, this term, this month, or even this week. One solution is to plan using the suggestions in Chapter 2: Time and Money.

Remember that an effective plan for the day does two things. First, it clarifies what you're choosing *not* to do today. (Tasks that you plan to do in the future are listed on your calendar or to-do list.)

Second, an effective plan reduces your day to a series of concrete tasks—such as making phone calls, going to classes, running errands, or reading chapters—that you can do one at a time.

If you feel overwhelmed, just find the highest-priority task on your to-do list. Do it with total attention until it's done. Then go back to your list for the next high-priority task. Do *it* with total attention. Savor the feeling of mastery and control that comes with crossing each task off your list.

**Don't believe everything you think.** According to Albert Ellis and other cognitive psychologists, stress results not from events in our lives, but from the way we *think* about those events.[12] If we believe that people should always behave in exactly the way we expect them to, for instance, we set ourselves up for misery. The same happens if we believe that events should always turn out exactly as we want.

There are two main ways to deal with such thoughts. First, don't believe them. Dispute such thoughts and replace them with more realistic ones: *I can control my own behavior, but not the behavior of others*. And: *Some events are beyond my control*. Changing our beliefs can reduce our stress significantly.

Second, you can just release stress-producing thoughts without disputing them. Mindfulness meditation is a way to do this. While meditating, you simply notice your thoughts as they arise and pass. Instead of reacting to them, you observe them. Eventually, your stream of thinking slows down. You might enter a state of deep relaxation that also yields life-changing insights.

Many religious organizations offer meditation classes. You can also find meditation instruction through health maintenance organizations, YMCAs or YWCAs, and community education programs.

**Remember that emotional pain is not a sickness.** Emotional pain has gotten a bad name. This reputation is undeserved. There is nothing wrong with feeling bad. It's okay to feel miserable, depressed, sad, upset, angry, dejected, gloomy, or unhappy.

It might not be pleasant to feel bad, but it can be good for you. Often, bad is an appropriate way to feel. When you leave a place you love, sadness is natural. When you lose a friend or lover, misery might be in order. When someone treats you badly, it is probably appropriate to feel angry. When a loved one dies, it is necessary to grieve. The grief might appear in the form of depression, sadness, or anger.

There is nothing wrong with extreme emotional pain. If depression, sadness, or anger persists, then get help. Otherwise, allow yourself to experience these emotions. They're often appropriate.

Sometimes we allow ourselves to feel bad only if we have a good reason. For example: "Well, I feel very sad, but that is because I just found out my best friend is moving to Europe." It's all right to know the reason why you are sad. It's also fine not to know. You can feel bad for no apparent reason. The reason doesn't matter. Because you cannot directly control any feeling, simply accept it.

There's no way to predict how long emotional pain will last. The main point is that it does not last forever. There's no need to let a broken heart stop your life. Although you can find abundant

# Choose to rest

A lack of rest can decrease your immunity to illness and impair your performance in school. You still might be tempted to cut back drastically on your sleep once in a while for an all-night study session. Instead, read Chapter 2: Time and Money. Depriving yourself of sleep is a choice you can avoid.

If you have trouble falling asleep, experiment with the following suggestions:

- Exercise daily. For many people, regular exercise promotes sounder sleep. However, finish exercising several hours before you want to go to sleep.
- Avoid naps during the daytime.
- Monitor your caffeine intake, especially in the afternoon and evening.
- Avoid using alcohol to feel sleepy. Drinking alcohol late in the evening can disrupt your sleep during the night.
- Develop a sleep ritual—a regular sequence of calming activities that end your day. You might take

a warm bath and do some light reading. Turn off the TV and computer at least 1 hour before you go to bed.

- Keep your sleeping room cool.
- Keep a regular schedule for going to sleep and waking up.
- Sleep in the same place each night. When you're there, your body gets the message: "It's time to go to sleep."
- Practice relaxation techniques while lying in bed. A simple one is to count your breaths and release distracting thoughts as they arise.
- Make tomorrow's to-do list before you go to sleep so you won't lie there worrying that tomorrow you'll forget about something you need to do.
- Get up and study or do something else until you're tired.
- See a doctor if sleeplessness persists.

9

advice on the subject, just remember a simple and powerful idea: This too shall pass.

Sometimes other people—friends or family members, for example—have a hard time letting you feel bad. They might be worried that they did something wrong and want to make it better. They want you to quit feeling bad. Tell them you will—eventually. Assure them that you will feel good again, but that for right now you just want to feel bad.

**Share what you're thinking and feeling.** Revealing your inner world with a family member or friend is a powerful way to gain perspective. The simple act of describing a problem can sometimes reveal a solution or give you a fresh perspective.

**Get help.** Remember a basic guideline about *when* to seek help: whenever problems with your thinking, moods, or behavior consistently interfere with your ability to sleep, eat, go to class, work, or create positive relationships.

You can get help at the student health center on campus. This is not just a service for treating colds, allergies, and flu symptoms. Counselors expect to help students deal with adjustment to campus, changes in mood, academic problems, and drug abuse and dependence.

Students with anxiety disorders, clinical depression, bipolar disorder, and other diagnoses might get referred to a professional outside the student health center. The referral process can take time, so seek help right away. Your tuition helps to pay for these services. It's smart to use them now.

You can find resources to promote emotional health even if your campus doesn't offer counseling services. Start with a personal physician—one person who can coordinate all of your health care. (For suggestions, go to your school's health center.) A personal physician can refer you to another health professional if it seems appropriate.

These two suggestions can also work after you graduate. Promoting emotional health is a skill to use for the rest of your life.

**Remember that suicide is no solution.** While entering higher education, people typically go through major change. For some people, this involves depression and anxiety. Both are risk factors for suicide—the second leading cause of death on college campuses.[13]

Most often, suicide can be prevented. If you suspect that someone you know is considering suicide:

- *Take it seriously.* Taking suicidal comments seriously is especially important when you hear them from young adults.

- *Listen fully.* Encourage the person at risk to express thoughts and feelings appropriately. If he claims that he doesn't want to talk, be inviting, be assertive, and be persistent. Be totally committed to listening.

- *Speak powerfully.* Let the person at risk know that you care. Trying to talk someone out of suicide or minimizing problems is generally useless. Acknowledge that problems are serious and that they can be solved. Point out that suicide is a permanent solution to a temporary problem.

- *Get professional help.* Suggest that the person see a mental health professional. If she resists help, offer to schedule the appointment for her and to take her to it.

- *Remove access to firearms.* Most suicides are attempted with guns. Get rid of any guns that might be around. Also remove all drugs and razors.

- *Handle the event as an emergency.* If a situation becomes a crisis, do not leave the person alone. Call a crisis hotline, 911, or a social service agency. If necessary, take the person to the nearest hospital emergency room, clinic, or police station.

If you ever begin to think about committing suicide, seek out someone you trust. Tell this person how you feel. If necessary, make an appointment to see a counselor, and ask someone to accompany you. When you're at risk, you deserve the same compassion that you'd willingly extend to another person.

Find out more from the American Foundation for Suicide Prevention at 1-800-273-8255 or **www.afsp.org**. Another excellent resource is the It Gets Better Project at **www.itgetsbetter.org**. ∎

**You're One Click Away...**
*from finding more pathways to robust emotional health online.*

## *Master Students* **IN ACTION**

" *I start every week with my Success Triangle: (1) Prioritize what needs to be done now and what can be done by others; (2) make a schedule, and check it daily (or more often as needed); and (3) reward myself—eat right, exercise, and get more rest. When I stick to my plan, there's less stress in my life.* "

—Karen Grajeda,
Boise State University

# ASKING FOR HELP

The world responds to people who ask. If you're not consistently getting what you want in life, then consider the power of asking for help.

"Ask and you shall receive" is a gem of wisdom from many spiritual traditions. Yet acting on this simple idea can be challenging.

Some people see asking for help as a sign of weakness. Actually, it's a sign of strength. Focus on the potential rewards. When you're willing to receive and others are willing to give, resources become available. Circumstances fall into place. Dreams that once seemed too big become goals that you can actually achieve. You benefit, and so do other people.

Remember that asking for help pays someone a compliment. It means that you value what people have to offer. Many will be happy to respond. The key is asking with skill.

iStockphoto.com/RTimages

## ASK WITH CLARITY

Before asking for help, think about your request. Take time to prepare, and consider putting it in writing before you ask in person.

The way you ask has a great influence on the answers you get. For example, "I need help with money" is a big statement. People might not know how to respond. Be more specific: "Do you know any sources of financial aid that I might have missed?" Or: "My expenses exceed my income by $200 each month. I don't want to work more hours while I'm in school. How can I fill the gap?"

## ASK WITH SINCERITY

People can tell when a request comes straight from your heart. Although clarity is important, remember that you're asking for help—not making a speech. Keep it simple and direct. Just tell the truth about your current situation, what you want, and the gap between the two. It's okay to be less than perfect.

## ASK WIDELY

Consider the variety of people who can offer help. They include parents, friends, classmates, coworkers, mentors, and sponsors. People such as counselors, advisors, and librarians are *paid* to help you.

Also be willing to ask for help with tough issues in any area of life—sex, health, money, career decisions, and more. If you consistently ask for help only in one area, you limit your potential.

To get the most value from this suggestion, direct your request to an appropriate person. For example, you wouldn't ask your instructors for advice about sex. However, you can share any concern with a professional counselor.

## ASK WITH AN OPEN MIND

When you ask for help, see whether you can truly open up. If an idea seems strange or unworkable, put your objections on hold for the moment. If you feel threatened or defensive, just notice

the feeling. Then return to listening. Discomfort can be a sign that you're about to make a valuable discovery. If people only confirm what you already think and feel, you miss the chance to learn.

## ASK WITH RESPONSIBILITY

If you want people to offer help, then avoid statements such as "You know that suggestion you gave me last time? Wow, that really bombed!"

When you act on an idea and it doesn't work, the reason may have nothing to do with the other person. Perhaps you misunderstood or forgot a key point. Ask again for clarity. In any case, the choice about what to do—and the responsibility for the consequences—is still yours.

## ASK WITH AN OPENING FOR MORE IDEAS

Approaching people with a specific, limited request can work wonders. So can asking in a way that takes the conversation to a new place. You can do this with creative questions: "Do you have any other ideas for me?" "Would it help if I approached this problem from a different angle?" "Could I be asking a better question?"

## ASK AGAIN

People who make a living by selling things know the power of a repeated request. Some people habitually respond to a first request with "no." They might not get to "yes" until the second or third request.

Some cultures place a value on competition, success, and "making it on your own." In this environment, asking for help is not always valued. Sometimes people say no because they're surprised or not sure how to respond. Give them more time and another chance to come around. ∎

9

# Choose to STAY SAFE

## While schools make every effort to promote student health and safety, you can always benefit from knowing how to protect yourself.

### TAKE GENERAL PRECAUTIONS

Three simple actions can significantly increase your personal safety. One is to always lock doors when you're leaving home. If you live in a dorm, follow the policies for keeping the front doors secure. Don't let an unauthorized person walk in behind you. If you commute to school or have a car on campus, keep your car doors locked.

The second action is to avoid walking alone, especially at night. Many schools offer shuttle buses to central campus locations. Use them. As a backup, carry enough spare cash for a taxi ride.

iStockphoto.com/Sherwin McGehee

Third, be prepared for a crisis. Ask your instructors about what to do in classroom emergencies. Look for emergency phones along the campus routes that you normally walk. You can always use your cell phone to call 911 for help.

Also, be willing to make that call when you see other people in unsafe situations. For example, you might be at a party with a friend who drinks too much and collapses. In this situation, some underage students might hesitate to call for help. They fear getting charged with illegal alcohol possession. Don't make this mistake. Every minute that you delay calling 911 puts your friend at further risk.

## Observe thyself

You are an expert on your body. You are more likely to notice changes before anyone else does. Pay attention to these changes. They are often your first clue about the need for medical treatment or intervention. Watch for signs such as the following:

- Weight loss of more than 10 pounds in 10 weeks with no apparent cause
- A sore, scab, or ulcer that does not heal in 3 weeks
- A skin blemish or mole that bleeds; itches; or changes size, shape, or color
- Persistent or severe headaches
- Sudden vomiting that is not preceded by nausea
- Fainting spells

- Double vision
- Blood that is coughed up or vomited
- Black and tarry bowel movements
- Rectal bleeding
- Pink, red, or unusually cloudy urine
- Discomfort or difficulty when urinating or during sexual intercourse
- Lumps or thickening in a breast
- Vaginal bleeding between menstrual periods or after menopause

If you are experiencing any of these symptoms, get help from your doctor or campus health service—*before* a minor illness or injury leads to more-serious problems.

## PREVENT SEXUAL ASSAULT

You need to know how to prevent sexual assault while you're on campus. This problem could be more common at your school than you think. People often hesitate to report rape for many reasons, such as fear, embarrassment, and concerns that others won't believe them.

Both women and men can take steps to prevent rape from occurring in the first place:

- Get together with a group of people for a tour of the campus. Make a special note of danger spots, such as unlighted paths and unguarded buildings. Keep in mind that rape can occur during daylight and in well-lit places.

- Ask whether your school has escort services for people taking evening classes. These might include personal escorts, car escorts, or both. If you do take an evening class, ask whether there are security officers on duty before and after the class.

- Take a course or seminar on self-defense and rape prevention. To find these courses, check with your student counseling service, community education center, or local library.

If you are raped, get medical care right away. Go to the nearest rape crisis center, hospital, student health service, or police station. Also arrange for follow-up counseling. It's your decision whether to report the crime. Filing a report does not mean that you have to press charges. And if you do choose to press charges later, having a report on file can help your case.

## PREVENT SEXUALLY TRANSMITTED DISEASE

People with a sexually transmitted disease (STD) might feel no symptoms for years and not even discover that they are infected. Know how to protect yourself.

STDs can result from vaginal sex, oral sex, anal sex, or any other way that people contact semen, vaginal secretions, and blood. Without treatment, some of these diseases can lead to blindness, infertility, cancer, heart disease, or even death.[14]

There are at least 25 kinds of STDs. Common examples are chlamydia, gonorrhea, and syphilis. Sexual contact can also spread the human papillomavirus (HPV, the most common cause of cervical cancer) and the human immunodeficiency virus (HIV, the virus that causes AIDS).

Most STDs can be cured if treated early. (Herpes and AIDS are important exceptions.) Prevention is better. Some guidelines for prevention follow.

**Abstain from sex.** Abstain from sex, or have sex exclusively with one person who is free of disease and has no other sex partners. These are the only ways to be absolutely safe from STDs.

**Use condoms.** Male condoms are thin membranes stretched over the penis prior to intercourse. Condoms prevent semen from entering the vagina. For the most protection, use latex condoms—not ones made of lambskin or polyurethane. Use a condom every time you have sex and for any type of sex.

Condoms are not guaranteed to work all of the time. They can break, leak, or slip off. In addition, condoms cannot protect you from STDs that are spread by contact with herpes sores or warts. Avoid condoms, lubricants, spermicides, and other products that contain nonoxynol-9, which can actually increase the risk of STDs.

**Stay sober.** People are more likely to have unsafe sex when drunk or high.

**Do not share needles.** Sharing needles or other paraphernalia with other drug users can spread STDs.

**Take action soon after you have sex.** Urinate soon after you have sex. Wash your genitals with soap and water.

**Get vaccinated.** Vaccines are available to prevent hepatitis B and HPV infection. See your doctor.

**Get screened for STDs.** The only way to find out whether you're infected is to be tested by a health care professional. If you have sex with more than one person, get screened for STDs at least once each year. Do this even if you have no symptoms. Remember that many schools offer free STD screening.

The more people you have sex with, the greater your risk of STDs. You are at risk even if you have sex only once with one person who is infected. The U.S. Centers for Disease Control and Prevention recommends chlamydia screening for all sexually active women under age 26. Women age 25 and older should be screened if they have a new sex partner or multiple sex partners.[15]

**Recognize the symptoms of STDs.** Symptoms include swollen glands with fever and aching; itching around the vagina; vaginal discharge; pain during sex or when urinating; sore throat following oral sex; anal pain after anal sex; sores, blisters, scabs, or warts on the genitals, anus, tongue, or throat; rashes on the palms of your hands or soles of your feet; dark urine; loose and light-colored stools; and unexplained fatigue, weight loss, and night sweats.

**Get treated right away.** If you think you have an STD, go to your doctor, campus health service, or local public health clinic. Early treatment might prevent serious health problems.

**Talk to your partner.** Before you have sex with someone, talk about the risk of STDs. If you are infected, tell your partner.

## PREVENT UNWANTED PREGNANCY

You and your partner can avoid unwanted pregnancy. There are many options, and choosing among them can be a challenge. Even birth control methods that are usually effective can fail when used incorrectly. To prevent pregnancy, make sure you understand your chosen method. Then use it *every* time you have sex.

To get updated information, go online to www.womenshealth.gov and search with the key words *birth control*. Also talk to your doctor. ■

9

# Alcohol, tobacco, and drugs:
## The Truth

The truth is that getting high can be fun. In our culture, and especially in our media, getting high has become synonymous with having a good time. Even if you don't smoke, drink, or use other drugs, you are certain to come in contact with people who do.

For centuries, human beings have devised ways to change their feelings and thoughts by altering their body chemistry. The Chinese were using marijuana 5,000 years ago. Herodotus, the ancient Greek historian, wrote about a group of people in eastern Europe who threw marijuana on hot stones and inhaled the vapors. More recently, during the American Civil War, customers could buy opium and morphine at neighborhood stores.[16]

Today we are still a drug-using society. Of course, some of those uses are therapeutic and lawful, including taking drugs as prescribed by a doctor or psychiatrist. The problem comes when we turn to drugs as *the* solution to any problem. Are you uncomfortable? Often the first response is "Take something."

We live in times when reaching for instant comfort via chemicals is not only condoned but encouraged. If you're bored, tense, or anxious, you can drink a can of beer, down a glass of wine, or light up a cigarette. If you want to enhance your memory, take a "smart drug," which includes prescription stimulants and caffeine. And these are only the legal options. If you're willing to take risks, you can pick from a large selection of illegal drugs on the street. And if that seems too risky, you can abuse prescription drugs.

There is a big payoff in using alcohol, tobacco, caffeine, cocaine, heroin, or other drugs—or people wouldn't do it. The payoff can be direct, such as relaxation, self-confidence, comfort, excitement, or the ability

to pull an all-nighter. At times, the payoff is avoiding rejection or defying authority.

In addition to the payoffs, there are costs. For some people, the cost is much greater than the payoff. Even if drug use doesn't make you broke, it can make you crazy. This is not necessarily the kind of crazy where you dress up like Napoleon. Rather, it is the kind where you care about little else except finding more drugs—friends, school, work, and family be damned.

Substance abuse is only part of the picture. People can also relate to food, gambling, money, sex, and even work in compulsive ways.

Some people will stop abusing a substance or activity when the consequences get serious enough. Other people don't stop. They continue their self-defeating behaviors, no matter the consequences for themselves, their friends, or their families. At that point, the problem goes beyond abuse. It's addiction.

With addiction, the costs can include overdose, infection, and lowered immunity to disease. These can be fatal. Long-term heavy drinking, for example, damages every organ system in the human body. And about 440,000 Americans die annually from the effects of cigarette smoking, including secondhand smoke.[17]

Lectures about the reasons for avoiding alcohol and drug abuse and addiction can be pointless. We don't take care of our bodies because someone says we should. We might take care of ourselves when we see that the costs of using a substance outweigh the benefits.

Acknowledging that alcohol, tobacco, and other drugs can be fun infuriates a lot of people. Remember that this acknowledgment is *not* the same as condoning drug use. The point is this: People are more likely to abstain when they're convinced that using these substances leads to more pain than pleasure over the long run. You choose. It's your body. ∎

VR Photos/Shutterstock.com

Givaga/Shutterstock.com

iStockphoto.com/Sergey Mostovoy

# WARNING:
# ADVERTISING
## *can be dangerous to*
# YOUR HEALTH

. . . . . . . . . . . . . . . . . . . . . . . . . . . . . . . . .

The average American is exposed to hundreds of advertising messages per day. Unless you are stranded on a desert island, you are affected by advertising.

. . . . . . . . . . . . . . . . . . . . . . . . . . . . . . . . .

Advertising serves a useful function. It helps us make choices about how we spend our money. We can choose among thousands of companies that provide goods and services. Advertising makes us aware of the options.

Advertising also plays on our emotions. And some ads are dangerously manipulative.

Consider how advertising can affect your health. Advertising alcohol, tobacco, pain relievers, and other health-related products is a big business. Much of the revenue earned by newspapers, magazines, radio, television, and Web sites comes from ads for these products. This means that advertisers are a major source of information about health and illness.

Advertising influences our food choices. The least nutritious foods often bring in the most advertising money. So, advertisers portray the primary staples of our diet as sugary breakfast cereals, candy bars, and soft drinks.

Ads for alcohol glorify drinking. Advertisers imply that daily drinking is the norm. Pleasant experiences are enhanced by drinking. Holidays naturally include alcohol. Parties are a flop without it. Relationships are more romantic over cocktails. Everybody drinks.

Advertising also targets our emotional health. The message behind many ads is: *Buying our product will make you okay*. This message is used to sell clothes, makeup, and hair products to make us look okay; drugs, alcohol, and food to make us feel okay; perfumes, toothpaste, and deodorants to make us smell okay. According to

many ads, buying the right product is essential to having the right relationships in our lives.

A related problem concerns images of women. Ads give us the impression that women love to spend hours discussing floor wax, deodorants, tampons, and laundry detergent—and that they think constantly about losing weight and looking sexy. In some ads, women handle everything from kitchen to bedroom to boardroom—true superwomen.

Images such as these are demeaning to women and damaging to men. Women lose when they allow their self-image to be influenced by ads. Men lose when they expect real-life women to look and act like the women on television.

Advertising creates illusions. The next time you're in a crowd, notice how few people look like those in ads.

Advertising often excludes people of color. If our perceptions were based solely on advertising, we would be hard-pressed to know that our society is racially and ethnically diverse. See how many examples of cultural stereotypes you can find in the ads you encounter this week.

Use advertising as a continual opportunity to develop the qualities of a critical thinker. Every time you're exposed to an ad, ask: What's the main message, and what's the evidence for it?

Stay aware of how a multibillion-dollar industry affects your health. ■

---

**JOURNAL ENTRY 17**
*Discovery/Intention Statement*

## Advertisements and your health

Think of a time when—after seeing an advertisement or a commercial—you craved a certain food or drink, or you really wanted to buy something. Describe a specific ad and exactly how it affected you.

I discovered that I . . .

_____

_____

_____

Now describe anything you'd like to do differently in the future when you notice that advertising affects you in the way you just described.

I intend to . . .

_____

_____

_____

9

# PRACTICING
# critical thinking 9

This exercise involves thinking at all six levels described in "Becoming a critical thinker" on page 160.

*Note:* If you'd like to keep your responses to this exercise confidential, then write on separate paper.

Do you **remember** your response to the Journal Entry that opened this chapter? If not, take minute to review what you wrote.

Now, after reading and completing the exercises in this chapter, do you **understand** your current level of health in a different way? Explain your answer:

_____

_____

_____

_____

Also take a minute to page through this chapter again and review the suggested strategies for protecting your health. List five strategies that you'd like to **apply:**

_____

_____

_____

_____

_____

Next, **analyze** your current level of health in more detail. If a statement does not apply to you, then skip it. As with the Discovery Wheel, the usefulness of this writing will be determined by your honesty and courage.

## Eating

What I know about the way I eat is . . .

_____

_____

What I would most like to change about my diet is . . .

_____

_____

My eating habits lead me to be . . .

_____

_____

## Exercise

The way I usually exercise is . . .

_____

_____

The last time I did 20 minutes or more of heart/lung (aerobic) exercise was . . .

_____

_____

As a result of my physical conditioning, I feel . . .

_____

_____

And I look . . .

_____

_____

It would be easier for me to work out regularly if I . . .

_____

_____

The most important benefit for me in exercising more is . . .

_____

_____

## Substances

My history of cigarette smoking is . . .

_____

_____

An objective observer would say that my use of alcohol is . . .

_____

_____

In the last 10 days, the number of alcoholic drinks I have had is . . .

_____

_____

I would describe my use of coffee, soda, and other caffeinated drinks as . . .

_____

_____

I have used the following illegal drugs in the past week:

_____

_____

When it comes to drugs, what I am sometimes concerned about is . . .

_____

_____

I take the following prescription drugs:

_____

_____

## Relationships

Someone who knows me fairly well would say I am emotionally . . .

_____

_____

The way I look and feel has affected my relationships by . . .

_____

_____

My use of drugs or alcohol has been an issue with the following people . . .

_____

_____

The best thing I could do for myself and my relationships would be to . . .

_____

_____

## Sleep

The number of hours I sleep each night is . . .

_____

_____

On weekends I normally sleep . . .

_____

_____

I have trouble sleeping when . . .

_____

_____

Last night, I . . .

_____

_____

The quality of my sleep is usually . . .

_____

_____

In light of your analysis, go back to the five strategies you listed earlier. **Evaluate** them by considering the aspect of your health that is most important to you right now. Then choose one strategy that you will definitely commit to use during the next 30 days. Describe that strategy below, making sure it is an action that you can take immediately:

_____

_____

_____

_____

Finally, experiment with the idea that your health is something that you **create** over the long term. Write a larger health-related goal—one that could make a big difference in the quality of your life over the next year. Also list the actions you will take to achieve that goal:

_____

_____

_____

_____

_____

_____

9

# masterstudentprofile

# Randy Pausch

(1960–2008) Pausch was a professor at Carnegie Mellon University, who, shortly after being diagnosed with pancreatic cancer, gave a "last lecture"—a reflection on his personal and professional journey—that became a hit on YouTube (this lecture was later adapted into a book of the same title). He devoted the remaining 9 months of his life to creating a legacy.

It's a thrill to fulfill your own childhood dreams, but as you get older, you may find that enabling the dreams of others is even more fun.

When I was teaching at the University of Virginia in 1993, a twenty-two-year-old artist-turned-computer-graphics-wiz named Tommy Burnett wanted a job on my research team. After we talked about his life and goals, he suddenly said, "Oh, and I have always had this childhood dream."

Anyone who uses "childhood" and "dream" in the same sentence usually gets my attention.

"And what is your dream, Tommy?" I asked.

"I want to work on the next Star Wars film," he said.

Remember, this was in 1993. The last Star Wars movie had been made in 1983, and there were no concrete plans to make any more. I explained this. "That's a tough dream to have because it'll be hard to see it through," I told him. "Word is that they're finished making Star Wars films."

"No," he said, "they're going to make more, and when they do, I'm going to work on them. That's my plan."

Tommy was six years old when the first Star Wars film came out in 1977. "Other kids wanted to be Hans Solo," he told me. "Not me. I wanted to be the guy who made the special effects—the space ships, the planets, the robots."

He told me that, as a boy, he read the most technical Star Wars articles he could find. He had all the books that explained how the models were built, and how the special effects were achieved. . . . I figured Tommy's big dream would never happen, but it might serve him well somehow. I could use a dreamer like that. I knew from my NFL desires that even if he didn't achieve his, they could serve him well, so I asked him to join our research team. . . .

When I moved to Carnegie Mellon, every member of my team from the University of Virginia came with me—everyone except Tommy. He couldn't make the move. Why? Because he had been hired by producer/director George Lucas' company, Industrial Light & Magic. And it's worth noting that they didn't hire him for his dream; they hired him for his skills. In his time with our research group, he had become an outstanding programmer in the Python language, which as luck would have it, was the language of choice in their shop. Luck is indeed where preparation meets opportunity.

It's not hard to guess where this story is going. Three new Star Wars films would be made—in 1999, 2002, and 2005—and Tommy ended up working on all of them.

On Star Wars Episode II: Attack of the Clones, Tommy was a lead technical director. There was an incredible fifteen-minute battle scene on a rocky red planet, pitting clones against droids, and Tommy was the guy who planned it all out. He and his team used photos of the Utah desert to create a virtual landscape for the battle. Talk about cool jobs. Tommy had one that let him spend each day on another planet.

© ABCNews.com

**RANDY PAUSCH . . .** was energetic.

**YOU . . .** can build energy with effective habits for eating, sleeping, and managing stress.

**You're One Click Away...**
*from learning more about Randy Pausch online at the Master Student Profiles. You can also visit the Master Student Hall of Fame to learn about other master students.*

Name _____

Date _____

1. How does the Power Process: "Surrender" differ from giving up?

2. List Michael Pollan's guidelines for nutrition.

3. List two ways you can build more physical activity into your day, outside of a scheduled time for exercise.

4. The text suggests two ways to "not believe everything you think." Briefly summarize those suggestions.

5. According to the text, emotional pain is a sickness that always calls for professional help. True or false? Explain your answer.

6. The suggested guidelines for asking for help include the following:
   (a) Ask with clarity.
   (b) Ask with sincerity.
   (c) Ask widely.
   (d) Ask with an open mind.
   (e) All of the above

7. List three things you can do to prevent someone from committing suicide.
   Answers will be three of the following:

8. General precautions you can take to stay safe at school include the following:
   (a) Lock doors when you're leaving home.
   (b) Avoid walking alone, especially at night.
   (c) Plan how to respond to an emergency.
   (d) All of the above

9. What are two questions that you can ask yourself every time you're exposed to an advertisement?

10. List five possible symptoms of sexually transmitted disease.

9

# CHAPTER 9 SKILLS Snapshot

Now that you've reflected on the ideas in this chapter and experimented with some new strategies, revisit your responses to the "Health" section of the Discovery Wheel exercise on page 30. Also think about ways to develop more mastery in this area of your life. Complete the following sentences:

## DISCOVERY

My score on the *Health* section of the Discovery Wheel was . . .

To monitor my current level of health, I look for specific changes in . . .

After reading and doing this chapter, my top three health concerns are . . .

## INTENTION

My top three intentions for responding to these concerns are . . .

## NEXT ACTION

I'll know that I've reached a new level of mastery with health when . . .

To reach that level of mastery, the most important intention for me to act on next is . . .

At the end of this course, I would like my *Health* score on the Discovery Wheel to be . . .

# What's Next?

Use this **Master Student Map** to ask yourself,

## WHY THIS CHAPTER MATTERS . . .

- You can use the techniques introduced in this book to set and achieve goals for the rest of your life.

## WHAT IS INCLUDED . . .

## HOW CAN I USE THIS CHAPTER . . .

- Choose the next steps in your education and career.
- Highlight your continuing success on résumés and in interviews.
- Experience the joys of contributing.
- Use a Power Process that enhances every technique in this book.

## WHAT IF . . .

- I could begin creating the life of my dreams—starting today?

**JOURNAL ENTRY 18**
*Discovery/Intention Statement*

## Revisiting what you want and how you intend to get it

Review the Power Process: "Discover what you want" on page 2. Then complete the following sentences with the first thoughts that come to mind:

I discovered that what I want most from life is . . .

_____

_____

_____

_____

_____

_____

_____

To get what I want from my life, I intend to . . .

_____

_____

_____

_____

_____

_____

© Ruslan Ivantsov/Shutterstock.com

# POWER process Be it

**U**se this Power Process to enhance all of the techniques in this book.

Consider that most of our choices in life fall into three categories. We can do the following:

- Increase our material wealth (what we have).
- Improve our skills (what we do).
- Develop our "being" (who we are).

Many people devote their entire lifetime to the first two categories. They act as if they are "human havings" instead of human beings. For them, the quality of life hinges on what they have. They devote most of their waking hours to getting more—more clothes, more cars, more relationships, more degrees, more trophies. "Human havings" define themselves by looking at the circumstances in their lives—what they have.

Some people escape this materialist trap by adding another dimension to their identities. In addition to living as "human havings," they also live as "human doings." They thrive on working hard and doing everything well. They define themselves by how efficiently they do their jobs, how effectively they raise their children, and how actively they participate in clubs and organizations. Their thoughts are constantly about methods, techniques, and skills.

In addition to focusing on what we have and what we do, we can also focus on our being. That last word describes how we *see* ourselves.

All of the techniques in this book can be worthless if you operate with the idea that you are an ineffective student. You might do almost everything this book suggests and still never achieve the success in school that you desire.

Instead, picture yourself as a master student right now. Through higher education, you are simply gaining knowledge and skills that reflect and reinforce this view of yourself. Change the way you see yourself. Then watch your actions and results shift as if by magic.

Remember that "Be it" is not positive thinking or mental cheerleading. This Power Process works well when you take a First Step—when you tell the truth about your current abilities. The very act of accepting who you are and what you can do right now unleashes a powerful force for personal change.

If you can first visualize where you want to be, if you can go there in your imagination, if you can *be it* today, then you set yourself up to succeed.

If you want it, be it.

**You're One Click Away...**
*from from accessing Power Process Media online and finding out more about how to "be it."*

# Define your *values*;
## align your *actions*

One way to choose what's next in your life is to define your values. Values are the things in life that you want for their own sake. Values influence and guide your choices, including your moment-by-moment choices of what to do and what to have. Your values define who you are and who you want to be.

Some people are guided by values that they automatically adopt from others or by values that remain largely unconscious. Other people focus on short-term gain and forget about how their behavior violates their values over the long term (a perspective that helped to create the recent economic recession). All these people could be missing the opportunity to live a life that's truly of their own choosing.

The master student qualities explained in this book are based on a specific set of values:

- Focused attention
- Self-responsibility
- Integrity
- Risk taking
- Contributing

You'll find these values and related ones directly stated in the Power Processes throughout the text. For instance:

"Discover what you want" is about the importance of living a purpose-based life.

"Ideas are tools" points to the benefits of being willing to experiment with new ideas.

"Be here now" expresses the value of focused attention.

"Love your problems (and experience your barriers)" is about seeing difficulties as opportunities to develop new skills.

"Notice your pictures and let them go" is about adopting an open-minded attitude.

"I create it all" is about taking responsibility for our beliefs and behaviors.

"Detach" reminds us that our core identity and value as a person does not depend on our possessions, our circumstances, or even our accomplishments.

"Find a bigger problem" is about offering our lives by contributing to others.

"Employ your word" expresses the value of making and keeping agreements.

"Surrender" points to the value of human community and the power of asking for help.

"Be it" is specifically about the power of attitudes—the idea that change proceeds from the inside out as we learn to see ourselves in new ways.

In addition, most of the skills you read about in these pages have their source in values. The Time Monitor process, for example, calls for focused attention. Even the simple act of sharing your notes with a student who missed a class is an example of contributing.

Gaining a liberal education is all about adopting and acting on values. As you begin to define your values, consider the people who have gone before you. In creeds, scriptures, philosophies, myths, and sacred stories, the human race has left a vast and varied record of values. Be willing to look everywhere, including sources that are close to home. The creed of your local church or temple might eloquently describe some of your values. So might the mission statement of your school, company, or club. Another way to define your values is to describe the qualities of people you admire.

Also, translate your values into behavior. Although defining your values is powerful, it doesn't guarantee any results. To achieve your goals, take actions that align with your values. ■

**You're One Click Away...**
*from finding a sample list of values online.*

10

# Jumpstart your education with
## transferable skills

Few words are as widely misunderstood as *skill*. Defining this word carefully can have an immediate and positive impact on your career planning.

## IDENTIFY TWO KINDS OF SKILLS

One dictionary defines *skill* as "the ability to do something well, usually gained by training or experience." Some skills—such as the ability to repair fiber-optic cables or do brain surgery—are acquired through formal schooling, on-the-job training, or both. These abilities are called *work-content skills*. People with such skills have mastered a specialized body of knowledge needed to do a specific kind of work.

However, there is another category of skills that we develop through experiences both inside and outside the classroom. These are *transferable skills*. Transferable skills are abilities that help people thrive in any job—no matter what work-content skills they have. You start developing these skills even before you take your first job.

Perhaps you've heard someone described this way: "She's really smart and knows what she's doing, but she's got lousy people skills." People skills—such as *listening* and *negotiating*—are prime examples of transferable skills. Other examples are listed on this page.

## SUCCEED IN MANY SITUATIONS

Transferable skills are often invisible to us. The problem begins when we assume that a given skill can be used in only one context, such as being in school or working at a particular job. Thinking in this way places an artificial limit on our possibilities.

As an alternative, think about the things you routinely do to succeed in school. Analyze your activities to isolate specific skills. Then brainstorm a list of jobs where you could use the same skills.

Consider the task of writing a research paper. This calls for the following skills:

- *Planning*, including setting goals for completing your outline, first draft, second draft, and final draft
- *Managing time* to meet your writing goals
- *Interviewing* people who know a lot about the topic of your paper
- *Researching* using the Internet and campus library to discover key facts and ideas to include in your paper
- *Writing* to present those facts and ideas in an original way
- *Editing* your drafts for clarity and correctness

Now consider the kinds of jobs that draw on these skills.

For example, you could transfer your skill at writing papers to a possible career in journalism, technical writing, or advertising copywriting.

You could use your editing skills to work in the field of publishing as a magazine or book editor.

When meeting with an academic advisor, you may be tempted to say, "I've just been taking general education and liberal arts courses. I don't have any marketable skills." Think again.

Interviewing and research skills could help you enter the field of market research. And the abilities to plan, manage time, and meet deadlines will help you succeed in all the jobs mentioned so far.

Use the same kind of analysis to think about transferring skills from one job to another. Say that you work part-time as an administrative assistant at a computer dealer that sells a variety of hardware and software. You take phone calls from potential customers, help current customers solve problems using their computers, and attend meetings where your coworkers plan ways to market new products. You are developing skills at *selling*, *serving customers*, and *working on teams*. These skills could help you land a job as a sales representative for a computer manufacturer or software developer.

The basic idea is to take a cue from the word *transferable*. Almost any skill you use to succeed in one situation can *transfer* to success in another situation.

The concept of transferable skills creates a powerful link between higher education and the work world. Skills are the core elements of any job. While taking any course, list the specific skills you are developing and how you can transfer them to the work world. Almost everything you do in school can be applied to your career—if you consistently pursue this line of thought.

## FIND EXAMPLES OF TRANSFERABLE SKILLS

There are literally hundreds of transferable skills. In fact, one purpose of this book is help you gain a set of transferable skills for success in school and the workplace. For example:

Chapter 1 suggests ways to choose and apply new strategies for learning.

Chapter 2 is about setting goals and translating them into items on your to-do list.

Chapter 3 presents strategies for recalling facts and ideas when you're under pressure (such as during a test).

Chapter 4 offers techniques for previewing and remembering what you read.

Chapter 5 suggests that you use several different formats for taking notes.

Chapter 6 is about ways to use test results and other assessments to improve your performance.

In Chapter 7, you'll find techniques for thinking critically about what you find on the Internet.

Chapter 8 includes ideas for speaking with "I" messages.

Chapter 9 presents strategies for maintaining your emotional health.

This chapter presents techniques that you can use to plan your career.

All of these are transferable skills. And they are just a small sample of what's possible for you to gain.

One key to developing transferable skills is simply being aware of how many of them exist. To find more examples of transferable skills, check out O*Net OnLine, a Web site from the federal government at **www.onetonline.org/**. There you'll find tools for discovering your skills and matching them to specific occupations. Additional information on careers and job hunting is available at CareerOneStop at **www.careeronestop.org** and my Skills my Future at **www.myskillsmyfuture.org**.

## ASK FOUR QUESTIONS

To experiment further with this concept of transferable skills, ask and answer four questions derived from the Master Student Map.

***Why* identify my transferable skills?** Getting past the "I-don't-have-any-skills" syndrome means that you can approach job hunting with more confidence. As you uncover these hidden assets, your list of qualifications will grow as if by magic. You won't be padding your résumé. You'll simply be using action words to tell the full truth about what you can do.

Identifying your transferable skills takes a little time. And the payoffs are numerous. A complete and accurate list of transferable skills can help you land jobs that involve more responsibility, more variety, more freedom to structure your time, and more money. Careers can be made—or broken—by the skills that allow you to define your job, manage your workload, and get along with people.

Transferable skills help you thrive in the midst of constant change. Technology will continue to develop. Ongoing discoveries in many fields could render current knowledge obsolete. Jobs that

exist today may disappear in a few years, only to be replaced by entirely new ones.

In the economy of the twenty-first century, you might not be able to count on job security. What you *can* count on is "skills security"—abilities that you can carry from one career to another or acquire as needed. Even though he only completed 8 years of formal schooling,[1] Henry Ford said, "The only real security that a person can have in this world is a reserve of knowledge, experience, and ability. Without these qualities, money is practically useless."[2]

***What* are my transferable skills?** Discover your transferable skills by reflecting on key experiences. Recall a time when you performed at the peak of your ability, overcame obstacles, won an award, gained a high grade, or met a significant goal. List the skills you used to create those successes.

For a more complete picture of your transferable skills, describe the object of your action. Say that one of the skills on your list is *organizing*. This could refer to organizing ideas, organizing people, or organizing objects in a room. Specify the kind of organizing that you like to do.

***How* do I perform these skills?** You can bring your transferable skills into even sharper focus by adding adverbs—words that describe *how* you take action. You might say that you edit *accurately* or learn *quickly*.

In summary, you can use a three-column chart to list your transferable skills. For example:

| Verb | Object | Adverb |
| --- | --- | --- |
| Organizing | Records | Effectively |
| Serving | Customers | Courteously |
| Coordinating | Special events | Efficiently |

Add a specific example of each transferable skill to your skills list, and you're well on the way to an engaging résumé and a winning job interview.

***What if* I could expand my transferable skills?** In addition to thinking about the skills you already have, consider the skills you'd like to acquire. Describe them in detail. List experiences that can help you develop them. Let your list of transferable skills grow and develop as you do. ■

**You're One Click Away…**
*from learning more about transferable skills online.*

10

# EXERCISE 17

## Recognize your skills

This exercise about discovering your skills includes three steps. Before you begin, gather at least a hundred 3 × 5 cards and a pen or pencil. Or open up a computer file and use any software that allows you to create lists. Allow about 1 hour to complete the exercise.

**STEP 1** **List recent activities** Recall your activities during the past week or month. To refresh your memory, review your responses to Exercise 7: "The Time Monitor" in Chapter 2. (You might even benefit from doing that exercise again.)

List down as many of these activities as you can. (If you're using 3 × 5 cards, list each item on a separate card.) Include work-related activities, school activities, and hobbies. Spend 10 minutes on this step.

**STEP 2** **List rewards and recognitions** Next, list any rewards you've received, or other recognition of your achievements, during the past year. Examples include scholarship awards, athletic awards, or recognitions for volunteer work. Allow 10 minutes for this step as well.

**STEP 3** **List work-content skills** Now review the two lists you just created. Then take another 10 minutes to list any specialized areas of knowledge needed to do those activities, win those awards, and receive those recognitions.

These areas of knowledge indicate your *work-content skills*. For example, tutoring a French class requires a working knowledge of that language.

List all of your skills that fall into this category, labeling each one as "work-content."

**STEP 4** **List transferable skills** Go over your list of activities one more time. Spend 10 minutes looking for examples of *transferable skills*—those that can be applied to a variety of situations. For instance, giving a speech or working as a salesperson in a computer store requires the ability to persuade people. Tuning a car means that you can attend to details and troubleshoot.

List all your skills that fall into this category, labeling each one as "transferable."

**STEP 5** **Review and plan** You now have a detailed picture of your skills. Review all the lists you created in the previous steps. See whether you can add any new items that occur to you.

Save your lists in a place where you can easily find them again. Plan to update all of them at least once each year. Your lists will come in handy for writing your résumé, preparing for job interviews, and doing other career-planning tasks.

# Create your CAREER *now*

Terry Vine/Getty Images

There's an old saying: "If you enjoy what you do, you'll never work another day in your life." If you clearly define your career goals and your strategy for reaching them, you can plan your education effectively and create a seamless transition from school to the workplace.

Career planning involves continuous exploration. There are dozens of effective paths to take. Begin now with the following ideas.

## YOU ALREADY KNOW A LOT ABOUT YOUR CAREER PLAN

When people learn study skills and life skills, they usually start with finding out things they don't know. That means discovering new strategies for taking notes, reading, writing, managing time, and the other subjects covered in this book.

Career planning is different. You can begin your career planning education by realizing how much you know right now. You've already made many decisions about your career. This is true for young people who say, "I don't have any idea what I want to be when I grow up." It's also true for midlife career changers.

Consider the student who can't decide whether she wants to be a cost accountant or a tax accountant and then jumps to the conclusion that she is totally lost when it comes to career planning. It's the same with the student who doesn't know whether he wants to be a veterinary assistant or a nurse.

These people forget that they already know a lot about their career choices. The person who couldn't decide between veterinary assistance and nursing had already ruled out becoming a lawyer, computer programmer, or teacher. He just didn't know yet whether he had the right bedside manner for horses or for people. The person who was debating tax accounting versus cost accounting already knew she didn't want to be a doctor, playwright, or taxicab driver. She did know she liked working with numbers and balancing books.

In each case, these people have already narrowed their list of career choices to a number of jobs in the same field—jobs that draw on the same core skills. In general, they already know what they want to be when they grow up.

## YOUR CAREER IS A CHOICE, NOT A DISCOVERY

Many people approach career planning as if they were panning for gold. They keep sifting through the dirt, clearing the dust, and throwing out the rocks. They are hoping to strike it rich and discover the perfect career.

Other people believe that they'll wake up one morning, see the heavens part, and suddenly know what they're supposed to do. Many of them are still waiting for that magical day to dawn.

**10**

You can approach career planning in a different way. Instead of seeing a career as something you discover, you can see it as something you choose. You don't find the right career. You create it.

There's a big difference between these two approaches. Thinking that there's only one "correct" choice for your career can lead to a lot of anxiety: "Did I choose the right one?" "What if I made a mistake?"

Viewing your career as your creation helps you relax. Instead of anguishing over finding the right career, you can stay open to possibilities. You can choose one career today, knowing that you can choose again later.

## PLAN BY NAMING NAMES

One key to making your career plan real and to ensuring that you can act on it is naming. Include specific names whenever they're called for. For example:

- *Name your job.* List the skills you enjoy using, and find out which jobs use them (you can begin by going online to **www.onetonline.org**). What are those jobs titles? List them. Note that the same job might have different names.

- *Name your company—the agency or organization you want to work for.* If you want to be self-employed or start your own business, name the product or service you'd sell. Also list some possible names for your business. If you plan to work for others, name the organizations or agencies that are high on your list.

- *Name your contacts.* Take the list of organizations you just compiled. Find out which people in these organizations are responsible for hiring. List those people, and contact them directly. If you choose self-employment, list the names of possible customers or clients. All of these people are job contacts.

- *Name your location.* Ask whether your career choices are consistent with your preferences about where to live and work. For example, someone who wants to make a living as a studio musician might consider living in a large city such as New York or Toronto. This contrasts with the freelance graphic artist who conducts his business mainly by phone, fax, and e-mail. He might be able to live anywhere and still pursue his career.

Now expand your list of contacts by brainstorming with your family and friends. Come up with a list of names—anyone who can help you with career planning and job hunting. Write each of these names on a 3 × 5 card. You can also use a spiral-bound notebook, computer, or smartphone.

Next, call the key people on your list. Ask them about their career experiences, tell them about the career path you're considering, and probe their knowledge of the industry you're interested in. After you speak with them, make brief notes about what you discussed. Also jot down any actions you agreed to take, such as a follow-up call.

Consider everyone you meet as a potential member of your job network. Be prepared to talk about what you do. Develop a "pitch"—a short statement of your career goal that you can easily share with your contacts. For example: "After I graduate, I plan to work in the travel business. I'm looking for an internship in a travel agency for next summer. Do you know of any agencies that take interns?"

## DESCRIBE YOUR IDEAL LIFESTYLE

In addition to choosing the content of your career, you have many options for integrating work into the context of your life. You can work full-time. You can work part-time. You can commute to a cubicle in a major corporation. Or you can work at home and take the 30-second commute from your bedroom to your desk.

Close your eyes. Visualize an ideal day in your life after graduation. Vividly imagine the following:

- Your work setting
- Your coworkers
- Your calendar and to-do list for that day
- Other sights and sounds in your work environment

This visualization emphasizes the importance of finding a match between your career and your lifestyle preferences—the amount of flexibility in your schedule, the number of people you see each day, the variety in your tasks, and the ways that you balance work with other activities.

## TEST YOUR CHOICE—AND BE WILLING TO CHANGE

Career-planning materials and counselors can help you test your choice and change it if you decide to do so. Read books about careers. Search for career-planning Web sites. Ask career counselors about skills assessments that can help you discover more about your skills and identify jobs that call for those skills. Take career-planning courses and workshops sponsored by your school. Visit the career-planning and job placement offices on campus.

Once you have a career choice, translate it into workplace experience. For example:

- Contact people who are actually doing the job you're researching, and ask them a lot of questions about what it's like (an *information interview*).
- Choose an internship or volunteer position in a field that interests you.
- Get a part-time or summer job in your career field.

If you find that you enjoy such experiences, you've probably made a wise career choice. And the people you meet are possible sources of recommendations, referrals, and employment in the future. If you did *not* enjoy your experiences, celebrate what you learned about yourself. Now you're free to refine your initial career choice or go in a new direction.

Career planning is not a once-and-for-all proposition. Rather, career plans are made to be changed and refined as you gain new information about yourself and the world. You might not walk straight into your dream job right after graduation. And you can approach *any* position in a way that takes you one step closer to your career goal. Do your best at every job, and stay flexible. Career planning never ends, and the process is the same, whether you're choosing your first career or your fifth.[3] ■

**You're One Click Away...**
*from finding more strategies online for career planning.*

# ✅ EXERCISE 18

## Create your career plan—now

Write your career plan. Now. Start the process of career planning, even if you're not sure where to begin. Your response to this exercise can be just a rough draft of your plan, which you can revise and rewrite many times. The point is to get your ideas in writing.

The final format of your plan is up to you. You might include many details, such as the next job title you'd like to have, the courses required for your major, and other training that you want to complete. You might list companies to research and people that could hire you. You might also include target dates to complete each of these tasks.

Another option is to represent your plan visually through flowcharts, time lines, mind maps, or drawings. You can generate these by hand or use computer software.

For now, experiment with career planning by completing the following sentences. Use the space provided, and continue on additional paper as needed. When answering the first question, write down what first comes to your mind. The goal is to begin the process of discovery. You can always change direction after some investigation.

1. The career I choose for now is . . .

_____

_____

_____

_____

_____

_____

_____

_____

_____

_____

_____

_____

2. The major steps that will guide me to this career are . . .

_____

_____

_____

_____

_____

_____

_____

_____

_____

_____

_____

_____

3. The immediate steps I will take to pursue this career are . . .

_____

_____

_____

_____

_____

_____

_____

_____

10

# ✓ EXERCISE 19

## Make a trial choice of major

The article "Thinking about your major" on page 171 explains four strategies for choosing a major. Now that you've thought more about what your career plan is, the purpose of this exercise is to take action on the strategies of choosing a major that will support your career plan. First, take a few minutes to review the article and your career plan from Exercise 18. Then complete the following steps:

**STEP 1** **Discover options** Look at your school's catalog or Web site for a list of majors. Make a photocopy of that list or print it out. Spend at least 5 minutes reading through all the majors that your school offers.

**STEP 2** **Make a trial choice** Next, cross out all of the majors that you already know are not right for you. You will probably eliminate well over half the list. Scan the remaining majors. Next to the ones that definitely interest you, write "yes." Next to majors that you're willing to consider and are still unsure about, write "maybe."

Now, focus on your "yes" choices. See whether you can narrow them down to three majors.

Finally, write an asterisk next to the major that interests you most right now. *This is your trial choice of major.*

**STEP 3** **Evaluate your trial choice** Congratulations on making your choice! Now take a few minutes to reflect on it. Does it align with your interests, skills, and career plans? Set a goal to test your choice of major with out-of classroom experience. Examples are internships, field experiences, study abroad programs, and work-study assignments. Note that these experiences might confirm your trial choice—or lead to a new choice of major.

......................................................................

# ✓ EXERCISE 20

## Create your academic plan

An academic plan is a road map for getting the most out of your education. This document is a list of all the courses you plan to take and *when* you plan to take each one. (At some schools, it is called a *degree plan.*)

**STEP 1** You probably started an academic plan when you registered for school. If you have any notes or materials from that experience, then review them. Also review your school's course catalog and Web site.

**STEP 2** Using all of the information you've gathered so far, create your list of planned courses on separate paper. Another option is to use your computer and create your list with word-processing, outlining, or spreadsheet software.

Consider formatting your plan as a chart:

- In the first column, list the name of each course.

- Use a second column to write the number of credits for each course.

- In the third column, note the term you plan to take each course (for example, *Spring 2016*). Be sure to check your college catalog for course prerequisites or corequisites.

**STEP 3** Now evaluate your academic plan. Make sure that it:

- Gives you the total number of credits you need to graduate.

- Meets your school's requirements for general education.

- Meets the requirements for your major, your minor, or both.

Reach out to instructors and advisors for help. Use available resources to create an academic plan that fuels your success.

# TRANSFERRING TO A
## new school

The way that you choose a new school will have a major impact on your education. This is true if you're transferring from a community or technical college to a 4-year school or if you're choosing a graduate school.

Even if you don't plan to go through the process of choosing schools again, you can use the following ideas to evaluate your current school.

**Gather information.** To research schools, start with publications. These include print sources, such as school catalogs, and school Web sites. Next, contact people—academic advisors, counselors, other school staff members, and current or former students from the schools you're considering. Contact the advisor at the new school to find out what the acceptance and graduation requirements will be.

Use your research to dig up key facts such as these about each school you're considering:

- Location
- Number of students
- Class sizes
- Possibilities for contact with instructors outside class
- Percentage of full-time faculty members
- Admissions criteria
- Availability of degrees that interest you
- Tuition and fees
- Housing plans
- Financial aid programs
- Religious affiliation
- Diversity of students and staff
- Course requirements
- Retention rates (how many students come back to school after their freshman year)

To learn the most about a school, go beyond the first statistics you see. For example, a statement that "30 percent of our students are persons of color" doesn't tell you much about the numbers of people from specific ethnic or racial groups.

Also, you could transfer to a school that advertises student–instructor ratios of 15 to 1 and then find yourself in classes with 100 people. Remember that any statement about average class size is just that—an average. To gain more details, ask how often you can expect to enroll in smaller classes, especially during your final terms.

Take trips to the two or three schools that interest you most. Ask for a campus tour and a chance to sit in on classes.

In addition, gather facts about your current academic profile. Include your grades, courses completed, degrees attained, and grade point average (GPA). Standardized test scores are important. They include your scores on the Scholastic Assessment Test (SAT), American College Test (ACT), Graduate Record Examinations (GRE), and any advanced placement (AP) tests you've taken.

Also find our how many course credits that you've already earned will transfer to another school. The more credits you can transfer, the more tuition money you will save.

**Choose your new school.** If you follow the suggestions given, you'll end up with stacks of publications and pages of notes. As you sort through all this information, remember that your impressions of a school will go beyond a dry list of facts. Also pay attention to your instincts and intuitions—your "gut feelings" of attraction to one school or hesitation about another. These impressions can be important to your choice. Allow time for such feelings to emerge.

You can also benefit from putting your choice of schools in a bigger context. Consider the purposes, values, and long-term goals you've generated by doing the exercises and Journal Entries in this book. Consider which school is most likely to support the body of discoveries and intentions that you've created.

As you choose your new school, consider the needs and wishes of your family members and friends. Ask for their guidance and support. If you involve them in the decision, they'll have more stake in your success.

At some point, you'll just choose a school. Remember that there is no one "right" choice. You could probably thrive at many schools—perhaps even at your current one. Use the suggestions in this book to practice self-responsibility. Take charge of your education no matter which school you attend.

**Succeed at your new school.** At your new school, you'll be in classes with people who have already developed social networks. To avoid feeling left out, seek out chances to meet people. Join study groups, check out extracurricular activities, and consider volunteering for student organizations. Making social connections can ease your transition to a new academic environment.

**Check credits.** No two schools offer the same sets of courses, so determining credits is often a matter of interpretation. In some cases, you might be able to persuade a registrar or the admissions office to accept some of your previous courses. Keep a folder of syllabuses from your courses for this purpose. Ask your academic advisor for help. Taking care of these details can help you graduate from your new school on time, with the education that you want. ■

**You're One Click Away...**
*from learning more online about changing schools.*

**10**

© 2014 Cengage Learning. All Rights Reserved. May not be scanned, copied or duplicated, or posted to a publicly accessible website, in whole or in part.

# Use résumés, networking, and interviews to "hire" an employer

## SEE YOUR RÉSUMÉ AS A WAY TO SET AND ACHIEVE GOALS

A résumé is much more than a list of your qualifications. This document says a lot about who you are, what you love to do, and how you contribute to the world by using your skills. You can gain a lot from thinking about those things now, even if you don't plan to apply for a job in the near future. Start *building* your résumé now, even if you don't plan to *use* one for a while.

## FOUR THINGS TO REMEMBER ABOUT RÉSUMÉS

First, there is no one right way to write a résumé. When you go to your school's career planning office, ask to see sample résumés—especially from alumni who got hired. Go online to find even more. You'll notice many differences in style and format.

Second, the main purpose of a résumé is to get you to the next step in the hiring process. This is usually a job interview. See your résumé as a piece of persuasive writing, not a dry recitation of facts or a laundry list of previous jobs. Neatness, organization, and correct grammar and punctuation are essential. And, they are paths to meeting a larger goal—making a strong impression on someone who has the power to hire you. If your résumé does that, then it works.

Third, people who read your résumé are pressed for time. Assume that they're reviewing hundreds of them, and that they only have 10 seconds to scan yours. With this in mind, make your résumé easy to read. Keep it short—one page. Use every line to document a specific accomplishment. Also avoid paragraphs and go for lists instead.

For more ideas about résumé writing, start with the résumé guide at CareerOneStop, a Web site posted by the federal government at **www.careeronestop.org/ResumeGuide/**.

## FINE-TUNE YOUR COVER LETTER

The purpose of a cover letter is to persuade someone to look at your résumé. In your first sentence, address the person who can hire you and grab that person's attention. Make a statement that appeals directly to her self-interest. Write something that moves a potential employer to say, "We can't afford to pass this person up. Call him right away to set up an appointment."

To come up with ideas for your opening, complete the following sentence: "The main benefits that I can bring to your organization are . . ." Another option: "My work experience ties directly to several points mentioned in your job description. First, . . ."

Perhaps someone the employer knows told you about this job opening. Mention this person in your opening paragraph, especially if she has a positive reputation in the organization.

## NETWORK LIKE A PRO

When people say "There are no jobs in this economy," maybe what they really mean is, "My current job hunting method is not working."

Supplement your résumé and cover letter with one of the strongest job-hunting methods—building a strong network. Get to know people in your career field. Do research to discover organizations that interest you. Find out who does the hiring at those organizations. Then contact people directly for an information interview.

Some people hear the word *networking* and wince. They think of it as sleazy or a waste of time. In reality, information interviews can be effective and fun.

Everyone has a network. The key is to discover it and develop it. Begin by listing contacts—any person who can help you find a job. Contacts can include roommates, classmates, teachers, friends, relatives, and their friends. Also list former employers and current employers.

Next, send a short e-mail to a person on your list—someone who's doing the kind of work that you'd love to do. Invite that person to coffee or lunch. If that's not feasible, then ask for a time to make a phone call. Explain that you'd like to have a 20-minute conversation to learn more about what people in your career field do, and about how they get hired. Again, you're asking for an information interview rather than a job interview. Whenever possible, make this contact after getting an introduction from someone that both of you know.

## BEFORE YOU GO TO A JOB INTERVIEW

When your résumé, cover letter, and networking leads to a job interview, prepare for it. Learn everything you can about each organization that's interested in you. Find out about the following:

- The organization's products and services
- Major developments in the organization during the past year
- Directions that the organization plans to go during the upcoming year
- Names of the organization's major divisions
- Names of people who could hire you
- The types of jobs they offer

Next, prepare for common questions. Many interviewers have the following questions on their mind, even if they don't ask them directly:

- How did you find out about us?
- Will we be comfortable working with you?
- How can you help us?
- Will you learn this job quickly?
- What makes you different from other people applying for this job?

## DURING THE INTERVIEW

Plan to arrive early for your interview. While you're waiting, observe the workplace. Notice what people are saying and doing. See whether you can "read" the company culture by making informal observations.

When you meet the interviewer, do three things right away: smile, make eye contact, and give a firm handshake. Nonverbal communication creates a lasting impression.

After making small talk, the interviewer will start asking questions. Draw on the answers you've prepared. At the same time, respond to the *exact* questions that you're asked. Speak naturally and avoid the impression that you're making a speech or avoiding a question.

Stay aware of how much you talk. Avoid answers that are too brief or too long. Respond to each question for a minute or two. If you have more to say, end your answer by saying, "Those are the basics. I can add more if you want."

A skilled interviewer will allow time for *you* to ask questions about the company. Use this time to your full advantage. Some good questions to ask:

- When does the job begin?
- What is a typical day like?
- What would I work on if I were to get the job?
- What training is offered for this job?
- Are there opportunities to advance?
- Who will supervise me in this job?
- Could I take a tour of the workplace?

Save questions about benefits, salary, and vacation days for the second interview. When you get to that point, you know that the employer is interested in you. You might have leverage to negotiate.

Be sure to find out the next step in the hiring process and when it will take place. Also ask interviewers for their business cards and how they want you to follow up. Some people are fine with a phone call, fax, e-mail, or other form of online communication. Others prefer a good, old-fashioned letter.

If you're truly interested in the job and feel comfortable with the interviewer, ask one more question: "Do you have any concerns about hiring me?" Listen carefully to the reply. Then respond to each concern in a polite way.

> make your résumé easy to read. Keep it short—one page. Use every line to document a specific accomplishment.

## AFTER THE INTERVIEW

Congratulate yourself for getting as far in the hiring process as an interview. Write a Discovery Statement that describes your strengths, along with what you learned about your potential employer. Also write an Intention Statement about ways to be more effective during your next interview.

Now comes follow-up. This step can give you the edge that leads to a job offer.

Pull out the business cards from the people who interviewed you. Write them thank-you notes, following each person's preference for paper-based or online contact. Do this within 2 business days after the interview. If you talked to several people at the same company, then write a different note to each one.

If you get turned down for the job after your interview, don't take it personally. Every interview is a source of feedback about what works—and what doesn't work—in contacting employers. Use that feedback to interview more effectively next time.

Also remember that each person you talked to is now a member of your network. This is true even if you do not get a job offer. Follow up by asking interviewers to keep you in mind for future job openings. Using this approach, you gain from every interview, no matter what the outcome. ■

**You're One Click Away...**
*from discovering more job-hunting strategies online.*

10

# ✓ EXERCISE 21

# THE DISCOVERY WHEEL—COMING FULL CIRCLE

This book doesn't work. It is worthless. Only you can work. Only you can make a difference and use this book to become a more effective student.

The purpose of this book is to give you the opportunity to change your behavior. The fact that something seems like a good idea doesn't necessarily mean that you will put it into practice. This exercise gives you a chance to see what behaviors you have changed on your journey toward becoming a master student.

Answer each question quickly and honestly. Record your results on the Discovery Wheel on this page. Then compare it with the one you completed in Chapter 1.

The scores on this Discovery Wheel indicate your current strengths and weaknesses on your path toward becoming a master student. The last Journal Entry in this chapter provides an opportunity to write about how you intend to change. As you complete this self-evaluation, keep in mind that your commitment to change allows you to become a master student. *Your scores might be lower here than on your earlier Discovery Wheel.* That's okay. Lower scores might result from increased self-awareness and honesty, as well as other valuable assets.

**Note:** The online version of this exercise does not include number ratings, so the results will be formatted differently from those described here. If you did your previous Discovery Wheel online, do it online again. This will help you compare your two sets of responses more accurately.

**5 points** = This statement is always or almost always true of me.

**4 points** = This statement is often true of me.

**3 points** = This statement is true of me about half the time.

**2 points** = This statement is seldom true of me.

**1 point** = This statement is never or almost never true of me.

 **You're One Click Away...**
*from having your Discovery Wheel scores calculated automatically for you online.*

1. _____ I enjoy learning.

2. _____ I understand and apply the concept of multiple intelligences.

3. _____ I connect my courses to my purpose for being in school.

4. _____ I make a habit of assessing my personal strengths and areas for improvement.

5. _____ I am satisfied with how I am progressing toward achieving my goals.

6. _____ I use my knowledge of learning styles to support my success in school.

7. _____ I am willing to consider any idea that can help me succeed in school—even if I initially disagree with that idea.

8. _____ I regularly remind myself of the benefits I intend to get from my education.

_____ **Total score (1) Attitude**

1. _____ I set long-term goals and periodically review them.

2. _____ I set short-term goals to support my long-term goals.

3. _____ I write a plan for each day and each week.

4. _____ I assign priorities to what I choose to do each day.

5. _____ I am confident that I will have enough money to complete my education.

6. _____ I make regular deposits to a savings account.

7. _____ I pay off the balance on credit card accounts each month.

8. _____ I can have fun without spending money.

_____ **Total score (2) Time and Money**

1. _____ I am confident of my ability to remember.

2. _____ I can remember people's names.

3. _____ At the end of a lecture, I can summarize what was presented.

4. _____ I apply techniques that enhance my memory skills.

5. _____ I can recall information when I'm under pressure.

6. _____ I remember important information clearly and easily.

7. _____ I can jog my memory when I have difficulty recalling.

8. _____ I can relate new information to what I've already learned.

_____ **Total score (3) Memory**

1. _____ I preview and review reading assignments.

2. _____ When reading, I ask myself questions about the material.

3. _____ I underline or highlight important passages when reading.

4. _____ When I read textbooks, I am alert and awake.

5. _____ I relate what I read to my life.

6. _____ I select a reading strategy to fit the type of material I'm reading.

7. _____ I take effective notes when I read.

8. _____ When I don't understand what I'm reading, I note my questions and find answers.

_____ **Total score (4) Reading**

1. _____ When I am in class, I focus my attention.

2. _____ I take notes in class.

3. _____ I am aware of various methods for taking notes and choose those that work best for me.

4. _____ I distinguish important material and note key phrases in a lecture.

5. _____ I copy down material that the instructor writes on the board or overhead display.

6. _____ I can put important concepts into my own words.

7. _____ My notes are valuable for review.

8. _____ I review class notes within 24 hours.

_____ **Total score (5) Notes**

1. _____ I use techniques to manage stress related to exams.

2. _____ I manage my time during exams and am able to complete them.

3. _____ I am able to predict test questions.

4. _____ I adapt my test-taking strategy to the kind of test I'm taking.

5. _____ I understand what essay questions ask and can answer them completely and accurately.

6. _____ I start reviewing for tests at the beginning of the term.

7. _____ I continue reviewing for tests throughout the term.

8. _____ My sense of personal worth is independent of my test scores.

_____ **Total score (6) Tests**

1. _____ I have flashes of insight and think of solutions to problems at unusual times.

2. _____ I use brainstorming to generate solutions to a variety of problems.

3. _____ When I get stuck on a creative project, I use specific methods to get unstuck.

4. _____ I learn by thinking about ways to contribute to the lives of other people.

5. _____ I am willing to consider different points of view and alternative solutions.

6. _____ I can detect common errors in logic.

7. _____ I construct viewpoints by drawing on information and ideas from many sources.

8. _____ As I share my viewpoints with others, I am open to their feedback.

_____ **Total score (7) Thinking**

1. _____ I am honest with others about who I am, what I feel, and what I want.

2. _____ Other people tell me that I am a good listener.

3. _____ I can communicate my upset and anger without blaming others.

4. _____ I can make friends and create valuable relationships in a new setting.

5. _____ I am open to being with people I don't especially like in order to learn from them.

6. _____ I build rewarding relationships with people from diverse backgrounds.

7. _____ I can effectively plan and research a large writing assignment.

8. _____ I know ways to prepare and deliver effective speeches.

_____ **Total score (8) Communicating**

**10**

1. _____ I have enough energy to study and work—and still enjoy other areas of my life.

2. _____ If the situation calls for it, I have enough reserve energy to put in a long day.

3. _____ The way I eat supports my long-term health.

4. _____ The way I eat is independent of my feelings of self-worth.

5. _____ I exercise regularly to maintain a healthful weight.

6. _____ My emotional health supports my ability to learn.

7. _____ I notice changes in my physical condition and respond effectively.

8. _____ I am in control of any alcohol or other drugs I put into my body.

_____ Total score (9) Health

1. _____ I see learning as a lifelong process.

2. _____ I relate school to what I plan to do for the rest of my life.

3. _____ I see problems and tough choices as opportunities for learning and personal growth.

4. _____ I have a written career plan and update it regularly.

5. _____ I am gaining skills to support my success in the workplace.

6. _____ I take responsibility for the quality of my education—and my life.

7. _____ I live by a set of values that translates into daily actions.

8. _____ I am willing to accept challenges even when I'm not sure how to meet them.

_____ Total score (10) Purpose

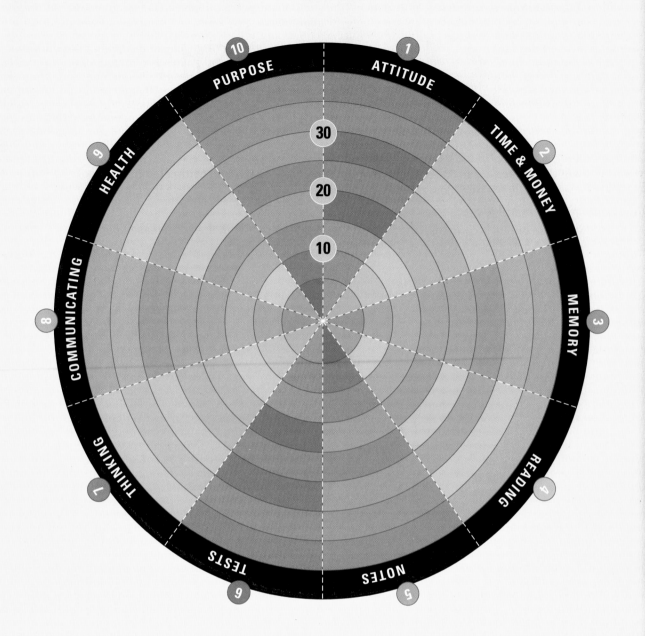

The wheel sections, clockwise from top, are labeled: PURPOSE (10), ATTITUDE (1), TIME & MONEY (2), MEMORY (3), READING (4), NOTES (5), TESTS (6), THINKING (7), COMMUNICATING (8), HEALTH (9). The rings are marked 10, 20, 30.

## FILLING IN YOUR DISCOVERY WHEEL

Using the total score from each category, shade in each section of the Discovery Wheel on this page. Use different colors, if you want. For example, you could use green to denote areas you want to work on. When you have finished, complete the following Skills Snapshot. ■

10

# SKILLS Snapshot

## Revisiting your Discovery Wheels

The purpose of this exercise is to (1) review both of the Discovery Wheels you completed in this book, (2) summarize your insights from doing them, and (3) declare how you will use these insights to promote your continued success in school.

Again, a lower score on the second Discovery Wheel does not necessarily indicate decreased personal effectiveness. Instead, the lower score could result from increased honesty and greater self-awareness.

Enter your Discovery Wheel scores from both chapters in the space below.

|  | Chapter 1 | Chapter 10 |
|---|---|---|
| Attitude | _____ | _____ |
| Time and Money | _____ | _____ |
| Memory | _____ | _____ |
| Reading | _____ | _____ |
| Notes | _____ | _____ |
| Tests | _____ | _____ |
| Thinking | _____ | _____ |
| Communicating | _____ | _____ |
| Health | _____ | _____ |
| Purpose | _____ | _____ |

Comparing the Discovery Wheel in this chapter with the Discovery Wheel in Chapter 1, I discovered that I . . .

In the next 6 months, I intend to review the following articles from this book for additional suggestions I could use:

# Now that you're done—
# BEGIN

If you used this book fully—if you actively participated in reading the contents, writing the Journal Entries, doing the exercises, practicing critical thinking, and putting the suggestions to work—you have had quite a journey.

Recall some high points of that journey. The first half of this book is about the nuts and bolts of education—the business of acquiring knowledge. It helps prepare you for making the transition to higher education and suggests that you take a First Step by telling the truth about your skills and setting goals to expand them. Also included are guidelines for planning your time, training your memory, improving your reading skills, taking useful notes, and succeeding at tests.

All of this activity prepares you for another aim of education—generating new knowledge. Meeting this aim leads you to the topics in the second half of this book: thinking for yourself, enhancing your communication skills, embracing diversity, learning to manage money, living with vibrant health, and creating a unique place for yourself in the world. All are steps on the path of becoming a master student.

Now what? What's your next step?

As you answer this question, remember that the process of experimenting with your life never ends. At any moment, you can begin again.

Consider the possibility that you can create the life of your dreams. Your responses to any of the ideas, exercises, and Journal Entries in this book can lead you to think new thoughts, say new things, and do what you never believed you could do. If you're willing to master new ways to learn, the possibilities are endless. This message is more fundamental than any individual tool or technique you'll ever read about.

There are people who scoff at the suggestion that they can create the life of their dreams. These people have a perspective that is widely shared. Please set it aside.

You are on the edge of a universe so miraculous and full of wonder that your imagination, even at its most creative moment, cannot encompass it. Paths are open to lead you to worlds beyond your wildest dreams.

If this sounds like a pitch for the latest recreational drug, it might be. That "drug" is enthusiasm. It is automatically generated by your body when you are learning, planning, taking risks, achieving goals, and discovering new worlds inside and outside your skin.

**The first chapter in this book included articles about transition. You are about to make another transition—not just to another chapter of this book, but to the next chapter of your life.**

Even so, we might avoid thinking about what's next in our lives until we're feeling ready for such a big conversation. "Ready" might be next week, next month, next year, or some other time that sounds more convenient. Other people reinforce this notion by telling you that your life will *really* start on the day when you . . . (Fill in the blank with phrases such as *graduate from college, get married, have kids, get promoted*, or *retire*.)

Agreeing with these statements can condemn us to a life of perpetual waiting. Using this logic, we could wait our whole life to start living. And that doesn't sound like much fun.

However, there is another option: You can give up the myth of "someday." You can start choosing the next steps now. You can start making commitments for the future that change your action in the present. Set goals that might take years to accomplish—and then enjoy every step along the way.

The first chapter in this book included articles about transition. You are about to make another transition—not just to another chapter of this book, but to the next chapter of your life. Engage with what you have learned to explore your skills, choose your major, plan your career, find your place in the global economy, and otherwise create the life of your dreams.

Use these pages to choose what's next for you. ∎

10

# "Use the following suggestions to continue ..."

**Keep a journal.** Write about your hopes, wishes, and goals. Keep a record of significant events. Continue using the format of Discovery Statements and Intention Statements that you learned in this book.

**Read, watch, and listen.** At any point in your life, you can enroll in "Internet university." Audio programs, videos, and courses from many colleges and universities are available online, often for free. To find them, start with the list available online at Open Culture (**www.openculture.com**). If you have access to iTunes, also check out iTunes U. Search for content from reputable instructors, and remember to think critically about everything you find online.

In addition, explore your campus and community libraries. Look for announcements of upcoming workshops and seminars.

**Take an unrelated class.** Sign up for a class that is totally unrelated to your major. If you are studying economics, take a physics course. If you are planning to be a doctor, take an accounting course. Take a course that will help you develop new computer skills and expand your possibilities for online learning. You can discover a lot about yourself and your intended future when you step out of old patterns.

**Travel.** See the world. Visit new neighborhoods. Travel to other countries. Explore. Find out what it looks like inside buildings that you normally have no reason to enter, museums that you never found interesting before, cities that are out of the way, forests and mountains that lie beyond your old boundaries, and far-off places that require planning and saving to reach.

**Get counseling.** Solving emotional problems is not the only reason to visit a counselor, therapist, or psychologist. These people are excellent resources for personal growth. You can use counseling to look at and talk about yourself in ways that might be uncomfortable for anyone except a trained professional. Counseling offers a chance to focus exclusively on yourself—something that is usually not possible in normal social settings.

**Form a support group.** An organized support group can help you reach goals in other areas of your life. Today, people in support groups help one another lose weight, stay sober, cope with chronic illness, recover from emotional trauma, and overcome drug addiction.

**Find a mentor—or become one.** Seek the counsel of experienced people you respect and admire. Use them as role models. If they are willing, ask them to be sounding boards for your plans and ideas. Many people are flattered to be asked.

**Consider further education and training.** Your career plan might call for continuing education, additional certifications, or an advanced degree. Remember that the strategies in this book can help you gain new knowledge and skills at any point in your life.

**Redo this book.** If you didn't get everything you wanted from this book, it's not too late. You can read part of it or all of it again at any time.

Also redo portions of the book that you found valuable.

 **You're One Click Away...**
*from finding more suggestions online for continuing the path toward mastery.*

---

 **EXERCISE 22**

## This book shouts, "Use me!"

**B**ecoming a Master Student is designed to be used for years. The success strategies presented here are not likely to become habits overnight. There are more suggestions than can be put into action immediately. Some of what is discussed might not apply to your life right now, but it might be just what you could use in a few months.

Plan to keep this book and use it again. Imagine that your book has a mouth. (Visualize the mouth.) Also imagine that it has arms and legs. (Visualize them.)

Now picture your book sitting on a shelf or table that you see every day. Imagine a time when you are having trouble in school and struggling to be successful as a student. Visualize your book jumping up and down, shouting, "Use me! Read me! I might have the solution to your problem, and I know I can help you solve it."

Sometimes when you are stuck, all you need is a small push. At those times, hear your book shout, "Use me!"

# PRACTICING critical thinking 10

This exercise will give you practice in thinking at **Level 5: Evaluating**. Test questions that call for this level of thinking begin with words like these:

- Critique
- Evaluate
- Judge
- Justify
- Rank
- Recommend
- Suggest
- Support

Your courses will often involve this level of thinking. For example, an English literature instructor might assign several short stories for you to read and then ask, "Which story did you like best, and why?"

Suppose that a friend says to you, "I want to get the most value from the money and time I invest in higher education. What are the most important things for me to do?" Your answer to this question involves evaluating.

Based on your experience with *Becoming a Master Student*, list the top three strategies that you would **suggest** for your friend that will **support** success in school.

_____

_____

_____

_____

_____

_____

# ✓ EXERCISE 23

## Do something you can't

Few significant accomplishments result from people sticking to the familiar. You can accomplish much more than you think you can. Doing something you can't involves taking risks. This exercise has three steps.

**STEP 1** Select something that you have never done before, that you don't know how to do, that you are fearful of doing, or that you think you probably can't do. Perhaps you've never learned to play an instrument, or you've never run a marathon. Be smart. Don't pick something that will hurt you physically, such as flying from a third-floor window. Use the space below to describe what you have chosen.

_____

_____

_____

**STEP 2** Do it. Of course, this is easier to say than to do. This exercise is not about easy. It is about discovering capabilities that stretch your self-image. To accomplish something that is bigger than your self-perceived abilities, use any of the tools you have gained from this book. Develop a plan. Divide and conquer. Stay focused. Use outside resources. Let go of self-destructive thoughts. Summarize the tools you will use.

_____

_____

**STEP 3** Write about your results of this exercise here.

_____

_____

_____

_____

# masterstudentprofile

# Lisa Ling

(1973– ) Lisa Ling, host of National Geographic Channel's *Explorer*, special correspondent for *The Oprah Winfrey Show*, and a former cohost of ABC's *The View*, was one of the youngest reporters for *Channel One News*, whose programming is aimed at middle and high schools.

I had heard about auditions for a teen magazine show called *Scratch*. They were holding auditions in a mall, and one Saturday in Sacramento I showed up along with hundreds of other students. They chose four of us to host this show—a fun teen magazine where I interviewed celebrities and did makeovers and silly things like that. But what was cool was that it was produced by a local news affiliate, and I used that entrée into the station to get an internship in the newsroom. I hung out with the writers and learned to run the teleprompter. I was sort of an eager and aggressive young kid who wanted to learn about the business, and I would show up at the TV station at 4:30 or 5:00 in the morning before classes.

After doing three years on a teen magazine show, I was ready to go to college. Then the director of Channel One called me and said, "We'd like you to come audition." I did and got the job. It was based in Los Angeles, so I ended up going to the University of Southern California while doing Channel One at the same time.

Channel One has been plagued by . . . controversy because it airs commercials within the broadcast. But for me as a reporter it was the most incredible opportunity, and the editorial content of Channel One I would put up against any network news show. I was a 19- and 20-year-old kid covering the civil war in Afghanistan, the Russian referendum elections, the civil war in Algeria, the drug war in Colombia, overpopulation in China, globalization in India. I would work on a series about the democracy movement in Iran in 1995 that would run about twenty-five minutes throughout the course of a week. And at that time, what news outlet would cover Iran for twenty-five minutes?

I actually think that was some of my best journalism. While I did do research on the various stories and countries, I kind of went in to them not knowing so much—just being open and not having a lot of preconceived ideas or notions. You know, these days we are almost brainwashed. When our leadership characterizes entire countries as evil, how do you *not* go into stories with preconceived ideas? What we did as young people was pick these places in the world that no one was covering and went there. We didn't tell our viewers what to think. We just gave them an opportunity to experience what *we* were experiencing.

I majored in history because I wanted to have as broad-based an education as I could possibly get. My history background and my political science background and my travels have been my biggest assets as a journalist.

People are always asking me: How did you get your job? And my answer is, I just got it. I just kind of willed it into existence. I just kind of created this situation.

My advice to young people: Before you get hampered by a job and family and financial obligations, try to get out of your comfort zone. If you can, live in another country for a year or so. You won't regret it.

© Michael Quan/ZUMA/Corbis

**LISA LING . . .** is inquisitive.

**YOU . . .** can keep inquiring about new possibilities for your life.

*Source:* Excerpted from "Journalist and Correspondent Lisa Ling," broadcast on *Profiles*, a radio program from WFIU, Indiana University, and hosted by Owen Johnson, November 11, 2007, http://wfiu.org/profiles/lisa-ling.

**You're One Click Away...**
*from learning more about Lisa Ling online at the Master Student Profiles. You can also visit the Master Student Hall of Fame to learn about other master students.*

# QUIZ

Name _____

Date _____

1. List the three categories of choices explained in the Power Process: "Be it."

2. Explain how *work-content skills* and *transferable skills* differ.

3. List two examples of work-content skills.

4. List five examples of transferable skills.

5. According to the text, you can create a career plan through the process of "naming names." True or false? Explain your answer.

6. Give three examples of ways to test your career choice.

7. According to the text, the main purpose of your résumé is to:

   (a) Get to the next stage of the hiring process—usually a job interview
   (b) Help you choose which courses to take in school
   (c) Help you choose which skills to develop
   (d) All of the above

8. Describe two strategies you can use to make your résumé easy to read.

9. If your scores are lower on the Discovery Wheel the second time you complete it, this means your skills have not improved. True or false? Explain your answer.

10. List at least three ways in which you can continue on your path of becoming a master student after completing this book.

# SKILLS *Snapshot*

If you fully participated with this chapter, you've got a lot of answers to the opening question: What's next? Reflect on these answers in light of your responses to the Purpose section of the Discovery Wheel in this chapter (page 230).

## DISCOVERY

My score on the *Purpose* section on the Discovery Wheel was . . .

One work-content skill that I've already developed is . . .

One transferable skill that I've already developed is . . .

When thinking and talking about my career plan, I feel . . .

## INTENTION

Three new work-content skills that I want to develop are . . .

Three new transferable skills that I want to develop are . . .

What I want most from any career I choose is . . .

What I want most from my education is . . .

## NEXT ACTIONS

The three most important things I can do in the next 6 months to achieve my career and educational goals are to . . .

# Endnotes

## INTRODUCTION

1. Excerpts from *Creating Your Future*. Copyright © 1998 by David B. Ellis. Adapted by permission of Houghton Mifflin Company. All rights reserved.
2. U.S. Department of Labor, Bureau of Labor Statistics, "Education Pays . . . ," May 27, 2010, www.bls.gov/emp/ep_chart_001.htm.
3. Randy Moore, "The Importance of Admissions Scores and Attendance to First-Year Performance," *Journal of The First-Year Experience & Students in Transition, 2006* 18, no. 1, (2006): 105–125.
4. U.S. Census Bureau, "Facts for Features: Back to School 2007–2008," June 14, 2008, http://www.census.gov/newsroom/releases/archives/facts_for_features_special_editions/cb07-ff11.html.
5. Richard Malott, "Self Management Checklist," Counselling Services, University of Victoria, 2003, accessed October 13, 2006, from http://www.coun.uvic.ca/learning/motivation/self-management.html.
6. Brad Isaac, "Jerry Seinfeld's Productivity Secret," *Lifehacker*, July 24, 2007, accessed November 8, 2012, from http://lifehacker.com/software/motivation/jerry-seinfelds-productivity-secret-281626.php.
7. B. F. Skinner, *Science and Human Behavior* (Boston: Free Press, 1965).

## CHAPTER 1

1. David A. Kolb, *Experiential Learning: Experience as the Source of Learning and Development* (Englewood Cliffs, NJ: Prentice-Hall, 1984).
2. Douglas A. Bernstein, Louis A. Penner, Alison Clarke-Stewart, and Edward J. Roy, *Psychology* (Boston: Houghton Mifflin, 2006), 368–369.
3. Howard Gardner, *Frames of Mind: The Theory of Multiple Intelligences* (New York: Basic Books, 1993).
4. Neil Fleming, "VARK: A Guide to Learning Styles," 2012, accessed November 8, 2012, from www.vark-learn.com/.

## CHAPTER 2

1. Alan Lakein, *How to Get Control of Your Time and Your Life* (New York: New American Library, 1973; reissue 1996).
2. Mei-Ching Lien, Eric Ruthruff, and James C. Johnston, "Attentional Limitations in Doing Two Tasks at Once: The Search for Exceptions," *Current Directions in Psychological Science* 15, no. 2 (2005): 89–93.
3. Clive Thompson, "Meet the Lifehackers," *New York Times*, October 16, 2005, www.nytimes.com/2005/10/16/magazine/16guru.html.
4. John Medina, *Brain Rules: 12 Principles for Surviving and Thriving at Work, Home, and School* (Seattle, WA: Pear Press, 2009), 87.
5. "Education Pays 2010," College Board, 2010, http://trends.collegeboard.org/education_pays.

## CHAPTER 3

1. Donald Hebb, quoted in D. J. Siegel, "Memory: An Overview," *Journal of the American Academy of Child and Adolescent Psychiatry* 40, no. 9 (2001): 997–1011.
2. Siegel, "Memory: An Overview."
3. Daniel L. Schacter, *The Seven Sins of Memory: How the Mind Forgets and Remembers* (Boston: Houghton Mifflin, 2001), 13–15.
4. Schacter, *The Seven Sins of Memory*, 35–36.
5. Alzheimer's Association, "Brain Health," 2012, accessed November 8, 2012, from www.alz.org/brainhealth/overview.asp.

## CHAPTER 4

1. National Endowment for the Arts, "To Read or Not to Read: A Question of National Consequence," December 3, 2007, accessed November 8, 2012, from http://www.nea.gov/research/ToRead_ExecSum.pdf.
2. Jeffrey D. Karpicke and Janell R. Blunt, "Retrieval Practice Produces More Learning than Elaborative Studying with Concept Mapping," *Science* 20 (January 2011), accessed January 21, 2011, from www.sciencemag.org/content/early/2011/01/19/science.1199327.abstract.
3. O. Pineño and R. R. Miller, "Primacy and Recency Effects in Extinction and Latent Inhibition: A Selective Review with Implications for Models of Learning," *Behavioural Processes* 69 (2005): 223–235.

## CHAPTER 5

1. Gayle A. Brazeau, "Handouts in the Classroom: Is Note Taking a Lost Skill?" *American Journal of Pharmaceutical Education* 70, no. 2 (April 15, 2006): 38.
2. Walter Pauk and Ross J. Q. Owens, *How to Study in College*, 10th ed. (Boston: Cengage Learning, 2011).
3. Tony Buzan, Use Both Sides of Your Brain (New York: Dutton, 1991).
4. Gabrielle Rico, *Writing the Natural Way* (New York: Penguin, 2000).

## CHAPTER 6

1. Jonathan D. Glater, "Colleges Chase as Cheats Shift to Higher Tech," *New York Times* May 18, 2006, accessed November 8, 2012, from www.nytimes.com/2006/05/18/education/18cheating.html.
2. Gerardo Ramirez and Sian L. Beilock, "Writing About Testing Worries Boosts Exam Performance in the Classroom," *Science* 331 (January 14, 2011): 211–213.
3. This article incorporates detailed suggestions from reviewer Frank Baker.

## CHAPTER 7

1. Quoted in Theodore A. Rees Cheney, *Getting the Words Right: How to Rewrite, Edit and Revise* (Cincinnati, OH: Writer's Digest Books, 1990).
2. Martin E. P. Seligman, *Authentic Happiness: Using the New Positive Psychology to Realize Your Potential for Lasting Fulfillment* (New York: Simon and Schuster, 2002).
3. Quoted in Alice Calaprice, ed., *The Expanded Quotable Einstein* (Princeton, NJ: Princeton University Press, 2000).

## CHAPTER 8

1. Thomas Gordon, *Parent Effectiveness Training: The Tested New Way to Raise Responsible Children* (New York: New American Library, 1975).
2. Daniel Goleman, *Emotional Intelligence: Why It Can Matter More Than IQ* (New York: Bantam, 1995), xiv–xv.
3. David Allen, "The GTD questions you can use every day," *Productive Living*, e-mail newsletter, January 12, 2011.
4. Diane de Anda, *Bicultural Socialization: Factors Affecting the Minority Experience* (Washington, DC: National Association of Social Workers, 1984).

## CHAPTER 9

1. Centers for Disease Control and Prevention, "Health Habits of Adults Aged 18–29 Highlighted in Report on Nation's Health," February 18, 2009, accessed March 15, 2011, from http://www.cdc.gov/media/pressrel/2009/r090218.htm.
2. University of Minnesota, "Health and Academic Performance: Minnesota Undergraduate Students," accessed April 10, 2009, from www.bhs.umn.edu/reports/HealthAcademicPerformance-Report_2007.pdf, 2007.
3. Kay-Tee Khaw, Nicholas Wareham, Sheila Bingham, Ailsa Welch, Robert Luben, and Nicholas Day, "Combined Impact of Health Behaviours and Mortality in Men and Women: The EPIC-Norfolk Prospective Population Study," *PLoS Medicine* 5, no. 1 (2008), accessed November 8, 2012, from www.plosmedicine.org/article/info:doi/10.1371/journal.pmed.0050012.
4. U.S. Department of Agriculture, "Dietary Guidelines for Americans, 2010," January 31, 2011, accessed November 8, 2012, from http://www.cnpp.usda.gov/DGAs2010-PolicyDocument.htm.
5. Michael Pollan, "Unhappy Meals," *New York Times*, January 28, 2007, accessed November 8, 2012, from www.nytimes.com/2007/01/28/magazine/28nutritionism.t.html.
6. Harvard Medical School, *HEALTHbeat: 20 No-Sweat Ways to Get More Exercise* (Boston: Harvard Health Publications, October 14, 2008).
7. Jane Brody, "Exercise = Weight Loss, Except When It Doesn't," *New York Times*, September 12, 2006, accessed November 8, 2012, from www.nytimes.com/2006/09/12/health/nutrition/12brody.html.
8. Harvard Medical School, *HEALTHbeat Extra: The Secret to Better Health—Exercise* (Boston: Harvard Health Publications, January 27, 2009).
9. Mary Duenwald, "The Dorms May Be Great, but How's the Counseling?" *New York Times*, October 26, 2004, accessed November 8, 2012, from https://www.nytimes.com/2004/10/26/health/psychology/26cons.html.
10. American College Health Association, American College Health Association–National College Health Assessment II: Reference Group, Executive Summary Fall 2008, accessed March 15, 2011, from www.acha-ncha.org/docs/ACHA-NCHA_Reference_Group_ExecutiveSummary_Fall2008.pdf, 2009.
11. Morita Masatake's ideas are discussed in David Reynolds, *A Handbook for Constructive Living* (New York: Morrow, 1995), 98.
12. Albert Ellis, *Overcoming Destructive Beliefs, Feelings, and Behaviors*: New Directions for Rational Emotive Behavior Therapy (Amherst, NY: Prometheus, 2001).
13. M. Schaffer, E.L. Jeglic, and B. Stanley, "The Relationship between Suicidal Behavior, Ideation, and Binge Drinking among College Students," *Archives of Suicide Research* 12 (2008): 124–132.
14. Minnesota Department of Health, "Sexually Transmitted Disease Facts" November 16, 2010, accessed November 8, 2012, from http://www.health.state.mn.us/divs/idepc/dtopics/stds/stdfactssummary.html.
15. Centers for Disease Control and Prevention, "Trends in Reportable Sexually Transmitted Diseases in the United States, 2007" (2009), accessed March 15, 2011, from http://www.cdc.gov/std/stats07/trends.htm.
16. Andrew Weil and Winifred Rosen, *From Chocolate to Morphine: Everything You Need to Know About Mind-Altering Drugs* (Boston: Houghton Mifflin, 1993), 45.
17. U.S. Centers for Disease Control and Prevention, "Tobacco-Related Mortality," March 21, 2011, accessed November 8, 2012, from http://www.cdc.gov/tobacco/data_statistics/fact_sheets/health_effects/tobacco_related_mortality/.

## CHAPTER 10

1. Encyclopaedia Britannica Online Reference Center, "Ford, Henry," accessed April 15, 2011, from www.library.eb.com/eb/article-22461.
2. FordCarz, "Henry Ford Quotations," 2003, accessed November 8, 2012, from www.fordcarz.com/henry-ford-quotations-about-cars.html.
3. Adapted from Dave Ellis, Stan Lankowitz, Ed Stupka, and Doug Toft, *Career Planning*, 3rd ed. Copyright © 2003 by Houghton Mifflin Company.
4. Kate Zernike, "College, My Way," *New York Times*, April 23, 2006, accessed November 8, 2012, from https://www.nytimes.com/2006/04/23/education/edlife/zernike.html.

# Additional Reading

Adler, Mortimer, and Charles Van Doren, *How to Read a Book: The Classic Guide to Intelligent Reading* (New York: Touchstone, 1972).

Allen, David, *Getting Things Done: The Art of Stress-Free Productivity* (New York: Penguin, 2001).

Belsky, Scott, *Making Ideas Happen: Overcoming the Obstacles Between Vision and Reality* (New York: Portfolio, 2010).

Bolles, Richard N., *What Color Is Your Parachute? A Practical Manual for Job-Hunters and Career-Changers* (Berkeley, CA: Ten Speed, updated annually).

Boston Women's Health Book Collective, *Our Bodies, Ourselves: A New Edition for a New Era* (New York: Touchstone, 2005).

Buzan, Tony, *How to Mind Map: Make the Most of Your Mind and Learn to Create, Organize and Plan* (New York: Thorsons/Element, 2003).

Chaffee, John, *Thinking Critically*, 10th ed. (Boston: Cengage, 2012).

Colvin, George, *Talent is Overrated: What Really Separates World-Class Performers from Everybody Else* (New York: Portfolio, 2008).

Coplin, Bill, *10 Things Employers Want You to Learn in College* (Berkeley, CA: Ten Speed, 2003).

Covey, Stephen R., *The Seven Habits of Highly Effective People: Powerful Lessons in Personal Change* (New York: Simon & Schuster, 1989).

Davis, Deborah, *The Adult Learner's Companion*, 2nd ed. (Boston: Cengage, 2012).

Downing, Skip, *On Course: Strategies for Creating Success in College and in Life*, 6th ed. (Boston: Cengage, 2011).

Elgin, Duane, *Voluntary Simplicity* (New York: Morrow, 1993).

Ellis, Dave, *Becoming a Master Student*, 13th ed. (Boston: Cengage, 2011).

Ellis, Dave, *Falling Awake: Creating the Life of Your Dreams* (Rapid City, SD: Breakthrough Enterprises, 2000).

Facione, Peter, *Critical Thinking: What It Is and Why It Counts* (Millbrae, CA: California Academic Press, 1996).

Fletcher, Anne, *Sober for Good* (Boston: Houghton Mifflin, 2001).

*From Master Student to Master Employee*, 3rd ed. (Boston: Cengage, 2011).

Gawain, Shakti, *Creative Visualization* (New York: New World Library, 1998).

Glasser, William, *Take Effective Control of Your Life* (New York: HarperCollins, 1984).

Godin, Seth, *Linchpin: Are You Indispensable?* (New York: Portfolio, 2010).

Golas, Thaddeus, *The Lazy Man's Guide to Enlightenment* (New York: Bantam, 1993).

Greene, Susan D., and Melanie C. L. Martel, *The Ultimate Job Hunter's Guidebook*, 5th ed. (Boston: Cengage, 2008).

Hallowell, Edward M., *Crazy Busy: Overstretched, Overbooked, and About to Snap!* (New York: Ballantine, 2006).

Keyes, Ken, Jr., *Handbook to Higher Consciousness* (Berkeley, CA: Living Love, 1974).

Kolb, David A., *Experiential Learning: Experience as the Source of Learning and Development* (Englewood Cliffs: Prentice-Hall, 1984).

Levy, Frank, and Richard J. Murname, *The New Division of Labor: How Computers Are Creating the Next Job Market* (Princeton, NJ: Princeton University Press, 2004).

Newport, Cal, *How to Win at College* (New York: Random House, 2005).

Nolting, Paul D., *Math Study Skills Workbook*, 4th ed. (Boston: Cengage, 2011).

Pirsig, Robert, *Zen and the Art of Motorcycle Maintenance* (New York: Perennial Classics, 2000).

Raimes, Anne and Maria Jerskey, *Universal Keys for Writers*, 2nd ed. (Boston: Cengage, 2008).

Ram Dass, *Be Here Now* (Santa Fe, NM: Hanuman Foundation, 1971).

Robinson, Adam, *What Smart Students Know: Maximum Grades, Optimum Learning, Minimum Time* (New York: Crown, 1993).

Ruggiero, Vincent Ryan, *Becoming a Critical Thinker*, 6th ed. (Boston: Cengage, 2009).

Schacter, Daniel L., *Searching for Memory: The Brain, the Mind, and the Past* (New York: HarperCollins, 1997).

Toft, Doug, ed., *Master Student Guide to Academic Success* (Boston: Cengage, 2005).

Trapani, Gina, *Lifehacker: 88 Tech Tricks to Turbocharge Your Day* (Indianapolis, IN: Wiley, 2007).

Ueland, Brenda, *If You Want to Write: A Book About Art, Independence and Spirit* (St. Paul, MN: Graywolf, 1987).

U.S. Department of Education, *Funding Education Beyond High School: The Guide to Federal Student Aid*. Published yearly, available at http://studentaid.ed.gov/resources#funding.

Watkins, Ryan, and Michael Corry, *E-learning Companion: A Student's Guide to Online Success*, 3rd ed. (Boston: Cengage, 2011).

Wurman, Saul Richard, *Information Anxiety 2* (Indianapolis: QUE, 2001).

# Index

comprehension
    in critical thinking, 160
    faster reading and, 108
    monitoring through highlighting, 102
computer-graded tests, 146
concept errors, on tests, 148
conclusion, in presentations, 192
conclusions, jumping to, 166
concrete experience, 33, 35, 90
condensing, in note taking, 130
condoms, 207
conflict management, 184–185
contacts, naming in career planning, 222
context, inferring word meaning from, 109
contingency plan, developing for online coursework, 132
copying, in note taking, 123
cornell method of note taking, 124–125
counseling, 234
courage, 5, 27
cover letter, 226
cramming, 142
creating (level 6 thinking), 47, 75, 92, 113, 133, 161, 173, 211
creating meaning, as memory technique, 84
creative serendipity, 164–165
creativity, 5, 164–165
credibility, of information, 112
credit, managing, 73
credits, transferring between schools, 225
critical thinking
    developing skill, 160–163
    highlighting and, 102
    Internet use and, 167
    note taking and, 121
    overcoming math anxiety, 151
    overcoming test anxiety, 150
    practicing, 47, 75, 92, 113, 133, 139, 161, 173, 193, 210–211, 235
    question-opinion-support chart, 85–86
cue column, 124–125
culture
    communicating across, 186–188
    conflict management and, 185
curiosity, 4
currency, of information, 112

# D

daily reviews, 141
daily to-do list (ABC), 60
davis, Sampson, 194
de Anda, Diane, 187
debate, postponing for note taking, 120
decision making
    emotional intelligence and, 183
    gaining skills at, 168
decoding, in memory, 81
define the problem, 169
defining terms, 162

delegating tasks, 17
detach (Power Process), 138, 217
diagrams, in note taking, 123
dictionary, 109
diet, 200
difficult reading, dealing with, 107
direct quotes, 190
disagreement, postponing for note taking, 120
discomfort
    changing habits and, 21
    with Discovery Statements, 12
    First Step technique, 25–27
    motivation and, 19
    willingness to accept, 5
Discover What You Want (Power Process), 2, 217
Discovery and Intention Journal Entry system
    continuing throughout life, 234
    explanation of, 10–11
    guidelines, 12
    as memory aid, 90
Discovery Statements. *See* Discovery and Intention Journal Entry system
Discovery Wheel (exercise activity), 28–32, 228–231
Discovery/Intention Statements. *See* Discovery and Intention Journal Entry system
discrimination, speaking up against, 188
disease, preventing, 207
distractions, listening and, 180
distribute learning, as memory technique, 87
diversity
    communication and, 186–188
    in conflict management, 185
    critical thinking and, 162
    in higher education, 13, 18, 22
do something you can't (exercise activity), 235
documentation, of information on the internet, 167
doing, learning by, 33, 35
drawing, as memory technique, 85
drugs, 208

# E

earnings, increasing, 68
eating disorders, 200
editing notes, 127
editing, as transferable skill, 218
education by the hour (exercise activity), 74
education. See Higher Education
educational objectives, 160–161
elaboration, as memory technique, 87
elaborative rehearsal, 90
Ellis, Albert, 203

emergencies, preparing for, 206
emotion
    allowing in conflict management, 184
    basing arguments on, 166
    listening and, 180
    as memory technique, 86
    public speaking and, 183
emotional health, 202–204, 209
emotional intelligence, 183
Employ Your Word (Power Process), 178, 217
employers, support for higher education, 17
encoding, in memory, 81
energy, 4
English as a Second Language (ESL), 110
english language, Standard, 110
English Language Learner (ELL), 110
essay questions, 146, 147
evaluating (Level 5 thinking), 47, 75, 92, 113, 133, 161, 173, 211, 235
evidence, considering in critical thinking, 163
exercise, and health, 201, 203
expectations, noticing and letting go, 98
expenses, 67
Experimenting with Muscle Reading (Discovery/Intention Statement), 105
explore your feelings about tests (Discovery Statement), 140
express your emotions, 183
extracurricular activities, benefits of, 44
eye contact, 180, 192

# F

fallacies, 166
false cause, 166
family
    reading time with, 107
    study time with, 66
Federal Deposit Insurance Corporation (FDIC), 72
feedback
    changing a habit and, 21
    in cross-cultural communication, 187
    grades as, 153
    listening and, 180
feelings
    in "I" messages, 182
    learning by, 33, 35
fill-in-the-blank tests, 146
Financial Aid for higher education, 74
financial plan, 72
Find a Bigger Problem (Power Process), 158, 217
First Step technique, 25–27, 151
fix-the-world brainstorm, 165
flag answers, in muscle reading, 100, 103
flash cards, for test review, 142
fleming, Alexander, 164–165

selectivity, as memory technique, 84
self-awareness, 4, 27
self-concept, cheating and, 149
self-deception, critical thinking as antidote to, 159
self-direction, 5
self-discipline, 19
self-discovery
    choosing a major and, 171
    cross-cultural communication and, 186
self-evaluation, 26
self-sabotage, 12
sentences, as mnemonic devices, 91
serendipity, 164–165
service learning, 45
sexism
    in advertising, 209
    avoiding in communication, 188
sexual assault, preventing, 207
sexually transmitted disease (STD), preventing, 207
short answer tests, 146
shorthand, 129
short-term goals, 59
short-term memory, 82, 86–87
sincerity, in asking for help, 205
skills
    improving, 216
    transferable, 218–219, 220
skinner, B. F., 21
sleep, need for, 203
social interaction
    brain health and, 90
    extracurricular activities, 44
    importance of, 15, 17
solutions, focusing on in conflict management, 184
songs, as mnemonic devices, 91
sorting ability, 4
sources
    considering in critical thinking, 163
    evaluating on the internet, 167
    listing in papers, 190
    recording in research, 130–131
spatial order, 84
speaking
    and listening, 180–181
    public, 191–192
speaking notes, 192
Sperry, John, 126
spontaneity, 5
stafford loan, 73
Standard English, 110
Stine, R. L., 114
strengths, First Step technique, 26
stress management, 150–151, 203, 205
stretch goals, 2
student loans, managing, 73
study checklists, 141–142
study errors, on tests, 148
study group, 144, 152

study techniques, 65–66
studying. *See also* Reading
    in groups, 144, 152
    for math tests, 152
    methods, 15
    regular study area, 66
    shorter sessions, 87
    for tests, 141–142, 144
    time management techniques, 65–66
substance abuse, 208
success
    First Step technique, 25–27
    in higher education, 16–17
    instructors and, 18
    learning styles and, 35–36
suicide, preventing, 204
summarizing
    avoiding plagiarism, 190
    citing sources, 131
    instructions for essay question, 147
    mind maps in test review, 142
    for reading comprehension, 104
    for reviewing notes, 127
support and support groups, 19, 21, 234
surrender (Power Process), 198, 217
suspending judgment, 4, 12, 180
synthesis, and recitation, 104

# T

take a First Step about your health (Discovery Statement), 197
taking notes under pressure (exercise activity), 129
taking the First Step (exercise activity), 27
tasks
    ABC daily to-do list, 60
    delegating, 17
teacher. *See* Instructor
teaching
    as memory technique, 88
    as test preparation, 144
teaching styles, 13
teams, study groups as, 144
technology
    attitude towards, 5
    cheating on tests, 149
    computer-graded tests, 146
    group study and, 144
    learning to use, 14
    for note taking, 128
    online coursework, 132
test anxiety, 139, 150
test error, sources of, 148
test mechanics errors, 148
tests
    after the test, 148
    before the test, 141–142
    cheating, 149
    Discovery Wheel, 29, 229
    during the test, 145–148

essay questions, 146–147
    as feedback, 153
    group study, 144
    math tests, 151–152
    misconceptions about, 139
    overcoming test anxiety, 150
    predicting test questions, 143
    reading test questions, 145–146
textbook reconnaissance (exercise activity), 1
Tharp, Twyla, 174
thesis statement, 189
thinking. *See also* Critical thinking
    creating ideas, 164–165
    decision-making skills, 168
    developing critical thinking skills, 161–163
    Discovery Wheel, 30, 229
    learning by, 33, 35
    levels of, 47, 160–161
    logical mistakes, 166
    thorough thinking, 159
    problem solving, 169
this book shouts "use me" (exercise activity), 234
thorough thinking, 159. *See also* Critical thinking
thoughts, in "I" messages, 182
3x5 cards
    career contacts, 222
    choosing a major, 171
    keeping track of ideas, 165
    money management, 6
    note taking, 123, 130
    public speaking, 192
    studying in waiting time, 657
    test review, 142
    to-do lists, 60, 61
    vocabulary development, 109
    writing specific goals, 59
three-ring binder, using for notes, 123
time. *See also* Time management
    characteristics of, 53
    Discovery Wheel, 29, 228
    estimate for to-do lists, 60
    finding for reading, 106
time limits, in brainstorming, 164
time lines, 12, 85–86
time management
    ABC daily to-do list, 60
    avoiding procrastination, 64
    and emotional health, 202–203
    essay questions, 146
    getting the most from study time, 65–66
    importance of, 53
    long-term planning, 62–63
    multitasking, 61
    online coursework, 132
    out of class time, 15
    setting and achieving goals, 59
    as transferable skill, 218